# The JLC Guide to
# Production Carpentry

### Proven Techniques for Framing and Finish

From the Editors of
## The Journal of Light Construction

*A Journal of Light Construction Book*

*www.jlconline.com*

hanley▲wood

Cover Design: Colleen Kuerth
Cover Photos: Don Dunkley, Bob Grant, Bob Joynt, Matthew Thompson

Project Editor: Steven Bliss
Editorial Direction: Sal Alfano, Don Jackson
Managing Editor: Emily Stetson
Editorial Assistant: Jody Ciano

Graphic Designer: Terence Fallon
Illustrator: Tim Healy
Production Director: Theresa Emerson

International Standard Book Number:
    ISBN 10: 1-928580-40-8
    ISBN 13: 978-1-928580-40-9
Library of Congress Control Number: 2008934247

Printed in the United States of America

*A Journal of Light Construction Book*
The *Journal of Light Construction* is a trade name of Hanley Wood, LLC.

The Journal of Light Construction
186 Allen Brook Lane
Williston, VT 05495

# Acknowledgments

We wish to thank the many *JLC* authors who contributed to this book, largely drawn from the pages of *The Journal of Light Construction*. *JLC*'s strength lies in its authors: they are among the best builders and remodelers working in the field and among the most generous in their willingness to share their hard-won knowledge. This book represents their collective wisdom, benefiting all throughout the building industry and ultimately the owners of the homes they build and remodel — all of us. For their contributions, we wish to thank the following: Paul Alves, Byron Beck, Bob Blodgett, Don Bollinger, Howard Brickman, Chas Bridge, Thomas Buckborough, Frank Caputo, Rick Castillo, John Connor, Rob Corbo, Jim Craig, Bob Dausman, Michael Davis, Andrew P. DiGiammo, William Dillon, Gordon Dixon, Jed Dixon, Don Dunkley, David Frane, Jack Galt, Chuck Green, Mike Guertin, Carl Hagstrom, Dave Haines, Ron Hamilton, John Harman, Dave Holbrook, Gary Katz, Keith Kelly, Jeff Kent, Dave Kostansek, Trevor Kurz, Ed Ladouceur, Lee McGinley, Blaine Miller, Tom O'Brien, Mark O'Neil, Robert Page, Bill Posey, Rodney Proctor, Gary Pugh, George Schambach, Len Schmidt, Peter Schrader, Mike Sloggatt, John Spier, Marie Tupot Stock, Tim Uhler, Emil Wanatka, Ross Welsh, David West, and Scott Woelfel. Our apologies to anyone we inadvertently left off the list.

# Contents

## PART 1
### FRAMING

# Introduction

"Production carpentry" often refers to the blazing-fast assembly of tract housing by specialized crews who are paid by piecework. To produce work at this pace, every step of the job must be planned in detail, and the on-site work must be approached systematically with the right tools and equipment. There's not a lot of time for head scratching, test cuts, mockups, or mistakes. With their emphasis on speed, however, production builders are often known more for their efficiency than for their quality of work.

Applying these same principles of efficiency to custom building is the focus of this book. The book's contributors are all successful custom builders who have pioneered ways to build at production speeds without sacrificing quality — thus combining the speed of the tract builder with the quality of the craftsman. This requires an even greater level of planning and organization, along with specialized tools, innovative materials, and the well-honed skills needed to put it all together on time and on budget. Some of the book's authors cut their teeth on the California tracts and later adapted their hard-won knowledge to the world of custom building and remodeling. Others, out of necessity, have devised their own innovative approaches to producing high-quality work at production speeds. In all cases, the best techniques come from the people in the trenches — the real experts on production.

The accomplishments of these authors clearly prove that the days of skilled craftsmanship are far from over. Granted, compared with previous generations of builders, much has certainly changed. New challenges are presented by declining lumber quality, unfamiliar composite materials, more stringent codes, and more demanding designs. But with each new generation of construction, new skills are mastered by an influx of talented, motivated craftspersons. Buildings must still be erected square and level, the framing must be accurate, the finish work must be precise, and everything must be designed and built to stand the test of time.

What stays the same from generation to generation is the commitment of builders to master the tools and materials of the day in order to efficiently produce durable, attractive, and affordable living spaces. That commitment to both quality and efficiency is the essence of production carpentry, as so clearly outlined here.

This book is written by veteran builders who have mastered the art of building fast and building well. It contains job-tested approaches to every phase of carpentry, from setting the sills to coping the crown moldings. You'll also learn about a host of innovative materials and techniques that enable contractors to produce custom details at affordable prices. Most important, because good planning is the key to success, you'll find the planning and prep work covered with the same attention to detail as the carpentry. We hope this collection of contractors' wisdom will help you continue to produce the best possible work on time and on budget, providing great value to your clients and a healthy bottom line for your company.

*Steven Bliss*
*Project Editor*

# Chapter 1:
# Framing Prep

- **Getting Organized for Fast Framing**

- **Framing: Day One**

# Getting Organized for Fast Framing

by Tim Uhler

Bring the right tools, break down the job into simple tasks, and have materials delivered when needed.

It's a great feeling when everything clicks during a house-framing job — the work goes quickly and turns out right, and the crew has a good time doing it. But smooth, glitch-free projects don't happen by accident. They require good organized, the right tools, and a production mindset.

Our company builds 10 or more houses per year; we frame them in-house with a four-man crew that also does exterior finish. We can produce this amount of work because we've broken the framing process down into a series of tightly organized tasks. What follows is an explanation of how we squeeze maximum efficiency out of each step of our process.

## Prepping the Crew

No matter how experienced the members of a crew are, only one person can be in charge. Production falls off quickly when every decision must be discussed or decided democratically. But that doesn't mean the person running the crew should treat the other carpenters like a bunch of robots.

As chief of my crew, I want everyone to understand what we're going to build. Therefore, I give each framer a copy of the material takeoff and a set of prints with the understanding that he should study them before we start the job. For the most part, the guys have been very good about doing this.

We'll pay each framer for up to two hours of study time. It's a worthwhile expense because it reduces the time I have to spend explaining things: the framers know what to do and are ready to work the moment they arrive on site. We also buy them framing books and send them to trade shows, where they can learn more about building.

## Ordering Material

You can't be productive unless materials and supplies arrive when you need them. We let the lumberyard do takeoff for the floors and walls. But if the roof is stick-framed, I do that part of the takeoff myself; when the lumberyard folks do it they provide various-length pieces for the jack rafters, and it can take a lot of head-scratching to figure out which rafter comes from which piece of stock. In short, it's just easier if we make the list.

I want the stock to be long enough to get two jacks — a long and a short — out of each piece; that way, there will be fewer sizes to keep track of and fewer pieces to handle. Since we don't want all the lumber to be delivered at once, we order it by task: first-floor framing, first-floor walls, second-floor framing, second-floor walls, and — finally — the roof. This saves us from having to sort through large piles of lumber and leaves more room to move around on site.

*Scheduling.* In most cases we have the first-floor framing delivered before we get to the job site. We tell the lumberyard which material should be on top. I like to schedule delivery of the framing package for the first-floor walls for midmorning on our first day, so if we finish framing the floor we can start cutting door and window packages.

We schedule deliveries two to five days in advance. If we are going to need I-joists, we order them a couple of weeks ahead of time because our lumberyard doesn't have many in stock. After receiving the materials, the lumberyard puts the order together, bands it, and leaves it sitting there until the day of delivery.

## Setting Up on Site

About four years ago, we bought a forklift. A good used one might cost $30,000 to $40,000 — but it saves an incredible amount of labor.

Ours changed the way I look at framing. Before the forklift purchase, I'd have the lumberyard drop the load close to the house, and we'd work our way down through the pile. But now, with the forklift, we can spread material around in such a way that groups of carpenters can work on various tasks or in different areas without having to go far for stock.

When we're framing walls, for example, we use the forklift to put the stud material in the middle of the floor, within easy reach of all the framers. Since there isn't always room to put 20-foot plate stock on the deck, we place it where the framer who's plating can reach it without leaving the floor. As soon as the first wall is up, we can put material where the wall was when it was lying down (**Figure 1**).

We also use the forklift to stand walls and lift beams too heavy to lift with the available manpower (**Figure 2**, next page). The machine saves us from a lot of other lifting, too — not just the heavy stuff, but any material higher than the first-floor top plates. This reduces our fatigue level, so we make fewer mistakes and have fewer aches and pains at the end of the day.

*Cut station.* We usually set up a cut station in the garage, with a sliding-compound miter saw opposite sawhorses stacked with stock for sills and cripples. The horses are at the same height as the cut station; to get material, all the framer has to do is turn around and grab it.

If there's enough space, we put the wall sheathing on the floor next to the stack of wall studs. Otherwise, we leave it on the forklift just off the edge of the deck, at a height where it's easy to reach. If we need the forklift for something else, we simply put the load down and then pick it up again later when the forklift is free.

**Figure 1.** Plate stock is stacked on sawhorses at a cut station on the garage slab (top), from where the material can easily be moved to the deck. When there's no room for cutting on the deck, the forklift comes in handy (center). Carpenters use a cart to move precut studs to where the walls are being framed (above).

**Figure 2.** A forklift places joists right where they're needed (left) and takes the strain out of lifting a long ridge beam (right).

## Assembly-Line Framing

No matter what kind of work you do, breaking the job into small, simple tasks will increase production. Doing a lot of the same thing all at once is always faster than switching back and forth between different tools and materials. If one carpenter is cutting door and window packages, I don't want him to stop until all of them are cut for that floor of the building. Or if a couple of guys are assembling walls, I want the two of them to do all the walls at once.

I try to divide the work into tasks that take about the same amount of time to complete; that way, we all finish at once and can team up differently on the next set of tasks.

Breaking the job down this way is also a good way to train new carpenters, because they can learn the process one simple step at a time. Once the crew has been through our framing process a couple of times, everyone knows how to perform every task — which means that if one person finishes his task early, he can go on to the next one, or help someone else finish what he's working on. In anticipation of this possibility, I always try to let people know what to work on next.

We don't have the same carpenters perform the same tasks every day or on every project. Instead, we switch around, so everyone stays fresh and no one gets bored.

***Making parts.*** The framing goes faster if you precut and preassemble as many parts as possible. For example, when we're framing walls, one framer uses the miter saw to cut all the door and window cripples and window sills (**Figure 3**), and another cuts all the headers, labels them by size, and stacks them nearby.

**Figure 3.** A carpenter precuts the cripples, rough sills, and headers for the first floor of the building and stacks them out of the way. A framer assembles king stud–trimmer combinations from precut parts (left). Cripples, headers, and rough sills await assembly (right).

**Figure 4.** Using the right tools for gang-cutting saves time. A chain saw works well for joists (left), while a worm drive in a swing table speeds the cutting of birdsmouths (below left). The 10-inch Big Foot can cut three 1 1/8-inch LVL stair stringers at a time (below).

There's no need to nail headers together because we cut them from solid stock.

Parts like corner studs and king stud–trimmer combinations do have to be nailed together, which we like to do in advance. We use a circular saw to cut trimmers at the lumber pile; then we assemble the pieces nearby. Once the parts are nailed together, we stack them on the deck next to the stud pile, or put them on a cart so we can move them out of the way or bring them close to where we're framing.

*Less cutting time.* One way to reduce cutting time is to order precut studs. Another way is to gang-cut rafters, joists, stair stringers, garage-wall studs, and the like. Gang-cutting is not only faster — it's more precise, because all the parts are the same (**Figure 4**).

If we have a lot of small pieces of the same size to cut, we set a stop and cut them on our miter saw. This is how we cut window sills, cripple studs for doors and windows, and many other elements.

## Tooling Up

Having the right tools at the right time can really boost production. Although a forklift is a big-ticket item, there are plenty of less expensive tools that can also make a difference.

*Layout tools.* If you're not using a construction calculator, you're wasting a lot of time. We use a Construction Master to lay out diagonals, figure out rafter cuts, calculate gable studs, estimate materials (it's easiest to work in feet/inches), and perform countless other tasks.

For long measurements, we use a 100-foot steel open-reel tape. The smaller, cheaper, pouch-size reels aren't as good; they wind slowly and get lost easily. Steel tapes last longer and are more accurate because they stretch less than fiberglass.

Stud layout sticks really speed up layout, too. I've been using them for about four years; currently we have a fixed-arm model from Big Foot

**Figure 5.** Good layout tools make a difference. At left, a carpenter measures wall diagonals with a 100-foot steel tape, which is more accurate than fiberglass tape because it doesn't stretch. An aluminum layout stick is well worth the $30 investment (right).

(www.bigfoottools.com), which can do 16-inch and 24-inch on-center layout (**Figure 5**). At $30, it's paid for itself many times over.

Some carpenters think layout sticks cause cumulative error because they're short (4 feet long) and must be "walked" down the stock. When walls are long enough for this to be an issue, I make a mark every 20 feet (an even multiple of 16 inches) along the plate and restart layout from there.

We rarely use spirit levels for layout; lasers are faster and more accurate. To plumb walls, create square lay-

out for mudsills, and project layout up to joists and rafters, we use a PLS5 (Pacific Laser Systems, www.plslaser.com). And to create level reference lines for tasks that require level layout — such as installing windows and building soffits — we use a rotary laser.

***Cutting tools.*** We keep a chain saw in the truck for cutting beams and headers and for gang-cutting joists. It's a good tool for demolition, which is sometimes necessary even on new construction.

We like to gang-cut our roofs. To do so we use a chain saw with a custom-made guide — similar to the

**Figure 6.** The author's crew uses a router and flush trimming bit to cut out window openings because it's faster and neater than using a recip saw (left). Whenever possible, they install hardware with a dedicated metal-connector nailer (center) or, in tight quarters, a palm nailer. Finally, cleaning with a backpack blower (right) takes less time than sweeping with a broom.

Headcutter — and a Big Foot circular saw with a swing table. With its 10-inch blade, this saw can cut 3¾ inches deep. We use it to gang-cut plates, stair stringers, and anything else too thick to cut with a 7¼-inch saw.

To cut out window openings, we use a plunge router with a flush trimming bit. This method eliminates the need to measure and mark, and it's faster than using a recip saw and cleaner than using a chain saw (**Figure 6**).

*Fastening tools.* In our area, it's necessary to install a lot of framing hardware — joist hangers, straps, hold-downs, and so forth. To avoid nailing everything on by hand, we use a metal-connector nailer and, when space is tight, a palm nailer. I can't imagine installing hardware without these tools.

Some hardware must be fastened with Simpson's SDS screws (www.strongtie.com). Since the holes aren't piloted, and driving them takes a lot of torque, we put them in with a big right-angle drill — the kind a plumber might use.

A few years back, we switched to coil framing nailers because they hold about five times as many fasteners as stick guns. The nailers are heavier, but they reduce the amount of downtime needed to reload. To me, the tradeoff is a no-brainer.

*Other equipment.* Although the subs who form and pour our foundations do a pretty good job, they occasionally make errors. They'll put a hold-down strap in front of a door opening, for example, or place a J-bolt where a post needs to be. Then we have to cut the piece of hardware off and replace it with a bolt epoxied into the foundation. This happens often enough that we keep a rotary hammer around so we can drill holes in concrete as needed.

In addition to sawhorses, we have a wheeled metal cart that we stack material on. With the cart, we can move items like studs, corners, and king stud–trimmer combinations around the floor without using the forklift.

About a year ago, we bought a backpack leaf-blower for cleaning off the deck. This machine gets the job done faster than a broom and makes it easier to keep a clean, safe work area.

## Maintaining a Production Mindset

It's important for the entire crew to approach the work with a production-oriented attitude. This doesn't mean "just slap it together" — it means being open-minded enough to ask on a regular basis, "How can we do this more efficiently?" We encourage everyone — not just the lead carpenter — to be imaginative about everything we do. Some of our least experienced framers have come up with some very good ideas — maybe because they look at things with fresh eyes.

Thanks to the Internet, I've been able to communicate with framers around the country, and I've learned a lot from them. But I've noticed that not everyone is capable of listening to others and learning something new. I've run into framers who are so invested in how they learned to frame that they're unwilling to try anything different. In the past, that approach may not have been a problem. But today, with tools, materials, and code requirements changing so quickly, I believe that framers who don't adapt will be left behind.

*Tim Uhler is a lead framer and exterior trim carpenter for Pioneer Builders in Port Orchard, Wash.*

# Framing: Day One

## by Don Dunkley

At its best, framing is a series of well-thought-out and coordinated steps. Of those steps, the first one can be the most important. I've learned that the ability to start off a project at full speed creates momentum that carries over throughout the entire job. Conversely, a job that stumbles right out of the gate eats up a lot of valuable time that you may not recover.

As a framing contractor, some of my best time spent was the time invested in preparing and organizing for the first day of a job. In this business, time is money, and neither is well spent when the first day at the job finds your crew mulling about waiting for you to figure out what to do with them while you're still trying to make sense of the plans. Nor is it a good use of daylight spending the first day or two laying out a floor with one other carpenter while the rest of the gang is on hold waiting for you to get it ready for them.

To start any job off with a bang, I organize my crew to be task specific the minute we get on site. My optimum choice in a crew size is five, including me. I set up two of the crew to break down the lumber package and one to cut the frame package, leaving two for layout, plating, and detail. First, I square the deck. Then I snap, plate, and detail the garage, using one of the crew to help me pull diagonals and snap lines. By the time I have this done, the rest of my crew will have broken down the package into usable sections and out-fitted the cut man for his day with a radial arm saw.

With the garage set up for framing, I can now concentrate on the main house. The end of a good first day will result in the frame package cut, labeled, and stacked, the garage framed or in frame stage, and the main house laid out. But this kind of organization can't be done without some serious time spent studying and understanding the plans. Before I get to the site, I am already familiar with the plans (see "Wall Layout Rules of Thumb," page 30), and I have prepared a cut list for the wall-framing phase. I arrive at the job with all the proper tools and supplies, and all of the lumber already dropped off at a previously marked-out location. Complete familiarity with the plans comes with good organization.

To make Day One successful, I use the following procedure to organize the site and crew for this crucial first step.

## What to Show Up With

I. **Tools** (other than usual carpentry tools)
*Must have:*
- two 100-foot steel tape measures
- transit and/or laser
- two dry lines minimum
- two chalk lines of different colors, spanish red mortar dye for permanent lines, blue or other color for changes
- keel for everyone on the crew, one color for marking crowns, two other colors for layout
- calculator (Construction Master is ideal)
- anchor bolt marker or combination square
- different sized auger or spade-style drill bits for anchor and hold-down bolts
- material to cover framing package (6-mil plastic is fine)

*Nice to have:*
- spray paint, any color
- clear lacquer spray (keeps lines from being washed away in rain)
- masonry chisel
- 2-pound hammer
- electric demo or chipping hammer
- extra sawhorses

II. **Information**
*Prints.* If you are the builder, you should have read every word on the prints by now. At the very least, right now you need:
- rough openings for all doors and windows
- head heights for every opening
- all wall heights, plus drop for every opening
- any unusual details noted: hold-downs, beam pockets and posts, transom windows, etc.

**Figure 7.** After breaking down the lumber package, a worker selects the straightest material for plate stock and marks it for cutting.

- location of openings or rough-in for plumbing, HVAC, and electric noted
- complete understanding of roof frame, rake wall requirements, exterior elevation needs, staircase layout such as radius for site-built circular stairs

*Materials takeoff list* or your order for the framing package (what's supposed to be there and what it's being used for)

*A cut list for rough openings that shows:*
- header sizes and the total number of each size
- the number of jack (trimmer) studs required of each length
- the number of king studs required of each length
- the number of sills of each size
- the number and length of cripples and studs for special-height walls, tall or balloon-framed walls, pony walls, rake walls

*An assembly list that shows:*
- the number of openings of each R.O. size and the wall height if this varies anywhere
- the number of channels for wall intersections
- the number of corner posts that need to be made up

III. **People.** Five crew members: two for layout, two to break down the package and frame, one cut man

## Prepping the Job

I. **Be there before the lumber package is dropped** to direct the driver or make sure you have marked clearly where the package is to be dropped. Give yourself enough room to break the package down without crowding yourself; get it close enough to the building that you don't have to walk too far but not so close that it's in your way. The package will usually be stacked for the driver's convenience, not yours. Most often, the plate material and the floor joists will be under the plywood. While you are snapping lines with one of your helpers, the other two workers should be breaking down the package and sorting it out (**Figure 7**).

## II. Sort out lumber by size into separate stacks.
Pay attention to what it's going to be used for as you do this.

- As you work, cull out unsuitable materials, and restack them near driveway for lumberyard pickup. At the end of the day, make a list of bad materials to be picked up so the driver can bring the replacements from the yard.
- As you handle each board, crown it now. Make big, visible crown marks with keel, arm's distance from the ends of the board. This is so you don't cut the crown mark off, and so you can see it from either end.
- Stack boards with crowns facing the same way. I crown all studs, too, especially 2x6s.
- Stack all materials on stickers 4 feet apart, off the ground. This helps keep the lumber in better shape, makes it easier to handle, and keeps the job site neater.
- After the lumber is sorted, check it against the delivery ticket and the takeoff.

## III. Set up a cut station right next to the pile. I prefer a radial arm saw with roller tables on each side.

**Figure 8.** Top and bottom plates are laid out and accurately marked for all studs, openings, and other wall-framing details.

- Cut all headers. Make a clear crown mark on each header. Write the length with keel as you go. Stack each size separately. We use 4-by header stock on the West Coast. If you're using 2-by lumber, you'll want to assemble headers at this point.
- Cut all jacks (trimmers).
- If different lengths, mark them and stack separately.
- If using solid-sawn 4-by header stock, cut all trimmers in place during framing to account for variations in width.
- Cut all sills, mark length as you go.
- Cut all cripples, throw in separate piles as you go.
- Cover anything you aren't going to use right away — sun is just as bad as rain on lumber.

**Figure 9.** After cutting R.O. packages, the crew builds prefabbed window and door headers (left), marks them clearly, and stacks them for fast wall assembly (right).

## Framing Begins

**I. Two carpenters start to load the cutting bench** while you square up the deck and snap, plate, and detail the garage (**Figure 8**, previous page). Once the load is broken down, the garage area can start being framed up.

- The cut man should be prepping all R.O. packages, including headers, sills, and cripples (**Figure 9**, previous page). These should be clearly marked so they can be spread to the proper location during framing.
- As the R.O. packages are completed, the cut man marks the headers clearly across the exterior side of the header with the door or window callout that matches the prints (Window A, Door 7, etc.).

**II. Layout.** During breakdown, the layout crew should go around and knock all the concrete chunks off the anchor bolts and sweep slab or deck clean.

- Check the slab or deck for elevation, level, and square.
- Check the overall dimensions of all the concrete at this point, too. Make sure they're the right length and width.

**III. Snapping.** If it's all good, square up the slab/deck and snap out all garage walls. If the weather is even a little bit shaky, spray clear lacquer over the lines to keep them in place.

**IV. Detailing the plates.** Plate and detail the garage. This can be done by the framing crew if they break down the package early.

## Full Steam Ahead

At this point, the framing team can start on the garage walls. I move on with my helper to snap out the main house. The cut man continues prepping R.O. packages for the main house, while the framers work on the garage. By the time the garage is framed, I'll often have the main house snapped out and detailed so the framers can move over and keep working.

*Don Dunkley is a framing contractor in Cool, Calif.*

# Chapter 2: Floor Layout & Framing

■ **Wet-Set Mudsills**

■ **Installing the Mudsill and Deck**

■ **Floor Framing With I-Joists**

With careful layout, placing sills directly into the wet concrete can save time.

# Wet-Set Mudsills

## by John Spier

In an ideal world, foundations would be level and square, and all the anchor bolts would be in exactly the right places. Of course, nothing is ever that easy. Setting sill plates onto a less-than-perfect foundation can be a time-consuming process of measuring, squaring, and shimming.

A few years ago, I came up with a method that works better for me. Before the foundation is poured, I cut and assemble the sill plates. I do the framing layout on them, and I drill and install the anchor bolts in the plates exactly where I want them. Then, just after the concrete is poured, I set the plates in place, bolts and all. I do a little thumping and tweaking, and soon the plates are ready for framing.

### Engineers' Lament

I can already hear the structural engineers saying, quite correctly, that foundation bolts should be held in place and the concrete poured around them.

Pushing bolts into partially cured concrete displaces the stone and coarse aggregate, leaving them sitting in a soup of cement, water, and fine sand, a mix weaker than the design strength of the rest of the concrete.

The method required on engineered structures in seismic or high-wind zones is to position the bolts before the pour, which is typically done with scrap lumber, wire, or a specialized product like Simpson's AnchorMate connector (www.strongtie.com).

Often, though, on less demanding sites, anchor bolts are placed into wet concrete. If this is done immediately, before the concrete begins to tighten up, the aggregate flows back around the bolts and little strength is lost.

### Advantages of Wet-Set Sills

We're all aware of the things that can go wrong with anchor bolts, no matter what method is used to set them. The most careful preplacement rarely survives the process of pouring and pulling the concrete through the forms — and handing a bucket of bolts and a tape measure to the average laborer is a recipe for disaster.

Bolts often end up under studs, joists, or posts; as a result they get cut off or the framing members get notched. Others end up in doorways and are cut off. If bolts are set too deep, the sills have to be chiseled out to install washers and nuts, a code violation. If the bolts are set too high, there might not be enough thread length to tighten them down completely. With my method, the bolts always end up at the proper height.

We've all experienced out-of-level foundations. Shimming sills level or packing mortar under them can add hours to the framing schedule. Wet-setting the sills eliminates this problem.

## Bolt Layout

For simple frames, it's enough just to start the layout and locate the bolts so that they don't land in the same places as the joists or studs. On more complicated jobs, you need a detailed framing plan showing the location of every piece of wood in the first level of the structure.

I used to draw the plan on paper, and then give the foundation contractor an anchor-bolt plan worked out to the inch. But I'd still have to fit the sills to the bolts and the framing to the sills, and hope that everything lined up. Now I do the initial framing plan directly on the sills, eliminating several steps. This saves time and minimizes errors.

Probably my biggest challenge used to be setting engineer-specified bolts for anchoring hold-downs. Making a mistake would require an expensive, time-consuming fix using epoxy and threaded rod.

On the project shown here, a simple two-story garage, the plans required hold-downs in shear walls at every corner. With the layout done ahead of time, the anchor bolts were perfectly aligned for the hold-downs to attach to the wall framing.

## Prepping the Sills

To begin, I cut the sills and assemble them in the lengths of the framed floors or walls. I'm careful to use straight stock, because there isn't any way to brace the sills straight in the forms.

In our area, we use double sills; the bottom one is pressure-treated, the upper one standard framing lumber. If there will be a conventional floor frame on the sills, the two layers can be permanently spiked together; if the upper sills are wall bottom plates (as on the slab foundation in the photos), I just tack them so that I can later remove the upper sill and build the walls lying flat.

Next, I establish a common layout for the building in both directions, which keeps the joists, studs, and rafters in line from sill to ridge. As I mark the layout on the sills, I can often shift other framing elements

**Figure 1.** With the garage-wall bottom plate tacked to the mudsill, the author marks the stud layout, making adjustments as needed so that the anchor bolts don't interfere with the framing (top). He checks the placement of a hold-down bolt (above left) using the actual hardware, and labels each set of plates (above right) in preparation for concrete.

slightly to reduce waste and avoid odd-sized bays (**Figure 1**). All the double studs for the shear walls in this garage, for example, incorporated one stud on the common layout.

I locate and mark any critical hardware, such as shear-wall hold-downs, so that no framing ends up in the way of these connectors. It's best to have the actual hardware on hand, or at least exact specifications, so the bolts can be set at the right distance from the members to which they attach. I also locate any bolts specifically called for by code, such as those within 12 inches of beam pockets or corners.

If the top sills are also wall bottom plates, I lay out the framing for the entire wall, including studs, cripples, openings, posts, shear-wall studs, and any other framing members. Then I locate the anchor bolts where they meet code and make sense. The building code or an engineer's spec, for example, might call for anchor bolts 32 inches on-center, but at a doorway it's clearly better to place the bolts just beyond the king studs on either side.

**Figure 2.** As soon as a section of wall is poured (top left), the author trowels the concrete to the correct level (top right). The plates — bolts and all — are then set into the wet concrete (above).

When I'm satisfied with the layout, I drill the holes and install the bolts in the sills. I label, organize, and store the completed sills, then wait for concrete.

## During the Pour

The guy who does my concrete formwork does a good job of stringing, squaring, and straightening the forms. To keep the sills square, I follow the forms, but I check his work with diagonal measurements. As each section of the forms is filled, I trowel the wet concrete smooth, working to grade nails set in the forms (**Figure 2**). Then I'm ready for the sills.

Handling the sills usually requires a couple of helpers. Together we set the sills in place inside the forms. Where the sills overlap at the corners, I tack the lapped corners together, squaring and straightening them carefully as I go. When I'm satisfied with the placement of the sills, I carefully push the bolts into the concrete as plumb as possible, making sure the nuts are threaded on the bolts consistently (**Figure 3**).

Next, I station a crewmember on a transit or laser level and check the sills for level. When I've found the lowest point, I go around and thump the rest of the sills down to that level with the head of a sledgehammer (**Figure 4**). I drive a nail through the forms every few feet to hold the sills in place while the concrete cures. Occasionally, I'll need to use a brace or block to hold a sill straight.

## Next Day

After the forms are stripped, I check the sills for square and level again. If minor adjustments are needed, I can always shim or plane them a bit. Small lateral adjustments can be made by shifting the upper sills and elongating the bolt holes slightly if necessary. But generally none of these tweaks are necessary.

**Figure 3.** As the pour proceeds, the crew works quickly to position the plates (left) and push the anchor bolts into the concrete (center and right).

**Figure 4.** While the concrete is still plastic, the crew finds the lowest point on the foundation and then uses a sledge to tap all the plates to that elevation (far left). Here, the author checks the short garage-wall plates for level (left).

**Figure 5.** After the forms are stripped (above left), the author uses a claw hammer to remove the irregular ridge of concrete along the side of the sill (above). The finished result is a square and level sill with accurately placed hold-down anchors and foundation bolts (left and far left).

The concrete tends to ride up along the sides of the sills, particularly in areas where they had to be thumped down. On the inside, this is not a problem, but on the outside, I flake off the excess concrete with a hammer claw so that the wall sheathing can be run down and nailed to the bottom plate (**Figure 5**).

On the garage shown, the entire sill-layout process took me a couple of hours before the pour. (I was working alone with no distractions.) Setting and adjusting the plates during the pour took less time than just measuring and setting the bolts would have.

*John Spier owns Spier Construction on Block Island, R.I., with his wife, Kerri Spier. All photos by Roe Osborn.*

# Installing the Mudsill and Deck

by Tim Uhler

**The work goes faster if you use a laser, install anchor straps instead of anchor bolts, and measure as little as possible.**

Our company builds a dozen or more houses a year. With a crew of only four carpenters, we can't afford to waste time, so we're always looking for systematic ways to approach the work.

Here, I'll describe our method for laying out and framing a first-floor deck. The techniques we've developed allow us to work quickly and accurately, and ensure that the rest of the framing goes well.

## Getting Started

We typically split into two teams of two carpenters. One team rolls out tools and gets the floor framing material ready while the other lays out the sills. The goal is for the sill layout to be dead square and perfectly parallel.

Framing errors and compromises tend to accumulate and show up in the roof; if the sills aren't square and parallel, the walls will follow, making the roof harder to frame. The error might even be visible when the job is done.

***Longest wall.*** The first thing we do is snap a line along the top of the longest wall, 5⅝ inches in from the outside face. This line represents the inside edge of the sill; its outside edge should be flush with the face of the wall. Sill stock is always a little bit wide,

which is why we offset the line 5⅝ inches rather than 5½.

On a straight foundation wall, the sheathing usually ends up ½ inch beyond the face. If the foundation bows out in the middle more than ½ inch, we'll shift the line out until there is no place where the sheathing will not be at least flush to the face of the wall. This may change the size of the house slightly, but that's better than having the foundation touch the back of the siding.

## Creating a Square Layout

Next, we snap a line square to the first line along the top of the longest intersecting 90-degree wall (**Figure 6**).

In the past we located this line using the 3-4-5 method or by calculating the length of the hypotenuse between the far ends of these walls. Now we use a PLS5 laser (Pacific Laser Systems, www.plslaser.com), which projects reference lines that are perfectly straight and square. It's faster than drawing right triangles, and there's no need to worry about inaccuracies caused by a sagging tape.

Using the laser, we can create square layout on a large foundation in a matter of minutes.

***Aligning the beam.*** We begin by making a mark

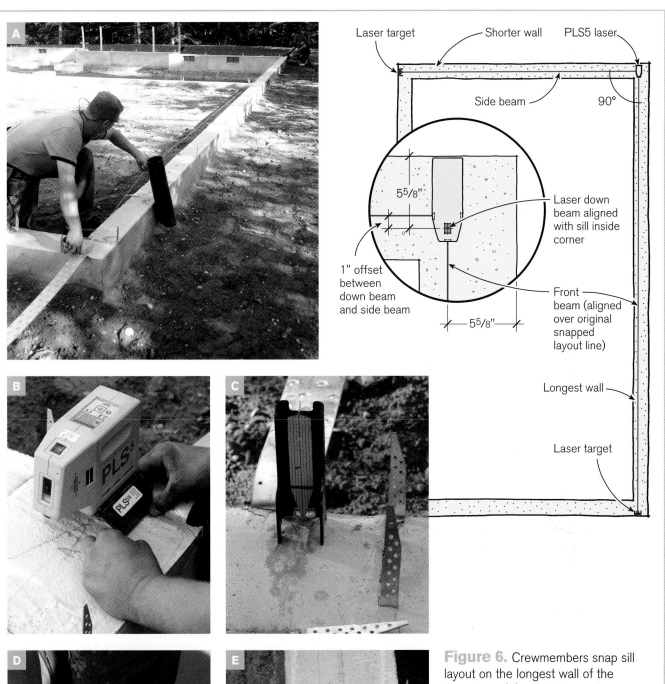

Laser target — Shorter wall — PLS5 laser

Side beam — 90°

5⁵/₈"

Laser down beam aligned with sill inside corner

1" offset between down beam and side beam

5⁵/₈"

Front beam (aligned over original snapped layout line)

Longest wall

Laser target

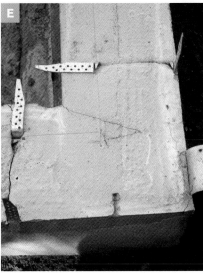

**Figure 6.** Crewmembers snap sill layout on the longest wall of the foundation (A), mark the inside corner, and align the laser over that point (B). Next, they place a target over the line at the far end of the wall and rotate the laser until the front beam hits the target dead center (C). Finally, they locate the perpendicular line by placing the target on the adjoining wall so that the side beam hits it dead center (D), mark that location, and measure in one inch to account for the offset between the down beam and side beam on the PLS5 laser. A line between this point to the inside corner will be square to the original line (E).

**Figure 7.** To lay out sills on a stepped foundation, most carpenters stretch the tape horizontally and use a level to plumb down (far left). A faster method is to stretch the tape, position the laser so the up beam hits the desired mark (left), and then mark where the down beam hits the foundation.

5⅝ inches in from the end of the line we made on the longest wall. This represents the inside corner where two sills will meet.

Next, we place the laser on the wall, align the downward beam with the corner mark, and aim the main horizontal beam toward the far end of the wall.

Our goal is to position the horizontal beam directly over the line on the wall. To do this, we position the laser target on the far end of the wall so that the pointer lands on the line. Then we rotate the laser so it projects a dot on the centerline of the target.

On a long wall, adjusting the laser takes very little movement; for fine adjustments, we tap lightly on the side of the laser. When the beam hits the target's centerline, we know it's aligned with the chalk line.

***Projecting a perpendicular line.*** The next step is to project a second line at a perfect 90-degree angle to the first and mark it on the adjoining wall.

The PLS5 projects three horizontal beams, two of which are perpendicular to the main horizontal beam. The main beam is already aligned with the line on the foundation, so to create a square layout we just have to determine where the side beam passes over the intersecting wall.

We do this by taking the target to the far end of the intersecting wall and positioning it so that the side beam hits it dead center. Then we mark where the pointer lands on the concrete.

With the PLS5, the side beams project at a one-inch offset from the vertical beam (in this case, one inch

**Figure 8.** A carpenter butts sill stock to the bolts, squares in from them (left), then measures the distance between each bolt and the layout line (center). After marking that distance on the stock, he drills the bolt holes (right).

**Figure 9.** Fastening sills with cast-in strap anchors (left) is faster than using anchor bolts. The carpenters place the sill stock on layout, tack it in place with a powder-actuated fastener (center), then fasten it by nailing on the strap (right).

too close to the outer face of the wall), so we measure over an inch and use the new mark to snap a line back to the corner where the two sills will meet.

## Laying Out the Remaining Walls

Now that we have two lines that are perfectly square to each other, laying out the rest of the walls is simply a matter of measuring off the first two lines. Difficulties arise only in places where the foundation walls step up and down or where we need to drop our layout onto a basement floor slab.

The traditional way to handle these areas is to stretch a tape horizontally and then use a plumb bob or level to carry the layout down. We find it faster and easier to stretch the tape and use the laser's up and down beams (the plumb beams) to carry the layout down (**Figure 7**).

## Installing Mudsills

Once layout is snapped, we gang up on the mudsill. If the sill is to be attached with anchor bolts, three framers mark bolt locations while one carpenter drills holes.

*Anchor bolts.* To locate the holes, we place the sill against the bolts, align a square with a bolt, and scribe a line across the sill at that location. We then measure the distance between the layout line (on the foundation) and the center of the bolt and make a mark that far in from the edge of the sill on the line we just scribed (**Figure 8**). The mark will be the center of our hole. It's important to do this accurately because the hole should not be greatly oversized.

We have tried using a specialized marking tool, the Bolt-Hole Marker (Big Foot Tools, www.bigfoottools.com), but found it difficult to balance a 2x6 plate on the stem wall while making the marks. This tool is much better suited for marking plates for slab foundations.

Once we're about halfway through marking and drilling, one framer breaks off from marking and begins to fasten the sills with nuts and washers. We tighten the nuts with an electric impact wrench, tak-

ing care not to overtighten them.

*Straps are faster.* Not long ago, we stopped using anchor bolts and started using a type of cast-in strap that wraps over the sill and is fastened to it with nails. We happen to use Simpson's MA6 anchors, but USP makes something similar, the ST1-TZ (www.uspconnectors.com).

On our crew, one carpenter cuts and places sill stock on the foundation, a second follows behind and tacks the sill on layout with a powder-actuated tool, and a third makes the structural connection by bending the straps over the sill and fastening them with a metal connector nailer. We tack down the sills to prevent them from moving while the straps are being nailed (**Figure 9**).

Using straps is much faster than using anchor bolts because there is no need to lay out and drill holes. Another advantage to using straps is that we never have to move a joist off layout because a bolt is in the way; since straps are thin, you can run joists and rim boards right over them.

To avoid having to use galvanized or stainless steel fasteners, we use borate-treated lumber for the sills (see "Fasteners for Treated Lumber," page 21). We frame quickly so that the sills are not exposed to the weather long enough for the borate to leach out.

## Using Girders to Break Up Spans

Most of the homes in our area are built over crawl-spaces, so we install rows of girders 8 or 9 feet apart to break up long floor spans and pick up point loads. This makes for a stiffer floor and eliminates the need for a stem wall at the center of the house.

We don't do this with basements, however, because that would require too many posts. Instead, we use larger joists, and — when necessary — break up the spans with bearing walls.

The tops of the girders should be flush to the tops of the sills. On large houses we install the sills that are perpendicular to girders first; that way, part of the crew can set girders while the rest of the sills are being installed.

**Figure 10.** With a crawlspace foundation, the author uses girders to break up the floor span. Instead of measuring, the crew lays the girder stock in rough position (top) and cuts the pieces so the joints land over footing pads (above left). The girders are supported by posts that land on pieces of rubber membrane and are tied to the footings with cast-in straps (above right).

**Figure 11.** After the girders are in, the crew installs rim boards (top), then places the joists in rough position (above).

We start by scattering the girder stock so we can cut the pieces where they go. The ends of the girders will be supported by posts that land on ribbon footings (long thin footings) or footing pads (**Figure 10**).

The footing pads vary in elevation, so each post has to be cut to a slightly different length to keep the girder level. To quickly measure post length, we stretch a string very tightly from sill to sill where each run of girders will be, measure up to it from the footing, and deduct the height of the girder.

If the run is more than 25 feet long, we add 3/16 inch to the height of the center posts to account for the sag in the string.

We have used a rotary laser to determine the height of posts, but that approach is slower than using a string. The laser is more accurate, but our primary objective is for the tops of the girders to be in a straight line between the sills. We don't care if a run of girders is slightly out of level — say, within 1/4 inch from end to end. (If the stem walls are off by more than that, we shim the mudsills.)

We cut the posts, stand them over a piece of PVC membrane, and install girders on top. The posts are

fastened to the footings with cast-in straps and to the girders with nailed 2x4 gussets. We sight the girders before nailing them off; if there is excessive crown, we'll cut the girder over an intermediate post.

The girders normally stop short of the stem walls, so it doesn't matter that they aren't treated. If the ends are less than an inch from the concrete, we cover them with PVC membrane.

## Laying Out and Installing Joists

Once the girders have been installed, we clean out the crawlspace and lay out the locations of joists and beams on the sills and girders. To minimize errors, only one carpenter does layout; the rest of the crew scatters the joists and sets beams.

*I-joists.* We use I-joists about half the time. Our supplier provides a "precut" package based on the plans, so we have to pay close attention to the lengths the manufacturer sends. The joists come several inches long and we trim them on site.

We like to scatter the longest joists first, just to get them out of the way. While one framer installs rim, another uses a forklift to boom the joists over the

## Fasteners for Treated Lumber

Unlike the old CCA (chromated copper arsenate) treated material, the new pressure-treating chemicals — ACQ (alkaline copper quat), ACZA (ammoniacal copper zinc arsenate), CA (copper azole), and CC (ammoniacal copper citrate) — are all very corrosive. Since conventional fasteners aren't compatible with this current crop of pressure-treated lumber, you'll need to use either hot-dipped galvanized or stainless steel fasteners for mudsills, plates, or other treated framing members.

Because my crew frames new homes, this issue affects how we fasten joists, rims, and sheathing to treated mudsills. Our initial response was to switch to hot-dipped galvanized stick nails when we were working with mudsills (stainless steel fasteners are just too expensive), but it's a big hassle to change fasteners every time you want to nail into the sill. Also, there still seem to be some questions about how well these fasteners stand up to the new pressure-treating chemicals over time.

Several months back, we stopped using pressure-treated lumber altogether and started using lumber treated with SBX (sodium borate) for sills. Borate-treated wood resists insects and rot and is nontoxic to humans and the environment. It's not appropriate for decks or ground-contact applications, but it's fine for mudsills because they're protected from water. And since borate-treated lumber doesn't corrode fasteners, we were able to go back to using conventional nails for the entire frame. There's one drawback to borate-treated lumber: it should not be exposed to the weather for very long, because the borate can leach out if it stays wet. Manufacturers indicate that it's okay for borate-treated lumber to be exposed to the weather during the "normal" construction process, but they don't say exactly how long that is; my understanding is that they're talking months rather than weeks. Our houses are dried in within three weeks, and when borate-treated material is on site we keep it under tarps.

Some building inspectors aren't familiar with borate-treated lumber, so be sure to get their approval before using it. On those rare occasions when we have to use pressure-treated lumber, we use framing hardware with extra corrosion protection, such as Simpson's ZMAX (www.strongtie.com) and USP's Triple Zinc G-185 (www.uspconnectors.com) connectors, as well as both companies' more heavily coated hot-dipped galvanized fasteners. — *T.U.*

foundation so that the other two guys can unload them (**Figure 11**). With the forklift, it takes only about 30 minutes to scatter all the joists for a 1,500-square-foot floor.

If the joists are less than 25 feet long, our preferred method is to use a chain saw to cut them while they're still banded together; if they're longer than that, they'll bend too much and throw off the measurement.

When the joists are more than 25 feet long, we leave off one of the rims, butt them to the opposite rim, snap a line for the cut, and cut them in place with a circular saw (**Figure 12**). We then install the last of the rim and begin to roll and fasten the joists.

**Figure 12.** Rather than measuring each joist, a carpenter butts them all to the opposite rim, snaps a line where the inner face of the rim will be (far left), and then cuts them in place with a circular saw (left).

**Figure 13.** To finish the frame, the author nails joists to the rim (top left) and sill (top right), then installs the required blocking (left).

*Nailing.* We follow the I-joist manufacturer's recommendation for nailing. We use RFPI Joists (Roseburg Forest Products, www.rfpco.com), which require one 8-penny nail through the rim into each flange and two 8-penny nails through the bottom flange (one on each side) into the rim (**Figure 13**). With solid-sawn joists, we use 10-penny nails to fasten every 1½ inches through the rim into the joists as well as to toenail the joists to the sill.

If we're using I-joists, the manufacturer supplies precut I-joist blocking, or LVL blocking when the engineer says it's necessary. With solid-sawn joists, we use solid lumber blocking.

Sometimes we're required to install double blocking under shear walls, in which case we make the blocks out of cutoffs from the 4-by girder material.

## Inspection

The building inspector needs to inspect the frame before we install subflooring. Framing the floor normally takes us five or six hours, so we schedule an inspection for the afternoon, and unless there are major problems we can sheathe the floor as soon as he leaves.

If the inspector asks for anything, it's usually that we add a few more pieces of framing hardware to tie the rim to the sill or that we add some extra anchor bolts to the foundation. When we need to add anchor bolts, we use ½-inch Kwik Bolts (Hilti, www.hilti.com), a type of wedge anchor.

If at all possible, we sheathe the floor and snap out the walls on the same day. That way, we can start framing the walls first thing the next morning. If we aren't finished when the inspector comes out, we have to call in for another inspection and we lose the next day on the job.

### Laying the Floor Sheathing

When we install subflooring, everyone sticks to a particular task until the floor is done. Since there are four of us, the first carpenter applies the glue, and a second packs material and beats the sheets together so that the T&G joints will close (**Figure 14**). A third packs material and cuts, and a fourth does nothing but nail.

We trade off on every house so that no one has to do the same thing all the time.

Gluing is the weakest link in the process. Even with a pneumatic glue gun — which is much faster than operating a gun by hand — the guy doing the gluing has to hustle to stay ahead of the rest of the crew.

We're very production-oriented about this; on a recent project we installed the subfloor on a 3,000-square-foot single-story home (95 sheets) in a little less than two hours, including trimming the edges.

During the drier months of the year, we sheathe floors with LP's midlevel OSB product, TopNotch Orange Plus (www.lpcorp.com).

But during the rainy winter months, we'll spend

**Figure 14.** When installing the subfloor, everyone has a particular job: one carpenter does nothing but glue, two carpenters cut and place the sheets and beat them together, and one just nails.

the extra $3 to $4 per sheet it costs to get AdvanTech (Huber Engineered Woods, www.huberwood.com), which is less likely to swell when it gets wet.

*Tim Uhler is a lead framer and exterior trim carpenter for Pioneer Builders in Port Orchard, Wash.*

# Floor Framing With I-Joists

## by Scott Woelfel

Fifteen years ago, when my company was building its office, showrooms, and warehouse, I had to find a way to frame the floor over a 40-foot-wide span. I considered using open web floor trusses, but I wasn't crazy about the price and they weren't readily available. The salesperson at my local lumber supplier called my attention to wood I-joists, a product they'd recently begun to carry and support. Sufficiently impressed with the apparent capabilities of this new (at least to me) technology, I decided to give it a try, and I haven't had a moment's regret — we've since used I-joists exclusively for all of our floor framing.

There's no reason I can think of not to use them. Maybe they take a little getting used to at first, but we've used them so often, for so long, that the details have become routine.

### Ordering I-Joists

When you work with I-joists, you're dealing with an engineered product with distinctly different perfor-

mance characteristics from solid lumber. Although you can simply refer to span charts in the manufacturer's product brochure for basic joist sizing, it's best to consult a product specialist before proceeding. Stairwell headers, doubled joists, cantilevers, long spans, and other framing complications call for some product-specific number crunching. You can't safely apply your old solid-lumber rules of thumb or "seat-of-the-pants" engineering. Typically, someone at the local lumberyard has been trained to design and specify I-joist framing systems, working with a take-off from your plans, usually for no extra charge.

***Review the plan.*** The first thing I do when I get a new plan is make a careful review of the framing requirements, locating all toilets, plumbing rough-ins, and any other element that creates a necessary deviation from uniform layout. You can't carve or modify an I-joist flange without destroying its structural integrity. I make my notes on the plan and hand it off to the engineered lumber specialist. He runs the numbers through proprietary I-joist design

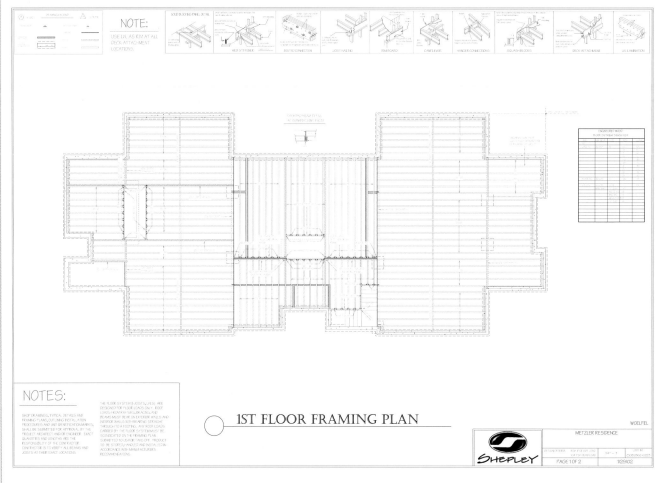

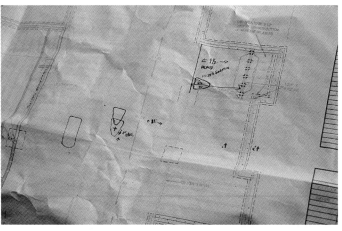

**Figure 15.** The distributor provides a floor framing plan and material takeoff using proprietary I-joist design software (above). The author checks this plan against the plumbing and HVAC layout for possible conflicts before placing the order (left).

software (our lumberyard uses Boise Cascade's BC Calc) to generate a floor framing plan and a bill of materials (**Figure 15**). When I get this plan, I check it over with my framer to make sure everything makes sense. If we have a question about any item or spec, we clear it up before placing the order.

*Engineered system.* I look at I-joists as part of a complete, prescriptive system. This system includes engineered rim joists, LVL girders and headers, solid I-joist bridging, and glued and nailed T&G plywood subflooring. If the prints suggest substituting dimension lum-

ber for any component of this prescriptive system, I'll ask the architect to reconsider. I-joists are dry, stable, and reliable, making them incompatible with solid-sawn lumber, which shrinks, twists, and splits. I see no reason to combine the two; it's asking for problems.

## Getting the Squeaks Out

One of the few early problems we noticed with the I-joist system was a tendency of the joists, when butted and hung on a flush header, to squeak underfoot. We could easily observe and pinpoint this phe-

**Figure 16.** To avoid floor squeaks, the author maintains a 1/4-inch gap between the hung I-joist end and the engineered header and makes certain that all holes in the joist hanger are properly nailed.

hangers we use have a hammer-down tab that wraps the bottom flange in a steel grip, reinforced by a nail (**Figure 17**). A positive-placement nail gun takes most of the pain away.

Hasty nailing of the deck plywood can be another source of squeaks. Even with a 2$1/2$-inch-wide flange, the gun nails can go astray and deflect out along the edge of the flange. When I walk the deck, I listen for squeaks and circle the spots. Before we put any ceilings up, somebody goes around and taps those nails back out. Subfloor adhesive is an integral component in the I-joist system, so properly placed nails stay put and quiet.

## Hanger Tips

The top-hung Simpson's ITTs cost about the same as face-mount hangers, about $2 each, but install faster because you don't have to hold them to a line and they require fewer nails. Some builders I've talked with use standard hangers because they think that the upper tab of a top-hung hanger might create a bump in the smooth plane of the subfloor, but we haven't found that to be a problem.

One thing that can trip you up is the unequal width of LVL lumber — sometimes there's as much as $3/8$ of an inch difference within a built-up beam. That can easily throw a top-hung hanger out of line. We typically power-plane the top edge of all our LVL members to avoid that problem (**Figure 18**).

## Rim Boards

Something to watch for is the irregular thickness of the engineered rim board, basically an oriented strand board product. When moisture gets to this material, it swells, affecting the inside span measurement. We've had to cut joists within the same run to

nomenon from below during the framing stage. Now we set the header in place, line and brace it, then measure the joist span. We deduct about 1/4 inch from the span and cut the joists to that length. After first nailing all of the hangers to the header, using an I-joist offcut as a hanger gauge block, we drop the joists into place, making sure they don't contact the header, and nail them through the hanger only (**Figure 16**).

I've also heard complaints about I-joists squeaking in the joist hangers — I haven't had trouble with that, maybe because we're scrupulous about nailing every hole in the hanger. The Simpson ITT series

**Figure 17.** The joist hangers used by the author have a bendable tab that wraps the bottom flange of the I-joist, preventing movement.

**Figure 18.** LVL planks are somewhat irregular in width. Power-planing the top edge of a built-up LVL header eliminates any bumps or level problems.

**Figure 19.** A thin plastic cutoff guide carries an 8-inch-diameter saw over the I-joist flanges and recessed web without overly compromising the depth of cut.

## Cutting and Handling

Cutting I-joists requires a jig, to bridge the 8-inch circular saw from flange to flange across the web. Trus Joist used to provide a handy plastic saw guide, but we can't seem to get them anymore. We're down to our last one in the company, and it's got a metal repair splice. Instead, the guys make custom guides out of lexan, a plastic panel that's durable and thin enough not to interfere with the depth of cut (**Figure 19**).

Using I-joists saves time. Because a single worker can easily sling a 40-foot joist, you can quickly spread your joists, and with less fatigue. The side-to-side floppiness of an I-joist can give you a little trouble when you're trying to send it across the span, especially the first piece. The best way is to catch the first joist's flange over the edge of the rim board and slide it to the opposite side of the deck. Once you roll your first joist into position and secure it, you can ship the rest of the joists out across the top flange of the preceding pieces (**Figure 20**). As the promotional literature says, every joist is dead-straight on edge, so you don't spend any time culling or crowning the framing material. And, because you can get I-joists delivered in lengths up to 48 feet, center laps can be eliminated, cutting out a lot of material handling.

If the I-joists aren't stored on edge, as recommended, but are laid flat on uneven terrain, they can take a side-to-side set, so you still have to pay attention and use layout marks when you plywood the deck.

## Installation Details

Solid blocking is required at midspan in an I-joist floor and is easy to precut because of the predictable flange dimension and resulting space between joists.

different lengths to compensate. The best strategy is to take delivery of your rim stock as late as possible, keep it dry, and use it right away. Once it's installed and covered by the deck ply, it should be fine.

When the plan includes an attached exterior deck, I substitute an LVL plank for the rim board at the deck location to provide more substantial holding for the carriage bolts that secure the deck ledger. This precaution isn't strictly necessary — the engineered rim board is approved for this application — but it's one I prefer to take.

**Figure 20.** The floppiness of a long I-joist is controlled by feeding it out along the edge of the preceding member to the opposite side.

**Figure 21.** Pressure blocking holds the joists upright on a recessed, inset mudsill.

We'll do a quick count and cut a bunch of the blocks at once. On our current job, the entire first-floor system is ledgered inside the foundation, to bring the finished floor closer to the final grade level. So, instead of rim joists, we used a lot of pressure blocks to hold the joists upright on the sill (**Figure 21**). I precut most of these in the shop on a radial arm saw. We convert job-site offcuts into blocking by running them through a table saw, because they're too short and awkward to handle with a circular saw and guide.

The computer-generated layout plans usually represent the blocking as a solid line, but we find it's easier to nail the blocking if it's staggered on either side of the centerline. Although staggering is common in solid-lumber framing, I double-checked this modification with my engineered lumber specialist to make sure we weren't compromising the system.

*Web stiffeners.* Certain applications call for web stiffeners to be added to the joists — for example, under a load-bearing partition, or when sistering two joists together. Occasionally, the local inspector requires us to close the gap left between the blocking and the joist flanges to create a firestop (**Figure 22**). We comply by packing out the web. This, and any two-sided web stiffener requirement, is a bit of a pain to do. The rim-joist material, at 1 inch thick, is ideal for packing the web out flush to a 2 1/2-inch-wide flange, but manufacturer's specs call for the nails to be clinched, or bent over, where they penetrate on the back side. The best way we've found to pack the web is to clamp stiffeners to both sides of it simultaneously and shoot them together. This leaves a 2 3/8-inch gun nail fully embedded and eliminates all that clinching.

*Keep off.* Even with blocking installed, attempting to walk the I-joists is a habit you want to break — it's that or your neck. All of the I-joists' stiffness is in the vertical orientation; if you try to walk the flanges, the joists can twist and buckle sideways and dump

you. Always stand on the deck sheathing, not on the joists. Running a course of temporary 1-by bracing every 6 to 8 feet is the recommended precaution to prevent rolling. We also loose-lay lengths of the engineered rim-joist material to serve as temporary walkways. The rim material isn't a scaffold plank and should never be used as one, but it spans less than 14 inches between joists in this application.

## Drilling and Modifying

I-joists have a series of 1 1/2-inch-diameter perforated knockouts in the web, which, if you pay close attention to the end-for-end joist alignment, supposedly makes cross-joist plumbing and wiring runs a relative breeze. Actually, this is usually a better idea in theory than in practice. The lumber distributor cuts the I-joists to rough length for delivery, we hope from a

**Figure 22.** In some jurisdictions, the inspector may require a fireblock in the gap left where one I-joist butts perpendicular to another.

**Figure 23.** When it's practical, cutting joists from the factory end ensures automatic hole alignment for cross-joist wiring or plumbing runs, but in the effort to maximize materials, this is not always possible. And drilling the OSB web is easy enough.

common end, typically using a chain saw. The painted factory end is immediately identifiable. The knockouts are spaced roughly 12 inches on-center, but closer to one flange than the other, so you also have to pay attention to the up-down orientation if you want to take advantage. When working with the joists on site, we try to make sure the factory ends are all together before we start measuring and cutting. If you mix ends, the knockouts won't line up and they'll be mostly useless (**Figure 23**). Of course, if you're cutting two joists out of a single length, you're not going to let the knockout location restrict you, anyway; after all, how tough is it to drill through a $7/16$-inch-thick OSB web? You can drill up to a $1 1/2$-inch-diameter hole anywhere in the web without compromising its performance.

You can cut an amazing amount of material out of the web, too, even from flange to flange, but not just anywhere or as much as you like. If you have to accommodate a duct or other large-diameter penetration, contact the product specialist for specific modification and cutting parameters. But you can modify I-joists in ways that would destroy a sawn-lumber joist.

Adding web stiffeners, and squash blocks under bearing partitions, and becoming familiar with the special capabilities and limitations of I-joists can seem like a lot of extra bother. But those requirements are actually a minor aspect of I-joist application and are more than offset by the ease, speed, exceptional flatness, and superior performance provided by the system as a whole. Once the benefits became clear, I started using I-joists on all of my floor frames and don't see any reason to go back to sawn lumber.

*Scott Woelfel is the owner and president of Francis E. Woelfel, Inc., in Harwichport, Mass.*

FRAMING

# Chapter 3:
# Wall Layout &
# Framing

- **Wall Layout Rules of Thumb**

- **Faster Wall Framing**

- **Plumbing and Straightening Walls**

- **Rake Wall Layout and Framing**

- **Building a Round Room**

# Wall Layout Rules of Thumb

## by Don Dunkley

I've been framing custom homes for more than 25 years, and I've learned that a well-planned layout is the key to an efficient job. Errors are bound to occur: clients are unpredictable, general contractors can forget to relay important details, framers are always in a hurry, and plans are often inconsistent. A job hindered by mistakes and changes goes slow, costs money, and becomes discouraging for everyone involved. But with a little planning and a well-detailed layout, I can often avoid these problems by following these rules.

## RULE 1:
## Study the Plans

I don't just roll up to a site, pull out a crisp set of unread plans, and pound away. Before I get to the site, I thoroughly review the plans and mentally put

the frame together. I study the roof frame first to determine my stud heights. I check the interior ceiling elevations, looking for any balloon frames and rake walls. I find all the beams that need to be installed. I study the elevations, looking for any conflicts. Failing to check for design errors at this stage is an invitation to a framing disaster.

*Plan quality.* Layout is always a challenge, and the quality of the plans plays a big part. Because of the high cost of hiring professional architects, builders can often get saddled with inadequate residential plans drawn by poorly trained building designers. Some of the designers I work with do excellent work, but many provide plans without specification sheets, with scant section views, and with inconsistent dimensions. The general contractor and the framing contractor usually wind up spending hours together

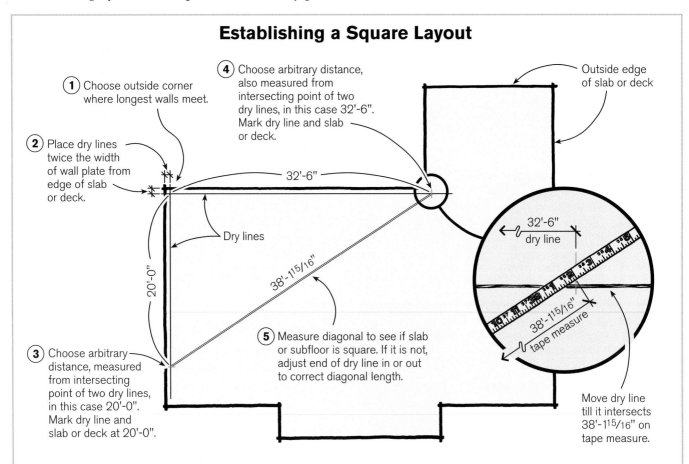

## Establishing a Square Layout

① Choose outside corner where longest walls meet.

② Place dry lines twice the width of wall plate from edge of slab or deck.

③ Choose arbitrary distance, measured from intersecting point of two dry lines, in this case 20'-0". Mark dry line and slab or deck at 20'-0".

④ Choose arbitrary distance, also measured from intersecting point of two dry lines, in this case 32'-6". Mark dry line and slab or deck.

⑤ Measure diagonal to see if slab or subfloor is square. If it is not, adjust end of dry line in or out to correct diagonal length.

Outside edge of slab or deck

Dry lines

32'-6"

20'-0"

38'-1⁵/₁₆"

32'-6" dry line

38'-1⁵/₁₆" tape measure

Move dry line till it intersects 38'-1⁵/₁₆" on tape measure.

**Figure 1.** Before any layout begins, the author establishes a "reference square" from which he pulls all his layout marks. Two dry lines, held two plate widths in from the edge of the slab or deck, form the legs of a large right angle. Using a Construction Master calculator, he figures the exact diagonal, and locates this dimension with a tape measure to establish an exact 90-degree angle (inset).

## Three-Step Layout

Framing layout includes three basic steps: snapping, plating, and detailing.

### Snapping

I measure and snap all the walls at one time. I prefer to use a geared chalk box for speed and fill it with standard red chalk blended with red mortar dye. This leaves a line that's not easily removed. I also carry a blue chalk line that is used to override errors.

### Plating

Once all the layout lines have been snapped on the deck, I spread long lengths of 2-by plate stock over the deck, and cut these to length, mirroring the lines snapped on the floor. In order to properly plate the walls, a carpenter must visualize how the walls will fit together. Plates must be cut so each end will either butt to a wall or receive one. Tight-fitting and clean, squarely cut plates are a must for a plumb frame.

### Detailing

Plate details are like a map, telling the carpenter what and where all the framing parts will go. With a series of pencil and crayon marks on the plates, I describe everything necessary to frame a wall, from stud lengths, beam pockets, and hold-down posts to window and door sizes. Clean and complete detailing is essential for a smooth and efficient framing job.

Two tools that come in handy for detailing are the channel marker and layout stick. The channel marker (below left) is a template tool that lets you quickly mark all corner and wall intersections. The layout stick (below right) is a 4-foot-long pattern that makes 16- and 24-inch on-center stud marks. These tools are available from Pairis Products (www.bestconstructiontools.com). — *D.D.*

**channel marker**

**layout stick**

making these half-baked plans work. I recommend the good designers whenever possible. But if my clients opt for someone else, I won't hesitate to tack on extra money at the bid stage for working with inadequate plans.

Once I have a basic understanding of how the frame will go together, I examine other critical details, including windows, interior trim, exterior finish, and structural requirements. As I gather the information I need, I write it directly on the layout pages of a set of job-site plans. And because the job site wreaks havoc on plans, I mark up an additional set of plans to keep at the office for future reference. Armed with a freshly marked set of plans, with no questions left unanswered, I'm ready to snap some lines.

## RULE 2:
## Make It Square

A slab or subfloor is almost never perfectly square, so the first thing I do is establish a set of square reference lines (**Figure 1**). Using a couple of 100-foot tapes and a calculator, I stretch two dry lines along the edges of a corner of the deck, set back twice the width of the future wall plates. I look for an outside corner where the two longest walls meet so the diagonal will be at least 30 feet. If the perimeter of the deck is too chopped up, I square the lines off a long interior wall.

To square up, plug the length dimensions into a Construction Master and calculate the diagonal, then adjust the lines until the measured diagonal matches.

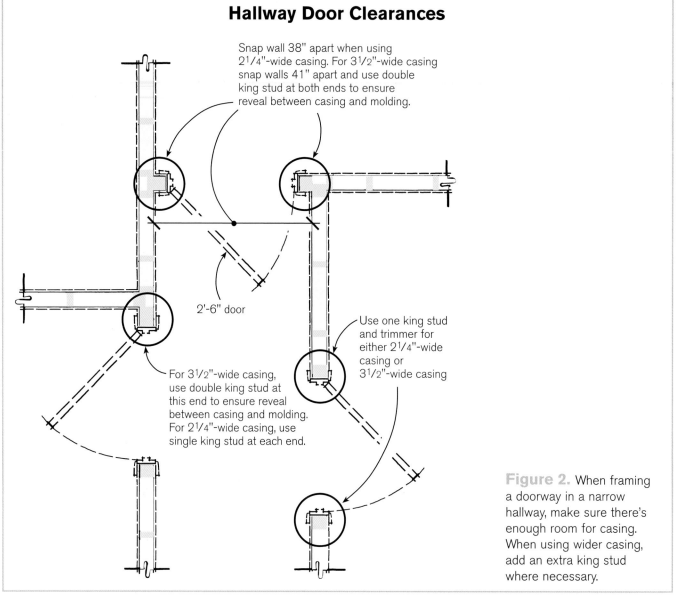

## Hallway Door Clearances

Snap wall 38" apart when using 2¼"-wide casing. For 3½"-wide casing snap walls 41" apart and use double king stud at both ends to ensure reveal between casing and molding.

2'-6" door

For 3½"-wide casing, use double king stud at this end to ensure reveal between casing and molding. For 2¼"-wide casing, use single king stud at each end.

Use one king stud and trimmer for either 2¼"-wide casing or 3½"-wide casing

**Figure 2.** When framing a doorway in a narrow hallway, make sure there's enough room for casing. When using wider casing, add an extra king stud where necessary.

Now find out how far out of whack the deck is by measuring from the edge of the deck to the dry lines. If needed, move the lines so the bottom wall plate will hang out over the edge of the deck a little, being careful to keep the lines square in relation to each other. When the lines are where you want them, measure toward the edge of the deck the width of the wall plates and make a set of marks, then snap the lines. You can now use this set of square base lines to pull all of the other dimensions.

*Exterior dimensions.* After my base line is set up, I snap out the exterior walls. The important thing here is to make the exterior dimensions match those on the plans as closely as possible. This is especially important on a house with roof trusses, because the truss manufacturer is building from plans received a month or so ago, not from what's built on site. For a house with a truss roof, I keep the exterior walls within ¼ inch of the plan. There's a little more wig-gle room with a stick-built roof, which can be cut to fit whatever dimensions the exterior walls get framed.

Once I have the outside dimensions under control, I move on to the inside walls.

## RULE 3:
## Lay Out With Trim in Mind

Don't overlook interior trim during framing. Before I start my layout, I find out what size trim will be installed. If it's not yet defined, I push the general contractor and client to choose the trim.

*Hallways* are typically planned small or get squeezed tight to make room elsewhere. The first place I look is the end of a hallway, where I'm almost sure to find the largest possible doorway being crammed into the narrowest possible space, leaving room for only the skinniest wisp of trim. Casing ends up being shoved tight to the drywall with no reveal, or worse, must be ripped down to fit. Knowing my casing size in advance, however, I can snap out the hallway to work for my trim.

To lay out enough room for a 2'-6" door, for example, with, say, a 2¼-inch door casing, the minimum hallway width required is 38 inches before drywall (**Figure 2**). This leaves room for a king stud and trimmer on either side of a 35-inch header, resulting in a 32-inch R.O. with 2 inches for the jamb and some shim space. Once drywall is on, a ½-inch reveal remains between each edge of the casing and the wall. For 3½-inch casing, I'll make the hallway 41 inches wide to leave a nice reveal. When "detailing" (see "Three-Step Layout," page 31), I mark an additional stud alongside the king stud for extra nailing for the trim.

Another tight spot is a bedroom door in a hallway that opens right against a perpendicular wall inside the room. To gain wall space in the bedroom, the designer typically crams the doorway tight to the adjacent wall. From the hallway side, there may be plenty of room for casing, but it's often a squeeze on the other side. In this case, measure from the inside corner the width of the casing, then add the drywall and the reveal. To keep the door tight to the wall but still leave a minimum reveal with 2¼-inch casing, plan for a single king stud.

*Bathrooms* are typically small and filled with lots of stuff. Often, a bathroom wall must fit both an entry door and a vanity (**Figure 3**, next page). To accommodate these, mark the vanity edge at 21 inches for the cabinet plus 1 inch for the counter nosing and ½ inch for drywall — a total of 22½ inches. To leave room for 2½-inch casing and a pleasing 1¼-inch reveal, mark the face of the king stud at least 24 inches from the wall. Check to see if the door will fit (don't make the door less than 2'-6"). If it looks like the casing will get hacked, widen the room.

*Kitchens.* Most kitchen base cabinets are 25 inches wide including the counter nosing. When a door has been placed tight to a cabinet, I allow a minimum of 27 inches from the intersecting rough-framed wall to the face of the king stud. This gives just enough room to fit in the casing.

## RULE 4:
## Know Your Windows and Doors

There's nothing quite so unsettling as realizing that the pile of windows that just arrived on the job site won't fit the framed openings. Before starting any job, make sure to confirm the window manufacturer's specs.

*Window R.O.* Most of the windows I install are aluminum or vinyl. Like wood and clad windows, they differ in size from manufacturer to manufacturer, typically ranging from ½ inch under to ½ inch over

the window dimensions called out on the plans. A call-out for a "3040" window (meaning 3'-0" by 4'-0") might require a 35½-by-47½-inch R.O. or a 36½-by-48½-inch R.O., or something between. A call to the manufacturer is the best way to be sure. In some cases, the call-out matches the R.O. exactly. But if there's any difference, I'll mark the correct opening size on the plan ahead of time to use when detailing.

Even if the plans include a spec sheet for wood window sizes, check them out beforehand. Don't count on them to be accurate. The burden of finding out the windows' proper R.O. falls to the framing contractor. If you don't check ahead of time and the openings turn out wrong, you'll be fixing them out of your budget.

Plenty of windows these days include half-round arches, elliptical arches, and transoms. Some are stacked on top of each other or mulled together. When the elevation shows such specialty windows, I always make a call to the supplier and get the lowdown on how to detail the rough openings.

*Egress.* Even though all plans where I build must be issued through a local building department for plan check, it's cheap insurance to double-check that all the bedroom window openings meet egress code. Remember, too, that any window that comes within 18 inches of the floor requires tempered glass. I always bring this to the client's attention, in case they want to raise the window sill height and save a few bucks.

When detailing the window locations on the framing plate, stay aware of local code requirements for a window's proximity to a gas meter. More often than not, the actual gas meter location will be different than what's indicated on the plans, or not noted at all.

*Window changes.* Nothing ruins a day like hearing the clients say, three weeks into a job, "We want wood windows instead of aluminum ones." The rest of the day gets spent yanking out headers and sills on a sheathed two-story wall. I try to nip this in the bud by insisting that the windows be a firm decision before layout stage — "no take-backs." Most clients don't realize windows aren't usually interchangeable by size, type, or manufacturer.

*Window headers.* To detail a standard window header, I add 3 inches to the R.O width. This accounts for the two trimmer studs. If the window or door opening is greater than 6 feet, the standard rule of thumb calls for double trimmers. Engineering may require an increase in header size, or a change to 4-by trimmer studs, so I always review the calc sheet attached to the plans (a requirement in California, where I work).

*Recessed windows.* I also check the elevations for recessed windows, common in stucco exteriors. Sometimes the floor plans show a standard opening, while the elevation shows a recessed detail. Recessed windows need extra framing, and the headers can

# Bathroom Layout Essentials

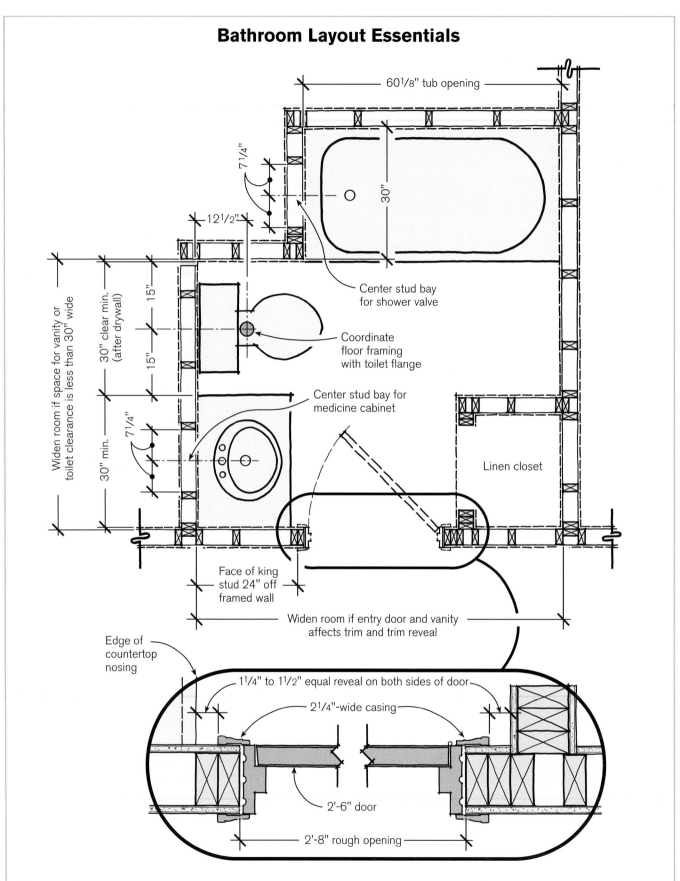

60¹/₈" tub opening

7¹/₄"

30"

12¹/₂"

Center stud bay
for shower valve

Coordinate
floor framing
with toilet flange

Center stud bay for
medicine cabinet

15"

15"

30" clear min.
(after drywall)

Widen room if space for vanity or
toilet clearance is less than 30" wide

7¹/₄"

30" min.

Linen closet

Face of king
stud 24" off
framed wall

Widen room if entry door and vanity
affects trim and trim reveal

Edge of
countertop
nosing

1¹/₄" to 1¹/₂" equal reveal on both sides of door

2¹/₄"-wide casing

2'-6" door

2'-8" rough opening

**Figure 3.** When a vanity butts the entry wall in a bathroom, make sure there's plenty of room for door casing and a reveal. Locate the inside face of the king stud at least 24 inches from the corner framing to allow for the drywall, vanity cabinet, and countertop overhang.

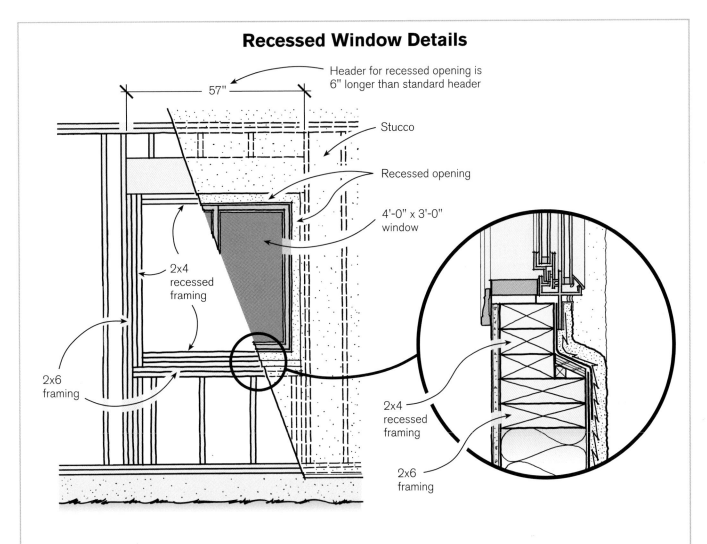

### Recessed Window Details

Header for recessed opening is 6" longer than standard header

57"

Stucco

Recessed opening

4'-0" x 3'-0" window

2x4 recessed framing

2x6 framing

2x4 recessed framing

2x6 framing

**Figure 4.** Recessed windows, common in stucco exteriors, require extra framing to create the recess. Therefore, the window headers have to be longer.

easily run an additional 6 inches in length (**Figure 4**).

*Door headers.* To detail door headers, I add 5 inches to the door call-out. For example a 3'-0" door requires a 41-inch header. This accounts for two trimmers, the door jamb, and shim room.

Pocket-door rough openings need 2 more inches in height than standard 6'-8" doors. On the West Coast, it's common to use solid 4x12 material as header stock for standard doors, and 4x10s for pocket doors. The R.O. width of a pocket door is figured by doubling the door width and adding 5 inches. For example, a 2'-8" pocket door has a 69-inch-long header (32 inches + 32 inches + 5 inches).

*Bypass doors.* Most of the closet door openings I frame are for bypass sliding doors. The R.O. is 1 inch smaller than a standard opening of that size, allowing the two doors to overlap. For example, while I'll frame a standard opening for a pair of 2'-6" doors using a header length of 65 inches, I'll cut the header to 64 inches for a bypass door.

## RULE 5:
## Work With Your Subs

I make sure that I take care of the subcontractors that follow the framing. It's easy to obstruct their access, so I plan ahead to keep framing out of their way. Look out for these folks, so when it comes time to ask for something to be moved or relocated, you've got a friend.

*Bathroom rough-in.* In the bathroom, the first thing I check is the toilet. Code requires the commode to have a minimum 30 inches of total clearance — 15 inches from the center of the flange to the walls on each side after drywall, as in Figure 3. Make sure there's enough space when there's a vanity next to the commode. If there's less than 30 inches for a vanity, I'll move a wall to gain more space.

When framing the subfloor, make sure a joist doesn't interfere with the toilet plumbing. I make a point of allowing at least 4 inches of joist clearance on each side of the toilet location.

## Simplifying Hold-Downs

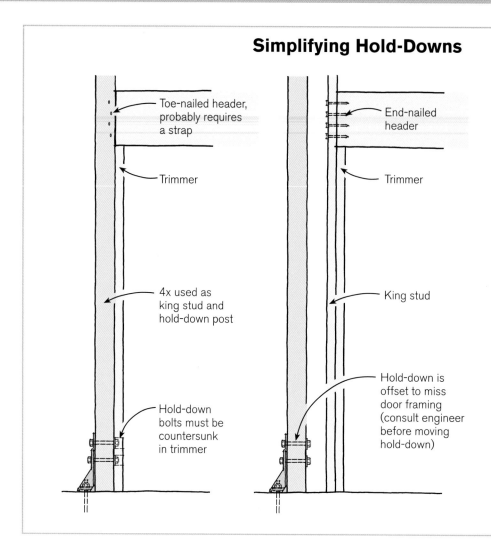

Toe-nailed header, probably requires a strap

Trimmer

4x used as king stud and hold-down post

Hold-down bolts must be countersunk in trimmer

End-nailed header

Trimmer

King stud

Hold-down is offset to miss door framing (consult engineer before moving hold-down)

**Figure 5.** When hold-down posts fall at the location of the king stud, the bolts must be countersunk in the trimmer (far left). Sometimes this can be avoided by moving the hold-down away from the opening (left), but check with the engineer before doing this.

The rough opening for a standard bathtub is 5 feet. I snap out the opening on the floor no less than 5 feet 1/8 inch and no more than 5 feet 1/4 inch. This gives the right amount of wiggle room to fit in a tub. A tub recess usually gets snapped out 30 inches deep. However, this typically puts a stud smack in the middle of the shower valve. To stay friends with the plumber, detail the plates so that studs land 71/4 inches from each side of center, creating a standard 141/2-inch stud bay with plenty of shower valve clearance.

I start the backing blocks to catch the top edge of the tub at 15 inches off the floor. When a tub-shower enclosure is used, center the blocking (2x4s turned flat) at 72 inches off the floor. Make sure a joist isn't in the way of the tub drain when framing the floor.

Most vanity tops are 22 inches wide, and when a half- or full-height privacy wall is drawn to separate the toilet and vanity, I snap out the privacy wall so that it's no less than 26 inches long. If you need to add a towel ring, add 12 more inches.

***Laundry rooms*** are usually crammed with cabinets and appliances, and it's important to know all the dimensions ahead of time. Washers and dryers are approximately 27 to 30 inches wide and about 26 to 28 inches deep, not including hoses and flex duct. This means a washer and dryer alcove must be at least 3 feet deep, and no less than 5 feet 6 inches wide (preferably 6 feet 0 inches). If a client requests a window behind the appliances, I keep the window sill no lower than 48 inches from the floor. Make sure any door is at least 2 feet 8 inches wide, or the dryer might not fit.

***Kitchens.*** Years ago, it was standard practice to install blocking for cabinets in the kitchen walls, but after years of framer neglect, most cabinet installers have given up expecting this. Most cabinet boxes today are made Euro-style, using a cleat fastened to the wall that matches a receiving cleat on the cabinet back. But I still offer continuous backing in the wall, using 2x6 or 2x8 blocks framed at a height of 90 or 96 inches, depending on the size of the uppers.

***Lighting.*** The hallway seems to be one place where ceiling joists invariably end up in the way of the electrician. Can lights are common here, so I check the electrical plan and confirm it with the general contractor. Because it's easy to forget about lighting, I put a reminder on the floor plan (or ceiling joist

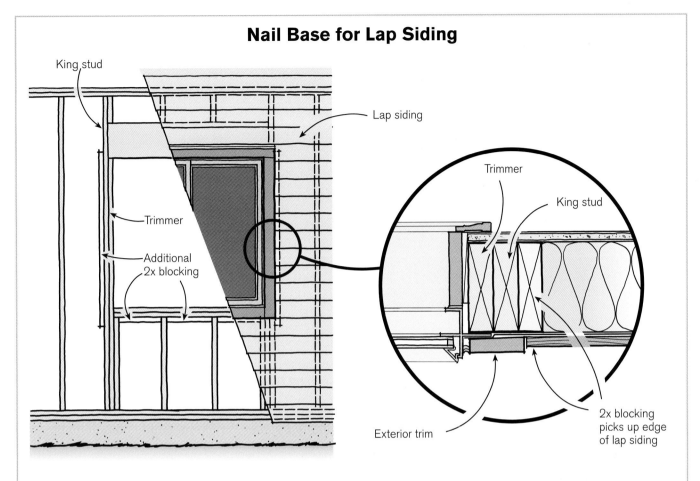

**Nail Base for Lap Siding**

King stud

Lap siding

Trimmer

Additional 2x blocking

Trimmer

King stud

Exterior trim

2x blocking picks up edge of lap siding

**Figure 6.** Where lap siding butts into the window trim, add additional 2-by backing as a solid nail base for the ends of the siding.

plan, if there is one) and on the floor itself. For can lights, I keep my ceiling joists at least 7¹/4 inches clear of center (a centered 14¹/2-inch-wide opening works in most cases).

Kitchen lighting can range from rows of mini-can lights to huge fluorescent light wells. Although this doesn't affect the initial wall framing, it's wise to nail down the kitchen light placement as soon as possible. The can lights aren't much of a problem, but the big recessed light wells can be. Once framed, these huge light boxes surrounded by doubled carrier joists will catch the eye of the client. Don't wait until you frame it to bring it to the client's attention. Avoid the punishment of having to reframe by snapping the light box out on the kitchen floor and letting the client mull over it.

## RULE 6:
## Look Out for Structural Needs

If structural engineering requirements are included with the plans, I study the calc sheet, making sure to note any changes and additions. Here are a few things to look for.

*Loads.* Beam loads that transfer down to a wall below are rarely pointed out in the first-floor layout. When detailing the plates, it's easy to overlook a second-story floor or roof beam, so I spend time locating all the structural support beams in the house. Heavy loads that land on a window or door opening must have a stronger header, which may require engineered lumber or more trimmers for greater bearing at the ends. If a beam load is placed over a stud or stud bay, a post the same width as the beam must be placed directly underneath. Other beams may require a pocket in the wall (commonly found in garage walls).

*Hold-downs.* If hold-down posts have been placed right next to an opening, they often act as king studs. This isn't too bad when it's a window opening, but for doorways it can be a real problem. The stud bolt has to go through the post but not stick past the face of the trimmer stud. This requires countersinking the nut and washer in the trimmer stud. I try to avoid this by calling the engineer to determine how much flexibility I have for moving the hold-down posts. Often there is enough wiggle room to locate the post shy of the king stud (**Figure 5**).

## Rules of Thumb for Window and Door Headers

### Windows

*Window width R.O. + 3 inches*

Sample R.O.: 3'-6" x 4'-6"

Header: 42 in. + 3 in. = 45 in.

Note: Check with window manufacturer for R.O.

### Doors

*Door width call-out + 5 inches*

Sample call-out: **2'-8" x 6'-8"**

Header: 32 in. + 5 in. = 37 in.

### Pocket Doors

*(Pocket door width call-out x 2) + 5 inches*

Sample call-out:

**2'-6" x 6'-8" POCKET**

Header: (30 in. x 2) + 5 in. = 65 in.

Note: For full-height pocket doors, headers must be one lumber size narrower than a standard door header to accommodate track.

### Bypass Doors

*(Single door call-out x 2) + 4 inches*

Sample call-out:

**PAIR 3'-0" x 6'-8" doors**

Header: (36 in. x 2) + 4 in. = 76 in.

Note: This accounts for a 1-inch overlap between doors.

## RULE 7:
## Consider the Exterior

Every exterior covering has an effect on the framing at some point. Stucco is the most common exterior I deal with, followed by horizontal lap siding (usually hardboard but occasionally redwood or cedar), T-1/11 plywood, and masonry (brick, rock, or manufactured stone).

*Horizontal lap siding.* If the exterior calls for horizontal lap siding, I find out whether it has a flat profile or a bevel. With bevel siding, it's a given that the trim boards go on first and the siding butts to it. If it's a flat profile, there is a choice, so I ask the general contractor or the client if they prefer the trim to go over the top of the siding or the siding to butt the trim. When siding butts up to trim, there is usually a backing problem. In almost all cases, the trim board will cover the framing on the sides of the windows, doors and corners, so there's no framing to fasten the siding to (**Figure 6**, previous page). In this case I detail on the plates where backing is needed (usually no more than a 2-by the length of the opening, nailed alongside the king stud).

*Stucco.* If stucco is called for, I like to know if it's a standard three-coat, or the popular two-coat foam board system. The two-coat system is approximately $1^{3}/_{8}$ inches thick, while the traditional three-coat is only $^{7}/_{8}$ inch thick. This extra thickness all but obscures the bottom edge of eaves blocking unless you hold it out an inch. Even though roof eaves blocking happens way down the road, I note this on the plans early so I won't forget it later.

Masonry also affects eaves blocking. For brick, I commonly hold the eaves blocks out $4^{3}/_{4}$ inches, but in the case of real or synthetic rock, it's best to check with the mason for an exact dimension.

## RULE 8:
## Write It Down

To make layout easier, I do the necessary homework. But let's face it: Time is limited for going over the plans with a fine-toothed comb, and no one can carry all the layout dimensions in his head. There are just too many to remember, and eventually they'll all get jumbled up — and many will change. The key for me is to keep a small notebook for each project that I constantly fill with all the important dimensions, and where I track changes as they occur.

*Don Dunkley is a framing contractor in Cool, Calif.*

# Faster Wall Framing

by Tim Uhler

Just about any framing job goes faster if you break it into small, simple tasks that can be worked on in parallel by different carpenters on the crew. This is definitely true of wall framing, which on our jobs begins after we snap wall layout on the deck.

I divide wall framing into three main stages: cutting and laying out the pieces, assembling the walls, and sheathing and standing the walls.

## Cutting and Layout

This stage has three distinct tasks, each of which can be done by one framer. There are currently three framers on our crew, including me. While I cut and lay out plates, the second carpenter cuts headers and window packages, and the third builds corners and king stud–trimmer combinations.

The exterior wall plates and window packages are cut from the same pile of 20-foot 2x6 material. We position it on horses in the garage, so it's within easy reach of both the layout person and the sawyer who cuts window packages (**Figure 7**).

***Laying out plates.*** I cut the plates in place, working to the snapped lines on the deck, and mark stud locations on them as I go. That way, if the other carpenters finish their tasks before I do, enough plates will be ready for them to begin assembling walls.

I cut the plates two at a time with a 10¼-inch Big Foot saw (**Figure 8**); www.bigfootsaws.com. If there's time, I also cut the double top plate. If the wall is shorter than 20 feet, I run the plates full length; if it's longer, I make the break at a 16-inch layout mark so that a stud centers on the joint.

On the plates that run through, I make a reference mark where they cross the intersecting wall, measure

**Figure 7.** The crew positions a pile of 20-foot 2x6s within easy reach of both the sawyer — who uses them to cut window packages and blocking — and the layout person, who uses them to make plates.

out another 5½ inches, and then cut them to length. Later, when we assemble the wall on the deck, we simply align the reference marks to the snapped layout so that the wall is automatically square when we nail it together. We still check diagonals to be sure, but we rarely have to rack the assembly.

After cutting plates, I mark door and window locations, then use a layout stick to mark stud centers. On eaves walls (those that run perpendicular to the floor joists), I always put the first stud at a joint between sheets of subflooring; that way the studs stack over the joists. We do this as standard practice because it makes the building stronger, leaves open bays for

**Figure 8.** The author cuts exterior wall plates two at a time with a Big Foot saw (far left). After marking the location of door and window openings, he uses a layout stick to space the studs (left).

**Figure 9.** It's faster to cut short pieces with a miter saw and stop than to measure and mark individual pieces and then cut them with a circular saw.

mechanicals, and provides continuous nailing for metal straps.

An important part of the layout person's job is to determine the most efficient order for framing and standing walls. The goal is to build as many walls as possible before standing any. I always start with the longest wall (usually the back one) and those parallel to it.

*Cutting window packages.* The sawyer does more cutting than anyone else, so he typically works in the garage with a miter saw and outfeed tables. Most of the windows are the same height, so he can set a stop and cut all the cripples at the same time (**Figure 9**).

This is the fastest way to cut multiples — much faster than marking each piece and cutting it with a circular saw.

Many framers say you should never move material to the saw because that's too much handling. In general, I agree — but not in this case: With 20-foot stock to work with, the sawyer might cut 12 cripples for each piece handled. Because the stock is nearby, all he has to do is grab it and put it on the saw.

When he's finished with the doors and windows, the sawyer cuts the scrap into $14\frac{7}{16}$-inch pieces for fire and panel blocking.

*Assembling trimmers and corners.* Working at a pile of studs in the center of the floor, the third framer builds all the corners and king stud–trimmer combinations with a nail gun and a circular saw (**Figure 10**). If we're using precut studs, he only has to cut trimmers. It's not just a cut-and-nail operation; he also culls badly crowned pieces and opposes the crowns when nailing trimmers to king studs. If there is wane on the trimmer, he faces it toward the king stud so there's a straight edge to follow later, when we use the router to cut the sheathing out of the openings.

After nailing trimmers to king studs, this framer makes up double 2x6s — or cuts 4x6s — to use at hold-down locations in shear walls. He then builds the two-stud L-shaped corners we use, which are sometimes called "California corners."

In the past we used these two-stud combinations where interior walls butt exterior walls (it was one less stud than the traditional three-stud channel and allowed the insulator to insulate the entire exterior wall).

Currently, we don't install any partition nailing; if the sheathing breaks at a partition, the nailer makes

**Figure 10.** A carpenter cuts trimmers from a pile of studs in the center of the deck (left). The finished corners and king stud–trimmer combos (right) are stacked next to the stud pile — close to where they'll be needed when the walls are assembled.

**Figure 11.** Working as a team, one carpenter packs material and crowns studs (top left) while the other tacks the bottom plate to the deck (right) and nails walls together (bottom left).

it difficult to install a stud exactly where it's needed.

We frame exterior walls without regard to partitions and nail up scrap for drywall backing after the partitions are in.

We stack the corners and king studs on an area of the deck where they're out of the way or put them on a cart so we can wheel them to where they're needed.

## Assembling Exterior Walls

We work together when assembling the walls (**Figure 11**). One carpenter nails framing together while the other two haul material, position door and window parts, and scatter and crown studs.

Though the traditional way to join walls is to lap the top plate over perpendicular walls, we no longer do that. Instead, we use galvanized steel tie plates, which are permitted under the IRC (section

R602.3.2). The plates must be at least 3 inches by 6 inches by .036 inch thick (20 gauge) and nailed on either side of the joint with six 8-penny nails. We use Simpson TP37 tie plates (www.strongtie.com) and, with our engineer's approval, eight 1½-inch metal connector nails per side (**Figure 12**, next page).

This approach allows us to cut and install both top plates and nail the sheathing to them while the wall is on the deck. We still occasionally lap top plates in some locations — for example, where a metal tie plate would make it hard to fasten a beam or framing connector.

Check with your building inspector and engineer before switching to tie plates. Some inspectors aren't familiar with them, and when they're covered by framing they're hard to inspect. We address this by installing the tie plates at the edge of the top plate so the inspector can see them from the ground.

**Figure 12.** Instead of lapping double top plates, the author's crew installs tie plates at the ends of walls (left) and uses them to hold the corners together (right). This method is permitted by the IRC, provided the plate is at least 3 inches by 6 inches by .036 inch thick and fastened on either side with a minimum of six 8-penny nails.

## Sheathing and Standing Walls

When we sheathe walls, two framers pack material and one does the nailing. The material packers place sheathing on the wall, tack it down, snap lines at the studs, and cut out openings with a router.

Because our area is seismically active, we're required to block all edges of sheathing panels. To reduce the amount of blocking needed, we run panels vertically and use material long enough to span from the top plate to the rim joist and mudsill below — or, if it's a second story, long enough to tie into the wall below. We use 9-foot panels for 8-foot walls, and 10-foot panels for 9-foot walls.

On long walls in two-story buildings, we align the sheathing with a line snapped ¾ inch down from the top of the double top plate (**Figure 13**). This keeps the top edge of the panels perfectly square to the studs; otherwise, small errors in placing the panels can accumulate and push a panel edge off a stud.

If the wall is short enough, we stand it with manpower alone. For walls too heavy to lift by hand, we use either a forklift or, if we can't reach with a forklift, pump-style wall jacks (**Figure 14**).

**Figure 13.** Sheathing will run off layout if it's nailed flush to a plate that isn't straight. To avoid this problem, the author aligns sheathing with a snapped line ¾ inch down from the top of the double top plate (left). After nailing it off, he cuts out openings with a router (right).

**Figure 14.** An all-terrain forklift can stand walls too heavy for a small crew to lift (left). When there isn't sufficient access for the machine, the author's crew uses wall jacks (right).

## Interior Wall Framing

While the crew finishes exterior walls, I lay out plates for interior walls. Around here, no one distinguishes between bearing and nonbearing interior walls — both get double top plates. While this method uses more material, it takes less labor because we can use the same precut studs in all the interior walls. And since we don't overlap the top plates, I can use the Big Foot saw to cut all three 2x4 plates on edge at the same time.

As I cut plates and do layout, the other carpenters frame behind me — one nailing and the other packing material. Once the walls are up, we plumb and align them (see "Plumbing and Straightening Walls," below), then move on to the floor or roof above.

*Tim Uhler is a lead framer and exterior trim carpenter for Pioneer Builders in Port Orchard, Wash.*

# Plumbing and Straightening Walls
## by Tim Uhler

It does no good to carefully lay out and snap lines for plates if you don't pay equal attention to plumbing and aligning the walls. Like many carpenters, I learned this the hard way. In the past, we've been forced to adjust the lengths of rafters, taper the drywall at ceiling corners, and even struggle to hang doors straight and trim them evenly — all because of poorly plumbed and aligned walls. Now we take the time to "plumb and line" the walls properly to ensure that the top plates end up directly above the bottom plates. It takes our three-man crew about 30 minutes to plumb, straighten, and brace all the walls on an average 1,200-square-foot floor of a house. On the following pages, I'll describe our method.

## Simple Tools, Basic Materials

It takes only a few basic tools to plumb and straighten walls — mainly a good level and some nylon dry lines. We like Stabila's Plate Level (www.stabila.com) because it can be extended the height of the wall and its offset design doesn't get thrown off by bumps and bows in the studs. And we recently started using a PLS5 point-to-point laser (www.plslaser.com), which lets the operator know the wall is plumb when both the down beam and the up beam hit the edges of the plates (**Figure 15**, next page). I also use a 3-foot stepladder; although two of the guys on my crew are tall enough to reach 8 or 9 feet up with a nail gun, I'm not so fortunate.

**Figure 15.** A plate level (left) is handy for plumbing walls because it extends from plate to plate. The author's crew uses a point-to-point laser to plumb walls by aligning the down beam (center) with the bottom plate and positioning the top plate overhead so that the up beam (right) just catches its edge.

Finally, we order 2x4 material for bracing. The braces should run at a 45-degree angle, so for 8- and 9-foot walls we use 12-footers.

## Plumbing Perimeter Walls

The process of standing and plumbing the outside walls really begins when we frame the deck, which we're careful to make level and square. Our walls are already sheathed when we stand them, which means they've been squared on the deck.

In most cases, when we stand the walls the outside corners are either dead-on or within ⅛ inch of being

— [Figure 16 image]

**Figure 16.** The author stretches a nylon line from end to end above the wall, then sights up from below to see whether the top plate is straight.

plumb. Now, I may take some heat for saying this, but I think it's acceptable for the corners of an 8-foot-tall exterior wall to be as much as ¼ inch out of plumb. I allow this tolerance because racking a wall once it's been sheathed is difficult. If the wall is less than 10 feet long, we might be able to rack it by pushing on the upper corner with a forklift, but that will get us only about ⅛ inch.

If we're really desperate, we might "remodel" the corner by pulling the sheathing nails from the corner studs, beating them plumb, then renailing the sheathing. But, in fact, because we're careful at the deck framing stage, this is almost never necessary, and the vast majority of our walls are on the money or less than ⅛ inch out of plumb.

## Straightening and Bracing

Next, we stretch our dry lines to gauge the straightness of the wall. Many framers I know stretch the string between 2x4 blocks nailed to the inside edge of the plates, which allows them to use a 2-by block to gauge the space between the plate and the line. We prefer to put the string ½ inch above the plates and in line with the inside edge (**Figure 16**). Then we stand under the wall and sight up the inside edge of the plates to see where they are in relation to the line, which is faster than using a gauge block.

Because we always cull the best plate stock, straightening the walls is fairly easy. The plate is either good where it is or has to come in or go out. It's unusual for our plates to be more than ½ inch out of parallel with the dry line.

If we like the plate where it is, we'll go ahead and nail diagonal braces between the deck and plate to

**Figure 17.** A carpenter nails the brace to the wall, then springs it down by sitting on it (left) before nailing it to the deck. When he gets off, the brace springs back up and pushes the wall farther out than it needs to go (center). Next, one carpenter sights the plate to the line and the other pulls the wall in by wedging a 2x4 under the brace (right).

hold it in place. Generally, we start bracing at one end of the wall and work our way toward the other end. But if there's a really big bow somewhere, that's where we'll start. It goes without saying that it's next to impossible to straighten a bowed header, so we're also careful to reserve the straightest stock for long headers.

*Spring braces.* We typically use spring braces to push the plates out or pull them in. If the top has to go out, we nail the 2x4 brace on the flat against the plates, sit against the middle to "shorten" it by springing it down, and then nail the bottom to the floor. We try to hit a joist; if we can't, we nail the

bottom of the brace to a cleat that's nailed to a joist.

When we get up off the brace, it springs back and pushes the wall out — usually too far, which is exactly what we want. We then take a 4-foot 2x4 scrap and wedge it between the bottom of the flat brace and the deck. This shortens the brace and pulls in the top of the wall. We wedge the 2x4 scrap in as tightly as needed to bring the top plate in line with the string (**Figure 17**), then nail it off.

We also use spring braces to pull walls in. The only difference is we don't sit on the spring brace when we first nail it in. If the wall proves really hard to

**Figure 18.** A normal-length brace may not have enough spring to bring a stubborn wall to plumb, so the crew uses a long pusher stick to move the wall before securing it with a regular brace.

## Adjustable Framing Braces

**by Carl Hagstrom**

How do you define a good tool? It must save time, improve accuracy, be reasonably priced, and nearly indestructible. When does a good tool become a great tool? When you can't wait to use the thing.

That's how I've come to feel about the Proctor wall braces I bought a couple years ago. There's not much glamour here, just an 11-foot piece of square steel tubing with a threaded insert in one end and a revolving nailing flange at the other. But when you're framing walls, this no-nonsense tool turns the tedious task of line bracing into a no-brainer.

***Time saver.*** I use these braces on every house and addition I build to quickly plumb and line the walls before the roof framing goes on. I also use them to plumb roof trusses, bring wooden beams in line, steady tall batter boards, and brace concrete forms.

Gone are the days when the crew struggles to steady a frame wall against a stiff breeze, waiting for the guy with the level to scream, "Nail it!" only to watch the laborer hit his shin instead of the nail in the brace.

With the Proctor braces, all that's necessary is to get the wall close to plumb and nail the brace to the wall and the floor deck. The threaded insert allows you to adjust the wall in or out about four inches by turning the square tubing. You don't need wrenches or forearms like Charles Atlas. Adjusting the walls in or out is literally a simple twist of the wrist.

***Accuracy.*** No matter how well you nail off a wooden line brace, the walls always seem to creep a little as the nails settle in, frustrating any attempts to achieve a high degree of accuracy. By contrast, the Proctor wall braces allow tolerances in the range of 1/8 inch. If the walls creep, or get a little out of whack during the course of the job, adjusting the braces brings the walls back in line. Being able to simply adjust these braces is particularly helpful when you come back after a weekend of rain and discover that your rain-soaked walls decided to

A carpenter brings a wall in line with a quick twist of a Proctor wall brace.

head off in crazy directions. A little wrist action tweaks them back where they belong.

***Durability.*** These braces are definitely rugged. I'm sure somebody could figure out a way to break one, but I have found them nearly indestructible. The mason working on a house I built dropped an 80-pound chimney block onto one from 16 feet up. It's bent, but still in use.

One more thing I appreciate about these braces as a contractor: they help make the job site a little safer. We no longer create booby traps when we forget to clean the nails out of wooden braces and their deck blocks.

***Price.*** At around $50 each (plus freight), Proctor wall braces are a pretty good buy. A dozen have served me well, but you could get by with six or eight if you had to. Plan on spending at least $400 for a set. You'll use them every time you frame, and I doubt you'll ever wear them out. For more information, contact Proctor Products (www.proctorp.com).

*Carl Hagstrom is a builder in Montrose, Pa.*

move in, we'll pull it slightly farther than necessary, knowing it will probably creep back out a bit. As an alternative to spring braces, some carpenters use adjustable braces such as those made by Proctor Products (see "Adjustable Framing Braces," above).

***Using a push stick.*** Sometimes a wall is so hard to move we can't budge it with a 12-foot spring brace. In

that case, we use a push stick, a 16- or 20-foot brace that can be sprung even more than a 12-foot brace. We wedge the push stick between the top plate and either a solid cleat on the deck or the bottom plate of a nearby wall (**Figure 18**, previous page). We leave the push stick in place long enough to secure the wall with a normal brace. There's usually so much tension on

**Figure 19.** An unsheathed wall can usually be racked square with muscle power alone (left). If the plate doesn't have to go far, it can be pushed into position with a brace nailed on edge (right).

the brace, we push the wall ⅛ to ¼ inch beyond plumb before bracing it. When we remove the push stick, the wall usually creeps back to a plumb position.

## Interior Walls

We frame most of the interior walls before installing the joists above, so we plumb and align those after the exterior walls. Interior walls go quickly because many of them intersect exterior walls, which are already plumb. Because they're framed with 2x4s and are unsheathed, interior walls are easy to rack square and straighten; we can usually muscle them straight without using spring braces (**Figure 19**).

We straighten the longest walls first, especially hallways, because it's particularly noticeable when they aren't straight. In most cases, hallway walls don't hit the exterior, so we start at one end, plumbing and bracing in both directions; plumb and brace the other end; then straighten between.

In halls and stairways with parallel walls, we straighten and brace only one side, then quickly straighten the other side by nailing temporary 2x4 spacers between it and the side that's already straight. After we're done with the interior walls, we go back and check all the door openings to make sure they're plumb enough for the finish carpenters.

## How Much Bracing Is Enough?

Some framers I know use so much bracing you can hardly walk through the house. I believe that if you

**Figure 20.** While working on a slab, a carpenter runs the brace in from an angle to avoid marring the concrete floor (left). At right, carpenters rack a wall square by nailing a diagonal to an outrigger fastened to the bottom plates.

place the bracing carefully, there will still be room to work inside. We usually put braces right at the corners and every 8 to 12 feet in between, taking care to avoid placing them in front of doorways.

It's not necessary to use a dozen nails at each brace, but you do have to make a solid connection. We put three nails at the top and two or three at the bottom of each brace. We make sure we haven't nailed into the joints between the plates, and we test every brace before moving on. We learned to do this after the bracing on a gable rake wall came loose. No one noticed the gable had moved out of plumb until it was too late, and the finish carpenter had to shim the tops of some cabinets way off the wall.

Sometimes you need to be creative about how to install braces. We don't want to nail into a basement or garage slab, so in those areas we angle in the braces from nearby walls or wood-framed floors (**Figure 20**, previous page).

## When to Remove the Bracing

The wall bracing doesn't come out until the floor or roof above is sheathed. On a two-story house, we'll leave the first-floor braces in place until we need to use them on the walls above. We leave the upper-floor braces in until the roof is stocked. This is especially important with heavy roofing material like tile, because stocking too much in one place can cause the rafters to push walls out of whack.

This happened to us about a year ago in a kitchen with a long-span cathedral ceiling. Even though the walls were braced and the rafters sheathed, there was enough weight in one spot to push the outer wall out of plumb, which we didn't notice until it was time to install the cabinets.

It's always a good idea after framing is complete to go back and check the walls for plumb. Even if you did a superior job of bracing, there's always some "creep" that happens when people start climbing around on the walls to set joists or trusses. This is particularly true if it rains a lot before the roof is tight to the weather — a common occurrence in our area. Drenched framing sometimes bows even more when it dries.

*Tim Uhler is a lead framer and exterior trim carpenter for Pioneer Builders in Port Orchard, Wash.*

# Rake Wall Layout and Framing

by Tim Uhler

I'm always impressed when I drive by a framing site and see rake walls up before the roof. In my opinion, that's a sign the framers know what they're doing.

The carpenter who taught me was uncomfortable laying out rakes, so he would frame the roof first, then fill in the rakes a stick at a time. It worked, but it was slower than framing the rakes and standing them up like any other wall — if for no other reason than we had to do the work from ladders or staging.

On the crew I run, we always frame the rakes flat on the deck. We've come up with a way to lay out and build rakes that is simple and about as idiot-proof as any framing method can be. I can't claim to have invented it, since it's based on methods I read about in the book *A Roof Cutter's Secrets,* by Will Holladay, and in trade magazines like *JLC.*

Although here I describe our approach to simple rake walls, these methods work equally well for complex rakes — ones where rafters start from different heights or where the pitch is not the same on both sides of the ridge.

**Full-scale layout on the deck using actual rafters is fast and accurate.**

# Rake Wall Layout

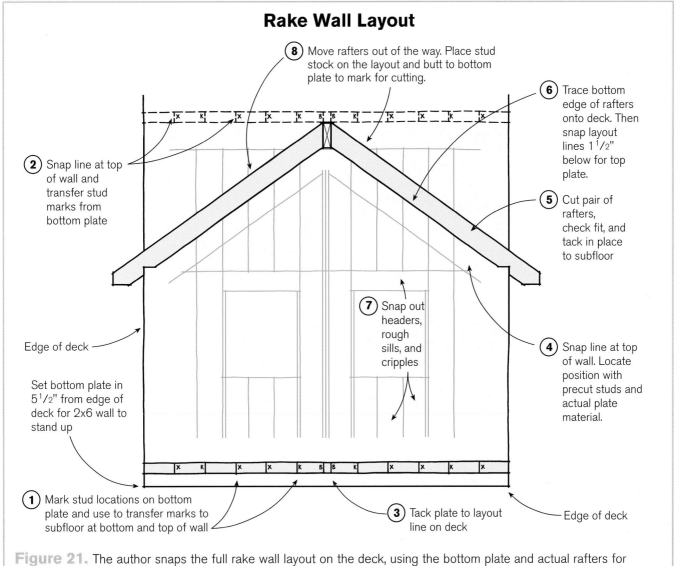

8 Move rafters out of the way. Place stud stock on the layout and butt to bottom plate to mark for cutting.

6 Trace bottom edge of rafters onto deck. Then snap layout lines 1$^1$/$_2$" below for top plate.

2 Snap line at top of wall and transfer stud marks from bottom plate

5 Cut pair of rafters, check fit, and tack in place to subfloor

Edge of deck

7 Snap out headers, rough sills, and cripples

4 Snap line at top of wall. Locate position with precut studs and actual plate material.

Set bottom plate in 5$^1$/$_2$" from edge of deck for 2x6 wall to stand up

1 Mark stud locations on bottom plate and use to transfer marks to subfloor at bottom and top of wall

3 Tack plate to layout line on deck

Edge of deck

**Figure 21.** The author snaps the full rake wall layout on the deck, using the bottom plate and actual rafters for accuracy. The bottom plate is used to transfer stud locations to the top of the wall.

## Toss the Tape

What's most unique about our approach is that we avoid measuring as much as possible; instead, we figure out most dimensions by laying down actual framing parts like studs and rafters. This simplifies the work and greatly reduces the chance for error. Other steps we take to save time are nothing out of the ordinary. We cut blocks without measuring and cut out window openings with a router, for example. We're not the only framers who use these labor-saving techniques, but I like to think that we're better than most at consistently using them.

## Full-Size Layout

There are a few things you need to know to frame a rake: the wall height in that part of the building, the roof pitch, and the size and location of door and window openings. Once you have this information, it's pretty easy to lay out and build the rake.

*Stud locations.* I like to snap the entire rake-wall layout onto the deck, because once that's done we can put away our tape measures and mark everything in place.

We mark the stud layout in two locations — along a plate line snapped along the edge of the deck, and along a parallel line snapped where the peak of the rake will be when it's lying flat (**Figure 21**). Then we snap lines between those marks to indicate stud locations when we cut and assemble the rake.

*Bottom plate.* If the rake wall is less than 20 feet long, we can use a single piece of lumber for the bottom plate. We mark the stud locations on the plate and use it as a story pole to transfer layout marks to the subfloor at the top and bottom of the wall (**Figure 22**, next page).

If the wall is more than 20 feet long, we'll need more than one piece of stock for the bottom plate. In that case, we do the stud layout directly on the deck, transfer it up to the plates, and repeat the layout farther up the wall.

**Figure 22.** The bottom plate does double duty as a story pole for transferring the rake-wall stud layout farther up the deck (top). After tacking the plate to the deck, the crew snaps lines between the layout marks (center) to indicate where each stud will go. The finished layout (above) is a full-size template for marking cuts and assembling pieces. There's no stud marked in the middle of this wall because there will be an opening there.

When we're done, we tack the plate or plates onto the deck on the layout line for that wall of the house. If we use 2x6 studs, the plate will be 5½ inches in from the edge.

We normally snap wall layout in black chalk because it won't wash away in the rain. To avoid confusion, we try to snap rake-wall layout in blue, but if it's rainy we have to snap it in black.

## Laying Out the Top Plate

In the past, we located the top of the rake wall by drawing the rafter on the deck. We would calculate the rafter cuts, measure the heel stand, and then figure out how far down from there the bottom edge of the rafter should be. But for some reason, when we did it this way the rafters on top of the rake wall never quite lined up with the other rafters in the roof.

***Tracing actual rafters.*** Now, we cut an actual pair of rafters instead and tack them onto the subfloor (**Figure 23**). This tells us exactly where the top plates should be in relation to the rafters and the bottom plate.

To ensure that the rafters are correctly positioned, we first snap a pair of lines across the deck to represent the wall height in that part of the building. We locate this line not by measuring but by taking the precut studs for that part of the house, butting them to the bottom plate, and capping them with a pair of top plates.

After doing this at each end of the wall, we snap a line across the deck in alignment with the upper edge of the top plates. This line represents the top of the wall; since it was laid out with actual pieces, it's closer to reality than numbers off a tape.

***Checking the fit.*** When the rafters go down, we align the seat cuts with the line representing the top of the wall. We can tell right away if something's wrong because the cuts will be off at the birdsmouths or ridge. Lately, to speed layout, we've been cutting rake rafters long and allowing them to butt at the center of the roof. When we install the ridge, it butts to these rafters and lands on a post in the wall.

Once the rafters are on the deck and all the fits look good, we tack the rafters down and trace along the lower edge. This line represents the upper edge of the rake-wall top plate.

To cut studs, we need to know where the bottom of the plate is, so we scribe or snap a line 1½ inches in from the line that we just traced.

We are now ready to cut and assemble the rake wall.

## Marking and Cutting Studs

We already have the regular studs for the ends of the wall, but the rest of the studs must be bevel-cut, each to a different length. There's no need to measure these cuts; all we have to do is move the rafters out of the way, place stud stock on the layout, butt it to the bottom plate, and mark where each piece crosses the layout line for the top plate (**Figure 24**).

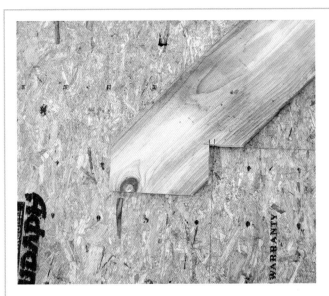

**Figure 23.** The author cuts a pair of rafters and tacks them down over layout lines or against the actual corner pieces of the wall. On this layout (above left), the blue line represents the top of the wall and the pencil line represents the face of a stud. With the rafters in position (above right), the author scribes a line along the bottom to mark the upper edge of the top plate. To mark the lower edge, he removes the rafters and snaps a parallel line 1½ inches in from the scribed one (left).

**Figure 24.** The full-size layout is used to mark the bevel cuts on rake studs. These studs have been placed on the stud layout; they butt to the bottom plate so the carpenter can mark where they cross the line representing the underside of the top plate (left). With the saw set to the bevel angle of the roof, the author cuts rake studs to length (right).

**Figure 25.** The layout is used to position studs as the wall is assembled. After nailing the studs between the plates (left), the carpenters nail the rake rafters on top of the wall (right). Door and window headers are installed as needed.

To prevent confusion about which way to cut the bevel, we mark the edge with an angled line. Then we set a saw to the roof angle and bevel-cut the tops of all the rake studs.

Besides making it easier to lay out the bevel cuts, working from a full-scale layout helps us keep track of the pieces; we don't always put all the rake studs down at once because sometimes the short ones come from cutoffs of longer pieces.

The same is true for window openings — we cut the studs over the header last so we can get them from scrap. Being able to look at the deck and see what's there makes it less likely we will miss something.

## Assembling the Pieces

After cutting all the pieces, we nail the wall together (**Figure 25**). The only thing we haven't cut is the fire blocking. We do this after the wall is assembled by holding scrap pieces of framing stock in position and cutting them by eye (**Figure 26**).

Once the blocks are fastened in place, we nail a pair of rafters to the top of the wall. Normally, the next step would be to square the wall — but we don't need to do this because we framed it on top of a full-size layout that was either drawn square to begin with or measured off a deck we knew to be square.

***Strapped to the deck.*** Before sheathing the wall, we slip short pieces of metal strapping beneath the bottom plate and nail them to the deck. We bend the other end of each strap around the bottom plate and nail the ends to the plate and to the edge of a stud. The straps will prevent the wall from slipping off the edge of the deck when we stand it up (**Figure 27**).

Typically we install two or three straps per wall, but

**Figure 26.** Rather than waste time measuring blocking with a tape, a carpenter lines up the saw by eye and makes the cut.

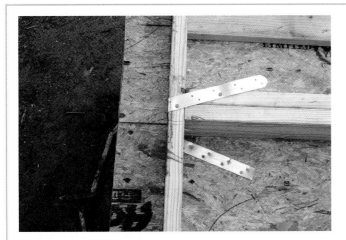

**Figure 27.** Metal straps (top left) function as hinges to prevent the wall from sliding off the deck during lifting. On large walls, the crew installs reinforcing straps (right) next to the studs where the lifting straps will go. Carpenters sheathe the wall in the usual way, then use a powerful router with a flush trimming bit to cut out openings (above left).

if the wall is really big, we install them every 6 feet or so. Once the straps are on, we sheathe the wall in the usual way, with ½-inch OSB.

***Fly rafters and rake trim.*** Framing rakes flat on the deck allows us to easily install parts that might otherwise have to be installed from staging or ladders. We like to install the rake overhangs and fly rafters — or bargeboards — before standing the wall. The overhang consists of a 2x6 nailed to short studs toe-nailed 24 inches on-center to a 2x6 cleat on the wall (**Figure 28**, next page). The fly rafters are 2x10 trim, which we nail to the overhangs. They run long at the bottom and are trimmed off later when we run the fascia.

***Two cuts at once.*** To avoid measuring, we lay the long pieces on the rake wall and trace the end cuts onto them. The outer pieces butt at the peak; to get that cut, we lap one over the other, square up, and draw the cut line.

We do something similar to get the miter cut where

the fly rafters meet. With the first piece nailed to the overhang, we lap the second piece over it and use the 3¾-inch cutting capacity of the Big Foot saw (www.bigfootsaws.com) to cut through both pieces at the same time. We then pull the second piece tight and nail it off. There's no need to caulk the joint; cutting it this way gives us a perfect fit.

If it weren't for the local inspectors wanting to examine the shear nailing, we'd paper the wall before we stood it up. And if we're doing the finish in-house, we might install windows and some of the siding — though we'd have to be careful not to make the wall so heavy we couldn't stand it up.

## Lifting the Wall

Rake walls are typically tall and heavy, so they can be dangerous to lift. Our four-man crew can safely lift small rake walls by hand, but large ones are beyond our ability.

**Figure 28.** It's easier to build overhangs while the wall is lying flat (A). Instead of measuring the outer piece of the ladder, a carpenter laps the stock, squares up to mark the cut, and cuts the piece in place (B). Fly rafters — or rake trim — are installed the same way. The first piece is nailed to the ladder, the second piece is lapped over it, and the joint is cut in place (C). The result (D) is a perfect fit.

Fortunately, we own a forklift, which we use to lift all but the smallest rakes. To prepare a rake for the forklift, we cut a couple of holes through the sheathing near the top of the wall and thread a strap through the holes; we try to put the strap about one-third the way down from the peak and spread it as wide as possible (**Figure 29**).

We're not concerned that the strap will break because it's rated for much more weight than our machine can lift.

***Strain of lifting.*** Lifting puts a lot of strain on a heavy wall. Since the tension on the strap squeezes sideways against the studs, we try to install the strap near a run of horizontal blocking.

Before sheathing a really big wall, we take yet another precaution: We use metal straps to reinforce the stud-plate-rafter connections closest to the lift-ing-strap holes. The sheathing would probably provide enough reinforcement, but the metal straps make us feel better.

Even with a machine, lifting rakes can be danger-ous, so for this part of the job we make ourselves slow down and check everything twice before mov-ing ahead. We plan all our moves in advance: where the forklift will go, where people will stand, and how we're going to brace the wall once it's up.

***Bracing the wall.*** The outermost braces can be pre-attached to the wall; once the wall is standing, all we have to do is nail them to the deck.

The center braces can't go in until the wall is part-way up, but we at least have the stock and framing guns there and ready to go.

When the wall is about 10 feet up, we stop lifting long enough to nail center braces to it. We put two

**Figure 29.** To prepare this wall for lifting, the author's crew puts a heavy lifting strap through holes in the sheathing, runs it across the inside face of the studs, then loops the ends onto the forks of an all-terrain forklift (top left). A carpenter uses hand signals to direct the forklift driver as he lifts the wall (top right). The crew quickly plumbs and braces the wall with prepositioned diagonal braces (above left). The project included several more rake walls, all raised in a similar manner prior to roof framing (above right).

nails very close together through each of the braces, so they can pivot down as the wall goes up. The carpenter who directs the forklift driver must pay close attention, because once the wall is partway up the driver can't see what's happening on the other side.

After the wall is partially braced, we let some of the tension off the lifting strap but do not remove it until the wall is plumb and securely braced in place. Sometimes we leave the strap and forklift there until the rake is fastened to the adjoining interior and exterior walls.

*Tim Uhler is a lead framer and exterior trim carpenter for Pioneer Builders in Port Orchard, Wash.*

# Building a Round Room

by Bob Blodgett

Creative use of plywood for plates and headers simplified the framing of this round tower.

**Figure 30.** A router on a pivot jig proved a necessity for making plates (top) and trimming subflooring (above).

Probably the most difficult project I've ever worked on was a large custom Victorian that included a pair of round two-story towers as its crowning touch. In the end it came out well and the owners were very happy with their new home. Here, I describe some of the trickier aspects of laying out and framing a round structure with a conical roof.

## Foundation First

The first order of business was to locate the center point of the 12-foot-diameter circle for each tower. We used this center point throughout the project, dropping a plumb bob to transfer it upward through successive stories.

The foundation contractor used 2-foot straight form sections, keeping them just inside the 6-foot radius. Because porches surround the tower, you can't see that the foundation is segmented rather than perfectly round.

*Sill plates.* At this point, the router became the most useful tool on the whole job. We mounted our trusty 1 1/2-horse Porter-Cable at one end of a long strip of plywood and put a 1/4-inch-diameter steel pivot pin at the other end (**Figure 30**). We used this pivoting jig to cut the sill plates and all the top and bottom plates for the walls. We moved the pivot pin as necessary to rout the outside and inside edges of the plates.

We used a double layer of 3/4-inch pressure-treated plywood for the sill plates and regular structural sheathing-grade plywood for the wall plates.

## Deck Framing

With the sill plates bolted in place, we installed the floor joists, letting them run a little long over the sill plates — they were cut off later. We then laid the plywood subfloor, letting it hang over a little as well. With the router jig, we trimmed the subfloor, using the same pin location as for the outside of the sill plate and working from the exact center of the room. We set the router cutter a little deeper than the subfloor thickness to mark where joists would need to be trimmed.

We decided not to make a curved box sill but instead installed short 2x6 cripple studs under the plywood, putting them 12 inches on-center, to carry the load from the walls above and provide nailing for sheathing.

## Wall Framing

The walls were also framed with 2x6s, again 12 inches on-center to provide a smooth continuous curve for the exterior finishes. We used doubled 3/4-inch plywood for the bottom plates and four layers for the top plates (**Figure 31**). This created a slight problem: When we got to the top of the wall, we found the round walls were slightly lower than the rest of the walls in the house and had to be packed out with 1/4-inch plywood. This was because 3/4-inch plywood is actually only 23/32 inch thick, so by the time we had stacked six layers for the top and bottom plates, we ended up losing 3/16 inch.

*Headers.* The next step was building curved headers. We ripped 9 1/4-inch-wide strips of 1/2-inch plywood, then kerfed them every 1 1/2 inches, 3/16 inch deep, so they would bend easily around a radiused clamping jig (**Figure 32**). Using construction adhesive, clamps, and screws, we made two triple-layer sandwiches for each header, then connected them top and bottom with the same 3/4-inch plywood that we had used for the wall plates. (We also used this plate material for the rough window sills.)

*Sheathing.* Sheathing the round walls was difficult.

**Figure 31.** A double layer of 3/4-inch plywood formed the bottom plates of the round walls; the top plates took four layers.

**Figure 32.** Carpenters made laminated window headers by bending three layers of 1/2-inch plywood around a form, and gluing it and screwing it together (far left). Each curved header has two triple-laminated pieces, joined at top and bottom by 3/4-inch-plywood plate material (left).

**Figure 33.** The conical roof framing was complicated by a hip rafter from the main roof that landed in the middle. To catch the end of the hip, the author used a double LVL beam, assembled like a rafter pair to match the profile of the vaulted ceiling.

Labels on image: Hip rafter, Peak of roof, Peak of ceiling, Double LVL beam

We used two layers of 1/4-inch plywood, running them horizontally around the wall and staggering the joints. This took three men, two to bend the plywood around the wall and one to screw it off. We even broke a few sheets in half trying to make the bend. (We first experimented with installing the sheathing vertically. It was easier to bend in this position, but it seemed too flimsy between the studs.)

## The Roof

The roof of the entire house was quite complicated to build, with loads of hips and valleys. The conical roofs, with their 23/12 pitch and 6/12 flare at the bottom, were no exception.

The basic round roof was figured the same as any other roof having a 6-foot run and a 23/12 pitch. The complicating factor was that the end of a hip rafter from the main roof landed right in the middle of the conical roof, about 3 feet up from the bottom of the rafters. We supported this hip with a double 12-inch LVL, but since the ceiling below was vaulted, the LVLs were more like rafters than a carrying beam (**Figure 33**).

*Roof sheathing.* Sheathing the roof was fairly tricky. Again, we used a double layer of 1/4-inch plywood. Each piece first had to be cut with a radius at the top and bottom. To mark the radius cuts, I first snapped a line on the deck to represent a rafter. I laid

## Scribing Curved Sheathing

Labels on diagram: Pivot pont (represents peak of roof); Rafter length; 1st sheet; 2nd sheet; 3rd sheet

**Figure 34.** The author laid out and cut roof sheathing three pieces at a time by swinging radiuses from a pivot point that represented the top of the rafter (left and center). The plywood was nailed off, then cut square to the rafters in place (right).

## A Simple Curved Partition

### by Chuck Green

The interior plans on a recent whole-house remodeling project included a 14-foot-long 36-inch-high curved half-wall at the edge of a mezzanine overlooking the stairs. This wall was framed more conventionally than the exterior bay. We drew the 9-foot 3-inch radius using the string-and-nail technique. Because the center of the circle was in midair, we had to erect a staging plank at the center location, to give us a surface where we could drive a nail to catch the end of the string. The curved wall ran from the front wall of the house to the stairway, so we had defined beginning and end points for our curve.

For the curved wall plates, we used a product called Flex-C Trac (Flex-Ability Concepts, www.flexc.com). This is a lightweight, flexible metal channel that comes in 10-foot lengths that join together easily for longer walls. We snapped two sections of Flex-C Trac together, curved the track to correspond to the radius we had drawn on the subfloor, then cut the track to length (**Figure A**).

We secured the bottom track to the floor with drywall screws and fastened 2x4 studs 12 inches on-center to the bottom plate by screwing through the light-gauge metal track. We snapped on the top plate, which was cut to the same length, then checked every stud for plumb before screwing it in place. Later, we framed a partition that intersected the curved wall near the center, helping to brace it.

Using our standard technique for stiffening half walls, we glued as well as screwed the 1/2-inch gypsum blueboard to the studs. Since the wall had a gentle curve, it was easy to bend the 1/2-inch blueboard — no need to wet the back or downsize to 1/4-inch or 3/8-inch drywall. The blueboard later received a coat of veneer plaster.

We trimmed the top of the wall with 3/4-inch birch plywood, edged with maple. To lay out the curve on the birch plywood, we set the sheet on top of the wall and traced the curve on the underside. We cut the curve with

**Figure A.** *Flex-C Trac metal plates save the time required to lay out and cut curved plywood plates. Studs attach easily with screws.*

a jigsaw, then sanded the edges, being careful to maintain a 90-degree edge. Finally, we glued and clamped on 3/4-by-3/4-inch maple edge strips, which were flexible enough to require only minor persuasion from our clamps.

The curved opening by the stairs, set off with the curved balcony wall, is now a main focus of the house.

*Chuck Green is a NARI-certified remodeler and owner of Four Corners Remodeling in Ashland, Mass.*

the first sheet of plywood perpendicular to this chalk line, with the line running right across the middle of the sheet (**Figure 34**). I then measured along the line from the bottom edge of the plywood to a point equal to the length of the rafter and drove in an 8-penny nail for a pivot point. With my tape measure and a pencil, I swung an arc along the bottom of the plywood. I then shortened the tape and swung a second arc at the top of the plywood, trying to get as much out of the sheet as possible.

Next, I lapped a second sheet over the first sheet, positioning it along the centerline so that its bottom arc would match the top arc of the previous sheet. Again, I swung arcs with my tape measure and pencil. I repeated this process, with increasingly shorter radiuses, until I reached the pivot point (the peak of the roof). We cut the plywood with a jigsaw.

As with the wall sheathing, it took three men to

**Figure 35.** Fascia, frieze, and exterior trim were kerfed on the back to make the bend.

install the plywood on the roof. We nailed from the center out toward the edges of the sheets, with two men holding and one nailing. We cut the ends square to the rafters right in place.

***Soffit, fascia, and exterior trim.*** After the rafter tails were cut, we routed 3/8-inch A-C plywood to the correct radius for the soffit. This created a smooth curve to bend the fascia around. For fascia and frieze boards (**Figure 35**), we used 3/4-inch pine, which we kerfed 3/8 inch deep on the back every 11/2 inches to make the bend (and even then we fought with it). We used cedar shingles as a drip-edge. We installed these before the shingle mold, so we could push the shingle molding up to the cedar for a tight fit.

For the shingle mold and crown, we used flexible moldings from Flex-Trim Industries (www.flextrim.com). These gave us a few problems. First, the stainless steel ring-shanked nails we used caused dimples. We first tried nailing at about 12 inches on-center. But as soon

as the sun hit the flexible trim, it sagged between nails. So we went back and nailed on 6-inch centers. The next day, the molding had sagged again, and we ended up nailing it about every inch to stop the sagging. We called Flex-Trim about the problem, and they pointed out that construction adhesive would help, but at that point it was too late.

***Flashing and roofing.*** We laid a self-sticking eaves flashing membrane over the cedar drip-edge and in all the valleys, since they were curved and since metal wouldn't have worked. The asphalt shingles on the conical roofs had to be cut with a radius, just like the plywood sheathing. (The roofer experimented with using straight sections, but it looked too chopped up.) Consequently, he ended up cutting all of them by hand. This reduced the courses to about 41/4 inches, and took twice as long as anticipated. He wove the shingles at the curved valleys.

## Custom Windows

We were pleasantly surprised to find that Marvin carries a line of radiused windows. The 6-foot radius we needed was a standard size, so we didn't have to pay extra for special setup at the factory. The windows came with full jambs, curved sills, and exterior casing, ready to install. They install just like any other window.

## Drywall, Plaster, and Interior Trim

Because of the tight radius, the drywallers felt that 3/8-inch drywall would work best. They poured water over the backs of the sheets and let them soak for an hour before bending them into place. The vaulted ceilings required installing the drywall in pie-shaped pieces, then building up the joints with Durabond for the smooth troweled finish. Overall, the drywall in the round rooms took about twice as much time as estimated.

***Plaster moldings.*** After the drywall was done, the

**Figure 36.** By swinging a sheet-metal screed from a pivot jig attached to the center point of the ceiling, the plasterer created a perfectly round crown molding (far left). Wood baseboards and window casings (left) had to be steamed and clamped into place to make the bend.

plasterers began the crown moldings, using a screed made out of sheet metal to shape the profile. For the straight sections of wall, we installed a perfectly straight wooden strip — a "ground" — for them to work to. For the round walls, they built a pivoting jig, much like the router jig we used for the plates, and installed it at the center point of the ceiling. With the screed attached at the end of the pivot arm, they were able to pull a perfectly radiused molding (**Figure 36**).

Again, the time the crown took was underestimated, so we were able to use plaster in only one of the two rooms that have crown. In the other room, we used a Flex-Trim product, which worked much better on the inside than on the exterior.

***Steam-bent trim.*** We started the interior trim by making the sills, again using the router jig. That was the easy part! The baseboards and window head casings, because they were concave, had to be steam-bent, a time-consuming process.

Even though we steamed the trim, we still had to use clamps to help pull it tight to the wall. And the moisture from the steam made the trim swell, so when it dried, the mitered joints opened up. This in turn made more work for the painter.

If there's a lesson in all of this, it's to overestimate the time it takes to build in the round. Figure out the time you think it will take to do the trickier tasks, then double it. Even then, you may come up short.

*Bob Blodgett is a builder in northern Vermont.*

# Chapter 4: Rafter Layout & Cutting

- **Roof Layout by Calculator**

- **Roof Layout With Scale Drawings**

- **Laying Out an Irregular Valley Rafter**

- **Rafter Cutting Basics**

- **Gang-Cutting Rafters**

# Roof Layout by Calculator

by Don Dunkley

When I started out as a framing contractor, I was often faced with complex roof structures that dwarfed my knowledge and experience. So I read a few books, cut a lot of lumber, and eventually got fairly good at putting roofs together.

Back then, I used the tried-and-true *Full Length Roof Framer* by A.F.J. Reichers to figure out my rafters. Short on text (12 pages) but long on span tables, generations of carpenters have used this little book to make their calculations.

Things changed in the late 1980s when I came across the Construction Master calculator (Calculated Industries, www.calculated.com). I used it through one whole job — from layout to roof framing — and I've never looked back. Now I use the Construction Master to work out a rafter cut list the night before framing begins. This saves me so much time that I now get to bed at a reasonable hour.

Over the years, using the Construction Master has helped me develop a quick and precise system for figuring out the rafters. Not only did it help me shave time off calculations, but it also increased my understanding and ability to frame more complex structures.

## The Calculator

Before the Construction Master, carpenters who wanted to use a calculator had to rely on a scientific model that dealt in trigonometric functions and decimals. Converting decimals to feet and inches is a pain, and dealing with secant, tangent, and cosine functions is guaranteed to cause most carpenters' eyes to glaze over. Since the Construction Master deals in feet and inches and uses the more common terms of rise, run, and diagonal, it's the ideal calculator for the job site.

The first step to calculating any rafter is a simple matter of entering the known **Run** (in feet, inches, and any fraction of an inch) and entering the known **Pitch**. For a basic gable rafter, punching the **Diag** key displays the resulting rafter length. To display the full height of the rafter off the plate, press the **Rise** key.

For a hip or valley rafter, press the **Hip/V** key (instead of **Diag**) for the length. To get the jacks for a hip or valley, you punch the **Jack** key to display the longest jack; keep pushing the **Jack** key to display successive jacks (the calculator has a default setting of 16 inches on-center, but any spacing can be entered). From a single **Run** and **Pitch** input, you get all those various rafter lengths. (Try that with a rafter table book!) If needed, you can use the conversion key (**Conv**) to find irregular hips and valleys and irregular jack rafters.

## Hip Roof Principles

To explain how the Construction Master works, I'll work through the calculations I make for framing a hip roof on a building that's 22 feet wide and 57 feet long. The rafter stock will be standard two-by mate-

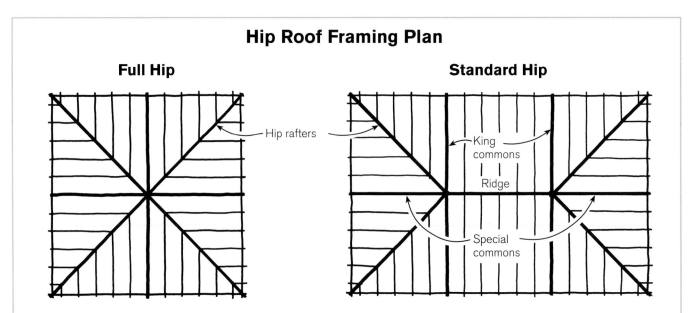

**Figure 1.** In plan view, hip rafters cross the diagonal of four squares on the end of the building. When the hips meet at the center, the roof is called a full hip (left). Hips separated by a ridge make a standard hip roof (right).

rial — 2x6 for the commons and jacks, and 2x8 for the hips and ridge board.

Now, you can't expect to punch a few buttons and know how to cut a roof. It's just not that simple. But by understanding a few basic principles, you can learn to build just about any roof.

*Hip terms.* When four hips come together in the center of a building, they make four squares (**Figure 1**). This is called a *full hip roof.* Separate the hips with a ridge board, attach commons, and you have the footprint of a *standard hip roof.* The standard hip corner is made up of three common rafters. Two are referred to as *king commons,* and the third, which is centered on the end wall, is the *special common.* Next to the king commons sit the jack rafters that fill in the hip.

*Span.* The first step is to measure the width of the building, or the *span.* In this case, the span is 22 feet. On the job site, I always measure the framed structure instead of relying on the plans. I prefer to measure from the top plates to ensure accuracy. Even a slight variation between the plans and the actual length can throw the roof off enough to make a difference.

*Pitch.* Divide the 22-foot span in half to determine the *run.* The run is the horizontal distance a rafter must cover to end in the center of the building. The *rise* is the vertical distance the rafter must travel from the top plate to the ridge. The ratio between rise and run is known as the roof slope, or *pitch,* which is expressed as the *unit rise* over the *unit run.* The unit run on common rafters is always 12 inches. The unit rise is also expressed in inches. The roof in this example has an 8/12 pitch — that is, 8 inches of rise for every 12 inches of run. The distance measured along the rafter from the outside wall to the top of the roof is the common rafter length. On a triangle this is called the hypotenuse, and on the Construction Master it's called the *diagonal* (**Diag** on the keypad).

*Layout.* When I sit down to make my cut list, I work through the layout in my head. The actual layout, of course, won't be done until the next day at the job site, but for the purposes of clearly explaining the calculations here, I'll walk through the steps as if I were on the job.

To prepare for the hip roof, the squares on the end of the building must be marked out to make sure the diagonally running hip rafters on each corner are of equal length. If the structure is out of square even slightly, the hips will not fit properly.

On the 22-foot-wide end wall, I measure in 11 feet from the outside plate. This marks both the center of the building and the center of the special common rafter. Using a Speed Square, I mark a square centerline and draw a "C" through it. On both sides of the centerline I measure ³/4 inch (half the thickness of the rafter) and make two more square lines. I've now marked the centerline of the building and the out-

## Calculating Common Rafters

Rafter Length:

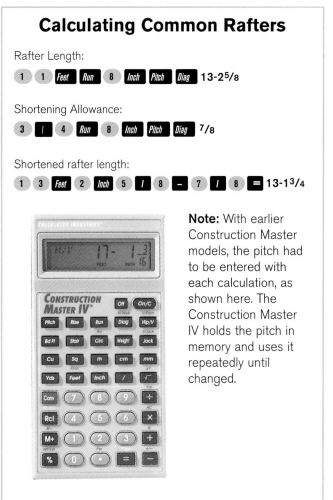

Shortening Allowance:

Shortened rafter length:

**Note:** With earlier Construction Master models, the pitch had to be entered with each calculation, as shown here. The Construction Master IV holds the pitch in memory and uses it repeatedly until changed.

**Figure 2.** On the Construction Master, all rafter calculations begin with the entry of dimensions for the run and pitch of the roof. Hitting the **Diag** key gives the length of a common rafter.

side edges of the special common.

I lay out the king commons on the 57-foot-long wall the same way, measuring in from the outside corner and marking a "centerline" at 11 feet, then adding lines for the rafter edges. Once I've marked both long walls, there should be 35 feet (57 minus 22) between the centerline marks of the king common rafters.

At this point, I measure the distance between the outsides of both king commons. This measurement will give me the full length of the ridge board — 35 feet 1¹/2 inches. I could build this roof with an uncut, or "wild," ridge, assemble most of the roof, then pull up the special common rafters to scribe and cut the ridge. However, I find it best to precut all ridge boards to length to ensure accuracy when dealing with complex roofs. Many times there will be no kings or common rafters to help establish a ridge board.

After I lay out the king commons and take the ridge length, I lay out the hip location. I use my Speed

## Hip Rafter Shortcut

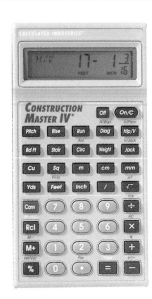

Shortening shortcut:
(when king common is 1¹/₂ inches thick)

[1] [1] [Feet] [-] [3] [/] [4] [=] [Run] [8] [Inch] [Pitch] [Hip/V] **17-1³/₁₆**

⌞_____⌟      ⌞_____⌟
Subtract to shorten Run    Calculate length of hip

(when king common is 3¹/₂ inches thick)

[1] [1] [Feet] [-] [1] [Inch] [3] [/] [4] [=] [Run] [8] [Inch] [Pitch] [Hip/V] **16-11⁵/₈**

⌞_____⌟      ⌞_____⌟
Subtract to shorten Run    Calculate length of hip

**Note:** The Construction Master IV automatically recognizes fractions as parts of an inch, so you don't need to hit the **Inch** key after entering a fraction like ³/₄. When entering 1³/₄ inches, however, you need to hit the **Inch** key after entering the 1; otherwise, the calculator will display ¹³/₄ inches.

**Figure 3.** Instead of subtracting the shortening allowance after finding the rafter length, the author adjusts the run of the hip rafter before calculating the rafter length. With standard two-by king commons, this shortens the run by ³/₄ inch (half the thickness of the commons). With wider 3¹/₂-inch commons, the run is shortened by 1³/₄ inches.

Square to draw a 45-degree line through the center of the outside corner of the wall. Because the rafter stock is two-by, I measure ³/₄ inch on each side of the line to mark the outside edges of the hip. I do this at all four corners.

In plan view, a hip rafter makes a 45-degree horizontal line through the 11-foot square from corner to ridge. This diagonal distance is the run of the hip. Since a square has equal sides, its diagonal is always 45 degrees, and this diagonal is always 1.414 times longer than the length of each side (by the Pythagorean theorem). Since the common rafter unit run is 12 inches, the unit run of the hip rafter is 1.414 times longer, or 16.97 inches (commonly rounded to 17). Therefore, the hip in this example has an 8/17 pitch. It has to travel 17 inches of run to match the rise of a common rafter that travels 12 inches of run. In this case, the hip will have to cover a total run of 15 feet 6¹¹/₁₆ inches to meet the king commons that have 11 feet of run.

### Calculating Rafter Lengths

Once I lay out the building and confirm measurements, it's easy to compute the rafters using the Construction Master. (*Note:* I used the Construction Master IV on this project. Newer models, including the Construction Master V and Pro, have reduced keystrokes for some operations and added new features, but work essentially the same way.)

*Common lengths.* To compute the length of the king common rafter, I enter **11 Feet** into the calculator, and push the **Run** key. Next, I enter **8 Inch**, and push the **Pitch** key. (*Note:* With the Construction Master IV, once you enter the pitch, the value

remains in the calculator as a constant — even after you turn it off. From then on, you don't have to enter the pitch when you do a calculation — it's always working in the background. With earlier versions of the Construction Master, you have to reenter the pitch with each calculation, as I've done above.)

To get the rafter length, I push the **Diag** key and the calculator displays 13 feet 2⁵/₈ inches. But this is not yet the correct dimension. Rafters and ridge boards are not just lines on paper — they occupy space. So I have to adjust to compensate for the thickness of the stock. With this full-length common rafter, I have to take into account the thickness of the two-by ridge. This is called the *shortening allowance*, and it is based on half the thickness of the ridge — in this case, ³/₄ inch.

To find the shortening allowance for ³/₄ inch, I enter ³/₄, hit **Run**, enter **8 Inch**, hit **Pitch**, then push **Diag**. The calculator will display ⁷/₈ inch. I deduct this amount from the result of the first calculation to get a final rafter length of 13 feet 1³/₄ inches (**Figure 2**, previous page).

*Hip lengths.* I next calculate the hip: Enter **11 Feet**, **Run**, **8 Inch**, **Pitch**, then punch the **Hip/V** key to get 17 feet 2³/₈ inches on the display. I also need to make a shortening allowance for the hip connection at the ridge. Unlike the deduction for the ridge on a common, the hip shortening allowance is half the 45-degree thickness of the common rafter. To calculate this, I enter ³/₄, **Run**, **8 Inch**, **Pitch**, then push **Hip/V**. The calculator displays 1³/₁₆ inches. I deduct this from the first hip length to get a final hip length of 17 feet 1³/₁₆ inches.

***Allowing for stock variations.*** In most conventional roof framing, the rafter and ridge stock are the same thickness. But when there is a difference in thickness, it affects the shortening allowance.

For example, the shortening allowance for the special common is based on half the thickness of the king commons — not the ridge. If the king commons are 3 1/2 inches thick, the ridge will grow by 1 3/4 inches rather than by 3/4 inch. The centerline at 11 feet remains the same, but because of the thicker rafter stock, the ridge will extend out farther to flush out at the edge of the king common. So, the special common will be shortened by half the thickness of the king commons — 1 3/4 inches — by whatever the pitch is. So, the length of a special common on an 8/12 pitch would be shortened by 2 1/8 inches. This same principle applies to the hip, and therefore the shortening allowance is based on the king commons thickness rather than the ridge.

***Shortcut.*** Once you become familiar with the basic principles behind hip framing, you can use a shortcut to make the calculations a little quicker. To avoid having to make the various shortening allowances, you can deduct the ridge and common thickness right off the span. Take, for example, the 22-foot-span building with a two-by ridge and rafters. I'll deduct 1 1/2 inches, representing the ridge, from the main span, leaving 21 feet 10 1/2 inches. I then divide this adjusted span by two to get an *adjusted run* of 10 feet 11 1/4 inches.

To find the lengths of the special and king commons on the calculator, I enter **10 Feet, 11 Inch, 1/4, Run, 8 Inch, Pitch.** Then I push **Diag** to display 13 feet 1 3/4 inches. I then push **Hip/V** to find the hip length of 17 feet 1 3/16 inches.

Another way to make the same calculations is to subtract half the thickness of the ridge (for commons) or commons (for the hips) from the run. For example, to find the hip, I would subtract half the thickness of the king common (3/4 inch) from 11 feet, then hit **Run, 8 Inch, Pitch, Hip/V** to find the length of 17 feet 1 3/16 inches (**Figure 3**). If the king commons were 3 1/2 inches thick, I'd subtract 1 3/4 inches from 11 feet, hit **Run, 8 Inch, Pitch, Hip/V** for a hip length of 16 feet 11 5/8 inches.

## Calculating Jack Lengths

The next rafters to be figured for a hip roof are the jacks. The jack rafters attach to the hip and get proportionally shorter as they follow the on-center layout on the plate from the king common toward the corner. This proportion is referred to as the *common difference*. To ensure a match on both sides of the hip, jacks are cut in pairs, making a right-hand and a left-hand jack. Our roof has eight jacks of each length, or four right- and left-hand sets. Since it's an equal-pitch hip roof, the plumb cut on all of the jacks is made on a 45-degree bevel.

The Construction Master has a **Jack** key that calculates the first, or longest jack, down to the last, or shortest, jack. Repeatedly pressing the key displays each successive jack length, deducting the common difference automatically. The Construction Master is programmed with a default setting for a 16-inch on-center jack spacing, but you can change it to whatever rafter spacing you are using. To do this on the Construction Master IV, clear the calculator, enter the on-center spacing, then press the **Jack** key. (On earlier versions, press the **Jack** key first, then enter the on-center spacing.) Then enter the run, the pitch, and press **Jack** again.

Now you're ready to calculate the length of the jack rafters. For example, to find the jacks for 2-foot on-center spacing, press **Jack,** and enter **2 Feet.** Then enter **11 Feet, Run, 8 Inch, Pitch.** Again, press **Jack,** and the calculator displays 10 feet 9 13/16 inches. Push **Jack** again and 8 feet 4 15/16 inches is displayed. Each jack is 2 feet 4 7/8 inches shorter than the previous one — the common difference for 24-inch on-center rafter spacing.

The jack rafters I calculated also need shortening to compensate for the thickness of the hip rafter. This shortening is based on the run of half the 45-degree thickness of the hip. The 45-degree length of the 1 1/2-inch-thick hip is 2 1/8 inches. Half of that is 1 1/16 inches. To find the shortening allowance, enter **1 Inch, 1/16, Run, 8 Inch, Pitch.** Then enter **Diag,** and the display reads 1 1/4 inches. The jack length is cut short by that amount.

## Shortcut for Jacks

The shortening allowance for jacks must be measured down the center top of the jack, since the lengths are calculated from center point to center point. This is quite inconvenient, especially when cutting large sets of jacks. To get around this, I use a shortcut that gives me the jack length from the long point of the bevel cut at the face of the hip to the outside of the plate. This allows for the tape to be hooked over the long point for easier measuring and accurate jack rafter spacing — important when the roof is sheathed in plywood.

To do this, I need to know the run from the face of the hip to the outside edge or long point of the first jack. To help visualize this distance, think about how the 1 1/2-inch-thick hip rafter sits at 45 degrees on the outside corner of the walls (**Figure 4**, next page). One half of its thickness (3/4 inch) projects past the side of the outside edge of the plate. Measured along the outside of the wall, this overhang is 1 1/16 inches long. The run measurement I want starts from this point — the face of the hip — and goes to the long point of the first jack. If I were on site, I could use the rafter layout marks to measure between these two points along the wall plate. But I can also work back-

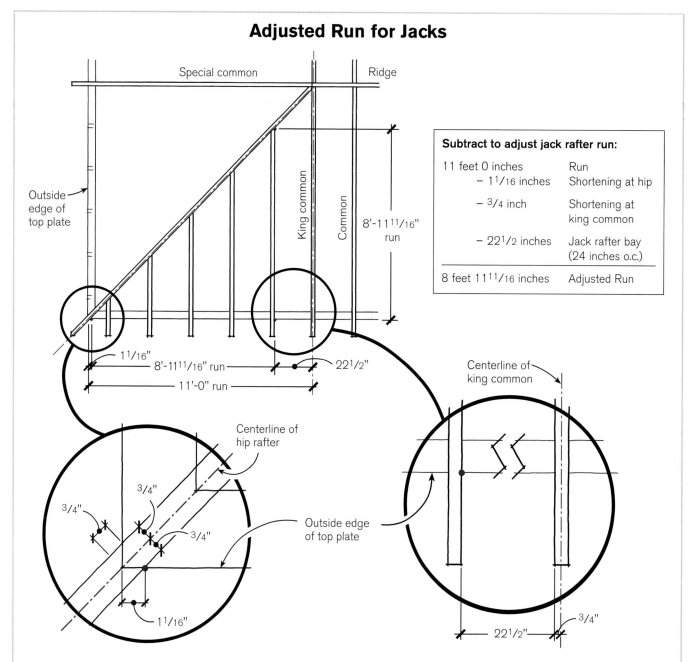

## Adjusted Run for Jacks

Special common | Ridge

Outside edge of top plate

King common | Common

8'-11¹¹/₁₆" run

**Subtract to adjust jack rafter run:**

| 11 feet 0 inches | Run |
| − 1¹/₁₆ inches | Shortening at hip |
| − ³/₄ inch | Shortening at king common |
| − 22¹/₂ inches | Jack rafter bay (24 inches o.c.) |
| 8 feet 11¹¹/₁₆ inches | Adjusted Run |

1¹/₁₆"
8'-11¹¹/₁₆" run — 22¹/₂"
11'-0" run

Centerline of hip rafter

Centerline of king common

Outside edge of top plate

³/₄" ³/₄" ³/₄"
1¹/₁₆"

³/₄"
22¹/₂"

**Figure 4.** It's easier to lay out a jack rafter when you can measure to the long point of the bevel cut instead of the centerline. One way to do this is to use the run of the longest jack, which can be measured or calculated from the rafter layout marks on the wall plate. In this example, from the run of 11 feet, first subtract the hip shortening allowance (1¹/₁₆ inch) — which is the same as the distance measured along the wall where the hip rafter overhangs the plate. Next, subtract half the thickness of the king common (³/₄ inch), then subtract the width of the last rafter bay (22¹/₂ inches).

ward from the 11-foot run, first subtracting half the thickness of the king common (³/₄ inch) then the width of the bay between the king common and the longest jack (22¹/₂ inches), and finally, the 45-degree thickness of the hip (1¹/₁₆). The result is a run of 8 feet 11¹¹/₁₆ inches — the total distance from the face of the hip to the long point of the longest jack rafter.

To find the jack length on the calculator, I enter **8 Feet, 11 Inch, ¹¹/₁₆, Run, 8 Inch, Pitch**. Then I punch the **Diag** key to get the first jack length of 10

feet 9⁷/₁₆ inches (**Figure 5**).

When calculating this way, the **Diag** key must be pushed to get the first jack, although this key is usually used to figure the common. (If you entered the **Jack** key, the first jack would be skipped, since the calculator thinks that it's using the common rafter run). Now press the **Jack** key to get the next jack length — 8 feet 4⁹/₁₆ inches. Hit the **Jack** key again to get 5 feet 11³/₄ inches, and so on, until the last, or smallest jack, is displayed.

## Shortcut for Jacks

Length of Jack from plate to long point:
(using Adjusted Run)

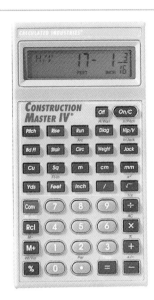

8 **Feet** 1 1 **Inch** 1 1 **I** 1 6 **Run** 8 **Inch** **Pitch** **Diag**    10-9$^7/16$

                                              **Jack**    8-4$^9/16$

                                              **Jack**    5-11$^3/4$

                                              **Jack**    3-6$^7/8$

                                              **Jack**    1-2$^1/16$

                                              **Jack**    0-0

**Figure 5.** Using the Adjusted Run, hit the Diag key to get the length of the longest jack (from plate to long point). Repeatedly hitting the Jack key gives the length of each proportionately shorter jack rafter.

**Further shortcut.** I used this example to explain how you can make the calculator figure to the framing face and not the centerline. Once you understand how to figure the jacks this way, you can use another shortcut. To the original run of 11 feet, add $^3/4$ inch. This gives the length of the run to the outside of the king common. Deduct 1$^1/16$ inches for the space taken by the hip at the corner. This gives a distance of 10 feet 11$^{11}/16$ inches from the inside face of the hip to the outside of the king common. On the calculator, enter **10 Feet, 11 Inch**, $^{11}/16$, **Run, 8 Inch, Pitch**. Now bypass the **Diag** key, and press the **Jack** key three times. The display will read 10 feet 9$^7/16$ inches. Again, this is the long point of the first, or

longest, jack. Keep pressing the **Jack** key to get the lengths of the remaining jacks.

### The Cut List

When I put together the rafter cut list, I put all the lengths down on a yellow legal pad. Knowing all the lengths enables me to accurately judge the lumber lengths I'll need to use on site. I organize my list carefully, labeling the various spans for easy identification, breaking down each section into its components, and then comparing it with the plans for any omissions or errors. Now it's time to make some sawdust.

*Don Dunkley is a framing contractor in Cool, Calif.*

# Roof Layout With Scale Drawings

## by William Dillon

During my 30 years as a carpenter, I have framed several hundred complicated roofs, and have read nearly every book on the subject. A particularly good one is *The Steel Square*, by H.H. Siegele, which uses drawing techniques rather than advanced math to illustrate complex rafter cuts.

I began using these drawing techniques because I wanted to better understand the geometry of roof planes. Not only did these methods help me grasp the way complex roofs fit together, but they also increased my cutting speed — and have been excellent teaching tools to boot.

Here, I'll show how I use this technique to develop the basic cuts for an irregular hip. The method explained here is accurate enough for concealed 2-by roof framing. Where accuracy is more critical — as in the timber-frame homes we build, where a half-degree error on an 8/12 timber valley really shows — I also use basic trigonometry, but that's another story.

### Thinking in Triangles

This method helps you think of a roof in terms of its component triangles and how they relate to each

**Use basic geometry and scale drawings to lay out rafter cuts for complex roofs.**

other. All the triangles that make up the roof are drawn on a flat surface. Think of the horizontal leg of each triangle — the run — as a hinge. Once the drawing is complete, the triangles can be mentally rotated on their hinges to form a three-dimensional model of the roof. When I teach this method, I use a cardboard model as a visual aid to show how each part of the roof relates to the others (**Figure 6**). Mastering the technique takes time — I'm still learning — but the basics can be grasped quite easily.

## Plywood Worksheet

I usually make my drawings on a piece of plywood, using the 12ths scale on the framing square. This makes sense on the job site, and lets me draw the cut angles full-scale. The only special tools I use are a large compass (Lee Valley Tools sells one; www.leevalley.com) and an oversized bevel square. The aluminum bevel square in the photos came from Germany, but any large one will work. (Quint Measuring Systems' contractor-grade True Angle Tool is available online in 24-inch and 36-inch lengths; www.quintmeasuring.com.)

The blueprints I'm typically given include only the most basic information about a roof: a plan view, an elevation, and the basic pitches. But this is enough information to develop the drawings, if you follow the correct steps. The easiest method is to break the drawing sequence down into discrete parts, each of which builds on the previous one.

- plan angle for the hip rafter
- common and hip lengths and cut angles
- hip backing angle
- roof surface

## Draw the Common and Hip Runs

The example roof has a 10/12 pitch on the hip end and a 5/12 pitch on the building's long dimension,

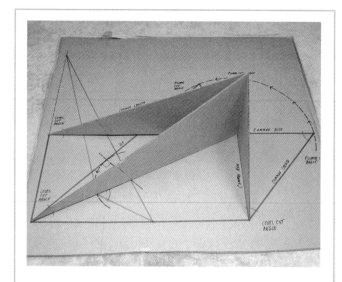

**Figure 6.** When teaching framing to novice carpenters, the author uses a simple cardboard model to help them "think in triangles."

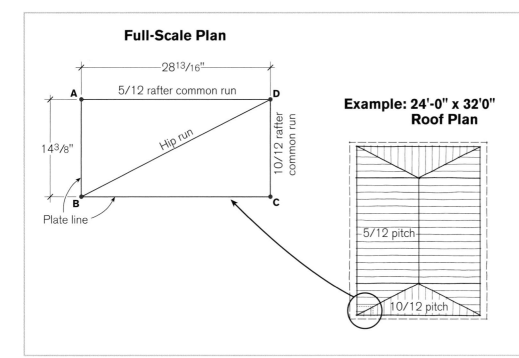

**Full-Scale Plan**

Plate line

**Figure 7.** The full-scale drawing for an irregular hip roof begins with a basic rectangle — a plan view that represents a corner of the roof. The sides are the two common runs; the diagonal is the hip rafter.

and the eaves meet at a 90-degree angle (**Figure 7**). Note that I'm ignoring the overhang and working from the plate line.

To get started, you first have to accurately draw the angle at which the hip rafter intersects the eaves at the corner. I start with an imaginary point on the hip rafter where the rise is 12 inches above the outside of

the plate, then determine the run of the common rafters from that point to the plate line. You can do this quickly with a calculator, but I just use a simple table I've printed out (**Figure 8**).

A 5/12 common rafter has a run of 28¹³/₁₆ inches at 12 inches of rise, while the 10/12 rafter runs 14³/₈ inches. I use these numbers to draw a rectangle,

# Finding the Run at 12 Inches of Rise

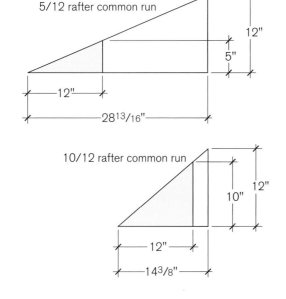

## Common Length at 12-Inch Rise

| Pitch | Length | Pitch | Length |
|-------|--------|-------|--------|
| 3/12 | 48¹/₆₄" | 14/12 | 10¼" |
| 4/12 | 36¹/₆₄" | 15/12 | 9⅝" |
| 5/12 | 28¹³/₁₆" | 16/12 | 9" |
| 6/12 | 24" | 17/12 | 8½" |
| 7/12 | 20⅝" | 18/12 | 8" |
| 8/12 | 18¹/₆₄" | 19/12 | 7⅝" |
| 9/12 | 16" | 20/12 | 7¼" |
| 10/12 | 14³/₈" | 21/12 | 6⅞" |
| 11/12 | 13³/₃₂" | 22/12 | 6½" |
| 12/12 | 12" | 23/12 | 6¼" |
| 13/12 | 11⅛" | 24/12 | 6" |

**Figure 8.** To start the full-scale layout drawing, the author finds the two common runs at 12 inches of rise; that is, he converts the 5-inch-over-12-inch roof pitch to 12 inches over 28¹³/₁₆ inches (left). Rather than do the math each time, he works from a chart (right).

# Common and Hips

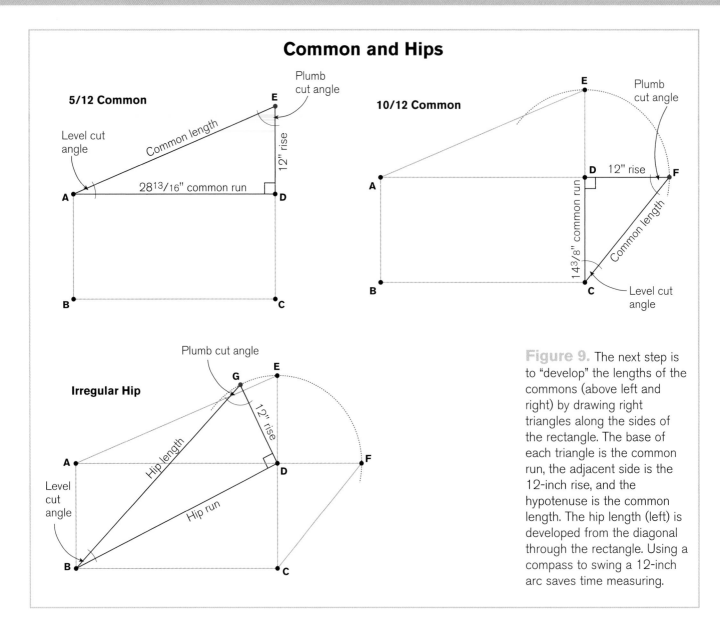

**5/12 Common**

Plumb cut angle

Level cut angle

Common length

12" rise

28¹³/₁₆" common run

**10/12 Common**

Plumb cut angle

12" rise

14³/₈" common run

Common length

Level cut angle

**Irregular Hip**

Plumb cut angle

Hip length

12" rise

Level cut angle

Hip run

**Figure 9.** The next step is to "develop" the lengths of the commons (above left and right) by drawing right triangles along the sides of the rectangle. The base of each triangle is the common run, the adjacent side is the 12-inch rise, and the hypotenuse is the common length. The hip length (left) is developed from the diagonal through the rectangle. Using a compass to swing a 12-inch arc saves time measuring.

which is the basis for all the drawings to follow. A diagonal across the middle (line BD) represents the hip in plan. If you've drawn accurately, you've already got the side cut angles for the jacks, which you can transfer to the stock with a bevel square.

## Draw the Common and Hip Rises and Lengths

Next, I draw the rise — 12 inches — of one of the common rafters by extending one end of the rectangle (**Figure 9**). So, for example, I extend line CD 12 inches to point E; this represents the rise of the 5/12 common rafter. Line AE represents the 5/12 common length.

Here's where the compass comes in handy. I set its points at D and E, then swing an arc around the end of the rectangle so I don't have to measure the rise three times. Next I draw the 10/12 common in exactly the same way as the 5/12, then the hip, using the framing square to draw its rise (DG) perpendicular to its run (BD).

You've now got the plumb cuts as well as the seat cuts for both commons and the hip.

## Draw the Hip Backing Angle

Figuring the backing angles for an irregular hip is usually tricky, but not with this method. Start by drawing a line perpendicular to the hip length, anywhere along its length. Extend the line to the hip run; this is line JK in the drawing (**Figure 10**).

Next, starting at point K, draw a line perpendicular to the hip run and extend it far enough in both directions that it crosses the plate lines (LM). You may have to extend one or both of the plate lines, as in the drawing, in order to intersect this new line.

Now I set the point of the compass on K and swing an arc from J to the hip run; the intersection is point N.

Finally, drawing lines from this point — N — to points L and M gives you the backing angle for the hip rafter.

## Hip Backing Angle

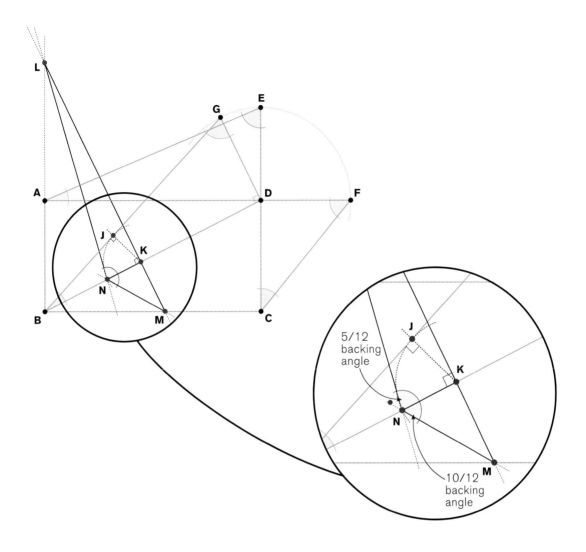

5/12
backing
angle

10/12
backing
angle

**Figure 10.** To develop the hip backing angle (angle LNM in the example), first draw a line perpendicular to the hip length extending to the base of the hip — from point J to point K. Next, draw a line from point K perpendicular to the hip run extending in both directions until it crosses the plate lines (LM). Then, using K as the pivot point, swing an arc from point J to the hip run — to point N in the example. Finally, draw lines from N to L and M; the resulting angle, illustrated in the cardboard model (photo, left), represents the top of the hip rafter.

# Roof Surface

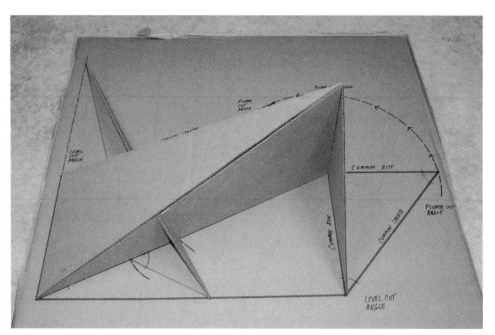

**Figure 11.** To draw the sheathing cuts at the hip corner, first extend both common runs well beyond the plate lines, then draw arcs from the tops of the common lengths to these new line extensions (arcs EO and FP). The cardboard model (left) shows how rotating triangle OAB creates a perfectly fitted roof surface.

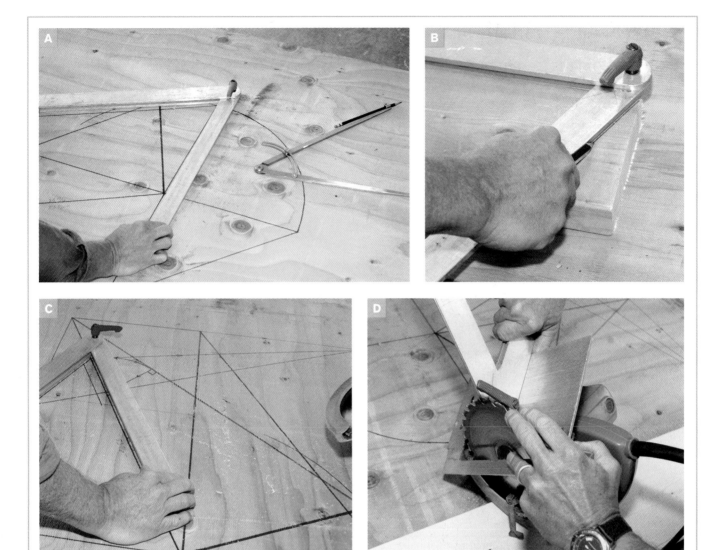

**Figure 12.** Pulling cut angles off the developed drawing is a matter of setting the bevel square and transferring the angles to the stock. Here, the author transfers the plumb cut for the 10/12 common (A, B) and sets the bevel angle for the 5/12 hip backing (C, D).

## Draw the Roof Surface

You can also easily figure out the angled cuts for the roof sheathing (**Figure 11**). Put the point of your compass at point A and the pencil end at E — the distance along the 5/12 common length. Then swing this arc in the opposite direction, make a mark, and extend the 5/12 run line (AD) until it intersects at point O. Draw a line from O to B; the triangle you've drawn represents the roof surface on the 5/12 side of the hip rafter.

Repeat these steps for the other side (triangle BCP).

At this point, you can transfer the cut angles to the stock for cutting (**Figure 12**).

*William Dillon is a job supervisor with South Mountain Co., an employee-owned design/build firm on Martha's Vineyard, Mass.*

# Laying Out an Irregular Valley Rafter

by Len Schmidt

With a couple of calculators and a methodical approach, you can leave your string and bevel gauges in the truck.

On a new house with some 26 different roof planes, our crew got lots of practice joining unequally pitched roofs. By the end of the job, we had settled on an accurate, efficient method for figuring the cuts on irregular hip and valley rafters. Here, I'll focus on a section of the roof where a lower bumpout with a 4³/4:12 pitch met the higher 6¹/2:12 main roof. We framed this section of the roof with a *major* (or supporting) valley rafter — a doubled LVL that extends all the way to the structural ridge and supports the *minor* valley, which intersects it lower down.

## Find the Angle in Plan

Locating where a hip or valley bears on an exterior wall is pretty straightforward on roofs with equal pitches — it's always located right over the outside corner, coming off at a 45-degree angle when viewed in plan. But on hips and valleys between roofs with unequal pitches, this can be a bit trickier. Most plans will call for the soffit to be the same depth all the way around. To make this happen when the intersecting roofs are of different pitches (as in our example valleys), the valley will come off the corner not at

45 degrees in plan, but at some irregular angle and skewed off-center toward the side of the shallower-pitched roof. This means having to determine the angle in plan.

There are many ways to find the angle in plan of an unequal-pitched hip or valley, but the one that works best for me uses a trig-function calculator (**Figure 13**). If you have two roof pitches given in inches, simply divide the shallower pitch by the steeper one and take the arc tangent (inverse tangent on the calculator). This gives you the angle in plan between the valley and a common rafter in the shallower-pitched roof. (If you divide the steeper pitch by the shallow pitch, you get the angle between a common and the valley on the steeper side.)

I make a note of this angle, 36.16 degrees: It's the setting for my circular saw table when making the plumb cheek cut at the top of the valley rafter, and I also use it when figuring out the bevel on top of the valley.

## Doubled-Up Hip and Valley Members

I usually double up 2x12s or LVL for the hip and valley rafters. The primary reason, even if it's not neces-

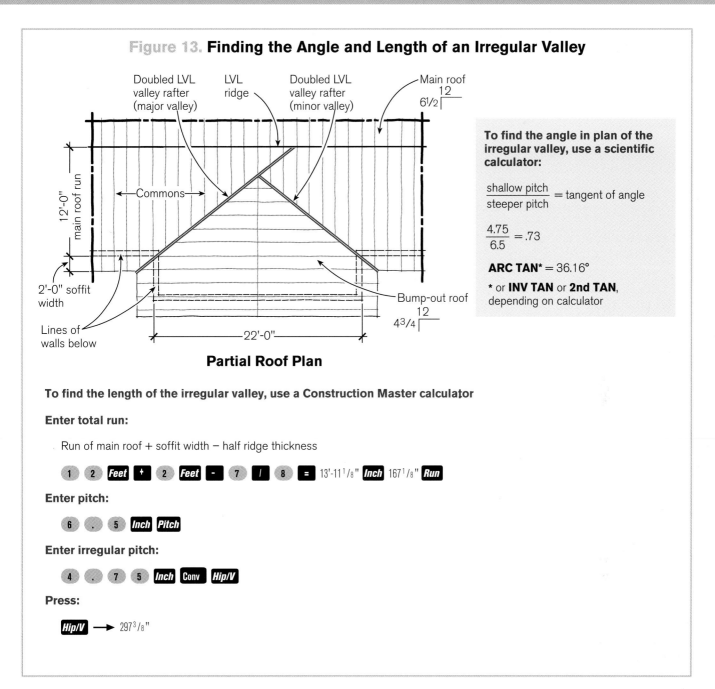

**Figure 13. Finding the Angle and Length of an Irregular Valley**

Doubled LVL valley rafter (major valley)

LVL ridge

Doubled LVL valley rafter (minor valley)

Main roof $6\frac{1}{2}\lfloor\overline{12}$

12'-0" main roof run

Commons

2'-0" soffit width

Lines of walls below

Bump-out roof $4\frac{3}{4}\lfloor\overline{12}$

22'-0"

**Partial Roof Plan**

To find the angle in plan of the irregular valley, use a scientific calculator:

$$\frac{\text{shallow pitch}}{\text{steeper pitch}} = \text{tangent of angle}$$

$$\frac{4.75}{6.5} = .73$$

**ARC TAN\*** = 36.16°

\* or **INV TAN** or **2nd TAN**, depending on calculator

**To find the length of the irregular valley, use a Construction Master calculator**

**Enter total run:**

Run of main roof + soffit width − half ridge thickness

( 1 )( 2 ) **Feet** **+** ( 2 ) **Feet** **−** ( 7 )( / )( 8 ) **=** 13'-11 1/8" **Inch** 167 1/8" **Run**

**Enter pitch:**

( 6 )( . )( 5 ) **Inch** **Pitch**

**Enter irregular pitch:**

( 4 )( . )( 7 )( 5 ) **Inch** **Conv** **Hip/V**

**Press:**

**Hip/V** → 297 3/8"

sary for strength, is that hip and valley length and the birdsmouth height measurements are always taken at the center of the rafter. If you are using a single-piece hip or valley rafter, it's difficult to lay out a length or height at the center when you have to draw on the face of a board. By using two pieces, one face of each piece will be at the centerline, where the layout dimensions are taken. Also, from a practical standpoint, this makes it much easier to rip the top bevel by following the corner of the board.

## Calculating the Length of the Irregular Valley Rafter

Before making any cuts, I calculate the lengths of the valley rafters. For this work, I use the

Construction Master calculator, which allows you to enter the common rafter run (half the building span), then convert it to a hip or valley run by hitting the **Hip/V** key.

The trick is to use the correct number for the run. For the major valley, this means using the total run of the main roof, 12 feet. I add in the soffit width (2 feet) and also subtract half the thickness (7/8 inch) of the ridge beam, a 1 3/4-inch-thick LVL. For an irregular valley, you have to enter both a "pitch" — the slope on the side of the valley you take the run from — and an "irregular pitch" — the roof slope on the other side of the valley. Then, hitting the **Hip/V** key gives you the length of the irregular hip or valley.

The process is similar for finding the length of the minor valley, except that I enter the run of the

**Figure 14.** **Finding Minor Valley Cheek-Cut Angle and Shortening Distance**

## Cheek-Cut Angle

**To find the cheek-cut angle, first establish the angle at which the minor valley intersects the major valley:**

$36.16° \times 2 = 72.32°$

$180°$ (in a triangle) $- 72.32° = 107.68°$

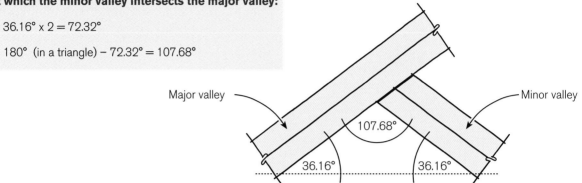

**Then, find the angle:**

$107.68° - 90° = 17.68°$

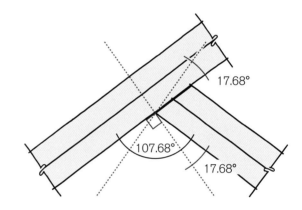

## Shortening Distance

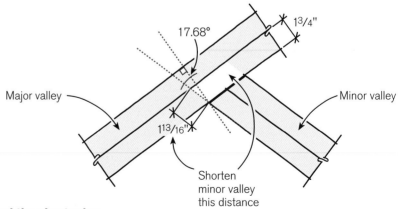

**Use the Construction Master to find the shortening distance for the minor valley cheek cut:**

17.68 **Pitch** 1.75 **Inch** **Run** **Diag** ⟶ 1.837 **Inch** 1¹³/₁₆"

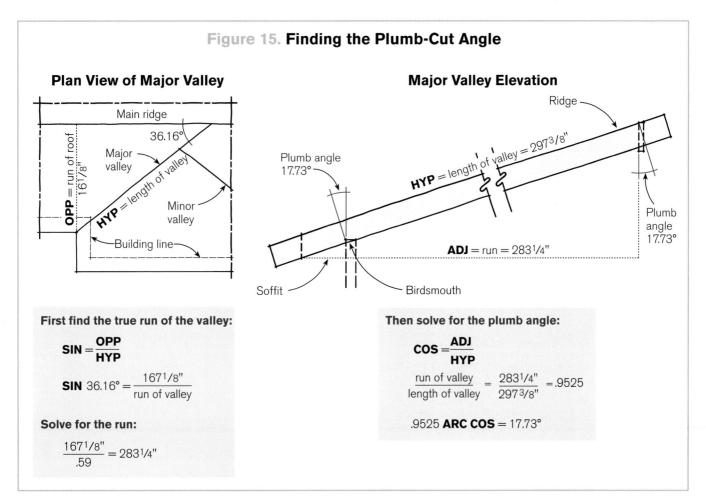

**Figure 15. Finding the Plumb-Cut Angle**

**Plan View of Major Valley**

Main ridge

36.16°

OPP = run of roof 167 1/8"

Major valley

HYP = length of valley

Minor valley

Building line

**Major Valley Elevation**

Ridge

Plumb angle 17.73°

HYP = length of valley = 297 3/8"

Plumb angle 17.73°

ADJ = run = 283 1/4"

Soffit

Birdsmouth

**First find the true run of the valley:**

$$SIN = \frac{OPP}{HYP}$$

$$SIN\ 36.16° = \frac{167\ 1/8"}{run\ of\ valley}$$

**Solve for the run:**

$$\frac{167\ 1/8"}{.59} = 283\ 1/4"$$

**Then solve for the plumb angle:**

$$COS = \frac{ADJ}{HYP}$$

$$\frac{run\ of\ valley}{length\ of\ valley} = \frac{283\ 1/4"}{297\ 3/8"} = .9525$$

$$.9525\ \textbf{ARC COS} = 17.73°$$

bumpout roof, 11 feet, in the Construction Master. This means the bumpout's roof slope is now the "pitch," while the steeper main roof is the "irregular pitch." Again, the soffit is added in, but it's easier to subtract half the thickness of the supporting valley just before making the cut. (See **Figure 14** for a simple way to find this shortening distance as well as the cheek-cut angle for the minor valley.)

## Finding the Plumb Angle and Birdsmouth Layout

Now it's time to lay out the plumb cuts at the ridge and birdsmouth (**Figure 15**). For this I reach for my trig calculator again. First I have to figure the true run of the valley rafter (as opposed to the main roof run). To do this, I divide the main roof run (167 1/8 inches) by the sine of the angle in plan (sine of 36.16 degrees = .59), yielding 283 1/4 inches. Then I solve for the cosine of the angle where the valley meets the top plate by dividing the run of the valley by its length. The angle turns out to be 17.73 degrees — the plumb-cut angle.

The seat-cut angle is simply the complement of this plumb angle, 72.27 degrees.

Now I can make the plumb cut at the top of the valley, setting my saw shoe at a 36-degree angle, as

calculated above. To actually locate the birdsmouth, I use the same process as for finding the length of the valley, except this time I subtract out the overhang to get the length to the outside of the top plate. This gives me the distance from the ridge cut to the plumb cut on the birdsmouth.

The height of the birdsmouth is the same as on all the common rafters, although the length of the seat cut will be longer. Remember that this layout is made at the centerline of the doubled rafter and that the birdsmouth plumb cut is also angled at 36.16 degrees to match the angle of the top plumb cut.

When making the birdsmouth cuts, I clamp the two rafter members together temporarily. I don't nail them off yet, though, because it's easier to rip the top bevels working on one piece at a time.

## Plumb Cuts at the Tail

The lower end of the valley rafter also gets angled to receive the fascia at the inside corner. Again, using a doubled member makes this easy. One piece gets a plumb cut at 36.16 degrees, while the other piece gets the complementary angle (53.84 degrees). At this point the rafter is almost ready to go up. All that remains is to bevel the top of the valley so the sheathing planes in correctly. This is more accurate and actually simpler than dropping the valley.

FRAMING

## Figure 16. Calculating Top Bevel Angles

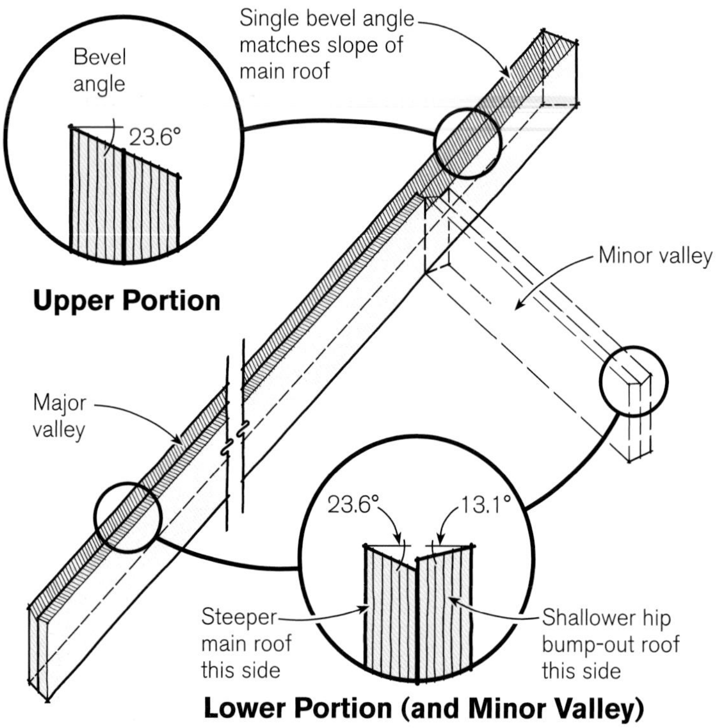

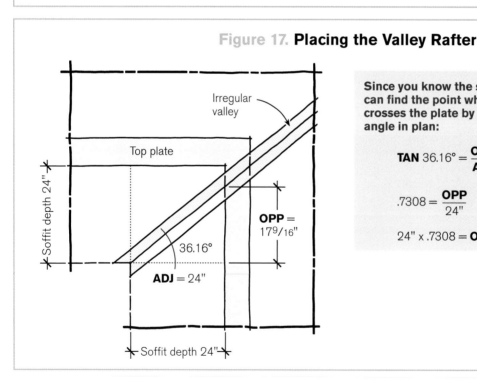

**Upper Portion**

Bevel angle

23.6°

Single bevel angle matches slope of main roof

Minor valley

Major valley

23.6°  13.1°

Steeper main roof this side

Shallower hip bump-out roof this side

**Lower Portion (and Minor Valley)**

To find the top bevel angle, use this formula on a scientific calculator:

**ARC TAN** (sine of angle in plan x roof pitch)

**For the shallow pitch:**

36.16° **SIN** = .59

$.59 \times \dfrac{4.75}{12} = .2336$

.2336 **ARC TAN** = 13.15°

For the steeper side, repeat using 6.5:12 as the slope and 53.84° for the angle in plan (the complement of 36.16°):

$53.84° \textbf{ SIN} \times \dfrac{6.5}{12} = .4373 \textbf{ ARC TAN} = 23.62°$

## Figure 17. Placing the Valley Rafter

Irregular valley

Top plate

Soffit depth 24"

OPP = 17 9/16"

36.16°

**ADJ** = 24"

Soffit depth 24"

Since you know the soffit depth is 24 inches, you can find the point where the valley centerline crosses the plate by using the tangent of the angle in plan:

$$\textbf{TAN } 36.16° = \dfrac{\textbf{OPP}}{\textbf{ADJ}}$$

$$.7308 = \dfrac{\textbf{OPP}}{24"}$$

$$24" \times .7308 = \textbf{OPP} = 17.54", \text{ or } 17 9/16"$$

## Finding the Top Bevel Angles

Both the minor valley rafter and the lower portion of the major valley rafter need two bevel angles, to plane into the pitches of the steeper and shallower intersecting roofs. But the section of the major valley that extends past the intersection with the minor valley has only a single bevel angle, to match the slope of the main roof (**Figure 16**).

I find it's easiest to figure the top rip angle using a trig-function calculator. For any hip between two roofs, the top-rip angle will be given by the formula:

**arc tan (sine of the angle in plan of valley x pitch of roof)**

This calculation must be done twice — once using the shallower pitch, with a plan angle of 36.16

degrees, and again using the steeper pitch and a plan angle of 53.84 degrees (the complement). In each case, the angle I derive with these formulas is the angle at which I set my saw table. I rip this angle with my saw table on the face of the board, with the blade following the corner along the edge. At the point where the minor valley intersects, the bevel angle on the shallow-side member reverses to match the steeper angle of the main roof.

## Placing the Rafter

It's helpful to know exactly where the irregular valley crosses the top plate, since it's not at the corner. Often, I'll use the angle in plan of the valley and find this working off the scaled plans. You can also figure it with some simple trig, as shown in **Figure 17**.

*Len Schmidt is the owner of Belgian Woodworks in Starksboro, Vt.*

# Rafter Cutting Basics

## by Don Dunkley

There are many ways to cut rafters. In more than 30 years of framing houses, I have learned a variety of techniques, from cutting rafters one at a time to production gang-cutting methods. But regardless of how you produce all the rafters that go into a house, the basic principles remain the same for every method. Rather than get too involved in different cutting techniques, here I'll concentrate on what is required to lay out hip and common rafters, and describe only a few shortcuts for cutting and stacking the roof. This follows "Roof Layout by Calculator" (page 64), in which I described how to calculate rafter lengths using the Construction Master calculator. The examples here use the same rafter lengths described in that earlier section — those required for a standard 8/12 hip roof on a 22-by-57-foot building. Once again, the Construction Master serves as an indispensable tool for figuring each rafter cut.

## The Common Rafter

Let's start with some fundamentals. A common rafter has three essential parts (**Figure 18**, next page).

*A ridge plumb cut.* Cut as an angle on the rafter, the *ridge cut* is held plumb, or vertical, when the rafter is installed at the face of the ridge board. It represents the top limit of the roof rise.

*A birdsmouth, for positive attachment to the outside walls.* This is made of two cuts: a vertical *heel cut* for the outside edge of the wall and a level *seat cut* that allows the rafter to bear on the wall.

*A tail cut, to define the overhang.* This consists of a plumb *tail cut* that ends the rafter, and a level *plancer cut* that keeps the tail cut from sticking past the bottom of the fascia board. If there's no overhang, then the rafter ends at the building line. If there's no fascia board or gutter, the plancer cut is eliminated.

## Common Rafter Layout

For accuracy, I use a framing square to lay out rafters. I use it initially to lay out a rafter pattern that contains all the necessary cuts for a particular set of rafters. I also use the Swanson Speed Square and the Swanson Big Twelve, a larger version of the Speed Square. But for my pattern layout, the framing square is key. It's also the best tool to use when starting out, since it gives you a visual representation of the unit rise and unit run.

*Ridge plumb cut.* To lay out a full-size common rafter on my example roof, I first look at my cut list and check to see what length material has to be used. In our example, the 11-foot run and 2-foot overhang calls for a 16-foot 2x6. With the framing square, I mark the ridge plumb cut (first making sure the rafter is labeled with the crown up). I place the cut mark as close to the end as possible. Of course, if the wood is split, you move down to avoid it.

Once marked, I make this cut. Then, hooking the tape over the long point, I pull down the rafter the calculated length of 13 feet 1¾ inches and place a mark on the top edge. From this point, I make another plumb line as I did at the ridge cut. This line represents the *building line* — the outside edge of the wall.

*Common birdsmouth.* To make the birdsmouth, I must first determine how deep the cut will be. To provide adequate bearing on the wall plates and to leave enough uncut material to support the overhang, I go by this rule of thumb: *At least two-thirds of the rafter stock must remain above the birdsmouth.* The size of the birdsmouth changes with the slope of the roof, so each roof pitch will have a different seat configuration. In this case, the two-thirds rule calls for a minimum 4⁵/₁₆ inches of the rafter above the outside wall plate. This distance is called the *heel stand* (shown in **Figure 20**, page 84). The remaining 2⁵/₁₆

# Parts of a Common Rafter

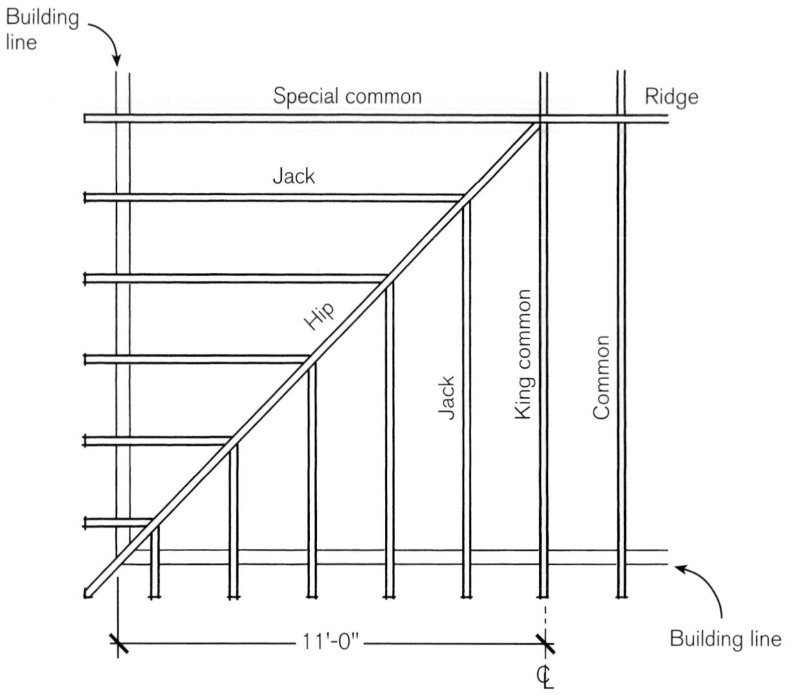

Building line

Special common

Ridge

Jack

Hip

Jack

King common

Common

11'-0"

℄

Building line

**Figure 18.** All commons, including king commons and special commons, are cut identically (though the special commons may have a different length). The author starts his layout by marking and cutting the ridge plumb cut, then measures down the rafter length and marks another plumb line to designate the "building line" at the outside wall plates. He locates the birdsmouth by measuring the heel stand along the building line, and also measures from this line to establish the tail cuts.

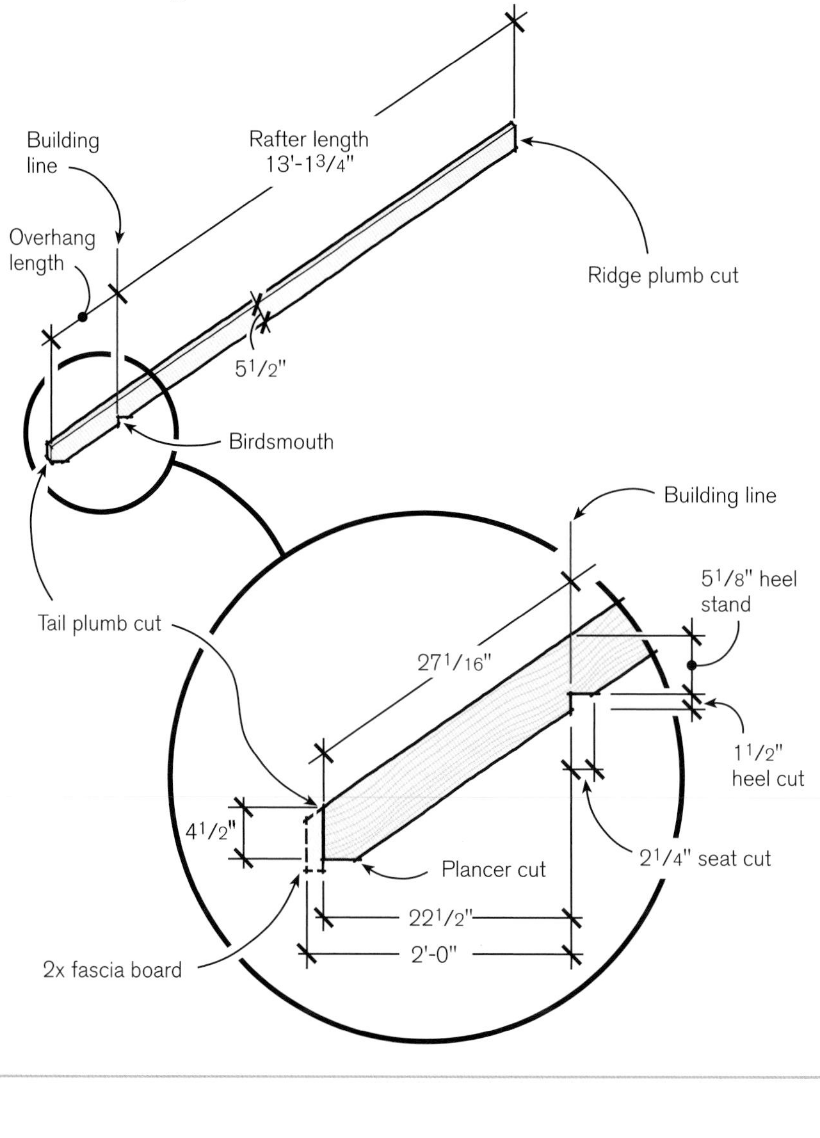

Building line

Rafter length
13'-1³/₄"

Overhang length

Ridge plumb cut

5¹/₂"

Birdsmouth

Building line

Tail plumb cut

27¹/₁₆"

5¹/₈" heel stand

1¹/₂" heel cut

4¹/₂"

Plancer cut

2¹/₄" seat cut

22¹/₂"

2'-0"

2x fascia board

inches — the heel cut — falls below the plate line. However, this deep heel cut covers most of the double top plate, leaving too little nailing for the exterior sheathing. So I increase the heel stand to 5$1/8$ inches, leaving a 1$1/2$-inch-deep heel cut. This results in a 2$1/4$-inch seat cut.

Keep in mind that the two-thirds rule relates to tail strength. Adding to the heel stand increases this strength. It is not necessary for the seat cut to bear on the full width of the top plate, but make sure you have at least 1$3/4$ inches of bearing.

To lay out the birdsmouth for cutting, I measure down the building plumb line and make a mark at 5$1/8$ inches. Then, at this point, I draw a line at 90 degrees from the building line in the direction of the ridge cut. This is the *seat cut line*. It represents the amount each rafter will bear on the plate.

***Common tail cuts.*** In the example, the plans call for a 2-foot overhang. All overhangs are measured on the horizontal projection from the building line. Don't just add 2 feet to the rafter length and call it a day; the actual rafter length needed will be longer. I use the Construction Master to figure this distance: 2 feet 4$7/8$ inches — the true overhang length along the rafter.

If fascia is used, deduct its thickness from the run. If the fascia board is a 2-by, then the run would be 22$1/2$ inches, giving a tail length of 2 feet 3$1/16$ inches (again, using the Construction Master). I measure down 27$1/16$ inches from the building plumb line along the top of the rafter and draw another plumb line. The rafter ends at this tail plumb cut.

For the plancer cut, if there is one, I check out the size of fascia board. In this case, it's a 2x6. Because 2x6 fascia is the same width as the rafter stock, the plumb cut on the tail will be wider than the fascia, so we need to trim down the tail cut to allow the fascia to hang below the tail cut. A 1-inch reveal is common, so I measure down 4$1/2$ inches on the tail cut

and draw a line 90 degrees to the tail plumb cut for the plancer cut.

## Making a Rafter Pattern

Once the birdsmouth and overhang are marked, I can make my cuts, giving me a completed common rafter. To simplify and speed production, I use a rafter pattern. The pattern is a template that I usually cut from plywood (for lightness) or from a scrap of rafter stock (for expedience).

This pattern has a plumb cut at the top, a birdsmouth laid out 12 inches down, and an overhang cut at the end. I nail 1-by scrap along the top edge (forming a "T" in cross-section) so the pattern can be laid over the rafter stock and held flush to the top edge. A 2-inch gap in this 1-by, located at the birdsmouth plumb line, allows me to reference the top of the building line for proper alignment (**Figure 19**).

## Hip Rafter Layout

A hip rafter is always cut from wider stock than the common rafter. This gives additional strength and allows extra width for nailing on the jacks. I make the ridge cut first. On a hip, the ridge cut is a little different from the commons because it must fit between two commons (**Figure 20**, next page). This cut, called a *double-cheek cut*, has a 45-degree bevel on each side.

***Cutting a double-cheek cut.*** To make a double-cheek cut, I place the framing square on the lumber so the tongue is set at 8 and the body is set at 17 (the run of a hip), and scribe a ridge plumb line down *both sides* of the 1$1/2$-inch-wide tongue (**Figure 21**, page 85). Then, with the table of my saw set at a 45-degree bevel, I cut along the first (outside) line, making the long point cut. I leave the line intact. I then cut in the opposite direction along the other

**Figure 19.** To speed layout on all commons and jacks, the author makes a rafter pattern. He attaches 1-by along the top edge for easy alignment. Note that he leaves a gap in this 1-by above the birdsmouth so he can find the building line mark on his rafter stock.

# Parts of a Hip Rafter

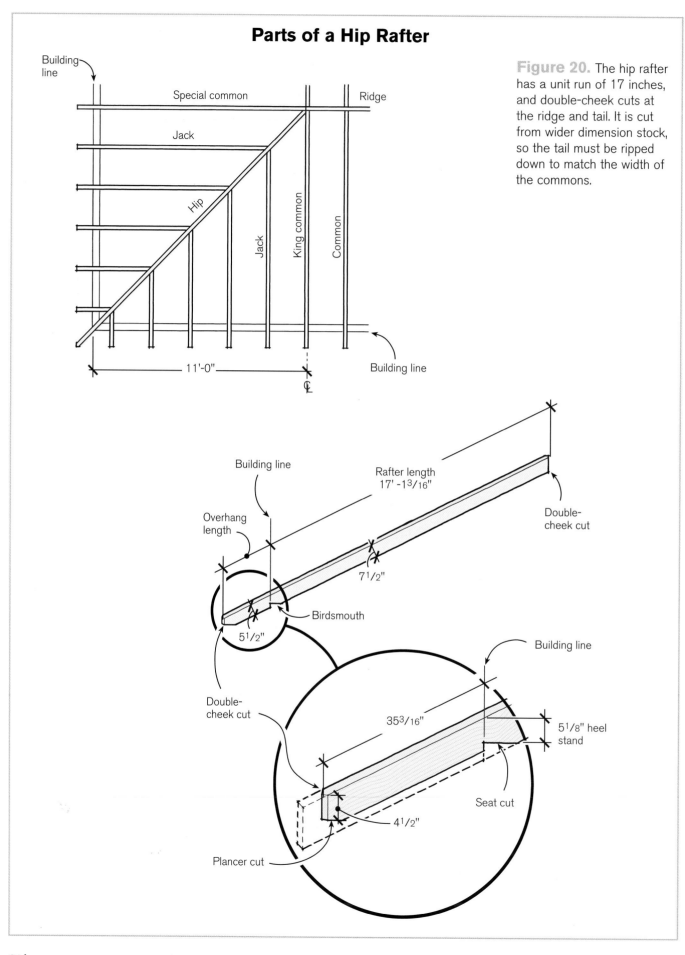

Building line

Special common

Jack

Hip

Jack

King common

Common

Ridge

Building line

11'-0"

C⌴

**Figure 20.** The hip rafter has a unit run of 17 inches, and double-cheek cuts at the ridge and tail. It is cut from wider dimension stock, so the tail must be ripped down to match the width of the commons.

Building line

Rafter length
17' -1³/16"

Overhang length

Double-cheek cut

7¹/2"

Birdsmouth

5¹/2"

Double-cheek cut

35³/16"

Building line

5¹/8" heel stand

Seat cut

4¹/2"

Plancer cut

line, making a short point cut. Again, I leave the line. This maneuver results in a pretty good double-cheek cut.

*Not a true 45.* It's important to note that this double-cheek cut is not a true 45-degree bevel, even though the saw is set at 45 degrees. Before power saws, this cut was made with a handsaw. But if a 45-degree line was made across the top of the rafter, and then cut with a handsaw, the resulting bevel cut would not fit properly. This is because the 45-degree bevel should be marked perpendicular to the ridge plumb line. This can't be done laying a Speed Square or tri-square on the top edge of the board and drawing a 45-degree line. This also goes for the jack rafters.

Since modern roofs use 2-by stock and are cut with power saws, a carpenter can easily overlook this. But if you're not aware of the issue, problems will arise when you use wider beam stock for the rafters, or when bevel cuts go beyond 45 degrees, as in the case of irregular roof jacks, turret jacks, and bay rafters. In these situations, the carpenter must understand basic rafter principles.

To lay out the ridge plumb cuts for a 6-by hip beam, for example, I first scribe the plumb line as usual (**Figure 22**, next page). Next, at a 90-degree angle from the ridge plumb line, I measure out the thickness of the stock (5$\frac{1}{2}$ inches), and place a mark. I then plumb through this mark with another ridge plumb line, giving me two plumb lines 5$\frac{1}{2}$ inches apart on the perpendicular. Across the top of the beam, I square two lines, one from the first plumb line and one from the second ridge plumb line. The intersection of two cross-diagonals between these two lines describes the proper bevel cut.

This can be done more efficiently with a framing square and the Construction Master. First, find the unit length of diagonal for the hip rafter at the pitch being used. Using the calculator, enter **8 Inch**, **Pitch**, **12 Inch**, **Run**, then push the **Hip/Val** key, which will display 18$\frac{3}{4}$ inches. This is the *unit diagonal length* of the hip with a 17-inch run. Since the tongue of the square is only 16 inches long, divide the numbers in half to get 9$\frac{3}{8}$ inches and 8$\frac{1}{2}$ inches. Place the framing square on top of the beam holding the tongue at 9$\frac{3}{8}$ and the body at 8$\frac{1}{2}$, and mark along both sides of the tongue. This is the proper bevel cut (it happens to be a 47.8-degree angle).

Some of the better framing squares will have tables printed on the blade that refer to this cut. They are usually referred to as "side cuts for a hip."

## Hip Birdsmouth

Once I make the double-cheek cut, I hook my tape over the end of the long point, measure down, and mark the top of the hip at the calculated length, 17 feet 1$\frac{3}{16}$ inches. Here, I make an 8/17 building line plumb mark. This designates the top of the building

**Figure 21.** To make a double-cheek cut on a hip, the author lays out a plumb cut with a framing square. He marks both sides of the 1$\frac{1}{2}$-inch tongue on the square (top). Leaving the line visible on the board, he then cuts along the outside line with the saw set at a 45-degree bevel, moving from the top edge of the rafter toward the bottom to cut the long point (center). Finally, he cuts in the opposite direction to cut the short point, resulting in a near-perfect double-cheek cut (above).

# Laying Out a Double-Cheek Cut in Wide Stock

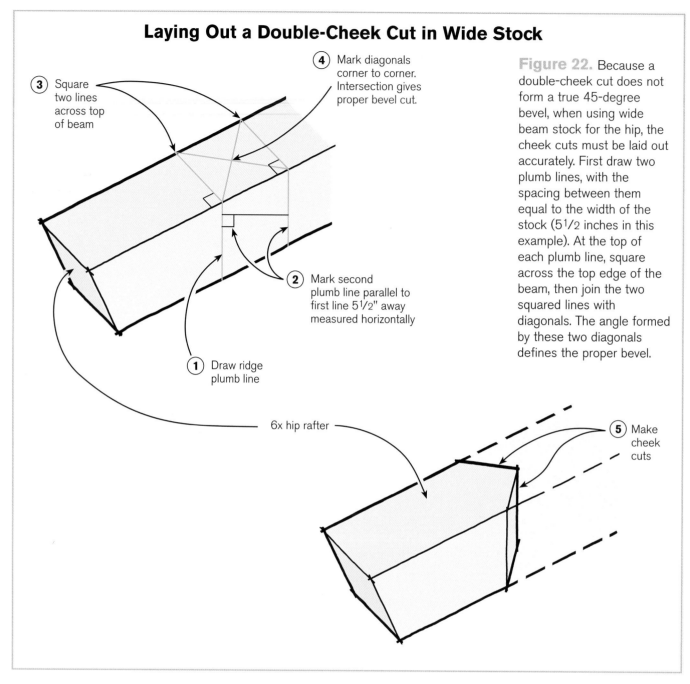

**3** Square two lines across top of beam

**4** Mark diagonals corner to corner. Intersection gives proper bevel cut.

**2** Mark second plumb line parallel to first line 5½" away measured horizontally

**1** Draw ridge plumb line

6x hip rafter

**5** Make cheek cuts

**Figure 22.** Because a double-cheek cut does not form a true 45-degree bevel, when using wide beam stock for the hip, the cheek cuts must be laid out accurately. First draw two plumb lines, with the spacing between them equal to the width of the stock (5½ inches in this example). At the top of each plumb line, square across the top edge of the beam, then join the two squared lines with diagonals. The angle formed by these two diagonals defines the proper bevel.

line and marks the position of the birdsmouth. Next, using the same heel stand measurement that I used for the commons, I measure down 5⅛ inches. At this mark, I draw a perpendicular (90-degree) seat cut line in the direction of the ridge. (When laying out birdmouths, always measure down from the top of the rafter. That way, if different widths of rafter stock are being used on the same roof, the tops of the rafters will plane in together.)

***Dropping the hip.*** After I lay out the birdsmouth, I must "drop the hip." This is done so the top edge of the hip will plane in with the other rafters. Because the hip rafter sits on the outside corner at a 45-degree angle from the other rafters, the outside face of the hip projects from the wall by half its

thickness. If you don't account for this, the top corners of the hip will stick above the roof plane. To correct for this, the seat cut must be cut a little deeper to drop the hip down.

To lay this out, I first measure along the seat cut line ¾ inch (half the thickness of the hip), starting from where the seat cut line meets the building plumb line (**Figure 23**). I then draw a second plumb line that goes right through this ¾-inch mark. From the top of this new plumb line, I measure down the heel stand of 5⅛ inches, make a mark, and draw another level seat cut line through this point going back toward the original birdsmouth. The ⅜-inch difference between the two seat cut lines is the drop for a 2-by hip on an 8/17 pitch. (This drop distance

## Dropped Hip Layout

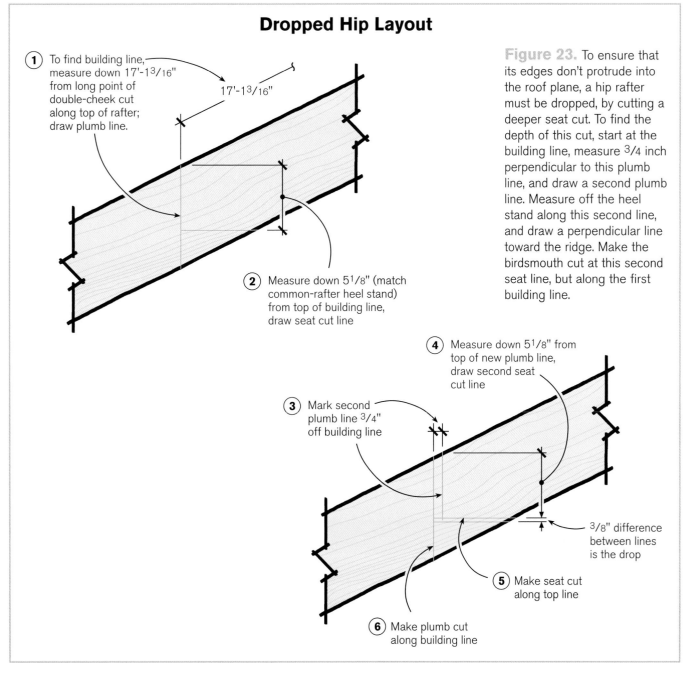

**1** To find building line, measure down 17'-1³/₁₆" from long point of double-cheek cut along top of rafter; draw plumb line.

17'-1³/₁₆"

**Figure 23.** To ensure that its edges don't protrude into the roof plane, a hip rafter must be dropped, by cutting a deeper seat cut. To find the depth of this cut, start at the building line, measure ³/4 inch perpendicular to this plumb line, and draw a second plumb line. Measure off the heel stand along this second line, and draw a perpendicular line toward the ridge. Make the birdsmouth cut at this second seat line, but along the first building line.

**2** Measure down 5¹/8" (match common-rafter heel stand) from top of building line, draw seat cut line

**4** Measure down 5¹/8" from top of new plumb line, draw second seat cut line

**3** Mark second plumb line ³/4" off building line

³/8" difference between lines is the drop

**5** Make seat cut along top line

**6** Make plumb cut along building line

varies with the thickness and pitch of the hips, so this procedure must be done on each different roof.) The second (top) seat line is the actual cut line, so I scratch out the first (bottom) seat cut line and the second plumb line.

*Hip tail cuts.* Before cutting the birdsmouth, I lay out the hip tail (**Figure 24**, next page). Because the hip is cut from wider stock, the tail that projects into the overhang must be ripped down to match the width of the commons. For now, I snap a chalk line on the tail part of the hip marking the new tail width, but I'll hold off making this cut.

I first figure the length of the hip overhang. Using the Construction Master, I enter the 8-inch pitch, the 22¹/2-inch run (for the horizontal projection minus

fascia), then hit **Hip/Val**, which will display 35³/₁₆ inches. I measure down the hip from the building line this distance and draw a tail plumb line. On each side of this plumb line, I mark half the thickness of the hip, or ³/4 inch, perpendicular to it, and draw two more plumb lines through each of those marks, as in **Figure 24**, next page. This gives me a total of three plumb lines at the tail. From the top of the hip, I measure 4¹/2 inches down the original (middle) plumb line to mark the location of the plancer cut, and draw a perpendicular line in the direction of the birdsmouth. (Make sure the plancer cut line is drawn before the tail bevel cut is made. If you don't, you have to measure down the center of the tail bevel, cut square over to the face, and then

# Laying Out and Cutting a Hip Tail

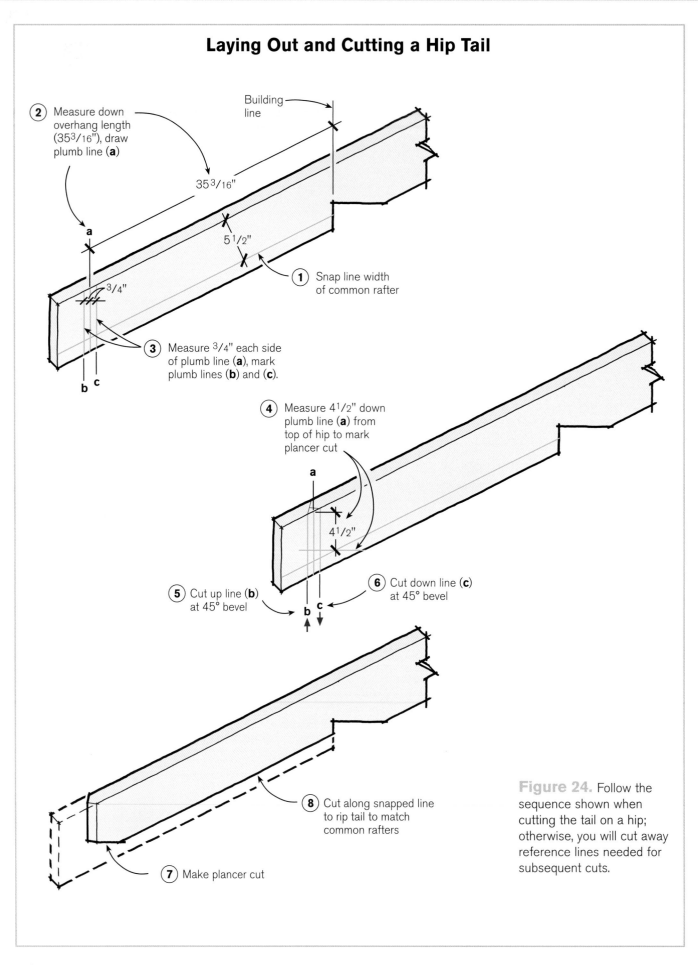

(2) Measure down overhang length (35³/16"), draw plumb line (**a**)

Building line

35³/16"

5¹/2"

(1) Snap line width of common rafter

3/4"

(3) Measure ³/4" each side of plumb line (**a**), mark plumb lines (**b**) and (**c**).

b c

(4) Measure 4¹/2" down plumb line (**a**) from top of hip to mark plancer cut

a

4¹/2"

(5) Cut up line (**b**) at 45° bevel

(6) Cut down line (**c**) at 45° bevel

b c

(8) Cut along snapped line to rip tail to match common rafters

**Figure 24.** Follow the sequence shown when cutting the tail on a hip; otherwise, you will cut away reference lines needed for subsequent cuts.

(7) Make plancer cut

**Figure 25.** The author cuts the jacks for all four hips in a roof in sets (four hips require eight jacks of each length). The photo at left shows the setup for the longest jacks. Similar setups would be required for each of the five jack lengths in the example roof.

lay out a perpendicular fascia cut line).

To cut the tail, I set the saw at a 45-degree bevel and make a double-cheek cut, just as I did for the ridge plumb cut. I cut down the furthest (outside) plumb line first, skip the middle line, and cut in the opposite direction along the third line. I then make the fascia level cut and finish off the tail by ripping the chalk line marking the width of the tail.

## Jack Rafters

Jacks are similar to commons as far as the birdsmouth and tail cuts. The difference is in the plumb cut at the top. The jack plumb cut is a compound bevel that fits tight against the side of the hip. Jacks are both right-hand and left-hand so they can sit on opposing sides of the hip. In our example, each of the four hips has two pairs of jacks, or eight of each length.

Because the jacks come in pairs and diminish in length as they progress down the hip, I stack the rafters in sets of eight, mark them for length, then scribe for the birdsmouth and tail cuts. In this method of production cutting, I add the tail length to each jack length to get a rough length for each of the various sets of jacks.

Starting with the longest jacks, I load up the sawhorses with eight rafters, crowns up. (If I'm using a cutting bench, I'll place the whole set of jacks from longest to shortest.) I square up the ends so the rafters can be measured together, and designate the pairs of rafters by marking four with a diagonal slash from the top right-hand side and four from the top left-hand side (**Figure 25**). I hook my tape over the top of the rafter on the outside of my stack, and measure down 10 feet 9$7/16$ inches — the length of the first, or longest, jack — and make a mark for the building plumb line. I do the same to the outside rafter on the other side of the stack, then draw a square line connecting the two marks. I now have all eight of the rafters of that set marked for length.

I lay out each jack by laying it flat according to the diagonal mark I placed at the end — the diagonal slash indicates the long point and must face up. I use the rafter pattern to scribe the plumb cut, building line, birdsmouth, and tail cut. The tails and birdsmouths are cut just like those on the commons; the plumb cheek cuts at the top are cut with the saw set at a 45-degree bevel.

*Don Dunkley is a framing contractor in Cool, Calif.*

# Gang-Cutting Rafters

by John Harman

In the 1960s and '70s, California tract builders were all gang-cutting their rafters. Since then, trusses have taken over in that market, and production cutting has become a dying art. Yet in many areas, carpenters continue to stick-frame roofs, and it's surprising how many of them cut rafters one piece at a time. Unlike most carpenters who gang-cut rafters, I did not learn this technique on the West Coast. About 20 years ago I got a job working for a builder in Massachusetts who production-cut all his roofs. I eventually moved back to eastern Pennsylvania and became a framing contractor, where I continue to gang-cut my roofs.

It doesn't matter whether there are 20 or 200 rafters to cut: it's always faster to gang them together and cut them all at once. When I frame a roof, the actual cutting time for the rafters is usually less than 15 minutes. This doesn't include layout or stacking the lumber on racks, but I'd be laying out the cuts and stacking the material on sawhorses anyway. To help with the heavy work, we use an all-terrain forklift. Once the rafters are cut, we lift them to the roof all at once.

## Setting Up

The first thing we do is build a set of temporary racks. They don't have to be elaborate, just sturdy and stable. I take a couple of 2x10s or 2x12s and brace the ends so they won't roll over (**Figure 26**). It takes less than a minute to build a set of racks. We build them low because they're more stable that way and it's a comfortable height to cut from. It's easier if you put the racks on a level surface, but they don't

**Specialized tools and production techniques make for much faster roof cutting.**

have to be perfectly level. The racks can run slightly up- or downhill. The important thing is for the top edges to be in the same plane.

The racks are usually about 14 feet long, but I'll make them longer if there are a lot of rafters to cut. Long racks can get kind of shaky under a heavy load of lumber, so if there are enough rafters I'll put a

**Figure 26.** The rafters are supported by a pair of simple racks and are kept upright by the triangular blocks at the ends.

**Figure 27.** Layout is done on the outer pieces (left), and a chalk line is used to transfer the cut lines to the pieces in between (center and right).

third rack under the middle of the stack.

*Racking.* Putting the lumber on the racks is called racking. To save time, I rack the entire roof package at once. This includes commons plus hip and valley jacks. It doesn't matter if the rafters are more than one length; they can still be in the same rack. One rack should be within a foot or so of the head cut and the other should be under the seat cut. If there are enough different lengths, we may build an intermediate rack to support one end of the shorter pieces. We could use a different set of racks for the shorter rafters, but there isn't always space to do it and it would require us to lay out an extra set of cuts. It's usually easier to do everything at once.

Since the birdsmouth is on the bottom of the rafter, we rack rafters with the crown side down. It's very important to stack the rafters tight; I use a hammer to beat them together. If the rafters are exposed, we'll use a piece of scrap to protect them from dents. We nail blocks to both ends of the racks to keep the rafters together. The blocks are shorter than the rafters so they won't interfere with the saw.

## Laying Out the Cuts

As with any roof-cutting project, there's a certain amount of prep work involved. I figure out all the cuts at home the night before I cut the roof. That way I don't waste time on the job or get distracted and make a mistake that ruins a whole pile of lumber. The last thing I want is to tell a builder to order 100 more 2x10s because I cut all the rafters 9 inches short.

However you figure the lengths, you have to put the cut lines on the bottom of the rafters. It's like working upside down, so it takes some getting used to. I mark the head cuts, seat cuts, and tail cuts on the two outside rafters and use a chalk line to transfer the marks to the rafters in between (**Figure 27**). I mark the head first, then determine rafter length and the seat cut from there.

Rafters of more than one length and for more than one roof pitch can be stacked in the same rack. I use 12-inch spacer blocks to separate different groups of rafters on the rack (**Figure 28**). This speeds the process because it allows us to fill the racks and get more cutting done in each setup. This also allows us to make the same cuts on one end but different cuts on the others.

## Production Cutting

The idea behind this method is to run the saw through all the rafters in a single pass. We do the head cuts first, the tail cuts second, and the birdsmouths third. Circular saws do not have the depth of cut to gang-cut the heads and tails. Instead, we use an adjustable table attachment on a chain saw to make the long straight cuts (**Figure 29**, next page).

**Figure 28.** Twelve-inch spacer blocks separate groups of rafters on the racks so that different cuts can be made, increasing the efficiency of both the stacking and cutting operations.

**Figure 29.** A chain saw has enough depth of cut to cut heads and tails in a single pass. This saw is attached to a custom-made shoe; an off-the-shelf model is available from Big Foot Tools.

We always make the head cuts first. That way we can recut them if the angle is a little bit off. A 2x4 nailed to the top of the rafters makes a good fence for the saw. We usually cut the tails before doing the seat and heel cuts because there's nowhere to nail the fence if the birdsmouths are already made.

We use a slow, smooth cutting action and let the saw do the work. The table should be held tight to the top of the rafters. If one side of the table comes off the work, the pitch will be wrong and there will be gaps where the rafter hits the ridge. A good coating of silicone spray on all chains, blades, and tables reduces friction and keeps blades sharper longer.

***Birdsmouth.*** The birdsmouth is the last thing we cut before unracking the rafters. If the roof pitch is steeper than 6/12, I'll remove the triangular piece of waste material by making a pair of bevel cuts with worm-drive saws. I'll set up a standard saw for the heel cut and another one with an oversized blade and a swing-cut table for the seat cut. The swing table is necessary because a conventional saw will not bevel more than 50 degrees, and seat cuts are often much steeper than that (**Figure 30**). For example, the seat cut for a 6-pitch roof is 63.5 degrees. The swing-cut saw I use takes a $10^1/_4$-inch blade and will cut up to a 75-degree bevel.

If the roof is 6/12 or less I use a dado saw to cut the birdsmouth in a single pass (**Figure 31**). I don't use it if the roof is steeper because the cut will be so deep that it would strain the saw to make it in a single pass.

At one time you could buy a kit that allowed you to put dado blades on a worm-drive saw. No one has sold anything like this for years. I got a local machine shop to take a standard worm-drive and turn it into a dado saw. It's not worth doing unless you make your living cutting roofs. It's cheaper, safer, and only a little slower to make all the seat cuts using a swing table.

## Hip and Valley Jacks

There are different ways to gang-cut hip and valley jacks. How I do it depends on the combination of parts I need. Most of the houses I frame have both hips and valleys. I gang-cut the fill as common rafters and then cut a hip jack and valley jack out of each one. The bevel cuts are made one at a time but taking the pieces out of commons allows me to gang-cut the heads and tails.

**Figure 30.** A swing-table saw makes possible the steep angles required for birdsmouths. Here, the birdsmouths on 50 rafters are made with just two long cuts.

## Rafter Cutting Tools

A standard circular saw will do for some ganged cuts, but you'll need specialized saws to make the others. The head and tail cuts are too deep to make with a circular blade. The only way to make them is with some kind of chainsaw. If you're going to production-cut the birdsmouths, you'll need a circular saw that bevels more than normal and has an oversized blade.

**Cutting with a chain.** At one time I used a Prazi Beam Cutter (Prazi USA, www.praziusa.com), a chain-saw attachment that bolts on to a circular saw (see photo). I rarely use the Beam Cutter anymore because the chain comes up through the work and splinters the layout line. These days I use a gas-powered chain saw with a specialized shoe and beveling attachment. I cut with the top of the bar; that way, the line remains intact and the chips and dust go down instead of up in my face.

A friend of mine uses an off-the-shelf attachment called the Headcutter (Big Foot Tools, www.bigfootsaws.com). I had a local welder custom-fabricate a similar device out of aluminum for me. The Headcutter bolts onto the bar of the chainsaw. The attachment I use is more stable because it bolts right through the bar of the saw.

**Specialized circular saw.** Another tool that's necessary for gang-cutting rafters is a swing-table saw. It consists of a standard worm-drive body equipped with an oversized blade and specialized base. The blade increases the depth of cut, and the base tilts well beyond the usual 45 or 50 degrees so you can make the steep bevel cuts required for birdsmouths.

Big Foot makes swing tables and swing-table saws.

*A Prazi Beam Cutter can be attached to a standard worm-drive saw. This one is being used to make tail cuts. The saw pulls the blade up through the work, which is why there are so many chips piled on top.*

Their 75-degree 10 1/4-inch swing-table kit fits Skil and Bosch bodies. You can buy a complete saw with swing table and guard for between $425 and $600, depending on which body you choose and where you buy it. Big Foot also makes a 14-inch model called the Big Boy, which comes with a 72-degree swing table and a Bosch body and costs $850 to $1,000, depending on the vendor.

Pairis Products (www.bestconstructiontools.com) sells a swing table that can be added to an existing saw.

Some of my saws have been rewired to run on 220 volts. It gives us a little more cutting power because there's less voltage drop at the end of a long extension cord. — *J.H.*

**Hip jacks first.** There are usually more hips than valleys, so it's necessary to cut more hip jacks than valley jacks. When I need extra hip jacks, I'll make tail cuts on both ends of some boards and cut two hip jacks out of each one. The birdsmouths are cut from above, so they have to face up on both ends of the boards (**Figure 32**, next page). The bevel cuts are made one at a time with a worm-drive saw. It takes two cuts and there will be a small piece of waste from the middle of the board.

**Valley jacks only.** It's rare around here, but sometimes a roof will have commons and valleys but no hips. In that case, I will gang-cut heads on both ends of some boards and get two valley jacks out of each one. If you figure the overall length correctly and make the head cuts parallel to each other, you can get two valley jacks with only a single bevel cut and no waste in between. The other way to do it is to use

**Figure 31.**
Here, the author uses a custom-made dado saw to hog out birdsmouths in a single pass.

**Figure 32.** Hip and valley jacks are usually cut from commons. In this case, the author only needs hip jacks, so he has put tails on both ends and will get two hip jacks out of each board.

two bevel cuts to get the valley jacks and make the head cuts closer to the ends.

*Layout tips.* It's easy to lose track of which hip and valley jacks have already been cut. To avoid this problem, I lay out all the bevel cuts while the boards are still in the rack. That way I can look at the pile and see if all the pieces are there.

For example, if there are two hips, there will be four of the shortest hip jacks, two lefts and two rights. I'll take these pieces out of the first four boards in the rack. Measuring up from the heel cut, I draw a line across the bottom edge of the board to indicate where the rafter will end and mark it with a slash to indicate which way the bevel runs. The jacks are laid out in pairs, so there will always be the correct number of lefts and rights (**Figure 33**). The next shortest set of jacks comes from the next four boards. I continue to lay out the jacks this way until the marks approach the midpoint of the boards. At that point I reverse direction and start measuring off the other end of the group. This allows me to get two jacks out of each board with only a small amount of waste in the middle.

Cutting the upper end of hip jacks is simply a matter of rolling the boards down one at a time, marking the roof pitch on the side (**Figure 34**), and making the cut with a saw that has been set to the proper bevel. I never have to guess which way to make the bevel cut, because it's already marked on the bottom edge of the board. It's a very fast and efficient way to cut hip jacks.

The tools and techniques are important, but not as important as having a good understanding of roof framing and how parts go together. Gang-cutting may seem complicated at first, but if you start with simple roofs and work your way up it soon becomes second nature.

*John Harman is a roof cutter and framing contractor in Northumberland, Pa.*

**Figure 33.** Hip jacks are laid out in pairs, lefts and rights (top). In the photo above, the three shortest pairs for two hips have been marked. The offcuts will be long enough to produce the next three pairs.

**Figure 34.** The bevel is ready to be cut on this pair of hip jacks. The birdsmouths have already been cut on the other end.

# Chapter 5: Roof Trusses

- ■ **Production-Style Truss Roofs**

- ■ **Assembling Truss Roofs on the Ground**

# Production-Style Truss Roofs

by Don Dunkley

Installing trusses successfully depends on a few easy routines. Over the years, I've developed several techniques that I use on all my truss jobs, regardless of whether they're on a huge production tract or a single custom home.

Doing prep work early on is where you can save the most time on a truss job. Although a truss roof can't go up until the trusses are delivered, there's a lot you can do while you're waiting for the load. The real benefit of prep work is that most of it can be done on the ground where the work is both safer and faster.

## Layout and Blocking

The first step should be to lay out the interior wall top plates with reference marks that will ensure the proper placement of the floating truss clips later on. This only takes a few moments when the building is not covered by a load of trusses. Don't bother laying out the exterior walls, because the eaves blocks will automatically do that for you.

Simultaneously, another carpenter can cut backing for ceiling drywall that will later be nailed flat to the top plates. By quickly scratching the truss layout on the floor, you can identify the walls that need backing. I prefer to use 2x6 backing where possible, and only use 2x4s when a truss chord runs down the middle of a wall or along one side. A good trick for measuring lengths is to spread the stock alongside wall partitions and cut it in place, allowing a few extra inches to run past the corners.

Once all the backing is cut, you can save time by temporarily hanging the material where it can be reached later on when standing trusses. Backing, eaves blocks, and outriggers with at least one nail started in them can be hung from nails placed on the inside of the exterior walls, a few inches down from where the stud butts the top plate. If you are using metal eaves vents, hang them up as well so they can be put in place as you stand the trusses. The metal flange on the ends is thin enough to allow it to be slipped in place between the two top plates. The important thing about hanging materials is to make sure that the pieces are completely out of the way below the plate line.

With large spans with no center walls to stand on when raising trusses, it's a good idea to build a catwalk. The most common areas for catwalks are in the garage and the living room. Keep the highest point flush with the top plate or just below. I prefer to use a flat 2x6, held on each end by a cleat fastened to the wall, with 2x4 legs nailed on for mid-span support. Catwalks should be plenty strong for safety's sake.

## Prepping Truss Braces

I use 1x4s nailed to the top chords to secure trusses as they are tipped up to their proper spacing. Other 1x4 bracing, called "lacing," is nailed in permanently at locations specified by the truss manufacturer's engineering plans. Truss installers have to follow the manufacturer's plans exactly to ensure that a truss roof system performs to its designed capacity.

To save time, I gang together as many pieces as I think I'll need for the top boards and the lacing, and lay them out all at once. This usually works out to

**Figure 1.** Small trusses (under 30 feet) can be spread evenly along the walls. The author prefers to stack larger trusses in bundles, so he only has to move them once. But if trusses are larger, say a 50-foot span with a 6/12 pitch, it ends up being too hard to move them twice. If there is room, he would rather load these so that they can be pulled off a bundle and stood one at a time.

about five to six times the length of the building. I use either 12- or 16-foot lengths because 8 and 10 footers are too short and pieces longer than 16 feet are too hard to handle. I mark the outside edges of the truss layout on the outer ganged pieces and transfer marks to the other pieces with a straight-edge. To designate which side of the layout marks the trusses should go on, I run keel lines parallel to the pencil lines to represent the leading edges. This avoids the hassle of making hundreds of small Xs.

*Fill package.* On most production jobs, the truss manufacturers send out a "fill" package with each truss order that contains cut-to-length eaves blocks, outriggers, and barge rafter stock. Smaller job-site fill packages might not include outriggers or barges. In these cases, they should be cut beforehand.

Once cut or removed from the fill package, it helps to mark and prep all the outriggers at one time by ganging them together and marking them at 22 1/2 inches and 24 inches from one end. This locates the end truss relative to the butt end that will be attached to the first interior truss. The remainder provides the extension for the overhang. Set a 16-penny nail in the face of the marked 1 1/2-inch space. Then set a toe-nailed 16-penny nail at the end that will butt into the receiving truss (the longer side). Hang the riggers up by hooking these nails onto other nails tacked at a convenient height along the gable-end wall.

*Sway braces.* At this time, I also cut a sway brace for each end. These braces run diagonally from the end wall top plate to the ridge block of the third regular truss and are used to plumb the first few trusses at each end. A 10-foot 2x4 works well for a typical 6-foot-tall truss. I prep the sway brace by cutting a 45-degree angle on one end, then hang it on the interior side of the end wall just below the top plate where I can reach it later.

## Loading the Trusses

When the trusses arrive on the site, there's still some ground prep work to do, but first the trusses have to be loaded on the building. Crane operators will put the trusses wherever the crew tells them to. In production situations, trusses aren't doled out one at a time. You'll get bundles dropped on the plate line as quickly as the crane operator can swing the boom, empty the load, and head back to the plant to load up for another delivery.

One thing to be on the lookout for, especially on the bustling tracts, are end-truss studs that have been knocked loose in a busy lumberyard. Once in the air, a bundle that contains a damaged end-truss can drop loose studs that fall like spears.

*Loading strategy.* The length of the building and the size of the trusses determine the best loading order. A truss that spans 30 feet and has a 4/12 pitch will only be 5 feet tall. Trusses in this ballpark, say 5

to 7 feet tall, are fairly easy to maneuver. I like to spread these out from one end of the building to the other before raising them (**Figure 1**).

However the trusses are loaded, I always make sure the end trusses will be in a position that allows them to be notched for outriggers before being stood. Climbing up an already raised gable truss, with saw in hand, to cut out spaces for outriggers is an excruciatingly slow job and is to be avoided.

After all the truss bundles have been loaded on the plates and the truck is gone, it's time to break into the fill package again to prep the eaves blocks. I place the blocks inside the house, butted together on edge along a wall. This aligns the blocks so that a toe-nail can be started into each one. I set the angle of the nail so that it will come out of the block with plenty of nail going into the truss. If set too flat, the blocks will fall off the nails when you try to hang them on the exterior walls. If set too steeply, the nails will not penetrate the trusses sufficiently.

The last preparation task to take care of is to precut the barge rafters. The length can be measured off a truss, and stock pieces can then be crowned up and cut plumb. It helps to nail a ridge block on one of each barge rafter pair. This block should be cut about 1/8 inch short to compensate for the truss plates. I also like to tack a small handful of 16-penny galvanized nails onto the top edge of the barge. This saves groping for stray galvanized nails later on when nail bags are full of 16-penny and 8-penny sinkers.

*Upright end-truss braces.* Before standing any trusses, temporary 2x6 braces are nailed vertically near the center of the gable-end walls to hold end trusses close to plumb while nearby trusses are raised. Avoid placing these uprights too close to the peak where they will get in the way when installing barge rafters. The 2x6s need to be long enough to reach from the bottom plate of an end wall, up along a stud, to the top chord of the end truss after it's raised.

If the trusses are over 8 feet tall, a separate upright brace is necessary on each side of an end truss. For tall trusses, you'll have to position upright braces farther from the center where you can still reach the top chord.

Once the uprights are in place, spread out the bracing pieces that were marked earlier. Lean the lacing high enough on the gable walls so you can easily pull them up into the truss cavities. This way they can be scattered into their locations as the trusses are stood, which is easier than fighting them into place afterwards. The remaining braces should be spread around the building exterior so that they lean a few inches below the plate where they won't interfere with spreading the trusses or walking on the plate.

*Outrigger notches.* With saws and nails placed up within reach of crewmembers on the top plates, it's almost time to spread and tip trusses. The final prep work involves notching the end trusses to accept out-

Figure 2. With the upright braces in position and toe-nails started along its bottom chord, an end truss is tipped into position and nailed off. On taller trusses, the author preinstalls the top outriggers to avoid difficulties in reaching them later.

riggers for the roof overhang. One foot down from the peak is a good measure for the top outrigger on each side. The rest are located 4 feet on-center down from these top notches (closer for tile roofs, to prevent sagging). I also like to place one close to the eaves to provide extra support for the barge rafter, especially when no fascia board is being used. At this point, I prefer to nail at least the upper outriggers into place because they can be very hard to reach later on.

Figure 3. Unless trusses are too big to handle twice, spreading out trusses along the top plate makes it easy to roll them into position later.

Before tipping a notched end-truss into place, I start 16-penny toe-nails along the bottom chord at 16 inches on-center. That way, when the truss is raised, I only have to lean over and finish driving the toe-nails as I adjust the chord flush to the edge of the wall with my foot. Raising an end truss often involves pushing on the truss studs. To be safe, it is vital to check that the studs are solidly attached before you begin to stand the truss. As a precaution, you can take this one step further and toe-nail the studs with 8-pennies to beef up the connections.

While one person is holding the truss upright, another positions it by moving it back and forth until the heel intersection of the bottom and top chords lines up with the outside edges of the wall. Once adjusted to position, tack the upper chord to the upright brace and nail the bottom chord to the plate (**Figure 2**).

## Standing Trusses

With the first end truss up, I like to spread the trusses if they aren't too big (**Figure 3**).

Spread them so that they end up leaning on top of one another in the same order you want to follow when you stand them up later on. Work in pairs, keeping an eye on your partner at all times. It's easy to knock one another off the building if your movements aren't coordinated. After the trusses are all spread out, prepare and raise the other end truss.

***Inside trusses.*** With the end trusses up, raise the first inside truss and adjust it into place. Sometimes the intersection of the bottom chord and the tail overhang of the top chord is not easily determined because the very tip of the bottom chord is broken or cut short. To be absolutely sure, I run a straightedge to mark the intersection on each truss. This way,

Figure 4. A carpenter nails off the top chord brace at the premarked layout line, automatically spacing the trusses. Note in the background how the outriggers have been installed in preparation for the barge rafters.

**Figure 5.** With the efficiency that comes from good preparation, an eaves block is installed (left), then the next truss is rolled up and nailed off (right).

when you are standing the trusses, a quick glance will tell you when you're on the money. This prevents you from ending up with a wavy roof line.

After the first interior truss is aligned and nailed down to the exterior walls with two 16-penny nails at each end, finish installing the outriggers to tie these two trusses together. Then, before tipping up more trusses, start a piece of temporary bracing on top of these first two trusses as close to the peak as you can reach. Use 8-penny nails and highnail them slightly so that they can be easily removed during the sheathing phase. On tall trusses, you'll need braces on both sides to reduce the risk of falling trusses.

From this point on, stand and space each truss using ridge and eaves blocks at top and bottom, and the bracing layout marks along the top chord (**Figure 4**).

***Installing the sway brace.*** On a typical roof, I'll install three regular trusses, then install a sway brace to rack the whole assembly plumb. (If I wait too long, there will be too many trusses and the roof will be hard to rack.) First, I pull up the drywall backing that was precut for the gable-end wall and nail that down to the top plate. Then I nail the 45-degree end of the sway brace on top of the backing and rest its other end on a nail placed in the side of the last ridge block I installed, the one between the second and third trusses. Finally, I rack the end truss plumb and nail the sway brace to the ridge block.

At this point, I like to change gears and install the barge rafters. After the barges are hung, I continue standing the remaining trusses (**Figure 5**).

In a production situation, it is important to establish a rhythm and a steady pace: Stand and align a truss, nail it to the top 1x4, pull up and nail in the eaves block as well as the ceiling drywall backing, pull up another 1x4 for the next set of trusses, install an eaves vent every fourth bay. With all the trusses

raised, plumb and brace the remaining end truss and install the barge rafters on that side.

***Lacing.*** Truss companies provide plans that show where various permanent braces, sometimes called "lacing," are meant to go. On production job sites, truss crews are usually well versed in bracing a standard plan, but these documents are necessary if the house is a new plan or a one-of-a-kind job. Building inspectors always check to make sure the lacing is in order after a roof is up (**Figure 6**).

As you stand the trusses, pull up the lacing and roughly spread it where it will be used. When nailing lacing, avoid nailing to the two end trusses until after they and the barge rafters have been adjusted. It is usually necessary to rack the barge and gable into a

**Figure 6.** Permanent bracing, which the author calls "lacing," is installed at specific locations identified in plans from the truss manufacturer.

**Figure 7.** Truss tails are marked with a string (left) and cut plumb (right).

straight line, and a braced web and bottom chord makes the assembly too stiff to work with.

While one carpenter is struggling with the lacing, another can be busy cutting the eaves overhang to the proper length (**Figure 7**). Use a chalk line to mark the lengths and a bevel square to mark the tails at the necessary pitch. If the roof is long, I mark pencil lines along the string (instead of snapping the line) to ensure a straight eaves line.

The final operation is straightening the barges and end trusses. One person can eye up the gable end from the ground and direct the other to spots where it has to go in or out. Nail a 2-by kicker to the side of the top chord at these points and angle it down to the bottom chords. Then nail a 2-by flat on the top of the bottom chords and extend it from the end truss back

several trusses. Rest the gable kicker on this bottom nailer and move the kicker until the adjustment looks straight from the ground, then nail it off. Several kickers may be necessary to tame the gable and barge.

With good prep techniques, standing a modest-sized truss roof is a single day's work. Because of the vast regional differences and building requirements, many aspects of trusses are not covered here. But one thing always remains the same: A carpenter is more efficient on the ground than climbing up, on, and around trusses. Learn to accomplish as much as possible on the ground before setting off eagerly to make a show out of raising a bunch of trusses, only to find yourself bogged down finishing off the details.

*Don Dunkley is a framing contractor in Cool, Calif.*

**Save time and decrease risk by assembling roof components on the ground.**

# Assembling Truss Roofs on the Ground

by Mike Guertin

Several years ago, while discussing how to lift trusses for a hip roof, our crane operator suggested that I preassemble some of the components on the ground. I decided to give it a try, so I worked a little late that day, attaching the jack trusses to the girder trusses (**Figure 8**, next page). The lift went off without a hitch. On the next hip roof house I built, I went further with the preassembly and attached the hip trusses and corner jacks while the assembly was still on the ground. Even factoring in some extra time for head scratching, the method saved us time.

Nowadays, on a single-story house, I usually just attach the jack trusses to the girder trusses before the crane lifts the assembly, since the rest of the components are easy to install in place. But on a two-story house, it's more efficient and safer to assemble as much as possible on the ground. These days I even sheathe the hip system before lifting.

## Laying Out the Girder Truss

I begin by squaring up and marking out one of the girder trusses while it's still lying flat on the pile of trusses. Trusses are sometimes fabricated out of dimension, especially at the tails, so when I lay out the jacks, I don't measure from the tails of the girder truss. Instead, I establish a line perpendicular to the top chord of the girder truss, in order to establish reference points for laying out the locations of the jack trusses (**Figure 9**, next page).

Generally, roof trusses are spaced 2 feet on-center, but one of the spaces between jacks will usually be less than the typical 22 1/2 inches.

***Installing the hangers.*** Jack trusses and hip trusses sit in hangers attached to the girder truss. Once I've marked the jack locations, I install the hangers, initially using only two 1 1/2-inch nails per hanger. Later, when the second girder truss is paired with the first, I'll finish nailing the hangers with 10-penny or 16-penny spikes that grab both girders.

To support the diagonal hip truss and the adjacent jack truss, several styles of hangers are available. I usually use a universal hanger that will fit either the left or the right hip trusses (**Figure 10**, page 103).

While the girder truss is still on the pile of trusses, I nail a single jack truss roughly in the middle of the

## Truss Components

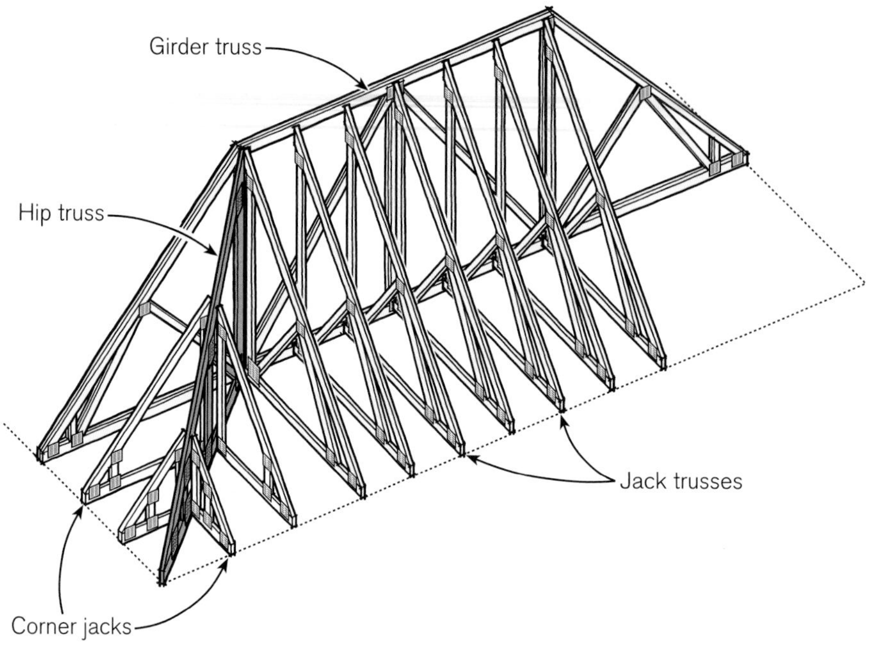

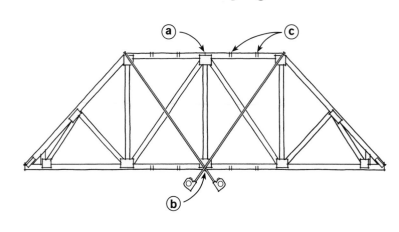

Girder truss

Hip truss

Jack trusses

Corner jacks

**Figure 8.** The girder truss (or hip girder) is the backbone of the hip roof truss assembly; most roofs require a double girder truss. Attached to the girder truss at right angles are the jack trusses (sometimes called the face jacks or end jacks). Extending at a 45-degree angle from the girder truss to the corners are the hip trusses (also called hip jacks, king trusses, or corner jacks). The short trusses that attach to the hip trusses are the corner jacks (also known, confusingly, as hip jacks or side jacks).

girder. Then I roll the girder upright and carry it to a flat location, accessible to the crane, to continue the assembly (**Figure 11**). The area doesn't need to be level, as long as it's fairly flat.

## Jacks and Kings to Open

Trusses with bottom chord overhangs or raised heels can be set up on the ground, because any unevenness can be corrected by blocking up the girder or jacks during assembly. But if we're assembling top-chord-overhang trusses, we have to block up the trusses on stacks of extra floor joists or wall plate stock to keep the tails from digging into the ground.

With the first girder truss upright at the chosen spot, I install the rest of the jack trusses to the first girder truss. I use a framing gun to nail off the jacks from behind, through the girder truss webs. When all the jack trusses are attached, I eyeball the bottom chord of the girder truss to see that it's still fairly straight, pushing it in and out until it's within 1/4 inch.

Next, I mark out a 1x3 brace to match the layout of the jack trusses, and I nail it across the bottom chords of the jacks near their tails (**Figure 12**).

***Beveling the tail.*** Hip trusses are fabricated in one of two ways: The tails are either cut to length or left long. In both cases, the tails are cut square by the fabricator, so they need to be beveled at 45 degrees in the field.

If the fabricator has left the tails long, I always calculate the desired length of the hip's bottom chord.

## Laying Out the Jack Trusses

Ⓐ Ⓒ

Ⓑ

**Figure 9.** To establish a 90-degree angle down from the girder truss's top chord as a reference, first mark the midpoint of the top chord (A). Then pull two tape measures from the top corners of the truss, crossing the tapes at the bottom edge of the chord (B). Adjust the tapes from side to side until they register the same measurement and mark that point as the midpoint of the bottom chord. The two midpoints can then be used as reference points for laying out the locations of the jack trusses (C).

**Figure 10.** This universal hanger supports both the hip truss and one of the jack trusses. This type of hanger is reversible and can be used on either the left or the right side.

Figure 11. A single jack truss nailed to the girder truss will hold it upright while the rest of the jack trusses are installed.

This chord is the hypotenuse of a right triangle; the other two sides of the triangle are the bottom chord of the abutting jack truss and the fascia length between the jack truss and the hip. I use the Pythagorean theorem ($a^2 + b^2 = c^2$) to calculate the length of the hypotenuse, which is the measurement to the tip of the trimmed tail. If the hip truss turns out to be too long, I trim it as necessary.

The square corners of the 2-by web are designed to nestle into the corner between the girder truss and the first jack (**Figure 13**). I insert the hip into the hanger, and holding the truss at roughly a 45-degree angle, I nail it home at the top, through both the girder and the jack. Again, I drive only a couple of nails through the hanger to hold the base of the hip; most of the hanger nails are installed after the second girder truss layer is assembled. To hold the tail of the hip in position, I tack a 1x3 across the tails of a couple of adjacent jack trusses.

## Doubling the Girder

Before installing the second girder truss, I need to straighten the first girder, so that I don't inadver-

tently brace the girder while it's crooked. I eyeball the top and bottom chords of the girder truss and then either lift or lower the ends of the jack trusses and hip trusses until the girder is fairly straight. Next, I square up the position of the jacks, using two tape measures to pull diagonals (**Figure 14**, next page). A 1x3 diagonal brace across the top of the jacks keeps things in place.

Now it's time to tack the second girder truss to the first, using just enough nails to close up any gaps between the top and bottom chords. One more time, I check to see if the girder trusses are straight. I use 1x3s and scrap blocks kicked into the earth to brace the bottom chords straight to a string (**Figure 15**, next page). It's inevitable that the steel truss plates will hold the chords somewhat apart when the two girders are sandwiched together, so I ignore these

**Figure 12.** Once the jack trusses are fastened to the girder, a long 1x3 holds the tails of the jacks in position.

**Figure 13.** The hip truss is installed tight to the corner where the outside jack truss meets the girder truss. Although the vertical web in the corner should not be trimmed with a bevel, the tail of the hip truss needs to be trimmed on site with two 45-degree bevels.

**Figure 14.** The jack trusses are squared to the girder truss by checking the diagonals across the top chords.

slight bulges when lining the girders to the string.

*Double-check the fastener schedule.* Before I start nailing off the girders, I always reread the truss documentation. Roof trusses are an engineered system; if the documents specify nailing or bolting "by others," I know that means me. The girders on the job shown in the photos required spikes 4 inches on-center staggered along the top and bottom chords, and 9 inches on-center staggered along all the webs.

Once the girders are nailed together, I finish nailing off the hangers. The universal hangers for the hip trusses and adjacent jack trusses usually have slots rather than round holes for nailing, making it possible to angle the nails so you can swing a hammer in the tight quarters (**Figure 16**). A pneumatic palm nailer is handy in these locations.

If the house has only one story, at this stage I'd call the hip system complete enough to raise. Installing the corner jacks to the hip trusses is fairly easy when you can work off a ladder, and the same goes for sheathing.

*Keeping things square.* After nailing the girders together, I recheck the strings and make adjustments as necessary. I verify that the jack trusses are square by checking the diagonals from the end of the bottom chord of the outermost jack truss where it meets the girder truss to the tail of the opposite outer jack truss. Once everything looks good, I nail a 1x3 diagonally across the top of the bottom chords. To prepare for sheathing, I replace the diagonal strap that I had

**Figure 15.** The second girder truss is paired with the first after the jack trusses and hip trusses have been installed. Before the two girder trusses are nailed together, they have to be straightened to a string. Diagonal 1x3s and kickers driven into the dirt are used to persuade the girder into position.

**Figure 16.** Once the two girder trusses are nailed together, the rest of the hanger nails can be installed.

**Figure 17.** Before installing the corner jack trusses, it's important to recheck the position of the end of the girder truss and the hip truss.

**Figure 18.** It's handy to have two people to help position the corner jacks on the hip trusses. The corner jacks are nailed at the top through the top chord of the hip truss.

nailed across the top chords of the jack trusses with one on the underside of the top chords.

## Installing the Corner Jacks

At this point I check the position of the hip truss, bracing it in place so it's equidistant from the girder and the nearest jack. I also check that the location of the tail of the hip matches the dimension on the truss plan (**Figure 17**).

Before I mark the locations of the corner jacks, I need to know how they were fabricated. If I'm unsure, I call the truss fabricator. Some corner jacks are fabricated to the correct length and are designed to be installed as delivered. The top and bottom chords have a square plumb cut, not a beveled plumb cut, and those chords contact the hip only at the corners of the cut. Because there is not much contact, I think this is a flimsy way of doing it. If

the trusses are delivered this way, I first nail the square ends to the hip truss. At the top chord, I then add a 2-by block with a bevel cut at the top end of the top chord to make a stronger connection with the hip truss.

If I have any say when the trusses are ordered, I ask the fabricator to leave them long. That way the top and bottom chords of the corner jacks have the same style plumb cut, but since they're long, they can be beveled on site. It's easiest if the length of the top and bottom chords corresponds to the long points of the 45-degree bevel cuts. It's important not to get the right-hand bevels and the left-hand bevels confused. To keep things organized, I pile the corner jacks near each hip by size.

*Corner jack layout.* Marking the positions where the corner jacks fasten to the hip trusses takes two people. The first step is to consult the "length hip or

**Figure 19.** To hold the tails of the corner jacks at 24 inches on-center, they're nailed to the 1x3 that was used to position the hip.

Figure 20. A subfascia ties the tails of the trusses together and stabilizes the truss assembly for lifting.

valley per foot run" line on a framing-square table. I follow the line across the table until I reach the roof pitch for the trusses I've got. The table is in inches and tenths of an inch per foot of run. Since roof trusses are generally set on 2-foot centers, I just double the number.

For example, if the trusses have a pitch of 10/12, the framing-square table would give me 19.70 inches per foot of run. For 2 feet of run (trusses on 2-foot centers), I would double the number, yielding 39.4 — about 39³/8 inches. Starting from the point where the hip touches the corner jack, I would mark down the top chord of the hip 39³/8 inches. Then I would place the end of my tape on that mark and measure the position for the next corner jack — again 39³/8 inches. Since my starting point would be the outer face of the last jack truss, my marks would indicate the locations of the short sides of the corner jacks.

I use the same stepping method to locate the attachment points for the corner jacks along the bottom chord of the hip truss. But for the bottom chords, there's no need to look up any numbers on the framing-square tables, since all 24-inch on-center trusses with 45-degree hip trusses have the same bottom-chord offset — about 33¹⁵/16 inches. I like to nail the corner jacks through from the hip truss as well as toe-nail them (**Figure 18**, previous page). After the top chords are tacked together, I check whether the bottom chords of the corner jacks and the hip truss are flush. If they're off by more than 1/8 inch, I probably made a mistake with the layout.

Next, I tack the tails of the corner jacks, spaced 24 inches on-center, to the 1x3 brace (**Figure 19**, previous page). Once the corner jacks are nailed in, I eyeball up the hip truss to see that it's still straight. If necessary, I use 1x3s nailed back to either the jack trusses or the

Figure 21. To facilitate fastening the trusses to the wall plates, the bottom course of sheathing can either be nailed loosely or be omitted.

girder trusses to straighten it out until the sheathing goes on. If the truss plan requires hangers for the corner jacks, I install them after I've nailed the bottom chords of the corner jacks to the hip truss.

## Subfascia and Sheathing

Although some builders don't install ~~~~~
find them especially us~~
trusses on the ground, because they ~
the end jacks and corner jacks in place (**Figu**
Before nailing a permanent subfascia to the tails
the jack trusses, I check that the girder trusses and
hip trusses are straight and that the trusses all line up
fairly well along their tails. (I usually don't install the
subfascia on the girder-truss tail side until the assembly is on the roof.)

On the ground, I sheathe only the end slope of the roof, not the return facets of the hip trusses. The lowest row of sheathing is either omitted entirely or tacked lightly in place, so it can be lifted up for toe-nailing the trusses to the wall plates. Sometimes I start with 24-inch rips of sheathing along the eaves, because they're easier to handle two stories up (**Figure 21**).

On one job, I rushed the assembly of one of the truss assemblies; once the crane dropped the assembly in place, it didn't sit evenly on the wall plates. We ended up having to pop off several sheets of sheathing to make corrections. The lesson: It's important to take the time during assembly to make sure the trusses are square and straight.

## Call in the Crane

Before the crane arrives, we mark the truss layout on the wall plates, paying special attention to the girder-truss location. We attach the fabric lifting straps to the hip-truss assembly through the top corners of the girder trusses, where the hip trusses are attached. We protect the lifting straps from the sharp edges of the truss plates by first wrapping the area with rags.

To balance the weight of the assembly so it flies level during the lift, I run additional straps out from the crane hook to the subfascia or tails of the jack

control if it
flies l~ ~ne subfascia
can be u~ ~uring the lift.

trusses. To make ~ ~ance the assembly, I like to use adjusta~ ~s or cable come-alongs. (There isn't nearly as ~ ~ch force on these straps or cables as there is on the primary straps; they're only needed to balance the load.) I have the crane operator lift the load until the girders are about a foot off the ground, and then I adjust the come-alongs until the system looks level.

I always assign one crewmember to use a tag line to control the assembly until it comes within reach of the crew on the staging (**Figure 22**). Once it settles onto the marks for the girder trusses, we slide the girders back and forth until the overhang is equal on both sides. The hip trusses should lie flat on the plates and should extend out from the corners of the walls. Once we're satisfied, we release the crane hook and nail the girders to the plates.

An added benefit of assembling a hip system on the ground is that it gives a stable point from which to brace back the rest of the roof trusses, making installation of the remaining trusses faster and safer.

*Mike Guertin is a custom home builder and remodeler in East Greenwich, R.I.*

# Chapter 6:
# Roof Framing Specialties

- **Building a Strong Cathedral Hip Roof**

- **Framing a Barrel-Vault Dormer**

- **Raising an Eyebrow Dormer**

# Building a Strong Cathedral Hip Roof

by David West

**Although its footprint is not large, the interior of this pool house is expansive, thanks to the cathedral ceiling and tall walls.**

On this architecturally designed pool house, I noted that the framing plan showed no collar ties, cables, or other means of bracing for the full cathedral hip roof covering the building. This wasn't an oversight but rather was intended to create an expansive interior space.

Still, with my background in architectural engineering, I recognized a structural challenge. Instead of taking the obvious route and persuading the client to accept a few ties in the final design, we decided to find another way to frame the roof to resist the outward thrust of the hips and the tendency of the rafters to sag under a snow load.

## Steel to the Rescue

Ultimately, we decided to use the four main building corners to lock the hips in position. We reasoned that as long as the corners couldn't move or separate, neither could the hips. But, rather than expect the sidewall sheathing, overlapping top plates, and framing nails to hold the corners together against the thrust of the hips, we opted to use custom-made steel L-braces on the top plates to reinforce the framing.

A local steel fabricator made the brackets, based on a plywood pattern I gave him to copy. We used 1/4-by-4-inch steel plate to make the 5-by-5-foot L-bracket arms. At the corners of each L are two rectangles of steel, welded on diagonally to form a saddle that

catches the ends of the hip rafters (**Figure 1**). The saddles have a 3 5/8-inch spread, giving us a little slack so we didn't have to fight the doubled LVL hips into place.

The brackets were drilled with 3/8-inch-diameter holes for lag-bolting to the plate, and the saddles were drilled to receive two 1/2-inch through-bolts to secure the hip rafters.

## Accurate Framing

We framed the walls with 2x6s on 16-inch centers, topped by a single plate. To ensure that we wouldn't be struggling to fit the heavy, 20-foot-long double LVL hip rafters, we took great care to square, plumb, and brace the four supporting corners to tight tolerances. The main square of the building was interrupted on three sides by the ells, so we stretched string lines from corner to corner across the gaps and left them in place for constant reference against possible movement. We set the lines on 2-by offset blocks inside the top plates and used a 2-by block as a feeler gauge to check the alignment.

While waiting for the steel brackets to be delivered, we went ahead and packed the plate between bracket locations with plywood to accommodate the thickness of the steel. After wrestling the steel into place, we installed a second 2x6 top plate over the assembly, first tracing the bolt-hole locations onto the

**Figure 1.** Four L-brackets custom-welded from 1/4-inch steel plate reinforce the corners of the building against the outward thrust of the double-LVL hip rafters. The saddle at the corner of each bracket is predrilled for a 1/2-inch bolt. The brackets were sandwiched between the top plates; lag screws hold the assembly together.

plates and predrilling them for lag screws. We then used 3 1/2-inch-long lags to tie the wood and steel layers together.

To work comfortably at the roof peak, which was 21 feet above the deck, we set up pipe staging inside the building. That involved pulling the temporary spring braces on the walls. We were pleased to find that the steel braces held the walls perfectly plumb throughout the roof framing process.

We used double 1 3/4-by-12-inch LVL hips, follow-ing the computer-engineered framing plan supplied by our lumber distributor. Each hip received a birdsmouth cut at the heel and a square-faced plumb cut at the ridge (**Figure 2**, next page). The hips butted against a 4x4 nailing block at the ridge. In addition to carrying the 2x12 rafters, each hip provided support for the ells' valley rafters. We framed each of these ell roofs with a combination supporting and supported valley.

## Cathedral Hip Roof

### Roof Framing Plan

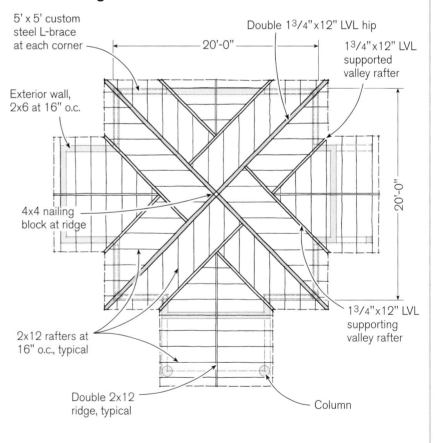

5' x 5' custom steel L-brace at each corner

Double 1³/4"x12" LVL hip

1³/4"x12" LVL supported valley rafter

20'-0"

Exterior wall, 2x6 at 16" o.c.

20'-0"

4x4 nailing block at ridge

1³/4"x12" LVL supporting valley rafter

2x12 rafters at 16" o.c., typical

Double 2x12 ridge, typical

Column

**Figure 2.** Restrained by the steel brackets at the corners, the structural hips bear against one another at the peak and need no further means of support. Supporting valley rafters running from top plate to hip rafter hold up the small ell gables.

**Figure 3.** Complex roofs are difficult to vent properly, so the author opted for an unvented "hot roof," using spray-in-place Icynene insulation to prevent moisture-transport problems.

## Hot Roof

Venting a hip roof is problematic because most of the rafter bays terminate against the hip rafter and not at the ridge, leaving no practical means of carrying air through from the eaves. We avoided the entire issue by blowing in Icynene foam insulation, creating an unvented "hot roof" (**Figure 3**).

Typical for our region, we applied 1x3 furring strips on 16-inch centers to the underside of the rafters in preparation for plaster board. With all the angles on this ceiling, the plasterer didn't mind not having any collar ties to cut around, and the clients are pleased with the final results. It's been over six months since completion, and there hasn't been a single crack in the finish. It appears that the bracing works just as we intended it to.

*David West owns Meadowview Construction in Topsfield, Mass.*

# Framing a Barrel-Vault Dormer

by Thomas Buckborough

**Keeping the ceiling joists independent of the rafters simplified the process.**

My design/build company recently completed a residential addition that included a 16-foot-wide dormer with an arched roof. Although the construction was challenging, the finished copper-roofed dormer, complete with a curved plaster ceiling, adds a dramatic element to the addition.

As I planned the dormer framing, I tried to anticipate the best way to create a crisp edge where the curved dormer ceiling intersects the flat sloping ceiling under the main roof. Clearly, it would be difficult to create the curve of the roof and the curve of the ceiling with the same rafters.

The solution was to frame the ceiling separately from the roof. This allowed us to concentrate on getting the proper bearing for the rafters without worrying whether the bottoms of the rafters established the desired ceiling curve. To clarify the design, I drew a section in both directions, as well as a standard framing plan (**Figure 4**).

## Curved Header

Fortunately, my lead carpenter had experience building curved structures on previous projects. The first step, just as for any dormer, was to frame a rectangular rough opening in the main roof. The LVL trimmer rafters and the LVL header at the high side of the opening were sized by a structural engineer. When we sheathed the main roof, we allowed the plywood to run wild into the rough dormer opening, to provide a

surface for drawing the curve of the dormer roof at the line where it intersected the plane of the main roof.

The dormer design included eight windows, all purchased from Eagle Window and Door (www.eaglewindow.com). The two largest windows were custom units with radiused tops.

The window header was assembled from five layers of CDX plywood — four layers of 3/4-inch plywood and one of 1/2-inch. Because the 31/2-by-151/2-inch header has a post at the midpoint of the 16-foot span, I felt confident that it was generously sized (**Figure 5**, page 116).

To draw the curves on the plywood, we made a 19-foot-6-inch trammel from scabbed-together 1-by boards. From the pivot point, we measured two radius lengths — 17 feet 101/2 inches and 19 feet 2 inches — corresponding to the inside and outside arcs of the header.

After scribing and cutting the plywood pieces, we assembled the header with plenty of nails and construction adhesive, staggering all the plywood joints. We nailed the header into place, and then we turned our attention to the dormer rafters.

## Dormer Rafters

To locate the line of the curved header on the plane of the main roof, we temporarily screwed 5/8-inch plywood over the roof sheathing, then used a laser pen to transfer the arc. One carpenter moved the

## Curved Dormer Details

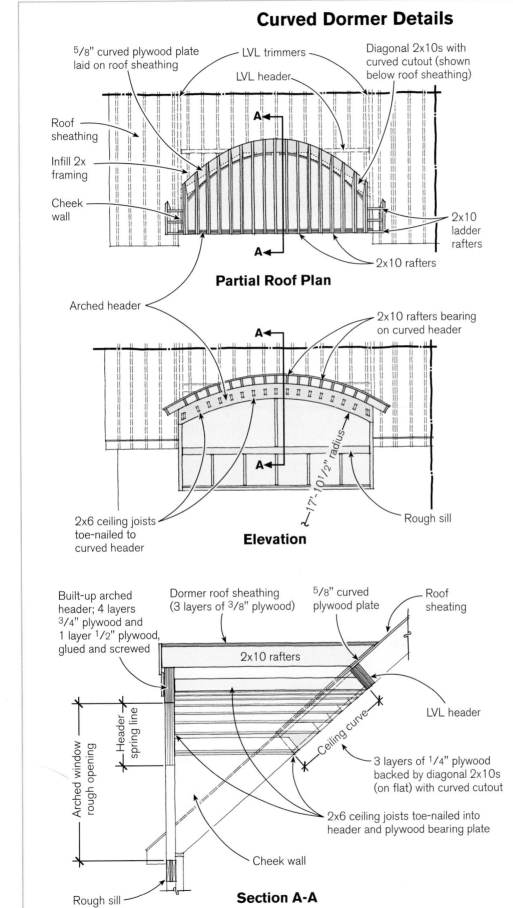

5/8" curved plywood plate laid on roof sheathing

LVL trimmers

LVL header

Diagonal 2x10s with curved cutout (shown below roof sheathing)

Roof sheathing

Infill 2x framing

Cheek wall

A

A

2x10 ladder rafters

2x10 rafters

**Partial Roof Plan**

Arched header

2x10 rafters bearing on curved header

A

A

17'-10 1/2" radius

Rough sill

2x6 ceiling joists toe-nailed to curved header

**Elevation**

Built-up arched header; 4 layers 3/4" plywood and 1 layer 1/2" plywood, glued and screwed

Dormer roof sheathing (3 layers of 3/8" plywood)

5/8" curved plywood plate

Roof sheating

2x10 rafters

LVL header

Header spring line

Ceiling curve

3 layers of 1/4" plywood backed by diagonal 2x10s (on flat) with curved cutout

Arched window rough opening

2x6 ceiling joists toe-nailed into header and plywood bearing plate

Cheek wall

Rough sill

**Section A-A**

**Figure 4.** To create a crisp edge on the interior where the curved dormer ceiling meets the sloped cathedral ceiling, the author framed the ceiling separately from the roof. This allowed him to get proper bearing for the roof rafters without worrying about whether they established the desired curve below.

**Figure 5.** LVL trimmers and header frame the dormer's rectangular opening (top). Short cheek walls at each end support the curved window header (above), which was laminated on site from five layers of plywood.

**Figure 6.** The rafters run from the top of the curved header to a curved plywood plate on the main roof (top). Because it provides low-slope protection, soldered copper was the roofing of choice (above).

**Figure 7.** To define the ceiling curve, the author installed a pair of angled 2x10s in the upper corners of the rectangular opening (left). The doubled 2x10s were cut to follow the curve of the header, then skinned on the inside with plywood to make a perfectly radiused nail base for the ends of the 2x6 ceiling joists (right).

laser pen along the header, using a simple site-built jig to keep it level, while another carpenter transferred the marks onto the 5/8-inch plywood. We then removed the plywood and cut out a curved plate to form a bearing surface for the dormer rafters.

Each 2x10 dormer rafter was individually measured and cut to length. We installed the rafters level, with one end resting on top of the window header and the other end, cut at an acute angle, resting on the main roof (**Figure 6**).

The dormer ended up with two small cheeks, which we closed in with 2x4 stub walls. The subfascia was made from 3/4-inch plywood. First we installed the curved subfascia on the face of the dormer, and then we installed the fascia returns back to the main roof. On each side of the dormer, the fascia return was attached to a pair of 2x10 ladder rafters supported by the cheek walls. Later, the subfascia pieces were covered with finger-jointed 1x12 cedar trim.

Since 5/8-inch plywood wouldn't easily bend to the roof's curve, we sheathed the roof with three layers of 3/8-inch plywood. We protected the roof sheathing with rubberized-asphalt eaves membrane; eventually, the roofing contractor arrived to install a flat-seamed soldered copper roof.

## Framing the Curved Ceiling

We drew an arc on the window header 4 inches up from the top of the window heads to mark the bottom of the ceiling joists. We then installed a pair of diagonal 2x10s in each corner of the rectangular rough opening and transferred the arc on the header onto the 2x10s, again using the laser pen.

We cut the curve with a jigsaw and then installed three layers of 1/4-inch plywood to create a smooth arc. The 2x6 ceiling joists were toe-nailed to this curved piece of plywood, defining the crisp edge I was looking for (**Figure 7**).

## Finishing

We insulated the dormer, then strapped the ceiling with strips of 1/2-inch plywood installed 12 inches on-center. Two layers of 3/8-inch blueboard conformed easily to the curve, without the need for moistening. Flexible corner bead installed at the transition between the main sloping ceiling and the curved ceiling established a near-perfect curve.

*Thomas Buckborough is a general contractor and designer-builder in Concord, Mass.*

# Raising an Eyebrow Dormer

by Jack Galt

One of the nicer elements to adorn Victorian and Queen Anne-style houses is the eyebrow dormer. But while it's graceful in appearance, the compound curves make for some tricky framing and finishing details. If you're attempting it for the first time, be sure to budget in a little head-scratching time. Here are a few tips I picked up while framing my first eyebrow, an 8-foot-wide, 2-foot-high dormer on a custom Queen Anne.

## Laying Out the Curves

For help in layout, I turned to *Audels Carpenters & Builders Guide*, which is usually very helpful, though not in this case. The section on eyebrow framing states that owing to the popularity of "this style of window, … some idea of its construction should be known to all carpenters." I had "some" idea, so I plowed ahead with not much more to guide me.

I established the curve of the window frame by connecting three intersecting curves of the same radius (**Figure 8**, next page). I did the layout on the deck until I had a pleasing shape, then made a plywood router template for cutting the curved pieces.

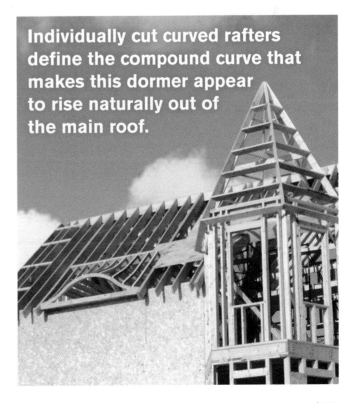

Individually cut curved rafters define the compound curve that makes this dormer appear to rise naturally out of the main roof.

# Framing Details

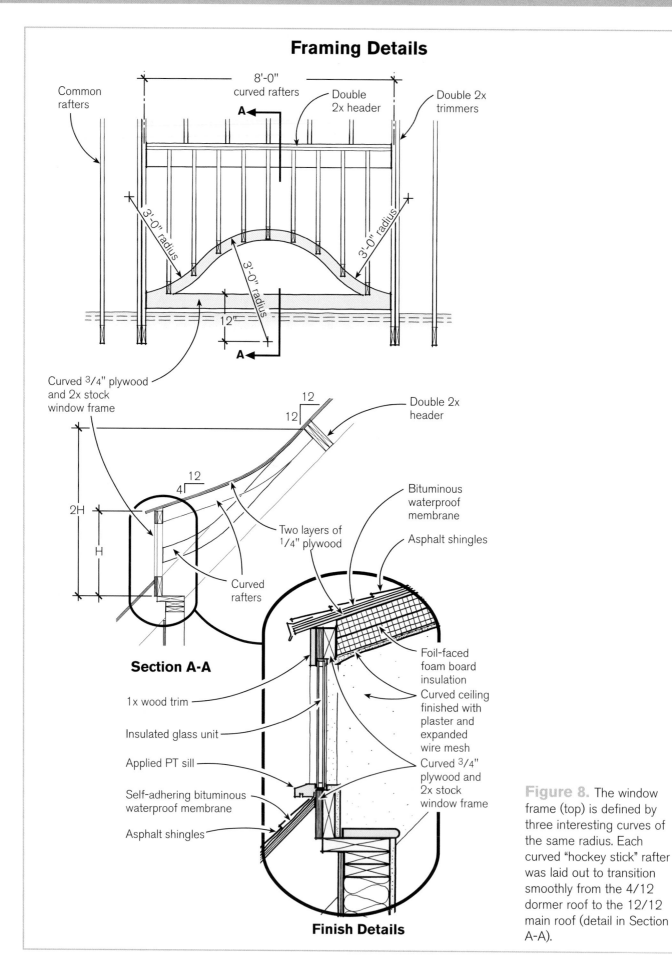

Common rafters

8'-0" curved rafters

Double 2x header

Double 2x trimmers

A

3'-0" radius

3'-0" radius

3'-0" radius

12"

A

Curved ³/4" plywood and 2x stock window frame

12
12

Double 2x header

12
4

2H

H

Two layers of ¹/4" plywood

Bituminous waterproof membrane

Asphalt shingles

Curved rafters

Foil-faced foam board insulation

**Section A-A**

Curved ceiling finished with plaster and expanded wire mesh

1x wood trim

Curved ³/4" plywood and 2x stock window frame

Insulated glass unit

Applied PT sill

Self-adhering bituminous waterproof membrane

Asphalt shingles

**Finish Details**

**Figure 8.** The window frame (top) is defined by three interesting curves of the same radius. Each curved "hockey stick" rafter was laid out to transition smoothly from the 4/12 dormer roof to the 12/12 main roof (detail in Section A-A).

**Figure 9.** The window frame is a sandwich of 2-by stock and 3/4-inch plywood, both cut with a router and template. The curved rafters were cut from clean 2x12s.

For the window frame, which supports the dormer rafters, I made a sandwich of 2-by stock and 3/4-inch plywood (**Figure 9**).

I framed the opening in the roof as I would for any dormer, with double trimmers on the side and a double header on top. I made the opening about twice as high as the window frame itself, measured plumb. This worked well with the 12/12 pitch of the main roof, though for shallower roofs I would have gone higher with the opening.

## "Hockey Stick" Rafters

I attached the window frame between the trimmers, bracing it as needed. Then, working from the center of the window, I established what seemed to be the right pitch for the eyebrow — 4/12, in this case. Using strings and straightedges, I found the point where the 4/12 pitch intersected the main roof. Holding a 2x12 in place, I marked the two pitches and the point of intersection. Working freehand, I rounded the point of intersection, coming up with a rafter shape that somewhat resembled a hockey stick.

I laid out four rafters on each side of the center one — that seemed like plenty for an 8-foot dormer. The other rafters were laid out the same way, except that the 4/12 pitch intersects the 12/12 at a lower point with each successive rafter.

As the eye travels down the curve of the eyebrow, the difference between its pitch and that of the common rafter becomes smaller. It is this change in pitch that gives the eyebrow dormer its compound curve, and makes it seem to rise naturally out of the main roof.

Because the curved rafters were cut from a 2x12, they ended up with a depth of 3 to 4 inches. I finished the rafters on one side and used those as templates for the other side.

## Sheathing and Roofing

With any compound curve, two layers of 1/4-inch sheathing works better than one layer of 1/2-inch. I ripped the plywood into 16-inch strips, which was easier than trying to get a full sheet to take the curve. I staggered the joints between layers and used screws to make sure the plywood stayed down nicely and formed a smooth curve (**Figure 10**).

Once the dormer was sheathed, I covered it with Grace's Ice & Water Shield (www.na.graceconstruction. com). I also protected the area where the base of the window frame meets the roof plane which extends below, forming a porch roof (**Figure 11**, next page).

The sheathing overhangs the edge of the eyebrow

**Figure 10.** A double layer of 1/4-inch sheathing covers the eyebrow. The author used screws for attaching the plywood to ensure a smooth curve.

by several inches. This creates a nice shadow effect, and also offers weather protection. I snipped and bent drip-edge around the overhang.

Traditional Queen Annes are often roofed with either slate or wood shingles, which offer great flexibility in making the roofing courses follow the lines of the dormer. On this roof, we used three-tab fiberglass shingles, which limits you to straighter lines. I found that being consistent with the shingle lines on the adjacent flat-plane roof meant that the curved courses weren't parallel with the edge of the eyebrow dormer roof. But this was barely noticeable from the ground and assured the best protection.

## Finishing

The outside of the eyebrow is trimmed with a cedar trim board that overhangs the window frame by $1^{1}/4$ inches — also routed with a template to follow the exact curve of the frame. Across the bottom is a painted pressure-treated sill, drip-kerfed and angled to shed water. The sash (a temporary piece of Plexiglass, until a custom IGU is made) rests against the inside of the trim board and sill. Glazing tape ensures a weathertight seal.

*Inside.* Since the curved rafters of the eyebrow are only 3 to 4 inches deep, I used foil-faced foam board for its higher R-value, cutting it to fit snugly between the rafters.

**Figure 11.** The eyebrow sits halfway down a sloping roof plane that continues over a porch, adding architectural interest to an otherwise unbroken expanse of roofing.

While drywall works fine on the flatter sections of the dormer ceiling, expanded wire mesh and plaster are the best way to finish the curves.

*Jack Galt is a former builder in northern Vermont.*

FRAMING

# Chapter 7: Pickup Work

■ **Framing a Hipped Tray Ceiling**

■ **Framing a Barrel-Vault Ceiling**

■ **A Simple Vaulted Ceiling**

# Framing a Hipped Tray Ceiling

by Tim Uhler

One of my favorite parts of framing a house is doing the interior-detail pickup framing — elements like arches, barrel vaults, and coffered ceilings. Here, I'll show a simple method for framing a hipped tray ceiling — a ceiling that looks like the underside of a hip roof except that it's flat on top (**Figure 1**).

There's nothing unusual about this shape, but we've gotten the process down to the point where we can lay it out quickly and hand most of the work off to the less experienced carpenters on the crew.

## Ceiling as Roof

To help newer framers visualize the ceiling, we use roof-framing terminology to describe the pieces. The members running up from the sides of the opening are called "commons" and the ones in the corners are "hips." These "rafters" butt against a lower rim board at the inside face of the soffit and angle up to meet the flat surface at the top of the tray. The flat area is bound by horizontal rim boards that catch the upper ends of the rafters and the tray ceiling joists that span from rim to rim.

The trays we build are small enough that all the framing members except the soffit rim can be made from 2x4s. The soffit rim should be at least as tall as the room's ceiling joists; we often make it from 2x12s.

*Sizing rule of thumb.* These ceilings typically go in master bedrooms. In rooms of that size, it generally looks good if the commons are about 3 feet long. They could be longer or shorter, but we've found

that regardless of the pitch, 3 feet is dramatic enough without overpowering the room. It's also a nice round number to work with.

We also have to determine what slope to use for the sides of the tray. On upper floors, we try to match the pitch of the roof so that the tray rafters near outside walls won't hit the roof rafters or come so close it's hard to insulate.

## Framing Calculations

We calculate our cuts and layout based on the 3-foot common-rafter length. The length of our tray rafters corresponds to the "line length" of a roof rafter — the distance between the head cut at the top and a line projected up from the plumb cut at the birdsmouth. Because the tray rafters butt to rim boards top and bottom, they don't need birdsmouths; instead, they have plumb cuts at both ends.

The photographs in this story come from a house with an 8/12 pitch roof, so that's the pitch we used for the tray ceiling. We knew the rafters would be 3 feet long, so the only thing we had to calculate was the length of a hip and the run of a common. The easiest way to do these calculations is with a Construction Master (**Figure 2**). I use a Construction Master Pro Trig Plus III set to round to the nearest 16th inch.

After entering the pitch (8) and the length of the common (3 feet), the calculator gives us the length of the hip (3 feet 10¹³⁄₁₆ inches) and the run of a common (2 feet 5¹⁵⁄₁₆ inches). We write both num-

**Figure 1.** A hipped tray ceiling (left) adds visual interest without a lot of additional framing cost. It's framed like a hip roof except that it's flat on top (right).

# The Geometry of a Hipped Tray Ceiling

To enter the line length of the common rafter and its pitch:

3 **Feet** **Diag** 8 **Inch** **Pitch**

These values are now stored in the calculator; you can do the next keystrokes in any order.

To find the length of the hip, enter

**Hip/V** and 3'-10¹³/₁₆" is displayed.

To find the run of a common, press

**Run** and 2'-5¹⁵/₁₆" is displayed.

**Figure 2.** Laying out a hipped tray ceiling — like the one in the drawing below — is like laying out a hip roof. The author usually starts with a known rafter length of 3 feet and often matches the pitch of the roof above. The calculations shown here are based on an 8/12 pitch. With this method, the only other dimensions the framer needs to know are the length of the hip and the run of the common, information that's easy to get from a Construction Master using the following keystrokes.

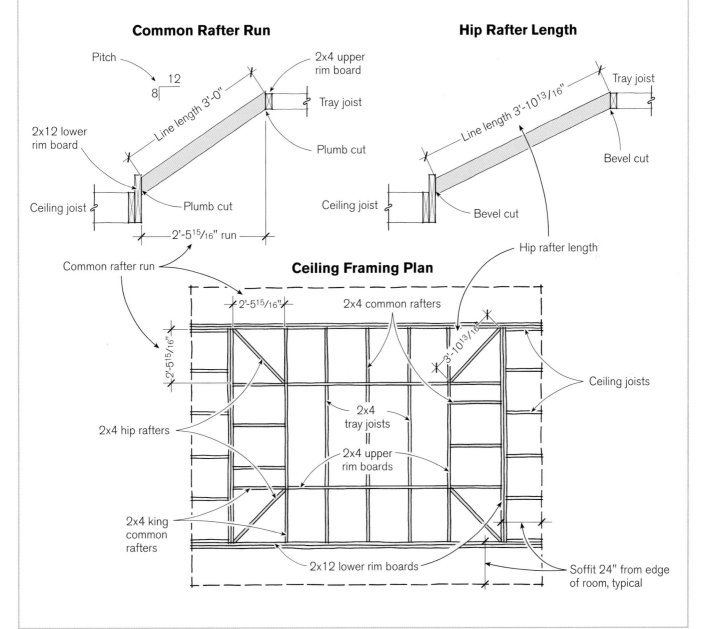

## Common Rafter Run

Pitch
12
8
Line length 3'-0"
2x4 upper rim board
Tray joist
Plumb cut
2x12 lower rim board
Ceiling joist
Plumb cut
2'-5¹⁵/₁₆" run

## Hip Rafter Length

Line length 3'-10¹³/₁₆"
Tray joist
Bevel cut
Ceiling joist
Bevel cut

## Ceiling Framing Plan

Common rafter run
2'-5¹⁵/₁₆"
2'-5¹⁵/₁₆"
Hip rafter length
3'-10¹³/₁₆"
2x4 common rafters
2x4 hip rafters
2x4 tray joists
2x4 upper rim boards
2x4 king common rafters
2x12 lower rim boards
Ceiling joists
Soffit 24" from edge of room, typical

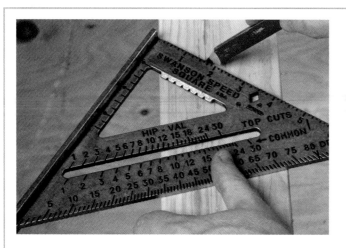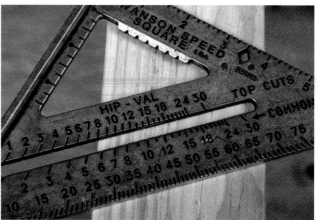

**Figure 3.** The rafters for a tray ceiling have plumb cuts on both ends. To use a Speed Square to lay out the 8/12 plumb cut on the end of a common, set the pivot point against the edge of the stock and align the number 8 on the "COMMON" scale with the edge of the stock (left). Use the same method to lay out the 8/12 plumb cut on the hip, but index off the "HIP-VAL" scale (right).

bers down and put the calculator away; that's it for the math.

Everything else from here on out is a matter of measuring, marking, cutting, and installing.

***Rise doesn't matter.*** If we were framing a roof, we'd want to know the rise of the commons to know how high above the plates to support the ridge while we installed rafters. But with a tray ceiling, the rise matters only if you're installing it in a dropped ceiling and need to fit it beneath the joists.

The ceiling shown here bumped into a large attic space, so we didn't have to worry about its height.

**Figure 4.** To save time cutting the commons, the carpenters stack the material and score the cut on the second piece while cutting the top piece.

## Laying Out Commons

To lay out the commons, we draw a pair of lines 3 feet apart and square across the edge of a 2x4. We then use the Speed Square to mark the two parallel lines, 3 feet apart on the 2x4's face, representing the plumb cuts at each end (**Figure 3**). We saw through the 2x4 at both lines and use this first common as a pattern to mark the others.

To save time, we stack the material for the commons, trace the plumb cuts onto the top piece, and make the cuts with a saw set deep enough to score the cut on the piece below (**Figure 4**).

## Laying Out Hips

We lay out the hips the same way, again with the Speed Square, but using the hip-valley scale this time.

***Bevel cuts.*** The ends of each hip get beveled with a saw set to 45 degrees so that the top will fit between the king commons and the bottom will fit the inside corner of the opening. Using the Speed Square, we mark the hip plumb cut at one end of the hip, then make a second line parallel to the first and 1½ inches — the thickness of the stock — away. (If the stock were 1¾ inches thick, the second line would be 1¾ inches away.)

We use these lines to guide the saw through the two bevel cuts that will produce the desired 90-degree point (**Figure 5**). With the saw set to a 45-degree bevel, we cut through the 2x4 at the line closest to the end of the board. Then, without flipping the board, we cut along the inner line (that's 1½ inches away), bringing the saw in from the other edge.

The two cuts cross at the center of the stock and give us the diamond-shaped point we're looking for.

***Getting the length right.*** We complete the hip by making a mirror image of this cut at the other end of

**Figure 5.** Here, a carpenter lays out the first set of bevel cuts on a hip by drawing parallel lines at the angle of the plumb cut on the hip. The distance between the lines is equal to the thickness of the stock — in this case, 1½ inches (A). It takes two 45-degree bevel cuts to cut the end of the hip. The first cut is made on the outer line with the blade angled toward the other end of the stock (B). The second cut is on the inner line with the blade angled toward the cut end (C). The result is a 90-degree point (D) in plan view that will fit the inside corner of the opening or between the king commons where they meet at the upper rim.

## Layout for Hip Bevel Cuts

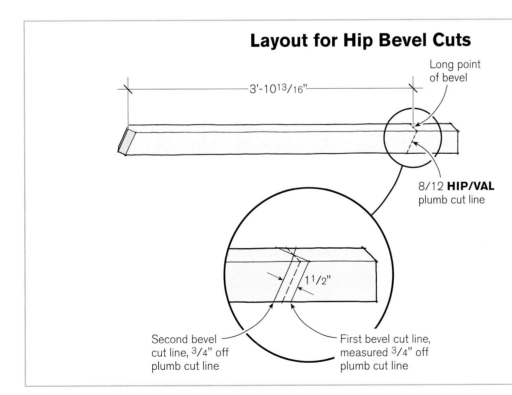

**Figure 6.** To lay out the second set of bevel cuts on the hip, the author first marks the calculated length of the hip, measuring from the long point on the other end. A pair of lines ¾ inch to either side mark the bevel cuts.

the stock. The finished piece should be 3 feet 10¹³⁄₁₆ inches point to point, so we measure this distance down the edge from the diamond cut we already made.

We make a mark, then use the Speed Square to draw an 8/12 plumb cut at the mark with the hip-valley scale. This new line represents the long point

of the diamond cut we want to make (**Figure 6**).

Next, we draw a second and third line parallel to the first and ¾ inch to either side of it. The first line is now centered between parallel lines that are 1½ inches apart. Our first 45-degree bevel cut is along the outer line with the blade angled back in. Our second bevel

**Figure 7.** The author's crew frames the opening by carefully trimming the joists in a straight line (left), then nailing on a 2x12 rim board (top right). Rafters will be installed above the line on the rim. On the outside wall, the rim is positioned plumb against the rafters using short nailing blocks (above right).

cut is along the inner line with the blade angled out. The cuts will cross to form a point at the center line, 3 feet 10¹³⁄₁₆ inches from the cut at the other end.

The tray has four hips, so we cut three more that are exactly the same as the first. The number of commons will vary with the size of the opening, but they all must be accurately cut because the way we install them leaves no room to fudge.

## Soffit Framing

While a more experienced carpenter is calculating and cutting the hips and commons, I'll have two less-experienced carpenters frame the soffit around the opening in the ceiling. We typically bring the soffit in 24 inches from the edge of the room. We usually know in advance that we're going to install a tray ceiling, so when we roll the joists we use pieces that run partway into the opening and stop. (We use bearing ridges on most of the houses we build, so it doesn't matter that the joists don't reach from plate to plate.)

If we're framing a 24-inch soffit and using a single rim board, we snap a line across the joists 22½ inches

in from the wall and trim the joists back to that line, making sure the cuts are plumb (**Figure 7**).

*Lower rim board.* Although the joists are usually 2x8s, we use 2x12s for the rim because the added height allows us to install rafters several inches up from the bottom of the opening. This leaves a vertical surface below the slope large enough to install a crown with cove lighting.

If we chose to, we could make the rim the same height as the joists and install the rafters flush to the ceiling.

We start by cutting rims and nailing them (crown side up) onto the ends of the joists. We then install a second pair of rim boards perpendicular to the first, 24 inches out from the walls at the ends of the opening.

We check to make sure the entire opening is plumb, square, and straight. If it's not, the precut hips and commons won't fit properly and it will show in the finished ceiling.

## Installing the Tray Ceiling

With the soffit framed and the hips and commons cut, it's time to install the rafters. But first we have to

**Figure 8.** King commons, which flank the hips, are positioned the same distance out from the corner as the run of a common — in this project, 2 feet 5$^{15}$/$_{16}$ inches (above left). The rafters install fast because toe-nailing holds them in place until the upper rim is installed. After the hips are nailed up (above right), the king commons and hips get nailed together at the top (left).

mark their layout. We like to install rafters 5 to 7 inches up from the bottom of the opening, so we snap a line at the right height on all four sides.

The hips land at the inside corners and the commons are spaced 24 inches on-center along the rims. But the commons on either side of each hip (the king commons) have to be a specific distance out from the corner, equal to the run of a common — in this case, 2 feet 5$^{15}$/$_{16}$ inches. This ensures that the hip and king commons converge at the same point.

***King commons and hips.*** Unlike roof rafters, which need immediate support at the ridge, tray ceiling rafters can be installed by toe-nailing them to the lower rim. They're so short and light that toe-nails will hold them until we get around to installing the upper rim (**Figure 8**).

Again, this is why we didn't bother to calculate the rise of the commons: if our cuts are accurate and we nail the hips and king commons tight to the rim, all the rafters automatically top out at the same elevation.

We measure out from the corners of the rim and nail the king commons in place. Next, we toe-nail the hips

in the corners. The hips and king commons will converge, and we nail them all together where they meet. (Be careful when positioning these pieces for nailing: if you hold on at the wrong spot, you could easily shoot a nail into your hand.)

***Upper rims.*** Once all the hips are nailed to the king commons, it's time to install the upper rim pieces. There's no need to calculate their lengths; all we have to do is measure from corner to corner where the hips and king commons meet. We cut the pieces from 2x4s and nail them at the corners (**Figure 9**, next page).

At this point, the upper rim goes all the way around the opening and is supported at the proper height. Next we install the commons 24 inches on-center between the king commons.

***Commons and joists.*** The only framing left is to install 2x4 ceiling joists between the upper rims. Once more, we install these pieces 24 inches on-center. If there's going to be a light or fan in the tray, we avoid running a joist across the center. There's no need to install hip jacks because the drywall will be

**Figure 9.** While it's possible to calculate the lengths of the upper rim pieces, the author finds it quicker and easier to install the hips and king commons (A), measure between them (B), and then cut the rim pieces to fit (C). Once the upper rims are in place (D), it's a simple matter to install the commons and run ceiling joists across the top.

able to span from hip to king common without any added support.

## Cost to Frame

A while back I timed how long it took me to frame a tray ceiling by myself. It took about two hours, but I was going all out. If I do the math and make a pattern for the hips and commons, the less experienced guys on our crew can frame a tray ceiling in about three man-hours.

Compared with the value that a tray ceiling adds to a new home, the material cost to frame one is almost negligible. The only things we have to go out of our way to get are the long 2x12s used for the lower rim. None of the 2x4s are very long, so we can usually get them from scrap.

*Tim Uhler is a lead framer and exterior trim carpenter for Pioneer Builders in Port Orchard, Wash.*

# Framing a Barrel-Vault Ceiling

by Tim Uhler

The company I work for builds spec homes. One of the ways we dress them up is by adding barrel-vault ceilings. Except for the layout, these impressive architectural details are not that hard to frame. A carpenter and helper can do it in four to five hours.

Our vaults are typically installed in a rectangular opening in a hallway or master bathroom. As a result, the opening is rarely more than 6 feet wide or 12 feet long. Framing a larger vault wouldn't be any different, but we've never had the space.

## Geometry of a Barrel Vault

The surface of the barrel is part of the inside surface of a cylinder; a section through it is an arc of a larger circle. The ends of the vault can be plumb and flat, or curved like the barrel itself. We usually make them curved.

*Like a hip roof.* The layout for this kind of barrel is similar to that of a regular hip roof — one where all the pitches are equal. On a hip roof, common rafters run up from the sides and meet at the ridge. On a barrel vault, half-arc segments run up from the sides and meet at the high point of the vault (**Figure 10**, next page). If the vault is small enough, you can make the entire segment from a single piece of plywood.

A hip roof has a single common rafter, called the king common, at each end. The king common runs from the top plate to the ridge board. The same is true of a barrel vault except that the end piece is half of an arc segment, and instead of hitting a ridge it meets the midpoint of the last full arc segment in the barrel.

*The hip is an ellipse.* The vault framing also includes hiplike pieces that come in from the corners at 45-degree angles. In plan, they look exactly like hips, but from the side you can see they're curved. Because they're formed by the 90-degree intersection of two cylindrical curves, their shape is actually an ellipse.

## Ceiling Opening

The first step in framing a barrel is to create an opening for the vault to go into. If it's on the top floor, we'll cut out some ceiling joists and head off the opening. That may not be possible on a lower floor, in which case we'll drop the surrounding ceiling by framing in a soffit (**Figure 11**, next page). The size of the opening might be specified by the designer; if not, we'll come up with a size that seems proportionate to the room. In the project photographed here, we framed the opening about 12 inches off the main walls of the room.

After the opening is framed, we double-check to make sure it's square and the sides are reasonably

To provide nailing for the drywall, flat 2x4 purlins are nailed between the curved plywood rafters.

parallel. Then we measure the distance across the opening at several points and use the average distance to determine the curves for the barrel.

## Determining the Radius

Once we know the size of the opening, we decide how tall the vault should be at its highest point, then calculate the radius required to hit both edges of the opening while passing through the high point. To put it mathematically, we know a chord length (the width of the opening) of a given circle, we know the plumb distance from the center of the chord to the circumference of the circle (the height of the barrel), and we need to find the radius of the circle.

The easiest way to get the answer is to use a construction calculator that has a trig function. I use the Construction Master Pro Trig Plus III. For the vault shown here, which is 48½ inches wide and 12 inches high, I punch in the following sequence:

The screen displays the radius of the arc, in this case 30½ inches. You can also use algebra to calculate the radius (**Figure 12**, page 131).

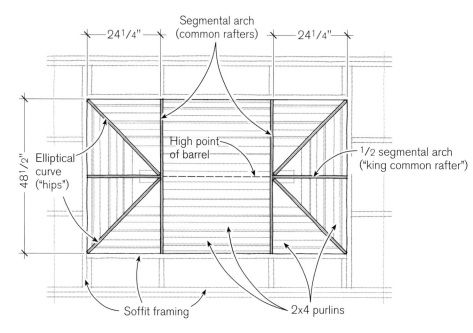

24¹/4"    Segmental arch
          (common rafters)    24¹/4"

High point
of barrel

48¹/2"    Elliptical
          curve
          ("hips")

¹/2 segmental arch
("king common rafter")

Soffit framing

2x4 purlins

**Figure 10.** The vault framing (above left) consists of radiused plywood "rafters" at the sides and ends, and elliptical plywood "hips" at the corners (drawing, left). Two-by-four "purlins" run between the plywood pieces. The surface is finished later with a double layer of ¹/4-inch drywall (above right).

**Figure 11.** On upper floors, the opening for a barrel vault can be created by heading off ceiling joists (left). In rooms with high ceilings, the vault may fit in a dropped soffit (right).

## Finding the Radius of an Arc

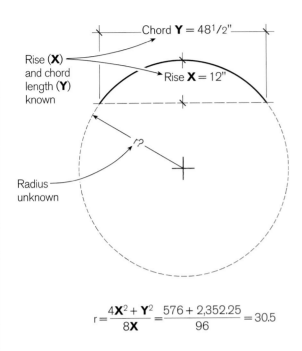

$$r = \frac{4\mathbf{X}^2 + \mathbf{Y}^2}{8\mathbf{X}} = \frac{576 + 2{,}352.25}{96} = 30.5$$

**Figure 12.** If the width and the height of a barrel vault or segmental arch are known, you can use this formula to calculate the radius of the curved arch pieces.

## Making Arc Segments

We make the arc segments out of plywood. You could use OSB, but that would make it harder to see the layout and make clean cuts. Whenever possible, we try to gang-cut the pieces with a jigsaw (**Figure 13**). We then cut one in half to make the king commons for the ends.

## Laying Out the "Hips"

The first time we framed this kind of vault, we didn't fully understand how to lay out the ellipses. When our initial efforts failed, we installed the segmental arches, or "commons," then scribed the ellipses by taping a pencil onto a 4-foot level and sliding the level along the plane of the barrel to mark the shape onto an oversized piece of plywood that had been inserted where the "hip" was to go. The method worked, but it was time-consuming and the curves weren't as fair as they should have been.

The next time around, I asked a cabinetmaker I know what we were doing wrong. He sent me a drawing that explained how to lay out the ellipses; without it I'd probably still be tracing the curves.

There are two numbers you need to know to lay out an ellipse: the length of the major axis and the length of the minor axis. If you have these numbers, you can also locate the two focus points. Once you have those points, all it takes is some picture-hanger wire and a pencil to draw the curve (see "Laying Out the Elliptical Hips," next page).

In a vault of this type, the minor axis matches the diameter of the cylinders from which the barrel is formed. Since we needed to draw only the top half of the ellipse, we used half the diameter, the radius of the circle — 30½ inches.

The major axis was a little trickier, but treating the elliptical "hips" like regular roof hips helped. Just as a hip runs 17 inches — actually 16.97 inches — for every 12 inches of common run, so does the elliptical hip. Using a calculator, we multiplied the common run, 30½ inches, by $\sqrt{2}$ to get the hip run — 43⅛ inches. Twice this would give the major axis of the ellipse, but since you use half the major axis to locate

**Figure 13.** The blanks for the arc segments are as long as the opening is wide. After marking the radius on the top piece (left), a carpenter cuts three arcs at once (right).

## Laying Out the Elliptical Hips

The "common rafters" of the barrel-vault ceiling featured in this article form a 12"-high segment of a circle with a radiuds of $30^1/2$". The "hips" are elliptical, and extend from the end of the barrel at 45-degree angles. Just as a regular hip rafter run can be found by multiplying the common run by the square root of 2, the run of the elliptical hip is $30^1/2 \times \sqrt{2}$, or $43^1/8$".

These two numbers — the circle radius and the hip run — are the basis for the minor and major axes needed to scribe the ellipse.

Note that for laying out this elliptical hip, you work from the full diameter of the circle that defines the ceiling's shape. After the ellipse is drawn, you then use only the top 12" of the ellipse, which matches the actual height of the vault.

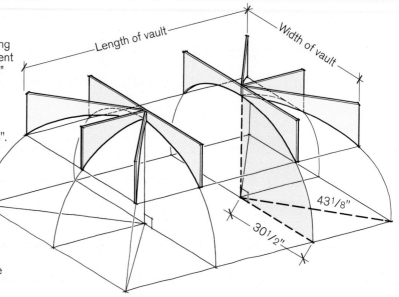

Two numbers are required for laying out an ellipse: the major axis (the length of the ellipse) and the minor axis (its overall height). In this case the major axis is twice the run of the elliptical hip, and the minor axis is the diameter of the circle that defines the vault. But for scribing what's essentially an elliptical arch, as in this case, you use half of each number — the $30^1/2$" radius and the $43^1/8$" hip run.

After snapping perpendicular lines to represent the major and minor axes, measure $30^1/2$" up the minor axis to locate the top of the ellipse. Using that as a fixed point, swing two $43^1/8$" arcs across the major axis to locate the focus points.

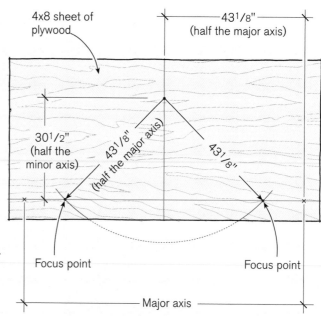

**3**

Picture-hanging wire works well for scribing an ellipse because it doesn't stretch like string does. Put a tack at each focus point and at the top of the minor axis, then run the wire from focus point to focus point over the top tack.

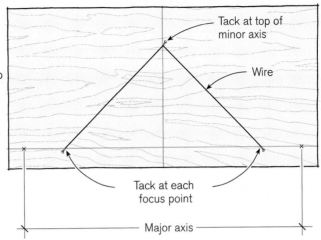

Tack at top of minor axis

Wire

Tack at each focus point

Major axis

**4**

Pull the top tack, then scribe the ellipse by pressing a pencil firmly against the wire and pushing it from one end of the major axis to the other.

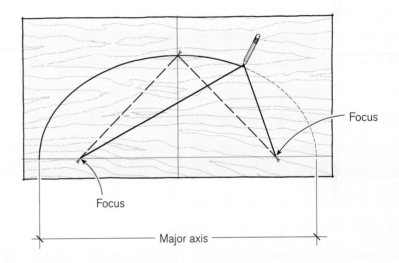

Focus

Focus

Major axis

Two elliptical hips

**5**

Because the barrel vault is 12" high, the elliptical hips are cut out of the top 12" of the ellipse. Cutting the arch in half yields two hips.

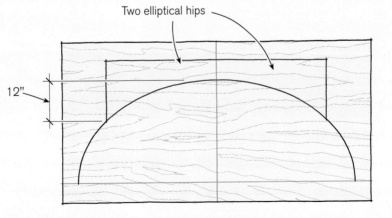

12"

**Figure 14.** After pulling the temporary tack, a carpenter inserts a pencil where the picture wire passes over the top of the minor axis (left). He then scribes the ellipse by sliding the pencil firmly against the wire, which he is careful to keep taut (right).

**Figure 15.** In this case, the elliptical curve is shallow enough to be cut with a circular saw. Only the top 12 inches of the ellipse — the height of the barrel — is needed.

**Figure 16.** The barrel portion — or the arch — is framed like an arched door opening with flat 2x4 purlins sandwiched between curved plywood pieces (left). This barrel was small enough to be lifted into place by two men (right).

**Figure 17.** After the barrel is positioned (left), the king common and the elliptical "hip" are installed. Here, a carpenter uses a straightedge to verify that the barrel surfaces are in the same plane as the hip end (right).

the focus points that allow you to scribe the ellipse, 43⅛ was the number we needed.

## Scribing and Cutting the Ellipse

We used picture-hanging wire rather than string to scribe the ellipse. We made sure to stretch it very tightly over the nail at the top of the minor axis when securing it to the nails at the two focus points. The final step was to pull the nail from the minor axis, then slide a pencil against the taut wire to scribe the curve (**Figure 14**).

Because the arch segments for the vault were 12 inches high, we needed only the top 12 inches of the elliptical arcs. This curve was flat enough to cut with a circular saw (**Figure 15**). To save time, we doubled up the plywood and cut two arches at the same time, then cut those in half to get the four hip pieces.

**Figure 18.** The purlins at the ends of the vault have straight cuts on one end and compound miters on the other.

## Putting the Pieces Together

Before building the vault, we needed to know the length of the barrel section. Again, I treated the opening as a hip roof, dividing the width of the vault in half (48½ inches ÷ 2) and measuring that distance in from each end of the opening.

Because it was small enough to be lifted into place easily, we built the barrel — basically flat 2x4 "purlins" sandwiched between a pair of ½-inch plywood arches at each end — on a bench (**Figure 16**). We nailed temporary 2x4 cleats across each end of the barrel, high enough up so they would land on the top of the framing and support the barrel while we positioned it and nailed it off. This barrel was small enough for two guys to handle; we've framed some that took six guys to lift.

Once the barrel was up, we installed the king commons and the elliptical hips, checking for alignment with a 4-foot level (**Figure 17**).

***End purlins.*** Though the purlins in the middle of the vault were cut square, the ones at the ends had to be compound beveled where they hit the hips (**Figure 18**). To get the miters and bevels, I simply held up a test piece where the lowest purlin would go and scribed the miter. Then I eyeballed the bevel and made the cut. After a couple of tries, I got it to fit and used a Speed Square to measure the two angles.

I knew the very top purlin would have a 45-degree miter with a 0-degree bevel, and I now knew the compound angle for the bottom piece. So, to get the angles for the rest of the purlins, I took the difference between the top and bottom angles and divided by the number of purlins. This gave me the number of degrees by which the bevel and miter angles would change as the purlins moved up the vault.

*Tim Uhler is a lead framer and exterior trim carpenter for Pioneer Builders in Port Orchard, Wash.*

# A Simple Vaulted Ceiling

by Emil Wanatka

To help give this large home a cottage-like feel, we incorporated an eyebrow into the fascia of the roof on both the front and back of the house. After seeing the revised drawings of the eyebrow above the patio doors to the great room, I thought how dramatic it would be if the curved shape could be carried through to the ceiling of the great room. The owner liked the idea. I assured her that building it would be no problem — then went into a huddle with the truss designer and framing contractor to figure out how best to build it.

## A Laminated Header

As described in "Framing a Barrel-Vault Dormer," page 114, we site-fabricated the curved header above the opening from plywood. This involved gluing and screwing together eight layers of 3/4-inch plywood to span the 20-foot opening. The laminated header is supported by a post at either side of the patio doors and carries only a short section of roof, so it doesn't have a lot to do structurally (**Figure 19**). The short rafter-framed section of roof above the header ends at a two-ply girder truss. Beyond that point, the great room ceiling was framed with scissors trusses.

**Windows.** The header dictated the shapes of the curved windows below, which were custom-made by

**Figure 19.** A site-built laminated plywood header defines the eyebrow profile above the patio doors. Short rafters extend from the eyebrow to the peaked roof beyond, which is framed with scissors trusses.

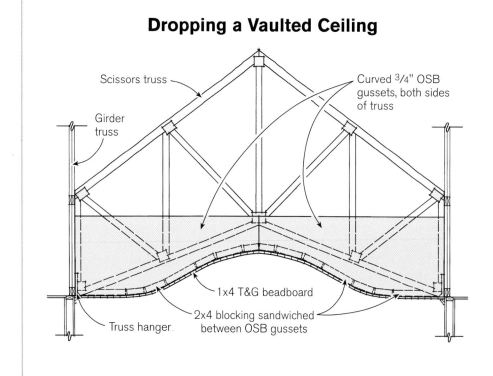

**Dropping a Vaulted Ceiling**

Scissors truss

Curved 3/4" OSB gussets, both sides of truss

Girder truss

1x4 T&G beadboard

2x4 blocking sandwiched between OSB gussets

Truss hanger

**Figure 20.** To carry the eyebrow shape into the living space, curved OSB gussets were nailed to each side of the scissors trusses framing the great room. Although the gussets and ceiling added little to the structural load, the roof trusses were engineered with the added weight in mind.

**Figure 21.** The finished ceiling of beaded fir boards was blind-nailed to blocking sandwiched between the OSB gussets.

**Figure 22.** Adding an eyebrow dormer to each side of an extended wing helped bring the large roof into scale and enhance the cottage-like feel the owner wanted.

Marvin from cardboard templates we provided. The three fixed clad-wood units cost $3,500 and involved an eight-week wait, but we were very happy with the way they fit the space.

## Dropping the Ceiling

To carry the eyebrow profile across the ceiling, we scribed the necessary curve on a series of identical gussets cut from 3/4-inch OSB. Establishing the shape of the first gusset involved some basic math, a compass made from a pencil and a long piece of string, and a certain amount of head scratching. Once we'd worked out the required curve, though, we were able to use the first gusset as a pattern for those that followed. All the gussets, including the first one, were marked and cut while lying flat on the deck.

We nailed a pair of gussets to each truss, sandwiching each truss between the two gussets, using string lines to keep everything in alignment (**Figure 20**).

***Blocking and beadboard.*** To provide a nailing surface for the beaded fir ceiling, we sandwiched 2x4

blocking between the OSB gussets. Depending on the amount of curvature, the lengths of blocking varied from 2 feet or so down to about 8 inches.

Instead of shaping the blocking to match the curve, we simply made sure it didn't project beyond the gussets at any point, which allowed the ceiling boards to bear against the OSB rather than the blocking. We angled the ends of the blocking so adjoining pieces butted tightly together end to end, eliminating the possibility of driving nails into gaps between lengths of blocking. Finally, we blind-nailed the 1x4 fir ceiling to the blocking (**Figure 21**).

The idea for this curved ceiling originated with the roof. The large size of the house and the client's desire for a fairly steep pitch led to a very prominent roof structure. The eyebrow dormers added to each side of an extended wing helped bring the roof into scale and enhance the quaint cottage-like feeling the owner wanted (**Figure 22**).

*Emil Wanatka is the owner of Timberline Builders in Durango, Colo.*

# Chapter 8: Precut & Panelized Framing

- **Framing With Precut Components**

- **Fast Framing With Panelized Walls**

- **Building With Structural Insulated Panels**

# Framing With Precut Components

by Michael Davis

Precut, prefabricated, and modular systems all have inherent benefits and drawbacks. My first attempt at prefabrication using an "automated" assembly line setup was a full wall panel on a multi-family project, calculated and drawn by hand. Although this approach was crude, it was surprisingly effective. I created a layout book and began building prefab walls. I took the book home at night and used Wite-Out for minor adjustments, redrawing and pasting in larger corrections. It changed day to day, but by the time the project was in full swing, we had a product that worked very, very well.

Prior to that, for about 10 or 15 years, we did everything we could think of in conventional prefab, including arches, drop ceilings, and framed roof details. Everything we did seemed to pay off. Most notable was the amount of waste, which was next to nothing. And as our construction company's market expanded from New Mexico into places like Aspen and Vail, Colo., where labor is both scarce and expensive, I thought prefabrication would still be the answer to all our clients' needs.

*Shipping air.* But I eventually discovered the Achilles' heel of panelized walls — freight costs. You can turn one tractor-trailer load of lumber into six truckloads of walls. Any savings you realize from the efficiency of panelization is eaten up by the cost of shipping. The term in the business is "shipping air." Somehow I had to use what I had learned about assembly-line techniques to achieve a competitive edge.

## A System Evolves

My answer to the problem was to do a partial, or hybrid, prefab. I would precut all the walls, lay out the plates, build the components, and ship packages of wall plates and bundles of components to the site for assembly. The advantage of this process is efficiency: speed, accuracy, quality control, no mistakes, no storage problems, and optimal use of labor.

*Halfway there.* We realized some of the benefits of factory-style fabrication, but there were drawbacks. The projects that we shipped were fairly complex, with up to 50 different units of components, including headers, trimmers, channels, and corners, all of various sizes. When a crew would break into a unit of precut, pre-laid-out lumber, they would spend half the day roaming a field of stacked components, gathering one of this, four of that, and so on.

This was not an efficient way to build. Many of the projects that we contracted for were on small sites, and we simply did not have the room to spread out. A different approach was required.

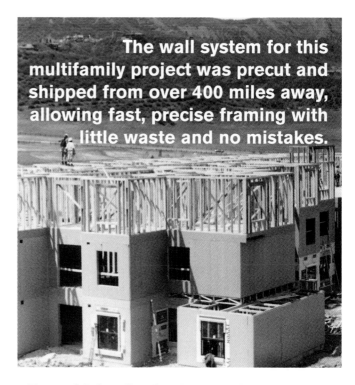

The wall system for this multifamily project was precut and shipped from over 400 miles away, allowing fast, precise framing with little waste and no mistakes.

*Freeze-dried walls.* The idea started to gel as I watched a documentary on climbers attempting to scale Mount Everest. I saw them huddled in their tents preparing freeze-dried meals thousands of feet above the nearest stove top. "Why not freeze-dried walls?" I thought. The idea is to bundle a plate, component, hardware, and nail package. Just add a little labor, and you have a panelized building package, miles away from the nearest prefab plant.

Of course, the thing about great ideas is that unless you have the right people to execute them, they remain just ideas. Luckily for me, I did have the right people. We are now turning out neat, easy-to-ship "freeze-dried" units — about four or five projects a year — 60,000 to 180,000 square feet each, and assembling them within about a 500-mile radius of our headquarters in Albuquerque, N.M.

## Hybrid Prefabrication

My process is not a true prefab operation because we don't actually assemble the plates and components into finished wall panels. It is actually a precut framing package (**Figure 1**), composed of everything required to frame a hotel or apartment unit completely. You may have seen similar packages on piece-work frames in California. We have taken that concept a few steps further. While we developed the system with multifamily projects in mind, it could work equally well for tracts or large custom projects.

**Figure 1.** Everything is fitted carefully to keep freight costs down and create a tight, solid, stackable package that will help reduce warping (left). "Hybrid prefab" packages contain everything you need to build walls, including precut plates, headers, trimmers, channels, corners, plus nails, hardware, and drawings (right).

On one semi-truck we can typically ship enough precut, labeled, and packaged material to cover a 20,000-square-foot area in walls. Each banded, wrapped, and numbered package measures 4 feet wide and 16 feet long. The height depends on the size and complexity of the unit. Units are designed to fit two abreast, three units end to end, and stacked 8 feet high — about 23,000 pounds.

Along with every prenailed subcomponent required (such as sills, cripples, headers, trimmer assemblies, corners, channels, nails, and hardware), our packages include every plate — cut to length and detailed per the plan. Every member is labeled, nailed, drilled, and fitted as required. Every package includes a dimensioned layout and placement plan and a plastic-wrapped shipping list with a printout of exactly what pieces are included. This includes a list of the wall plates, indicating the width and length of each wall, as well as elevations for walls where additional clarity would be helpful.

*Quality and efficiency.* Every step of our process has multiple quality controls built in. Quality is our foremost concern, because the product that we are shipping will be delivered to carpenters who are paid twice as much as our prefab team. Plus, the men in the field are working in far rougher conditions: limited space, snow, cold weather, and so on. Our goal is to take half the work and all the thinking out of framing.

## Where to Start

The process starts with a careful review of the plans, which enables us to catch discrepancies early on that might lead to problems in the field. My associate, Christopher Head, who has training in both architecture and framing, inputs data into a commercially available computerized wall-panel design system (**Figure 2**). He is very methodical, and when he prints out a set of walls, you know they are going to work like a charm.

Once the input and design have been completed and any problems resolved, a complete set of shop drawings is printed and forwarded to the project architect for review. These documents, along with any adjustments required by the architect, become our Bible for the project.

*Accurate cut lists.* Chris then works through the drawings to define logical areas or "units" that can be grouped into a package — such as apartments with identical floor plans. Wall-plate and component cut lists are compiled, and three copies of every list are printed. The lists are precise. The item counts are cross-referenced. Quantities are confirmed and totals balanced in much the same way an accountant might tie in figures on a financial statement. When

**Figure 2.** It all starts with a careful review of the drawings and a Keymark design system. Mistakes are a lot cheaper and easier to correct on paper than during cutting or assembly.

the field operation begins, everyone is provided with specific instructions on what is required to complete the work.

## Splitting Up the Tasks

The operation is broken into two production "lines" — wall plates and components. On the plate side, lumber is dropped at the cutting station, and I receive the first of the three wall-plate lists. I check the quality of each piece of lumber, and I use the premium lumber first for the longest lengths on our various cut lists. Material with defects, such as bows or excessively large knots, is trimmed and the defects removed. Shorter walls are then cut from the salvaged material. The smallest and least desirable materials are cut into blocks for channels and corners. Nothing goes to waste. By working from the longest to the shortest, we are able to use every section of lumber, even down to pieces as small as 6 inches.

*Dimensional consistency.* Often a CCA-treated 2x6 will measure 5 3/4 inches wide, while the nontreated plate is 5 1/2 inches. If walls are framed with the bottom plates wider than the top plates, problems occur during plumb and line. If the bottom plate of an intersecting wall is 1/4 inch too wide, then the top of the wall will be 1/4 inch out of plumb. This is a progressive error that gets worse the more walls you tie together. By running every piece of treated plate through a table saw, we ensure that the top and bottom plates are the same size. This ensures that plumb and line goes faster and smoother and that the finished product is better.

*Organizing the plates.* Once the plates have been cut to length, they are numbered. The wall designation is written on the top, bottom, and end of each plate as well. Experience has taught us that it is not always possible to view the bottom of the wall to read the number. By taking a few extra seconds per wall to write the designation on the end of each plate, we can save valuable time for those in the field.

The plates are then joined together — one nail within 12 inches of the end of the plate and one nail every 6 feet along the length of the wall. The fastening of the plates plays an important role in getting a straight wall to the site. The guys on the tables complain a bit about how hard it is to split the plates, but at least when they are separated, they are straight.

We are careful to nail through the top plate only. This way, once the wall is split and assembled, an 8d nail left sticking out will be hanging harmlessly from the top, as opposed to sticking up out of the bottom plate, waiting to impale an unsuspecting foot.

Wall plates are sorted, and each set of plates is checked off of the computer printout. The wall plates, along with the verified list, are bundled into a package. This package then moves from the cutting/ nailing station to the layout station.

## Layout

When Chris receives a package, he checks the list again to verify that it was completed. He then discards the list from the cut station and begins checking the length, plate dimension, and quality of each set of plates using a second copy of the wall-plate list as he lays them out (**Figure 3**). Anything that doesn't meet Chris's high standards is recut. Chris lays out the wall plates and stacks them. He double-checks the second copy of the panel list to ensure that the package is accurate and complete. Then he sends the package to the top plate prep station.

At this station, top plates are cut, labeled, and tacked to the wall plates. Also, in order to speed completion in the field, two 1/4-inch kerfs (or courtesy cuts) are made on the bottom plate to allow easy removal of door plates after erection. As plates and components are moved from one station to another

**Figure 3.** As wall plates are cut to length, they are labeled and nailed into sets (far left). Precut plates are then moved to the layout station, where workers lay out stud and component placement, top plate length and positioning, anchor bolts, and "courtesy cuts" at doorways (left).

**Figure 4.** Perfectly uniform two-way channels make backward installation impossible. Note the efficient use of lumber that might otherwise be scrap.

**Figure 5.** These timber cutoffs have been salvaged from the scrap pile and ripped down to 3 3/4 inches for use as cripples. This eliminates splitting problems, reduces waste, expedites assembly, and improves quality.

in the yard, they are bundled, reusing the banding from the original lumber bunks.

The project that we are fabricating now requires expansion anchors at 24 inches on-center at certain interior bearing walls. The bolt layout is included in our computer wall elevation. The bolt layout is done by Chris, and the holes are predrilled in the bottom plate. This eliminates the need for the field supervisor to determine which walls require bolting or to do a layout. He simply hands a carpenter's helper the box of expansion anchors that was included in the wall pack and instructs him to install an anchor in every predrilled hole.

## Components

While the plates are traveling through the various stations, the component crews are hard at work assembling headers, trimmers, channels, and corners from lists that are cross-referenced to the wall panel elevations. The header team gets one copy of the list to check off timber and engineered-lumber headers and posts. Another copy of the list is provided to the crew that nails up all the stud-based components, such as king stud/trimmers, corners, and channels. Each piece of cut lumber is clearly marked and then checked off the list.

Structural elements include dimensional lumber, Parallam and LVL headers, and king stud/trimmer assemblies ranging from single, double, triple, and quad trimmers, to Parallam trimmers and support columns. A wide range of rough openings and load-path considerations makes buildup a challenge. However, it is precisely this type of project that is best suited for our system. By placing all these various headers, trimmers, sills, and blocks together in one package, each piece clearly marked to match the layout, we make what would otherwise be a very difficult and confusing task a fairly simple "frame by number" assembly.

We normally use solid timbers in lieu of built-up header assemblies. The cutoffs from the timbers are recycled into solid blocks for channels. We use 4x4, 4x6, and 6x6 blocks to form two-way corners and channels. This is one more way that we take the thinking out of wall assembly and save time in the field. These components are universal, so you can't put a tee or corner in backward (**Figure 4**).

*Cripples.* We use these timber cut-offs to solve another common framing problem. If the header does not completely fill the space from the top of the opening to the bottom of the double top plate, cripples must be cut to fit in this space. Once dimensional lumber is cut to a length shorter than its width (for example, a 2x6 cripple cut shorter than 5 1/2 inches), it is likely to split when nailed. For example, to fill a 3 3/4-inch void between the top of a header and the bottom of the double plate in a 2x6 wall, we cut solid cripples from beam stock 5 1/2 inches wide (to match the 2x6 wall), 4 inches long, and 3 3/4 inches deep (**Figure 5**). These cripples can be toe-nailed to the top of the header with no danger of splitting.

The buildup crew is also responsible for hold-down assemblies. Posts for hold-downs are cut to length and marked with the bolt pattern for the scheduled hardware. The posts are then run through a two-step process on our drill press. First, we drill an oversized hole on the back side of the post to allow the nut and washer to be countersunk into the column, so as to not interfere with wall sheathing. Then the hole for the bolt is drilled through the post at 1/16 inch larger than the required fastener. Using a drill press ensures that the holes are straight and true. In many cases we will go ahead and bolt the hold-down onto the column. This assembly can be installed in the wall once concrete-embedded bolt locations are verified.

Any stud material that is not straight and true is

**Figure 6.** Carpenters assemble precut wall panels on site (above left). Wall plates are stacked at the far end of the table, while headers, sills, cripples, and tees are stacked to the left, with finished walls to the right. Everything required is in the package. The compact lumber packages will result in an enormous pile of wall panels. Two short walls at the bottom of the pallet are used to create clearance for the forklift (above right). Carpenters can spread and erect wall panels very quickly. Notice how clean the area is (left).

moved to the cut station, where it is used for cripples, blocking, or plates for small walls. Lumber will always move. Crowns become more pronounced. Twists and cups develop. We make sure that all the studs that go into our packages at least start out straight.

## Final Assembly

As the wall plates and components are completed, they move to the final assembly station. Yard foreman Dave Gonzales oversees this critical step as the triple check in our quality-control process. He begins assembling each package with the third copy of the wall and component lists. He verifies that the plate crew has provided every wall required and that the buildup crew has delivered the correct type and quantity of component assemblies. Dave is a real perfectionist. It's not uncommon to see him breaking out his power planer to smooth blocks in a channel that don't flush up just right. Anything that doesn't look good to Dave

is rejected. He knows that we count on him to catch any errors that might have slipped by the rest of us. We do not hurry him. If he is not 100% sure that a package is correct he knows that he won't catch any grief from us if he tears the whole thing down and starts over. When it leaves our yard it has to be right.

*Holding platforms.* We developed a set of small platforms to hold the stickers or support boards under the package. Each platform is designed to hold a double 2x4 sticker that is 48 inches long. The platforms provide a space so that banding material can slide through beneath the double 2x4. The 4-foot-long double 2x4 stickers come from materials that I deem to be "terminally crooked" at the cut station. Even the most unruly board will find a home and a useful life in our shop. Once the banding is in place, the sticker is secured to the package. This gives us a full 3-inch clearance for the forks on the lift. Providing ample clearance below the package enables the forklift operator to unload and stack unit packages unassisted. Furthermore, the stickers are laid out on a standardized grid, six to a package. This enables us to stack each package atop another without any additional blocking.

***Wrapping the package.*** All of our packages are wrapped to protect them from moisture and ultraviolet light. We order all our materials wrapped to help keep them in the best possible condition. We recycle all of our lumber wraps as covers for the completed product. When we run short of recyclable wrapping, we use a 6-mil black plastic cover.

## On Site

The walls are assembled in a prefab area on site (**Figure 6**), stacked, and the plastic cover reused to protect the finished walls until they can be installed (often this is the third useful life for these covers). In this way, fabrication can start well before the concrete slab is completed. By the time the slab is ready, all the walls for that building are framed and ready to be stood up.

Getting a head start on the walls can greatly reduce the time required for framing, thereby accelerating the overall project schedule. However, we feel that the greatest benefit from the system is realized by placing a framing table directly on the slab and assembling the walls near where they are to be used. Another small crew can then erect the walls once the unit is completed. This eliminates the need for stacking, banding, and moving the packages of finished walls, which is in itself a time-consuming process.

***No waste.*** When we started on our current project, we had a large dumpster delivered to the yard for all

**Figure 7.** This is all of the framing waste from a 60,000-square-foot project, plus somebody else's trash — barely a small pickup load.

the scrap that we expected to generate. After three weeks of operation we don't have enough waste to fill the back of a pickup truck (**Figure 7**).

I look at it this way: You pay for lumber, you pay to have it delivered, you pay to have it cut up, and if you throw it away, you pay to have it hauled off. So to me, careful use of materials and recycling is just good business. Whether you want to save the world or save a buck, you end up doing many of the same things.

Most important, the guys in the field love our packages because they are right. Not sort of, not really close, but right on the money!

*Michael Davis is the owner of MDI in Albuquerque, N.M., which offers hybrid prefab services to contractors on Colorado's Western Slope.*

# Fast Framing With Panelized Walls
## by Lee McGinley

Finding good help has always been tough, and the current boom economy has made it tougher. I tackled a recent labor problem by hiring a company to panelize a 2,400-square-foot house. By shifting the labor burden to the panelizer, I only had to hire an inexperienced helper and pay for some crane time, rather than assembling an entire crew. We erected the shell in four weeks, or about the same amount of time it would have taken an experienced four-person crew to stick-frame the same structure.

## Planning and Design

I shopped around among several panel manufacturers before settling on Sprowl Building Components in Searsmont, Maine — a relatively small shop that was willing to work with my custom design, rather than trying to steer me to a preset package. The company will also modify its framing details to suit customer preferences, as long as the details conform to code. For example, double rough window sills could be substituted for Sprowl's single-sill detail.

***Drawing the plans.*** I hired a residential designer to draw a set of floor plans and elevations for the 1¹/₂-story house, which has a shed dormer on the south and a gable dormer over the stairway on the north. The first floor has an open floor plan with a step down to the living room; bedrooms and two bathrooms are on the second floor.

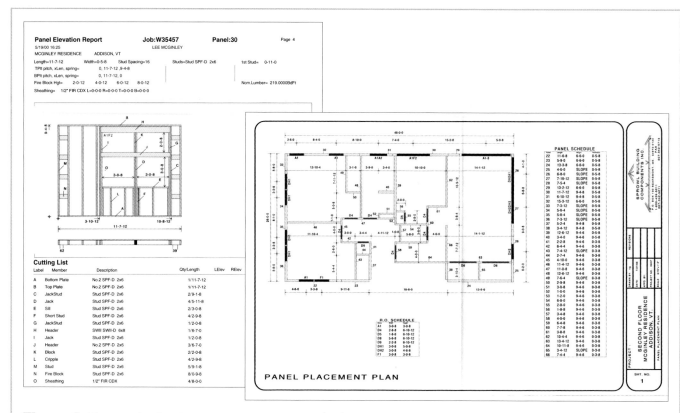

Panel Elevation Report     Job:W35457     Panel:30     Page 4

5/19/00 16:25              LEE MCGINLEY

MCGINLEY RESIDENCE     ADDISON, VT

Length=11-7-12    Width=0-5-8    Stud Spacing=16    Studs=Stud SPF-D 2x6    1st Stud=   0-11-0

TPlt pitch, xLen, spring=    0, 11-7-12 ,9-4-8

BPlt pitch, xLen, spring=    0, 11-7-12, 0

Fire Block Hgt=    2-0-12    4-0-12    6-0-12    8-0-12          Nom.Lumber= 219.0000BdFt

Sheathing=    1/2" FIR CDX L=0-0-0 R=0-0-0 T=0-0-0 B=0-0-0

**Cutting List**

| Label | Member | Description | Qty/Length | LElev | RElev |
|---|---|---|---|---|---|
| A | Bottom Plate | No.2 SPF-D 2x6 | 1/11-7-12 | | |
| B | Top Plate | No.2 SPF-D 2x6 | 1/11-7-12 | | |
| C | JackStud | Stud SPF-D 2x6 | 2/9-1-8 | | |
| D | Jack | Stud SPF-D 2x6 | 4/5-11-8 | | |
| E | Sill | Stud SPF-D 2x6 | 2/3-0-8 | | |
| F | Short Stud | Stud SPF-D 2x6 | 4/2-9-8 | | |
| G | JackStud | Stud SPF-D 2x6 | 1/2-0-8 | | |
| H | Header | SWII SWII-D 6x8 | 1/6-7-0 | | |
| I | Jack | Stud SPF-D 2x6 | 1/2-0-8 | | |
| J | Header | No.2 SPF-D 2x6 | 3/6-7-0 | | |
| K | Block | Stud SPF-D 2x6 | 2/2-0-8 | | |
| L | Cripple | Stud SPF-D 2x6 | 4/2-9-8 | | |
| M | Stud | Stud SPF-D 2x6 | 5/9-1-8 | | |
| N | Fire Block | Stud SPF-D 2x6 | 8/0-9-8 | | |
| O | Sheathing | 1/2" FIR CDX | 4/8-0-0 | | |

PANEL PLACEMENT PLAN

**Figure 8.** The panelizer's schematics detail each panel (left) and its place in the floorplan (right). The wall panel drawing labels components and provides a cut list. Similar information is given for truss layout and construction. Booklets shipped with the panels contain the final schematics for all components as well as bracing patterns for the roof and floor trusses.

Unlike some panelizers, Sprowl doesn't preinstall windows. I planned to use Eagle windows and doors, so the drawings noted the center-to-center distances between rough openings. Each opening was identified by a letter, and a separate window schedule gave rough opening dimensions.

**Figure 9.** The crew set, lined, and braced the first-floor wall panels in one afternoon with the help of a crane. Panelizing saved the builder more than $18,000 on the project.

I specified 2x6 exterior and plumbing walls, 2x4 framed interior walls, and 5-ply fir plywood sheathing, which I prefer to OSB. The floors and roof were framed with trusses.

Sprowl redrew the plans with their proprietary software (which will import AutoCad files, if you have your plans on disc), then printed out about 35 pages that detailed each panel and truss (**Figure 8**).

***Proofing makes perfect.*** Because the panel manufacturer works out all the details of the framing, you never have to do a takeoff. But another important responsibility takes its place: The necessity of going over each sheet, comparing it with the original plans, and making any necessary corrections. Once you've signed off on the manufacturer's plans, any inconsistencies are your problem.

I proofed the plans carefully, but I failed to catch one minor glitch. The original plans included a step down to the living room, and this should have been taken into account in the framing of the exterior walls. Because it wasn't — and because I didn't notice the omission in the proofs — I had to deal with it on the job site, by stick-framing a low wall to fill the gap. I'll be more careful next time.

## Assembling the House

About two weeks after I signed off on the plans, the panels and trusses were ready to ship. As luck would

**Figure 10.** Bundled second-floor trusses are set atop the first-floor walls. The lumberyard strapped together several sheets of plywood subfloor before delivering it to the job site. The 20-foot-high stairwell panels are visible in the background.

have it, the two flatbed trucks arrived at the site during pouring rain. We piled everything on the ground and called it a day.

When the weather cleared, we called the crane back to set the first-floor girder and floor trusses on the foundation, then stacked the subfloor sheathing on top. (Given better weather, we could have done this as part of the initial unloading and saved an hour or two of crane time.)

*Wall connections.* After spending a couple of days gluing and screwing down the subfloor, I scheduled an afternoon session with the crane to set, line, and brace the first-floor exterior wall panels (**Figure 9**). The exterior wall corners were framed with 12-inch-wide "ladders" at the end of one panel, to which the end stud of the adjoining panel is toe-nailed.

The next morning, I positioned and nailed the first-floor interior wall partition, while my helper readied the second-floor trusses and subflooring to be lifted into place (**Figure 10**). As with the exterior wall panels, partition walls were joined at "ladders" built into the framing. This worked very well and made it easy to align the walls while providing some flexibility in the floor plan (**Figure 11**). If it doesn't cause problems elsewhere, nonbearing partitions can easily be shoved one way or the other by a few inches to alter the size of a room or closet.

*Fasteners.* To avoid having to drag an air hose around while setting the panels, I'd planned to tack things together with a few fasteners from a Paslode Impulse nailer, then go back and finish up with a regular air nailer. As things worked out, though, we relied on the Impulse nailer almost completely. The absence of air hoses running over the deck made it easier to jockey the panels around.

*Finishing up.* It took two more return visits from the crane to get the structure closed in. The first came after we'd finished gluing and screwing the sec-

ond-floor deck, when we set the second-floor walls (**Figure 12**, next page). Once the two of us had finished setting the exterior walls, we had the crane place the interior walls in the center, then sent the operator home.

The second session came after we'd finished setting the second-floor partitions and were ready to begin on the roof trusses. The crane lifted the bottom halves of the piggyback trusses into place one at a time as we nailed them off (**Figure 13**, next page). We braced the trusses as directed by the manufacturer, loaded the roof sheathing on top, and raised the top halves of the piggyback trusses into place. That was it for the crane. At that point, we just had to slide the top sections into place, nail them off, and apply the sheathing.

**Figure 11.** Partition-wall intersections are simplified by the presence of framing "ladders." The end stud of the adjoining wall is nailed to the ladder, as shown here, making it easy to adjust the final position of nonbearing partitions as needed.

**Figure 12.** Second-floor exterior wall panels were lifted individually into place from the ground. The gable wall panels were framed floor to roof as single units to avoid a potential hinge effect that might arise with separate wall and gable panels.

Finally, I hired a three-man framing crew for a day to set the windows and exterior doors and run the plywood band between the first and second floors.

## The Bottom Line

Overall, panel quality was very good. All the pieces were cut to exact measurements, and the panels fit perfectly as drawn, except for the one I should have corrected at the proof stage. In a few cases, the panel sheathing overhung the end of a panel by a quarter

inch or so, but this was easily corrected with a power plane. One minor annoyance was the quality of the factory nailing at the partition backers. The toe-nails were left protruding and had to be hammered down by hand. I was very happy with the quality of the finished shell, which was comparable to one put up by a custom framing crew.

*No crane, no crew.* Panelizing cuts your labor requirements to the bone, but it increases your reliance on a crane and operator. I hired a crane service that had several machines available and was willing to give my job first priority in scheduling. In return, I agreed to give several days' notice when I needed the crane. Although the company was about 20 minutes away, the $65 hourly rate covered only the time on site, not travel time.

Even so, there was some unproductive crane time. At one point, we had to spend an hour or so straightening walls while the crane and operator sat and waited, because it didn't make sense to have them leave and come back. Next time, I might try to tighten up the crane schedule by adding another experienced carpenter, for a total crew of three.

*Costs and savings.* In all, the bill for the crane and operator came to just under $2,000. The panelized walls, floor trusses, and roof trusses came to just under $15,000, including $1,000 for trucking. (The panelizer makes local shipments with its own trucks, but because my site was a six-hour drive from the factory, I had to pay for shipment by common carrier.) The complete materials package — with me supplying the $1\frac{1}{8}$-inch plywood subflooring, $\frac{5}{8}$-inch plywood roof sheathing, and 2x bracing — came to less than $8 per square foot of floor area, or about what it would have cost me for the materials to stick-frame a comparable

**Figure 13.** The top half of the piggyback trusses went up next (left). The shed dormer houses the master and guest bathrooms. At right, the nearly finished house.

structure. (Note: All figures are in 2000 dollars.)

Because I had to pay only myself and a low-priced helper, though, labor costs were far lower. Our combined wages for the four-week job came to less than $5,500. If I'd been asked to bid on stick- framing an identical structure, I would have charged $10 per square foot for labor, or about $24,000.

***Fringe benefits.*** I figure that going with panels saved me a good $18,000 in labor. I saved another $500 by doing away with the usual job-site dumpster, since panels generate virtually no waste. By not having piles of framing material on site, I also simplified material handling and pilferage. I wouldn't hesitate to go with panels again.

*Lee McGinley is a builder living in Addison, Vt.*

# Building With Structural Insulated Panels

## by Gary Pugh

About 20 years ago, I watched a video about a house being built with structural insulated panels, or SIPs. It was the first time I'd seen the process: instead of framing one stick at a time, the carpenters were installing entire sections of wall, which had arrived on site sheathed on both sides and insulated.

It impressed me as a faster and better way to build, so I tried SIPs on my very next house. That first one was difficult because I had no one around to explain the technical details. But we stuck with it, and now my company builds only projects that include SIPs.

## What Are SIPs?

SIPs are made by bonding a sheet material — OSB, plywood, steel, or fiber-cement — onto both sides of an expanded polystyrene (EPS) or polyurethane foam core. By themselves, these materials are not strong enough to support loads, but once they're made into panels they can be used for structural elements like walls, roofs, and floors. The most common panels consist of OSB over EPS (**Figure 14**, next page).

Raw panels are produced in factories and then cut to size in fabrication plants, or sometimes on site.

***Size and thickness.*** OSB-faced panels come in sizes up to 8 feet by 24 feet. Foam cores are sized in thickness to match the width of standard framing lumber; that way, you can reinforce a panel or provide nailing by inserting a piece of framing stock. For example, a 6-inch panel is actually 6½ inches thick, made with a 5½-inch-thick piece of foam sandwiched between two sheets of ½-inch OSB.

Walls are typically made from 4- or 6-inch panels. Floors and roofs might be made from 6-, 8-, 10-, or even 12-inch panels.

SIPs produce a tight, well-insulated shell with less labor than an equivalent stick-framed building. Total building costs range from 1% less to 5% higher.

## Why Use SIPs?

We use SIPs because it takes less time — fewer labor hours — and less skill to assemble precut panels than it does to stick-frame. The parts of the building made from panels are straight and true, and they won't shrink or warp. Plus, panels are exceptionally well

**Figure 14.** The most common type of structural insulated panel is produced by sandwiching EPS foam between two sheets of OSB. The face material can also be plywood, steel, or fiber-cement, and the core can be polyurethane.

insulated and sealed against air infiltration.

Our clients want their homes to be "green," and SIP buildings qualify because they're energy-efficient and make good use of natural resources. The OSB skin is made from fast-growing trees that are plantation-grown specifically for OSB.

Also, there's very little job-site waste with SIPs; the panels are cut by a fabricator, who can easily recycle cutoffs or use them when smaller panels are called for.

## Insulation Value

The R-values associated with various building materials are misleading because they don't reflect how and where the material is installed. For example, 5½-inch fiberglass batts are rated R-19, but a wall insulated with these batts is not R-19, because there will be thermal breaks at every stud, plate, and header.

***Whole-wall R-value.*** A more realistic way to look at insulation is to consider "whole-wall R-value," a method developed at Oak Ridge National Laboratory (ORNL), in Oak Ridge, Tenn., for estimating the R-value of various assemblies. The whole-wall R-value includes the insulation plus everything else that's in the wall.

According to ORNL, a 2x6 wall framed 24 inches on-center with plywood sheathing, drywall, and 5½-inch batts has a whole-wall R-value of 13.7. The same wall built with 6-inch OSB SIPs has a whole-wall R-value of 21.6. Why the difference? The foam in the SIPs has a higher R-value than the batts, and the SIP assembly contains fewer thermal breaks.

## Ordering Panels

It's possible to buy raw panels and cut them to size on site, but it's better to pay a fabricator to do the cutting. Many fabricators have computer-controlled equipment that cuts panels far more accurately than we ever could.

***Design.*** Like any building, a SIP structure starts out as a set of plans. Just about any stick-framed plan can be converted to SIPs (**Figure 15**), although it's easier when the initial design is done with panels in mind.

Either way, the first step in any SIP project is to produce a detailed set of shop drawings that show door and window openings, corners, edges, and wiring chases, as well as how the pieces will be joined on site.

Once the drawings are approved, delivery of the panels takes six to eight weeks. The process is a lot like ordering trusses, except in our case we produce the shop drawings in-house.

The fabricator could draw them, but we prefer to do it ourselves because we gain more control over how the panels will go together.

***Handling.*** SIPs arrive at the site on one or more semitrailers. Small panels are light — a 4x8 6-inch panel, for example, weighs about 115 pounds.

Larger panels are heavy, so we rent an all-terrain forklift to handle those.

## Floor Structure

SIPs can be installed over any type of floor system. In our area of Northern California, most homes have wood-framed floors on stem-wall foundations with crawlspaces below.

Structurally, there's no reason we couldn't build the floor with SIPs. Doing so would be much faster

**Figure 15.** Panels can be used for any part of the building that isn't curved. The walls and roof of this traditional-style house are made from SIPs.

**Figure 16.** Plates are installed first. Here, a 3x6 has been screwed to the deck over a continuous bead of sealant. In preparation for standing the walls, a carpenter runs sealant along the face and edges of the plate (A). The crew then stands the panel over the plate (B), braces it plumb, and nails it to the sides of the plate (C). When walls land on concrete, the plate is installed over a wider strip of pressure-treated plywood, which is also sealed to the concrete (D).

than stick framing, and the insulation value would be very high.

But on most projects we still use conventional floor framing; even with the labor savings, SIP floors aren't always cost-effective in a mild climate like ours.

In colder areas, of course, where insulating the floor is a major concern, building a floor with SIPs might make more sense.

***Sound transmission.*** Even if they did cost less, we wouldn't use SIPs for upper floors.

The panels are good at preventing airborne noise from entering through the walls and roof, but walking on them creates a drumming effect that's annoying to the people below.

## Setting Walls

Our panels arrive on the job cut to size with door and window openings, but without solid lumber inserted.

The foam is recessed along the edges, so there's

room to make insertions: bottom plates to fasten panels to the floor; splines to join them edge-to-edge; and top plates to stiffen the top of the wall and provide nailing for the roof or floor above.

We install these lumber members over beads of sealant (provided by the panel manufacturer), then nail them in place through the face of the panel.

For an extra charge, some manufacturers will install the nailers for you.

***Plates.*** With SIPs, wall plates are nailed, screwed, or bolted to the floor and then the panels are slipped over them.

If the wall lands on a stem wall or slab, the plate and panel must be isolated from the concrete. To do this, we install a strip of pressure-treated plywood — sealed to the concrete with foam sill seal — and then install the plates over a bead of sealant.

Before installing the wall panel, we run sealant along the top and both edges of the wall plate, then stand the panel over it (**Figure 16**).

**Figure 17.** The OSB and foam were cut from the corner of this SIP shear wall so that a hold-down could be installed. Later the crew will foam in around it and replace the missing OSB.

After bracing the panel plumb, we nail it to the plate through the OSB skin.

*Hold-downs.* In many regions, this nailed connection is all that's needed to hold panels to the floor or foundation. But we build in a seismically active area, so some of the panels are designated as shear walls and must be tied to the foundation with hold-downs.

The old way to do this was to connect threaded rods to the foundation and run them all the way up through the panels.

An easier method is to put double studs in the edge of the shear panel, cut a hole in the OSB, remove some of the foam, and install a conventional hold-down inside (**Figure 17**).

The hold-down is then bolted to the foundation and the double studs.

Another method is to run a strap up from the foundation and screw it to the outside of the panel at a double stud.

## Joining Panels

We edge-join the panels with splines that fit into slots in adjoining edges and work like gussets.

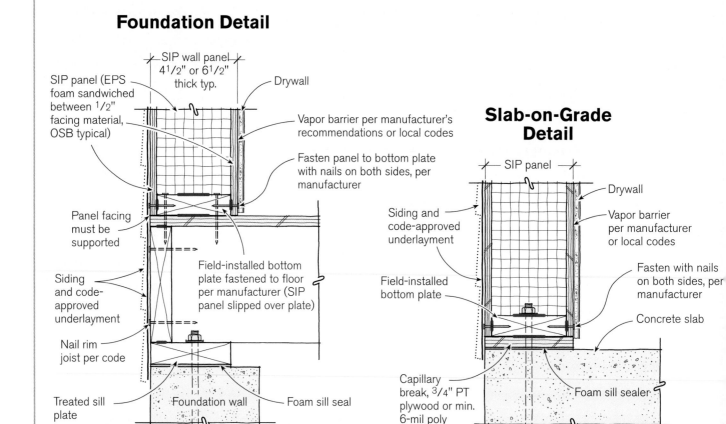

### Foundation Detail

SIP wall panel 4 1/2" or 6 1/2" thick typ.

SIP panel (EPS foam sandwiched between 1/2" facing material, OSB typical)

Drywall

Vapor barrier per manufacturer's recommendations or local codes

Fasten panel to bottom plate with nails on both sides, per manufacturer

Panel facing must be supported

Field-installed bottom plate fastened to floor per manufacturer (SIP panel slipped over plate)

Siding and code-approved underlayment

Nail rim joist per code

Treated sill plate

Foundation wall

Foam sill seal

### Slab-on-Grade Detail

SIP panel

Drywall

Vapor barrier per manufacturer or local codes

Siding and code-approved underlayment

Field-installed bottom plate

Fasten with nails on both sides, per manufacturer

Concrete slab

Capillary break, 3/4" PT plywood or min. 6-mil poly

Foam sill sealer

**Note: Areas with a continuous bead of sealant marked in RED**

They're installed over beads of sealant and nailed in place through the skin of the panel.

We use three types of splines: solid pieces of lumber; surface splines, which are 4-inch rips of OSB; and block splines, which are basically a smaller SIP that fits inside the edges of adjoining panels (**Figure 18**, next page). We prefer the foam block or surface splines because they don't produce thermal breaks.

We use solid lumber splines only where we need a doubled stud to carry a point load.

*Solid nailers.* Any vertical edge that is not joined to another edge with a spline must be filled with a piece of solid lumber. This provides nailing where there otherwise would be nothing to nail into.

Wall corners are made by butting the edge of one panel into the face of another and then screwing back through into the nailer (**Figure 19**, next page). The exposed foam edge of the overlapping panel is filled with lumber to provide nailing for the wall finish.

Once the walls are up, we insert top plates. This stiffens the walls and provides solid nailing for the second floor or roof.

## Sealing the Seams

There are a number of ways to seal the seams between panels. We run beads of panel mastic on mating surfaces, but you can also use polyurethane foam from a can.

As an added measure, some panel manufacturers require you to surface-seal the interior joints by covering them with SIP tape, a type of peel-and-stick membrane. This is primarily a concern with SIP roofs in very cold, wet climates, because warm interior air will carry moisture through the gaps and can cause the outer layer of OSB to rot.

In some locales, the building code may require that you install a continuous vapor barrier inside the building.

And to the extent that it reduces air leakage, a vapor barrier can be an improvement.

But the real issue with SIPs is not moisture diffusion through the panels — it's air leakage at the seams. In most climates, if you properly seal the seams you should not have problems, even without a vapor barrier.

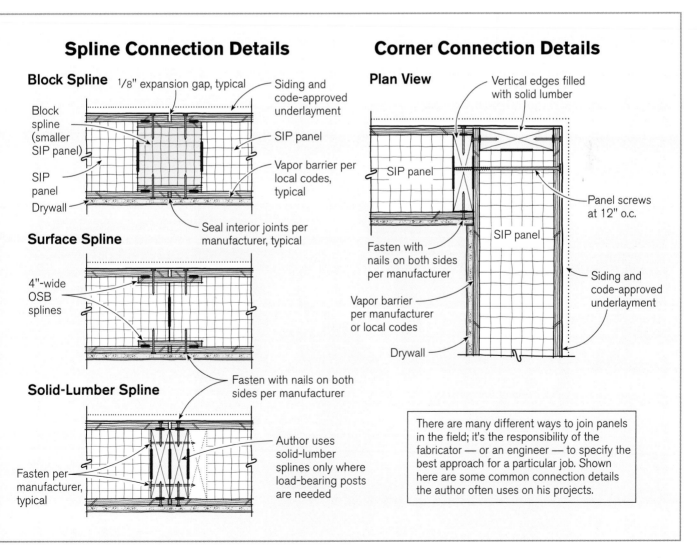

## Spline Connection Details

**Block Spline** 1/8" expansion gap, typical — Siding and code-approved underlayment

Block spline (smaller SIP panel)

SIP panel

SIP panel

Vapor barrier per local codes, typical

SIP panel

Drywall

Seal interior joints per manufacturer, typical

**Surface Spline**

4"-wide OSB splines

Fasten with nails on both sides per manufacturer

**Solid-Lumber Spline**

Fasten per manufacturer, typical

Author uses solid-lumber splines only where load-bearing posts are needed

## Corner Connection Details

**Plan View**

Vertical edges filled with solid lumber

SIP panel

Panel screws at 12" o.c.

SIP panel

Fasten with nails on both sides per manufacturer

Siding and code-approved underlayment

Vapor barrier per manufacturer or local codes

Drywall

There are many different ways to join panels in the field; it's the responsibility of the fabricator — or an engineer — to specify the best approach for a particular job. Shown here are some common connection details the author often uses on his projects.

**Figure 18.** Panels are connected edge-to-edge with splines. Here, a carpenter prepares to install a block spline over continuous beads of sealant (left). The spline functions as a gusset and is held in place with nails driven first into the loose panel (center) and then into the adjoining panel (right).

Because SIP buildings are so tight, it is necessary to mechanically ventilate them to remove excess humidity and provide fresh air. The best way to do this is to install a heat-recovery ventilator (HRV).

## The Roof

If the budget allows, a project might have a SIP roof. A truss roof is cheaper and, if the roof is complicated, easier to install. But a SIP roof is tighter and better insulated.

With a SIP roof, beams are required, except where the panels span from wall to wall. There is typically a bearing ridge and beams at hips and valleys. Roof panels are joined edge-to-edge in the same manner as wall panels, then screwed to the beam or wall below.

Many of the photos shown here are from a house with a flat — or, more accurately, very low-slope — SIP roof surrounded by a short parapet (**Figure 20**). The panels are supported by interior beams and ledgers screwed to the inside faces of the walls. The ledgers are sloped to drain the rubber membrane roof toward scuppers in the parapet; inside the house, we

**Figure 19.** At corners, the crew installs nailers flush to the edge of the panels, butts the panels together (far left), and uses screws to fasten through to the nailer beyond (left). These panels are 6½ inches thick, requiring 8-inch-long screws.

**Figure 20.** Roof panels are lifted with an all-terrain forklift (A) and lowered onto glulam beams and sloped ledgers screwed to the wall panels (B). This carpenter fastens a panel by screwing through to the beam below (C). The parapets terminate with a double top plate, specified by the engineer (D).

dropped the ceilings to make them flat, leaving space for ductwork and wiring above (**Figure 21**, next page).

## Door and Window Openings

Door and window openings are often cut right through the panel. Headers are not usually necessary unless the opening is more than 5 feet wide and or very close to the top. If the opening's large enough, you can save on material by piecing in around it. In such a case, the edges of the flanking panels should contain full-height studs plus jacks to support a panel or a header and panel above.

***Cutting in the field.*** Occasionally, the owner will want to add a window or make slight design changes after the panels are delivered. As long as the changes are minor, we can accommodate them by cutting the panels on site (**Figure 22**, next page).

After cutting, we use a hot knife to remove foam from the edge so there's room for a spline or nailer.

Because SIP buildings are engineered, we have to get changes okayed.

## Effect on Subs

As with any alternative method, using SIPs affects the subtrades.

Drywallers and finish carpenters love SIPs because they are flat and straight and they don't shrink or bow. Also, finding nailing is easy because the panels are continuously sheathed on both sides.

Roofing over SIPs is no different from roofing over any other sheathed roof.

***Mechanical trades.*** Since partition walls in SIP houses are normally stick-framed, the HVAC installer can easily run ducts in them. The only time there's a problem is when there's no attic and both the floor and roof are SIPs. Then we have to provide chases.

The plumber is in the same boat as the HVAC contractor — most of the pipes go in partition walls. If the kitchen sink is on an outside wall, we either run plumbing through the toe space or bring it up through the bottom of the cabinet (**Figure 23**, page 157).

We typically build an interior chase for the vent pipe; when necessary, we leave an open space

## Flat SIP Roof and Parapet

Metal cap flashing

Double 2x6 top plate

Rubber membrane roof and counterflashing

8d nails at 6" o.c. each side

8d nails at 6" o.c. top and bottom

Panel edge infilled with 2x8 solid lumber

$8^1/4$"-thick SIP roof panel

Panel screws, two rows at 24" o.c.

Panel screws at 12" o.c.

3x6 ledger screwed to interior wall face, sloped to drain

$6^1/2$"-thick SIP wall panel

2x6 ceiling joists at 16" o.c.

Panel screws at 12" o.c.

Joist hanger

Drywall

2x6 ledger

Stucco and code-approved underlayment

Drywall

**Note: Areas with a continuous bead of sealant marked in RED**

**Figure 21.** Many of the photos in this story are from a house with a low-slope SIP roof and parapet walls. The roof panels are supported by ledgers, which provide a slight slope toward drainage scuppers. Inside, the ceiling was dropped to provide space for ductwork and recessed lighting.

**Figure 22.** Mistakes and changes sometimes force the crew to alter panels in the field. Here, a carpenter trims a panel to size (left), then uses an electric hot knife (right) to neatly remove the foam so there will be room for a block spline.

**Figure 23.** To avoid putting pipes in the wall, the author had the plumber install the drain and supply lines for a sink just inside the panels at the sink-cabinet location (far left). If plumbing must go in an exterior wall, the author creates a chase by cutting out the panel and removing some of the foam (left). Once rough-in is complete, the author's crew uses spray foam to fill in around the pipes.

**Figure 24.** Wire chases are provided by panel manufacturers. The electrician accesses the chase by cutting a hole through the OSB and removing some of the foam. He can then fish wires through the chases and connect them to remodeling boxes in the panels.

between two panels for pipes, then fill the space later with EPS and spray foam.

*Electrical.* The electrician faces the greatest challenge because it's hard to avoid putting switches and receptacles in exterior walls.

We order panels with one vertical and two horizontal wire "chases" — 1¼-inch holes that run edge-to-edge through the foam (**Figure 24**).

The first horizontal chase is at outlet height, and the second is at switch height. Since they're marked on the OSB, their location is obvious.

The electrician accesses the chase by cutting a hole through the face of the panel and digging out some of the foam. He is then free to fish wires vertically and horizontally and install remodeling boxes as needed.

When the wiring is done, we seal everything with spray foam.

With a little planning, you can run most of the wire through interior walls and minimize the amount that runs through panels.

## Cost

Panels cost more than conventional framing material, but they require less labor.

In my business, building a house with SIPs costs somewhere between 1 percent less to 5 percent more than stick-framing the same plan.

Because a SIP house is tighter and better insulated, we can downsize the HVAC system — but we have to install an HRV.

We don't have to hire an insulation contractor, and our dumping fees are lower because there is much less waste.

*Gary Pugh owns Alternative Building Concepts, a green building company in Santa Rosa, Calif.*

# Chapter 9: Remodeler's Specialties

- **Replacing a Bearing Wall With a Flush Beam**
- **Fast-Tracking a Second-Story Addition**
- **A Pop-Top Shed Dormer**

# Replacing a Bearing Wall With a Flush Beam

by Mike Sloggatt

**A shallow steel-reinforced beam preserved headroom in this low-ceilinged room.**

When I'm reviewing the prints for a remodeling job, one of the first items I check for is the addition of new structural beams, which always require plenty of manpower and extra work. But prints don't always give you a clear picture of actual site conditions.

Such was the case with a split-level home we recently remodeled. To increase room size on the ground floor, the plans called for the removal of a bearing wall (**Figure 1**, page 162), which would be replaced with a 15-foot-long beam made from a pair of 1¾-inch-by-14-inch Microllam LVL joists. The problem was that setting this 14-inch-deep beam flush to the top of 2x8 floor joists would leave nearly 7 inches of Microllam hanging down into the room. Not very attractive, in my book.

Because the split-level had a ceiling height of only 7 feet 4 inches on the first floor, it wasn't difficult to convince the homeowner that installing a shallower 7-inch-high beam would be a better solution. Admittedly, our approach was more expensive than cutting a pair of stock LVLs to size, as shown in the original plan; but a beam designed to be installed

flush with the finished ceiling would result in an unobstructed ceiling and make the room much more attractive.

## A Better Beam?

Typically, a shallow 7-inch wood beam requires reinforcing with a steel plate or I-beam to give it enough strength to span 15 feet. In the past, I've always hired an engineer to design these wood-and-steel "flitch beams," then ordered the steel from a local fabricator and assembled them on site.

But the installation of large beams — which involves lugging around 350-pound plates and assembling them on a table, then hoisting a 600- or 700-pound beam overhead — is a daunting task with a small crew. At my age, I wasn't looking forward to the process.

Convinced there had to be a better way, I decided to try a prefabricated beam from the Better Header Co. (www.betterheader.com). I had seen this company's product at a trade show and promised myself that the next time I had to install a steel flitch beam, I'd give it a try. I wanted to see if the system was any better than my site-built approach.

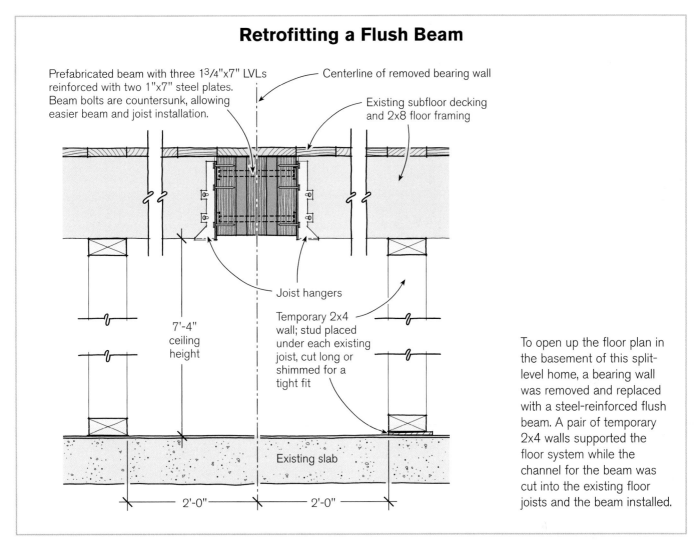

**Retrofitting a Flush Beam**

Prefabricated beam with three 1³/₄"x7" LVLs reinforced with two 1"x7" steel plates. Beam bolts are countersunk, allowing easier beam and joist installation.

Centerline of removed bearing wall

Existing subfloor decking and 2x8 floor framing

Joist hangers

Temporary 2x4 wall; stud placed under each existing joist, cut long or shimmed for a tight fit

7'-4" ceiling height

Existing slab

2'-0"

2'-0"

To open up the floor plan in the basement of this split-level home, a bearing wall was removed and replaced with a steel-reinforced flush beam. A pair of temporary 2x4 walls supported the floor system while the channel for the beam was cut into the existing floor joists and the beam installed.

To get a beam design that would work in my situation, I provided the company with the length of the span, the width of the structure above, and an estimate of all of the loads that the beam would have to carry. (Sales are typically handled through your local lumberyard.) I also provided a sketch of the existing structure's cross-section that showed the span of the floor above, the location of a second-floor bearing wall, and the ceiling above (see "Retrofitting a Flush Beam," above).

The price for a delivered beam was $1,100. At first, that seemed expensive, especially since I could purchase all the components for around $850. But when I considered the additional $200 for the engineering fee, and the two hours or more we'd have to spend assembling and lugging around the beam with four men, I decided that the prefabricated beam was the better deal.

I was promised delivery to the job site within a week. But one problem remained: This beam would be heavy. Built of three 1³/₄-inch-by-7-inch LVLs reinforced with two 1-inch-by-7-inch steel plates, all bolted together, the beam would weigh nearly 800 pounds. I needed to make sure that I was prepared to handle the load when the beam arrived.

## Supporting the Floor System

Delivery was scheduled for noon by boom truck. That gave us an entire morning to prepare the site for installation. The room was already gutted, and a plumber had relocated some pipes the day before. We had to work around a few wires, but most would be relocated later by an electrician.

To support the ceiling joists while we installed the beam, we needed to build a pair of temporary 2x4 walls. In general, temporary shoring should be built as close to the original beam as possible. In this case, placing the temporary 2x4 walls 2 feet on either side of the existing bearing wall's centerline would leave us with the 4-foot working area we'd need to accommodate our jacks.

With only a floor load and attic above to support, I felt that this 4-foot clear span wouldn't be a problem. But in more complicated cases where there is a posted ridge or other substantial load above, I always consult an engineer, who specs out distances, connectors, and the proper removal sequence.

After measuring, cutting, and laying out the plates for both temporary walls, we went ahead and installed the first one. (The other would have to wait until we

**Figure 1.** To open up the floor plan of a split-level home, the author removed this bearing wall and replaced it with an engineered beam. Matching the depth of the beam to the 2x8 floor framing maximized headroom and allowed the beam to be hidden by the ceiling finish.

**Figure 2.** After building the first temporary support wall, a carpenter removes most of the old bearing wall. Had the floor joists broken over the bearing wall, as is often the case, both temporary walls would have needed to be in place before removing the old framing.

had the beam positioned.) We began by fastening our top plates to the floor joists above, then positioned the floor plates directly below and placed one stud under each joist. To ensure a snug fit, we measured for each stud and then cut long by about 1/8 to 1/4 inch. If a stud still seemed loose, we ran a hardwood shim under the bottom plate and beat it in.

We held everything together with 3-inch-long #10 deck screws — two to three per stud connection — which would make it easy to take everything apart afterward and reuse the materials for other parts of the project.

Before loading the studs by removing the bearing wall, we ran horizontal 2x4s to connect the studs at midheight. This lateral bracing helps prevent individual studs from bowing. We also added a diagonal 2x4 brace at the end of each wall, fastened at the top, middle, and bottom to help prevent bowing or racking.

In addition, prior to removing any bearing structure, it's good practice to measure and write down the distance from the floor to the bottom of the existing joists in a number of places. I wrote these measurements right on the joists next to the beam, and used them later to determine whether the floor framing had dropped from its original position after the job was complete.

It's also good practice to go upstairs and make written notes of any unevenness in the floor, cracks in plaster or drywall, or problems with door swings and clearances, and to point them out to the homeowner so you don't end up owning existing problems. I also document these issues with a digital camera prior to any wall removal.

With the existing conditions documented and one temporary support wall installed and braced, we were ready to begin demolition. Since the joists above ran continuously over the bearing wall, we could remove the old bearing wall with only one support wall in place (**Figure 2**). More typically, the joists break over a center bearing wall, requiring two support walls prior to demolition.

As so often happens on the day of a big job, I was short one man, so installation of the big beam was up to just me and one helper. Fortunately, though, we were well prepared. That morning, I had rented two Hi-Jacks (Vermette Machine Co., www.vermettlifts.com) from the local tool-rental store. These freestanding jacks are capable of lifting 500 pounds each up to a height of 10 feet (somewhat less in interior spaces, where structures overhead may interfere with the lifting mechanism) and are easily transported and assembled on site.

I had also placed two furniture dollies outside on the sidewalk, thinking we would have to drop the beam onto them and roll it up to the house. But when the boom operator opted to send the beam right through the front doorway instead, he got no argument from me (**Figure 3**).

**Figure 3.** To get the 800-pound beam into the house, the boom operator dropped one end onto a jack inside and the other onto a dolly outside. The author and his helper rolled the beam through the front door, then slid a second dolly under the tail end and pushed the whole assembly the rest of the way into position.

After we transferred the beam onto both jacks, we rolled it into position. Then we assembled and braced the second temporary support wall for the other half of the room (**Figure 4**). With the second wall in place, we removed the last section of header from the old bearing wall.

## Cutting in the Beam Pocket

Next, we marked the location of the new beam on the floor joists, centering it on the old bearing wall. The beam actually measured almost 7½ inches wide, plus I added an extra ⅛ inch for wiggle room, so we marked a 7⅝-inch-wide channel to receive the beam.

To get clean, straight cuts, we started our kerfs with a circular saw and finished up with a reciprocating saw (**Figure 5**, next page). Even though a cut line that wandered ¼ to ½ inch wouldn't be a big problem structurally, square cuts look more professional, and they help justify the invoice later on.

After cutting the pocket, we cleaned up stray nails to make room for the beam (**Figure 6**, next page). We were careful to cut all metal flush with the recip saw so that the beam wouldn't push up the subfloor or finish floor when it was installed. And to accommodate a few stray telephone wires, we cut out a short section of the 1x6 subfloor to leave a ¾-inch-thick chase above the beam.

## Installing the Beam

Once the pocket was prepped, we proceeded to jack up the beam. The Hi-Jacks are stable and roll easily even when loaded, so the beam didn't have to be per-

fectly aligned with the pocket when we started lifting.

Because of their design, though, the Hi-Jacks couldn't lift the beam all the way up into the pocket. To hoist it the last 6 or so inches into place, we had to place cribbing between it and the lift. We did this by raising the beam as high as we could into the pocket (to keep it from rotating) and temporarily posting one end, which allowed us to lower the jack on that end and block under the beam with scrap 2-bys (**Figure 7**, next page). After using the same approach to install cribbing under the other end, we were able to jack the beam fully in place, lined up flush with the ceiling joists.

One common problem with site-built beams is bolt heads sticking out just where a joist is sitting. But this header's recessed bolts made it much easier to slide into position. Also, the rollers on the jacks made it easy to position the heavy beam precisely, even with the beam held up high.

With the beam in place, we installed tripled 2x6 posts below each end of the beam to lock it into position, and then lowered and disassembled the jacks.

To complete the installation, we fastened metal joist hangers to all of the floor joists; using a Paslode Positive Placement pneumatic nailer (www.paslode.com) made the job go a lot faster (**Figure 8**, page 165).

In cases where the bottom of the joist sat flush to the bottom of the beam, we notched the end of the joist to allow the hanger to sit flush (**Figure 9**, page 165). Once again, the recessed header bolts made installing the hangers much easier, because they didn't interfere with the hangers.

By rechecking the joist-height measurements I'd taken before removing the old bearing wall, I could easily find out how close the joists were to their orig-

**Figure 4.** Once the beam was in position on the floor beneath the pocket, the second support wall could be assembled. Lateral and diagonal bracing strengthened the temporary walls and helped prevent individual studs from buckling under load.

**Figure 5.** After laying out the new 7 5/8-inch-wide beam pocket, the author's helper snaps chalk lines (above left), then uses a small square to mark cut lines on the joists (above right). Starting kerfs with a circular saw (far left) and finishing up with a recip saw produced clean, straight cuts. The author set the recip-saw blade so that it just barely cut through the 2x8 joist, and he gave the tool a slight backward tilt to prevent the blade from wandering off the cut line (left).

**Figure 6.** Before the new beam could be raised into the pocket, any penetrating nails that might be pushed up through the subfloor above had to be either cut off or clinched over.

**Figure 7.** A worker uses 2x4 cribbing to lift the beam above the level of the jacks' support columns. Sections of the temporary wall's top plate were cut to make room for the jack arms.

**Figure 8.** The author uses a Paslode Positive Placement pneumatic nailer to fasten the joist hangers to the beam and floor joists.

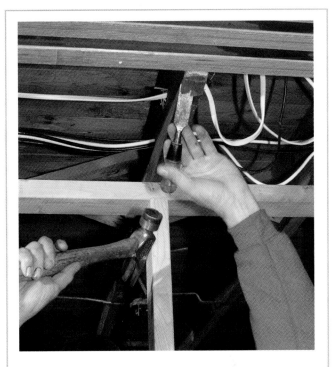

**Figure 9.** Where the floor joists are flush with the bottom edge of the beam, the author chisels out notches for the joist hangers.

**Figure 10.** Once the joist hangers were installed on one side of the new beam, the author removed the temporary supporting wall.

inal position. In this case, the floor wasn't level to begin with, while the beam was laser straight. Where joists were too low, I drove hardwood shims between the plate and the bottom of the joist to raise the joist until it was flush with the bottom of the beam; then I installed the joist hanger.

Meanwhile, on the other end of the beam, the tops of some of the joists were as much as 3/8 inch above the top of the beam. Since my measurements for the finished floor confirmed that nothing had moved, it was apparent that the sagging of the original structure prevented the beam from going completely flush with the existing framing.

Because the section above included a tile floor, I chose to leave the joists as they were and deal with shimming drywall rather than try to straighten out the sag and risk cracking the existing tile floor.

Once all the hangers were in place, we removed the temporary walls (**Figure 10**). The entire job took approximately 4.5 hours and required two men. We paid $140 to rent the pair of Hi-Jacks for the day, which was much less expensive than paying four borrowed carpenters for two hours. And the jacks don't break for lunch.

*Mike Sloggatt is a remodeling contractor in Levittown, N.Y.*

# Fast-Tracking a Second-Story Addition

by Dave Haines

Demolition of the existing roof — and framing and roofing of the new second floor — were completed in just four days with the help of wall panels and roof trusses.

As my clients were describing the extensive remodel planned for their 1950s cape, I realized that getting the roof off and back on again as quickly as possible would be critical to the project's success. My family had been planning a vacation for more than a year, and there was no way I could leave an extensive remodel in limbo for the two-and-a-half weeks I'd be gone — especially a job that involved ripping off the house's sloped-ceiling second floor and replacing it with a full second story.

Besides a new second floor, the job included a new kitchen, a rear deck, and a family-room addition on the back of the house.

## Tight Schedule Rules

As soon as I got home from that initial meeting, I created an 11-week construction schedule to ensure that most of the critical work would be done before our vacation.

The first two weeks of the project would be the most stressful — laying the family-room foundation, completing the demo, and getting the roof back on, all while the clients were living in the first-floor den. My goal was to demo the existing second story on a

Tuesday, frame the new second-story walls on Wednesday, set and sheathe the roof trusses on Thursday, and finish installing shingles by the end of Friday.

To keep up the pace, I decided to use wall panels supplied by the truss manufacturer. As usual, I had done the design work for the project in Chief Architect (**Figure 11**), so I supplied the truss company with accurate drawings of both existing conditions and the proposed construction. The company, in turn, provided engineer-stamped drawings to submit with the building-permit application.

## Dealing With Debris

With a permit in hand and the roof trusses and wall panels on order, I went about putting in the foundation for the family-room addition and gutting the second floor in preparation for ripping off the roof.

The site's narrow driveway meant I couldn't set a dumpster there because it would prevent the excavation and foundation contractors from reaching the back of the house for the addition. Instead, I used my excavator's dump-body trailer for the debris; it could simply be rolled out of the way when the need arose (**Figure 12**).

**Figure 11.** Plans drawn in Chief Architect helped the clients and the building inspector visualize the project, and were also supplied to the truss manufacturer.

**Figure 12.** Demo of the existing roof took half a day. A dump trailer provided by the excavation contractor handled the debris.

**Figure 13.** Flooring behind the original upstairs knee walls had to be filled in before the wall panels could be set. Two-by-ten blocks extended the tapered joist ends.

**Figure 14.** On its first visit, the crane lifted the second-story wall panels onto the deck. Wall framing took a day.

## Tuesday: The Tearoff

Fortunately, the weather turned nice the week of the tearoff. In keeping with the schedule, a crew of seven guys tackled the house with bars and recip saws. By lunch, most of the structure was down.

Using the dump-body trailer to catch the debris had another advantage beyond mobility: the axles underneath the trailer make it much taller than a conventional dumpster, so dropping in material from the second-floor level was relatively easy.

Demolishing the second floor and existing kitchen generated about 16 tons of debris, filling the trailer three times.

Later that day, the wall panels and trusses showed up. We had the driver drop them in the driveway as far back as he could, so there would be room for the crane.

We spent the rest of the day cleaning up smaller debris and adding rim joists and floor sheathing in areas that had previously been hidden behind the cape's knee walls (**Figure 13**). Though the weather looked clear, we tarped the house at the end of the day for good measure.

**Figure 15.** Because the existing floor was 2 inches out of square, the crew had to shorten one wall panel by removing the last stud (A), cutting off the plate (B), and replacing the stud (C). Another panel was lengthened with plywood spacers (D).

## Wednesday: Standing Walls

The next morning, we finished patching the floor framing and subfloor. When the crane arrived, just after lunch, we set the wall panels and trusses for the family-room addition. Then we had the crane lift the walls for the second story onto the floor deck, setting them directly over a bearing wall to avoid cracks in the finishes below (**Figure 14**).

Rather than keep the crane sitting around while we set the walls, I sent the operator away, which kept the bill to a three-hour minimum charge. This gave us the whole afternoon to set walls, so we spent a lit-tle extra time wrapping them with housewrap before standing them.

We measured the floor deck and found that it was about 2 inches out of square. This wasn't a surprise: I had known something was off when I measured the house during the design phase. Instead of trying to fig-ure out the exact problem then, I'd had the panel pro-ducer make the panels as if the house were perfectly square. I knew we could make field modifications later.

The out-of-square floor deck required that we shorten one wall panel and extend another. The pro-cess was easy: With two guys working, the alterations took about 10 minutes (**Figure 15**).

**Figure 16.** In preparation for the crane's second visit, the crew installed the girder truss for a small bump-out (A). The gable truss was prepped with building paper (B) and preinstalled blocking for the drywall ceiling (C). When the crane arrived, truss-setting moved quickly (D); note the vertical bracing for the gable truss, installed on the inside rather than the outside of the end wall.

**Figure 17.** Lifting trusses in pairs eliminates waiting: there's just enough time to set the two trusses (left), using precut braces marked with the layout (center), while the crane operator picks up the next pair. Unlike longer braces, the 49 1/2-inch-long pieces (right) don't get in the way of the next trusses to be set.

We finished out the day straightening the walls. The panels come with a single top plate; you add the double plate to stitch the wall together, then plumb and string it or site it as usual.

We were lucky that we had great weather, because effectively tarping the second floor with the walls standing and no roof would have been nearly impossible. If rain had been in the forecast, I probably would have kept the crane on site and worked as long as necessary to set the trusses. With the trusses up, I could have tarped the structure; luckily, this wasn't necessary.

## Thursday: Setting Trusses

The next day, while waiting for the crane, we installed a two-ply girder truss for a small intersecting gable over a bedroom bump-out (**Figure 16**). We knew having this in place would make setting the rest of the trusses go much faster. We also prepped the gable trusses and got some braces and spacers ready.

When the crane arrived, we began by lifting the interior wall studs and the roof sheathing up onto the second-floor deck, then started placing trusses. With the first gable in position but still suspended from the crane, we installed temporary bracing. Most framers place vertical braces on the outside of the building, which requires ladders or staging, but I like to put them on the inside because it can be done easily from stepladders.

The rest of the trusses were set very quickly. To keep things moving, we typically have the crane lift the trusses in pairs. The timing works perfectly: while we're setting and bracing two trusses, the operator

can pick up another pair and have them ready for us by the time we're done with the first two (**Figure 17**). We were able to stock the second floor with material and set all the second-floor trusses within the three-hour minimum crane charge.

Once the trusses were in place, we immediately started sheathing the roof. Handing the sheathing up from the second-floor deck, we tacked it in place, aligning the trusses as we went, then had one guy finish it off with a coil framing nailer. He was responsible for making sure all the sheathing was solidly nailed and that nothing was missed.

The main roof was completely sheathed by the end of the day. We could have stuck around for another hour or two and felted the roof, but with no rain in the forecast, we went home.

## Friday: Roofing

The roofers showed up Friday morning. They got started on the front side of the roof while we finished up filling in the valleys on the gable bump-out and installing subfascia on the back.

By noon the roof was shingled and I was able to breathe a little easier.

## Planning Paid Off

The following week, we built the porch roof, finished off the interior partitions, and moved on to doors and windows.

The rest of the job was a matter of scheduling subs to bring it all together. The granite countertops and custom shower doors were templated the day before I left on vacation. When I got back, the countertops

PHOTOS: BILL SCHLOO

**Figure 18.** The completed home (left) looks vastly different from the original structure (center) and has 1,000 square feet of additional living space. The family-room addition on the back of the house (right) contains a cathedral ceiling and a wood-burning fireplace.

and finished flooring had been installed, so I just had to arrange for the plumbing trim-out and for final inspections, and complete a few items on the punch list.

The house had gone through quite a transformation (**Figure 18**). In addition to gaining an extra 1,000 square feet of living space, it now had a luxury master bath, a porch, a back deck, and a wood-burning fireplace.

The project's $270,000 price tag might seem high, but in this area it's tough to find an existing home for less than $500,000, and you'd pay a similar amount for a 1/2-acre building lot — if you could find one.

*Dave Haines owns Haines Contracting in Doylestown, Pa.*

# A Pop-Top Shed Dormer

by Bob Dausman

Recently, some customers approached me about improving the upstairs of their modest, 1 1/2-story gable-roof home in upstate New York. Though it was in a beautiful setting with a large pond, the older home had low ceilings and little natural light. Their goal was to add a second-floor bath, get more usable floor space, and have taller, brighter rooms.

Simply installing skylights wouldn't address the headroom issue, and gable dormers, while charming, wouldn't add enough usable floor space. After discussing various options, we decided on a shed dormer that would span about two-thirds the width of the house. An existing closet and small bedroom would be converted into a full bath and a home office. The dormer would also allow us to add windows in the new bearing wall.

## Waste Not, Want Not

Shortly after the dormer decision was made, my dad, also a builder, recalled that early in his career he'd worked on a similar job. But instead of tearing off

**With proper support and a watchful eye, you can raise a shed dormer without exposing the house to the weather.**

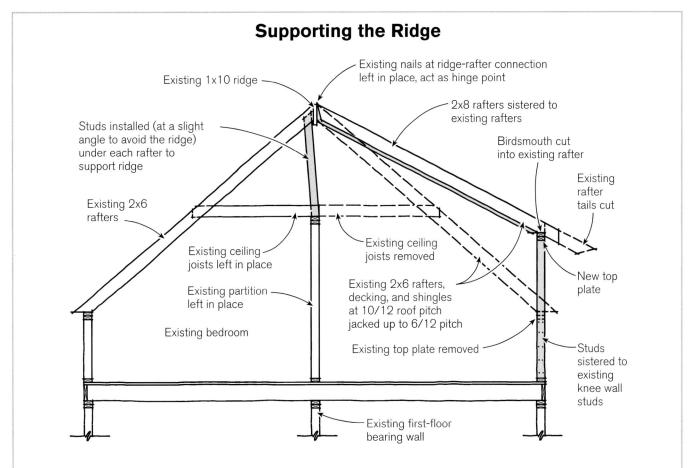

## Supporting the Ridge

Existing 1x10 ridge

Existing nails at ridge-rafter connection left in place, act as hinge point

2x8 rafters sistered to existing rafters

Studs installed (at a slight angle to avoid the ridge) under each rafter to support ridge

Birdsmouth cut into existing rafter

Existing rafter tails cut

Existing 2x6 rafters

Existing ceiling joists left in place

Existing ceiling joists removed

Existing partition left in place

Existing 2x6 rafters, decking, and shingles at 10/12 roof pitch jacked up to 6/12 pitch

New top plate

Existing bedroom

Existing top plate removed

Studs sistered to existing knee wall studs

Existing first-floor bearing wall

**Figure 19.** A structural wall, centered under the ridge, shoulders the roof load and eliminates the need for transverse ceiling joists or collar ties.

the original roof and building a dormer roof from scratch, they had jacked the existing roof into place. Although he couldn't remember all the details, I was intrigued by the idea. The present roof was less than 10 years old; the original roof had been stripped down to the skip sheathing and new plywood sheathing and shingles had been installed. Those facts, and the idea that the building and its contents could remain under the protective cover of the roof throughout the process, convinced me that jacking was the way to go.

***Supporting the structural ridge.*** One of the biggest

**Figure 20.** With the rafters cut free of the knee-wall plate, hydraulic jacks ease the roof up to its new elevation (left). Even as the roof gapes open, most of the weather is kept outside.

**Figure 21.** As the roof swings up, the rafter tails swing out, so the jacking point must be repositioned inward.

concerns when creating a shed dormer is connecting the common rafters across the building by ceiling joists or collar ties in order to keep the ridge from sagging and the walls from bowing outward. Instead, after gutting the interior of the second story, we framed a slightly angled supporting wall, from the top of the first-floor center-bearing wall plate to the underside of the rafters, just to one side of the 1x10 ridge board (**Figure 19**, previous page). This created a structural ridge that would carry the roof load, allowing us to eliminate the existing ceiling joists and permanently dispense with their replacement. We cut

the nails holding the joists to the rafters and took the chimney down to below the roof line, temporarily covering the hole in the roof with plastic.

Since the chimney encroached on the dormer area, its flashing would have tied the roof to the chimney and made it difficult to raise that section. And the rafters on either side were tight to the block and would have bound on the chimney as the roof swung up. We also wanted to take this opportunity to replace the unattractive cinderblock with a better-looking brick chimney.

## Hinge

We first transferred the dimensions of the dormer to the exterior of the roof and snapped the outline onto the shingles, then recipro-sawed through shingles and sheathing from the ridge down to the eaves. Next, we cut all the toe-nails holding the rafters to the top of the knee wall. We left the nails that held the rafters to the ridge on the assumption that they would pull out as needed but also act as a hinge. I was somewhat concerned that that assumption might be flawed, and that the considerable weight of the roof section might cause it to pull away from the ridge as we jacked it up. If the nails didn't hold, the only thing tying the roof section in place would be the cap shingles.

***Way, hay, up she rises.*** With the roof ready to jack, we started in, using a series of hydraulic jacks under a temporary 2x4 plate, installed flat and nailed to short blocks scabbed onto the rafter sides (**Figure 20**, previous page). We stood the jacks on a length of 2x6 to help distribute the temporary load across the floor. Despite my concern, and the worry expressed by the

**Figure 22.** New double-hung windows, sidewall shingles, and chimney top complete the exterior of the dormer.

owner when he stopped by the job, it was soon apparent that the integrity of the "hinge" was intact. The rafters showed no tendency to pull away from the ridge.

However, the arc described by the rising roof caused the plate to gradually swing out beyond the exterior wall (**Figure 21**). To compensate, we moved the plate in as needed and substituted longer jacking posts. The raising went smoothly, and in several hours the dormer roof was at the proper height.

Next, we plumbed up from the original knee wall, snapped lines across the underside of the rafter tails, and cut new birdsmouths. We nailed a top plate in place, added another plate below that, and then toe-nailed the studs in place, sistering them alongside the knee-wall cripple studs. After tarping the ends and the front wall to keep the weather out, we called it a day.

## High and Dry

We spent the next several days buttoning up the framing, extending the roof over the end walls, sheathing the dormer, and trimming the rafter tails for a new soffit. The front wall now provided suffi-cient height to install double-hung windows to match the existing. We extended the existing shingle siding and painted wood trim to complete the exterior and rebuilt the top of the chimney, adding to its original height to maintain proper clearance above the shallower roof slope (**Figure 22**).

To strengthen the existing rafters, we sistered full-length 2x8s alongside. This also enabled us to restore a proper plumb cut at the ridge and renail the rafters at the ridgeboard. To complete the interior, we installed polystyrene vent blockers to the underside of the roof sheathing prior to insulating with $5\frac{1}{2}$-inch-thick fiberglass batts. The ceiling was fin-ished "cathedral" style, with drywall applied directly to the underside of the rafters.

***Let it snow.*** All in all, the process went without a hitch, saved time, and eliminated a great deal of demo-lition and waste. One of the biggest advantages was that we kept the interior under continuous cover dur-ing what turned out to be a damp and snowy week.

*Bob Dausman is a principal owner of Dausman & Oley Construction, in Syracuse, N.Y.*

# Chapter 10: Exterior Trim

- **Building Traditional Cornice Returns**

- **Installing PVC Trim**

- **Trimming a Curved Portico**

CHARLES WARDELL

# Building Traditional Cornice Returns

by Gordon Dixon

Our company builds spec and custom homes that mimic New England farmhouses on the exterior but have more modern floor plans inside. Prominent features of the style — typically a simplified Greek Revival — are the wide frieze and corner boards, and, at the top of the corner boards, the cornice returns — the small projecting boxes where the eaves moldings turn the corner at the gable end.

The simplest version of the cornice return, and one we build often, uses all flat stock. It consists of a finish fascia board, a narrow buildup strip, and "poor man's cove" — flat stock that we bevel and use instead of crown molding, as did many builders here in Vermont before us (**Figure 1**). One big advantage of using flat stock instead of crown for this detail is that it allows us to turn the eaves molding up the rake without having to worry about the crown profile changing. With flat stock, we just rip the eaves piece to match and cut the compound angle on our sliding miter saw.

On a recent job, and the one featured here, we were called in late in the game to do all the exterior work — windows, siding, and trim — on an 8,000-square-foot house. The trim was fairly elaborate Greek Revival. The architect copied some of the details from a beautiful 1860s house that sits in a small village in northern Vermont. The drawings showed the traditional cornice — a wide ogee crown

The elaborate cornice details were adapted by the architect from a beautiful 1860s house in the village of Moscow, Vt.

running along the eaves and turning up the rake.

By the time we came on the job, the former GC had already ordered all the materials we would need. On our first day, two tractor-trailers pulled up filled with beautiful clear red cedar for the trim work. There was square-edge stock in several sizes and a variety of moldings. We sorted the material to size up what we had and found we only had one size of crown molding. I realized that the cornice detail wouldn't work as drawn with only one crown profile for the fascia — unless we fudged the corner where the eaves turns up the rake.

I discussed this with the designer and owner and we decided to modify the traditional Greek Revival detail rather than fudging and ending up with a sloppy corner joint. Instead, we would bring the eaves crown molding around the corner, wrapping the cornice return with standard 90-degree cuts (**Figure 2**). The rake crown would then follow the rake frieze buildup and die on the roof of the cornice return. This detail is common on many new traditional-style houses, and can be built with off-the-shelf crown from the lumberyard.

## Making Mockups

I started this job the same way I do any complicated exterior trim job — by completely mocking up one corner, including the soffit, the frieze, the capital

**Figure 1.** A simplified Greek Revival cornice treatment uses flat stock with beveled edges — "poor man's cove" — instead of a crown molding. Using flat stock makes it easy to turn the corner where the eaves meet the rake.

*continued on page 182*

# Cornice Details

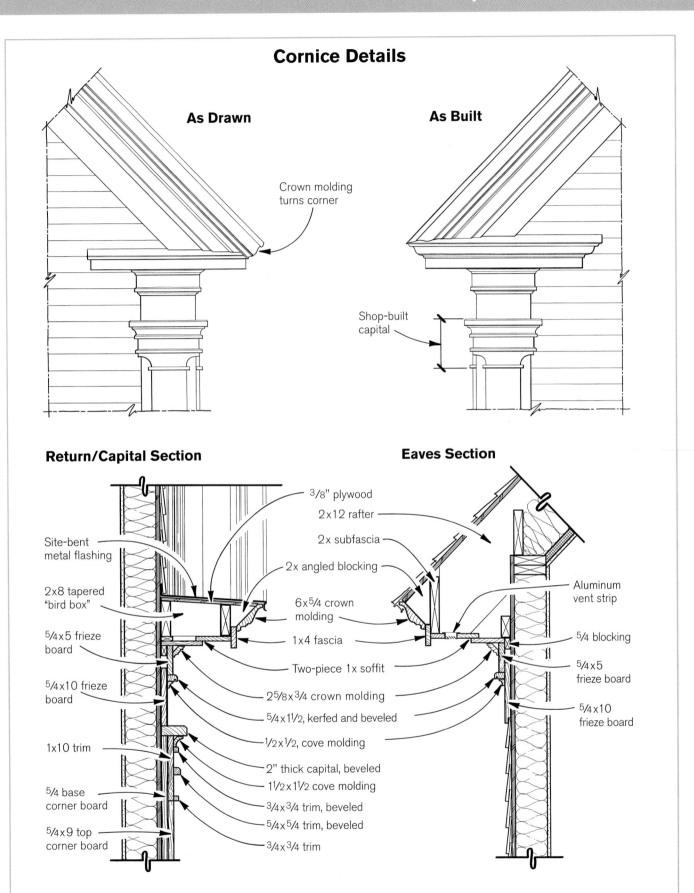

**As Drawn**

**As Built**

Crown molding turns corner

Shop-built capital

**Return/Capital Section**

**Eaves Section**

Site-bent metal flashing

2x8 tapered "bird box"

5/4x5 frieze board

5/4x10 frieze board

1x10 trim

5/4 base corner board

5/4x9 top corner board

3/8" plywood

2x12 rafter

2x subfascia

2x angled blocking

6x5/4 crown molding

1x4 fascia

Two-piece 1x soffit

2 5/8x3/4 crown molding

5/4x1 1/2, kerfed and beveled

1/2x1/2, cove molding

2" thick capital, beveled

1 1/2x1 1/2 cove molding

3/4x3/4 trim, beveled

5/4x5/4 trim, beveled

3/4x3/4 trim

Aluminum vent strip

5/4 blocking

5/4x5 frieze board

5/4x10 frieze board

**Figure 2.** As drawn, the cornice detail would have required two crown molding profiles in order to execute a crisp corner joint (top left). Instead, the author used the more common eaves return, which uses only one crown profile (top right). Except for that change, the details shown are replicas of an 1860s house in Moscow, Vt.

## Detail: A Simple, Stylish Return

**by Dave Holbrook**

The detail, developed by architect Francis Sullivan, cleverly updates the traditional, decorative cornice return in a contemporary and simple manner.

The concept is to miter the plumb fascia to what replaces the earboard, creating in effect a cornice return. For this detail, the rafter tails typically overhang about 8 inches and are cut plumb and level to outline the soffit. However, the detail works equally well without an overhang. Instead of running over the earboard and out into space, the rake board ends on top of the return. A narrower, decorative strip overlays the main rake, aligned

with its upper edge. The narrow rake piece miters to a companion "drip strip" on the fascia.

This feature, although simple, is probably the most complex piece in the whole assembly, in that it tilts out from the fascia. A bevel along the bottom edge of the drip strip establishes its angle perpendicular to the slope of the roof, or square to the rake angle. The rake miter is thus a simple 45-degree square cut, which is as complicated as this detail gets (**Figure A**).

Since there are a few more pieces to this return than the standard method, I didn't want to assemble it piece by piece at the top of a ladder. Instead, I decided to prefab all the returns and pre-attach them to the fascia

## Cornice Return Detail

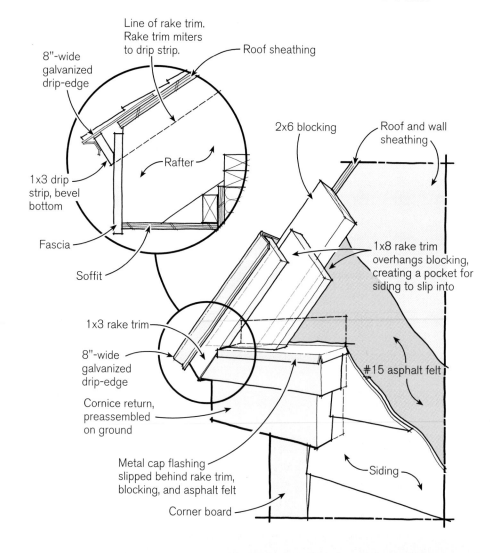

8"-wide galvanized drip-edge

Line of rake trim. Rake trim miters to drip strip.

Roof sheathing

Rafter

1x3 drip strip, bevel bottom

Fascia

Soffit

2x6 blocking

Roof and wall sheathing

1x8 rake trim overhangs blocking, creating a pocket for siding to slip into

1x3 rake trim

8"-wide galvanized drip-edge

Cornice return, preassembled on ground

#15 asphalt felt

Metal cap flashing slipped behind rake trim, blocking, and asphalt felt

Siding

Corner board

**Figure A.** *The author preassembled the cornice returns and fascia before nailing them up. The edge trim was installed in place. Polyurethane adhesive caulk keeps the miters from opening up.*

**Figure B.** *To look proportionate, trim details on the main roof (left) should be downsized on doghouse dormers (right). A 25% reduction looked right in this case.*

boards before nailing them up as assembled units.

Because the rake board installs over a build-out to give it visual relief and allow the siding to tuck under, the return must also be built out to the same plane as the rake.

A 3-inch-wide strip along the top edge of the return completes the detail. It's angled on one end to match the roof slope and is miter-returned to the wall at its opposite end. Because miter joints tend to open up when used outdoors, I used a polyurethane sealant to glue all the miters together and keep water out of the joints. I've worked with lots of red cedar trim and found that, unlike other sealant types, polyurethane bonds well to that resinous species.

For the two doghouse dormers on this project, I scaled the detail down by about 25% from the main roof to look proportionate with the smaller dormer roofs (**Figure B**).

With the fascia and returns assembled and installed, we cut the rake boards between the ridge and returns, and added the 3-inch-wide strips. The beveled-edge eaves strip was nailed to a chalk line. Although the top edge of the strip leans away from the fascia, a continuous run of 8-inch-wide galvanized drip-edge provides enough support and bridges the gap.

**Flashing**

It's common to use 1x6 fence board to pack out the rake trim. I like a stronger shadow line and used 2x6 instead. To keep things watertight at the cornice return, it's necessary to flash the upper edge of the return. All you need is a regular Z-bar profile, but the depth of the return — about 3 inches — exceeds anything you'll pull off your supplier's shelf. I had a local roofing outfit brake 8-foot lengths of red copper for my unfinished cedar trim, or white anodized aluminum to match painted trim. The flashing has to fit behind both the rake and the backing member — something to keep in mind when you're nailing up the backer.

The bottom end of the backer also has to be cut to a level line, struck from the bottom edge of the roof sheathing, to accommodate the flashing. I cut the backer a little high to eliminate interference and kept its lower end nail-free to allow me to flex it up just enough to slide the flashing behind it and the #15 asphalt felt underlayment that wraps the roof-to-wall transition.

*Dave Holbrook is a builder on Cape Cod, Mass.*

**Figure 3.** Angled blocks fastened with galvanized screws support the crown on the returns and up the rake (far left). A plywood lid caps the return (left).

details, and the "bird box" (the local term for the cornice return). We used short lengths of material for the mockups, substituting pine wherever we could. The idea was to work out all the details, including how much of each molding or lumber size we would need, what we would need to rip, and any pieces we would have to fabricate (like the small beveled pieces on the capital). This also gave us the chance to fine-tune the compound angles we would need to cut where the rake frieze lands on top of the return.

Once we established the exact angle for each of these cuts, we cut a sample piece of stock, labeled it, drilled a hole in it, and put it on a leather belt we call the "dog collar." Then every time we got to a new corner, the guy on the saw could find the angle from the sample piece and make the cut quickly and confidently. There were 10 cornice returns on the house, and we kept the same guy on the miter saw the whole time. Working out the details on the mockup saved us an enormous amount of time later.

I subbed out the capitals to our cabinetmaker. I figured he could handle the radius work and all the small buildup pieces better in the shop than we could. He preassembled the capitals and back-primed them so they were ready to go up. When we got to that stage later, installation was a breeze.

## Bird Boxes

Our first task was laying out the subfascia and building the bird boxes. We used 2x8 stock, which we tapered slightly to provide a slope on top (**Figure 3**). We added angled blocks to support the crown and capped the boxes with 3/8-inch plywood lids. We attached the blocks with construction adhesive and

**Figure 4.** Eaves membrane protects the finished returns (left) until metal flashing is installed (right).

**Figure 5.** The finished return: note how the cornice details on the dormer have been scaled down.

until the roofer came, we covered the plywood lids with Ice & Water Shield (**Figure 4**) (Grace Construction Products, www.graceconstruction.com). The roofer bent permanent flashings out of the same metal as the standing seam roof. After these were installed, we were able to run the trim up the gable ends.

## Durable Details

We used stainless steel nails throughout. We shot the smaller trim pieces in place with our Senco finish nailer. The larger pieces were first tacked with the finish gun, then nailed with hand-driven ring-shank nails. All the stock was back-primed, and some of it was primed on all four sides. Back-priming is a good idea, and we always do it, but the paint is definitely hard on saw blades.

A job like this only comes along every few years — where we have the chance to work with premium materials and clients who understand the time it takes to execute the kind of details the plans call for. It took our crew of four about six weeks to run all the exterior trim (**Figure 5**). Most of the first week was spent making mockups, prepping material, and doing layout. But the up-front head-scratching time kept us on schedule. Once we had figured out what we had to do, we picked up speed as we went along, and finished our job on schedule.

*Gordon Dixon is a builder in Stowe, Vt.*

two screws — one into the 2-by bird box stock and one down through the plywood lid. We also ran these blocks along the eaves and up the rake. When the blocks were in place, we cut back the plywood roof sheathing, which the framers had left hanging over.

Once the bird boxes were in place, we ran all the horizontal trim along the eaves. To protect the returns

# Installing PVC Trim

by Jeff Kent

The company I work for builds custom homes on the coast of Rhode Island. It's a harsh, damp environment that eats wood finishes and encourages mold and rot. Most homeowners here can look forward to spending a lot of time and money maintaining their exteriors. So when my supplier approached me in 2000 with a new PVC trim product that looked like painted wood but was immune to these problems, I was eager to try it. I already use fiber-cement siding and Trex decking, so PVC would let me offer my customers a totally maintenance-free exterior. I used it for the first time on a 5,200-square-foot Shingle-style house in southern Rhode Island. The material more than lived up to its promise. I now use it every chance I get.

Using PVC trim doesn't require any new skills. You can cut it, drill it, and fasten it with standard carpenter's tools (**Figure 6**, next page). But because the

For attractive and maintenance-free exterior trim, cellular PVC is hard to beat. But proper detailing is critical to good performance.

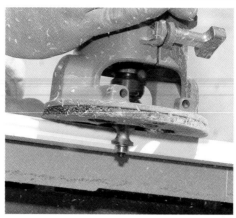

Figure 6. PVC trim stock cuts and routs much like wood. The dust tends to have a static cling, but it's not as fine or as abrasive as fiber-cement dust. PVC trim also won't dull blades any faster than wood.

material is more flexible than wood and expands and contracts more, you do have to vary your approach a bit. If you don't have good installation information, you're going to hate this product. However, if you learn to detail it right, it can save you expensive callbacks. The people I know who have learned how to use it, myself included, say they'll never go back to wood.

## The Material and Cost

The material used in PVC trim is called cellular PVC. The resin itself is similar to that used in plumbing pipes, but the term "cellular" refers to the trim material's lighter density. PVC pipe is much denser; the cut edge actually looks like glass. If you made a board out of the pipe material, it would be too heavy to lift and you would never be able to drive a nail through it. To make PVC trim boards, manufacturers mix the compound with a blowing agent that causes it to expand, giving the material a uniform cellular structure similar in density to white pine or clear cedar but it has no grain to warp or soak up moisture.

PVC trim comes in $1/2$-, $5/8$-, $3/4$-, and 1-inch thick-

nesses and in 18- and 20-foot lengths. Shingle mold, brick mold, crown mold, and beadboard are also available, as are PVC sheets in $1/2$-, $5/8$-, and $3/4$-inch thicknesses.

Most of the companies that make PVC trim seem to charge roughly the same price for it, but that doesn't mean all products are the same. The main variables I've found are porosity and color. Some brands have porous edges that are hard to sand smooth and finish, and some products aren't a true white — a problem if you don't intend to paint. Others have a white surface and a brown interior that shows on unfinished butt joints. In my experience, the best-quality PVC trim is made by Azek (www.azek.com) and Kleer (www.kleerlumber.com). Both companies make dense, nonporous boards that are easy to sand and finish. And they're a true white all the way through.

PVC costs about twice as much as finger-jointed pine and just a little less than clear cedar. It also takes a little more time to install than wood. However, we encourage our customers to look beyond the initial cost to the fact that it's a durable

Figure 7. PVC material has no organic material, so it is not prone to rot. This makes it ideal for coastal homes and any details exposed to harsh weather. Not only will all exterior trim, including everything on this entry (far left), hold up to wind and high humidity, but it also is an excellent material for outside showers (left). The author even shapes the soap dish from PVC.

**Figure 8.** While durable on the exterior, PVC has advantages for interior woodwork as well (far left). The author uses it for interior columns, pre-assembling a boxed column and then installing it around a structural post (left).

product that never needs maintenance.

Indeed, we feel the product's advantages make it well worth the cost. Since there's nothing organic, you don't have to worry about insects eating it. It won't soak up water, so you can set it right on concrete without fear of rot. Because there's no grain, it won't warp, twist, or bend. And when you glue two pieces together, they fuse into one, making the joint permanently watertight. These advantages make the product great for much more than simple trim. In fact, the more we use it, the more uses we find for it. They include:

- exterior railings and balustrades
- raised panels for exterior window treatments
- access panels for whirlpool tubs
- outside shower stalls (**Figure 7**).
- interior and exterior columns. We've had so much success with these that we made 100 three-sided columns in our shop. We slip the column over a structural post, then glue the fourth side in place on the job site (**Figure 8**).

We even used PVC once to make a 10-foot-long photographer's sink. The glue fused the joints, making it a single piece.

## Workability

The first thing you will notice about a PVC board is that it's a lot floppier than an equally sized wood board. It's so flexible that you can tie a 1-inch-wide strip into a pretzel shape. Because of this flexibility,

it takes two workers to rip the material (**Figure 9**, next page).

Some contractors, concerned that the PVC will flex between rafters or trusses, claim you need a subfascia. However, we don't use a subfascia and I've never had any deflection problems, even when spanning 2-foot distances between roof trusses.

The flexibility actually has an advantage. The same thermal blankets plumbers use to bend PVC pipe (available from any plumbing supply store) can be used to soften a PVC board. If you're installing arch-topped windows, for example, the softened board can then be placed in a jig to make a piece of curved head trim. It will cool in about 10 minutes.

Nailing and cutting are the same as for wood. The material won't pucker when you nail it, like some composites, and there's no more wear and tear on bits, blades, and tools than with wood. (Compare that with fiber-cement, which not only dulls blades, but its fine dust actually destroys tool motors.)

## Gluing

The biggest problem with PVC is that it expands and contracts with changes in temperature, and unlike wood, it actually expands more lengthwise. The manufacturers claim that you get only a $1/16$-inch expansion and contraction in a 14-foot board, but I haven't measured it. I do know that if you put it on a house during the summer when it's warm and don't glue the joints, you can come back in the winter and see big gaps. Manufacturers say that the greatest expansion comes

**Figure 9.** PVC trim stock is much more flexible than wood of comparable dimension. It will sag on a table saw, so two people are needed to rip it (far left). To demonstrate the material's flexibility, the author ties a 1-inch-wide strip into a pretzel (left).

after the last nail, so it's important to nail aggressively and close to the end, but in my experience the best way to prevent shrinkage is to glue all joints.

I use glue wherever one piece of trim touches another, and I always stagger the joints from one piece to the next. Without glue, the material will expand and contract in different directions. With glue, you control that expansion and contraction. In fact, the glue does more than bond two pieces, as with wood: it actually fuses them together to form a single piece (**Figure 10**). I've glued butt joints and given them to people to try and break. They can't do it. If they succeed in breaking anything, it's the board and not the joint.

I've used PVC plumber's glue, but wasn't altogether happy with it. It turns yellow over time, and it starts to set up in a matter of seconds, giving you little work time. I've since switched to Gorilla brand PVC glue (www.gorillaglue.com), a water-based product that does as good a job, doesn't yellow, and gives about five minutes' working time (**Figure 11**). That's plenty of time to get it on the edge of an 18-foot piece of trim. We've found the easiest way to apply the glue is from a plastic squeeze bottle. An empty drinking water bottle works great for this.

For corner boards, we rely on Kleer brand stock that comes with a lock miter that doesn't need to be glued (**Figure 12**). We preassemble the corner boards, using an Omer nail gun that shoots plastic nails. The nails fire through the material very easily, and a light sanding blends the heads in with the white trim. The plastic nails aren't structural (they're only meant to clamp the joint while the glue dries), so we still use stainless steel nails to fasten the boards to the house.

**Figure 10.** Once glued, the many pieces of a PVC cornice fuse together, creating a stiff assembly that remains seamless. These seams are hardly noticeable after three years on a house on the Rhode Island coast.

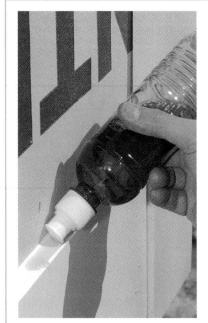

**Figure 11.** While plumber's PVC cement will bond trim stock, the author prefers Gorilla brand PVC glue — a water-based product that doesn't yellow and gives about five minutes' working time. He buys it in bulk and uses a water bottle to apply it.

**Figure 12.** Unlike many composites, PVC won't pucker at the surface when nailed. Some boards come with precut lock miters, which don't have to be glued.

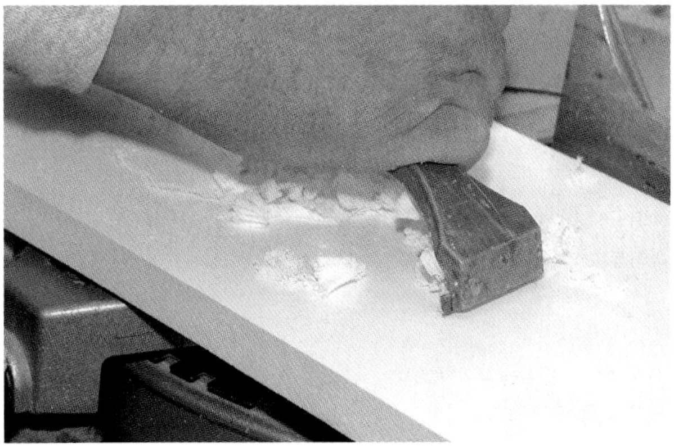

**Figure 13.** PVC trim holds paint much better than wood, and it will never require maintenance if left unpainted. Scratches, scuffs, and glue can be removed with a sharp scraper or light sanding.

## Finishing

PVC can be left unfinished or painted. Because the product is white, the first few times we used it, we figured we wouldn't have to paint. But glue drips, as well as glue-laden fingerprints and smudges, meant we spent a lot of time cleaning the stuff afterward. We finally concluded that we could offer a better result for less money by painting it. Another reason for painting PVC is to discharge the natural static, which is inherent to the product. (The static attracts dust and dirt.)

We use one coat of a good acrylic latex paint. We find that it actually holds up better on PVC than on wood because there's no moisture in the material to weaken the paint bond. We don't prime and we don't use oil paint. We don't use oil-based putty, either, because the oil in the putty will bleed through the paint. (I know of one contractor who dabs appliance paint on the nail heads with an artist's brush, but I haven't tried that.) Painted PVC is virtually indistinguishable from painted wood trim and the PVC will hold paint for up to 25 years. Homeowners will probably grow tired of a color before they need to repaint.

If you're not painting the material, use a paint scraper to clean up dried glue and remove scratches from the surface (**Figure 13**). Simply bear down on the scraper and pull on it. Although it takes several passes, it will eventually pull the scratch away.

*Jeff Kent is a project manager with EFC Construction Management in Pawtucket, R.I. All photos by Charles Wardell.*

# Trimming a Curved Portico

## by Mike Sloggatt

Not long ago, I was asked to build a curved portico by adding a roof structure and columns to an existing semicircular front porch on my client's Greek Revival–style home. The critical dimension for the new roof structure was the outside arc of the existing masonry porch below, which the new roof would have to match. And since the curved crown molding had to be special-ordered to size, accurate layout of the structure's outside arc was vital for a good fit.

Working on a circular rather than a rectangular shape requires a different mode of thinking. All of our layout would need to start at the outside of the crown and work inward toward the center. So instead of a lot of complex math and "air framing," I decided to take the same simple approach I use to build gable-end walls: lay out and cut everything on the ground.

## Using a Layout Table and Trammel

To minimize confusion, we built a layout table — basically an 8-foot-by-12-foot drawing and cutting board — with three full sheets of 3/4-inch plywood fastened to 2x4 sleepers on the garage floor. Because most of our layout would originate from the center of a circle, we snapped a centerline down the middle of the layout.

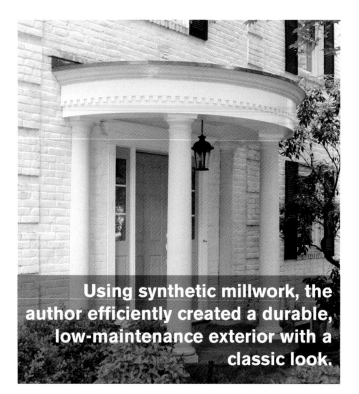

Using synthetic millwork, the author efficiently created a durable, low-maintenance exterior with a classic look.

**Figure 14.** To make a layout table, the author fastened full sheets of 3/4-inch plywood to 2x4 sleepers, then used a trammel to draw and cut out the parts of the portico, starting with the roof sheathing shown here.

Then we used scrap 3/4-inch plywood to construct a trammel arm. Fastened to the centerline with a screw acting as a pivot point, the trammel allowed us to quickly and accurately draw arcs and cut all the required curves for the project. We did our circular cutting with a router screwed to the trammel board.

Working in full scale from the architect's plans, we drew all of the construction details on the layout table, using the 10-foot 10-inch porch diameter as the reference dimension (see "Curved Portico Details," facing page). By working outward and adding together the trim elements, we were able to determine the exact

diameter of the crown molding; working toward the inside, we were able to determine dimensions and locations of the key framing elements and the various components of the semicircular structure underneath.

## Precutting the Parts

Once we were satisfied with the layout, we began using the trammel to cut out the parts, starting at the top with the roof sheathing. First we screwed three pieces of 3/4-inch CDX plywood to the layout table to give us a piece large enough to form the entire roof section. To cut around the roof's perimeter (**Figure 14**), we set the

**Figure 15.** Because the portico's architectural details were drawn to full scale, it was possible to locate columns and plan the framing without using complicated math (left). After cutting out the two sections of the plywood plate with the trammel-mounted router, the author fastened them to the layout table (right) before laying out and precutting the framing.

# Curved Portico Details

**Framing Plan**

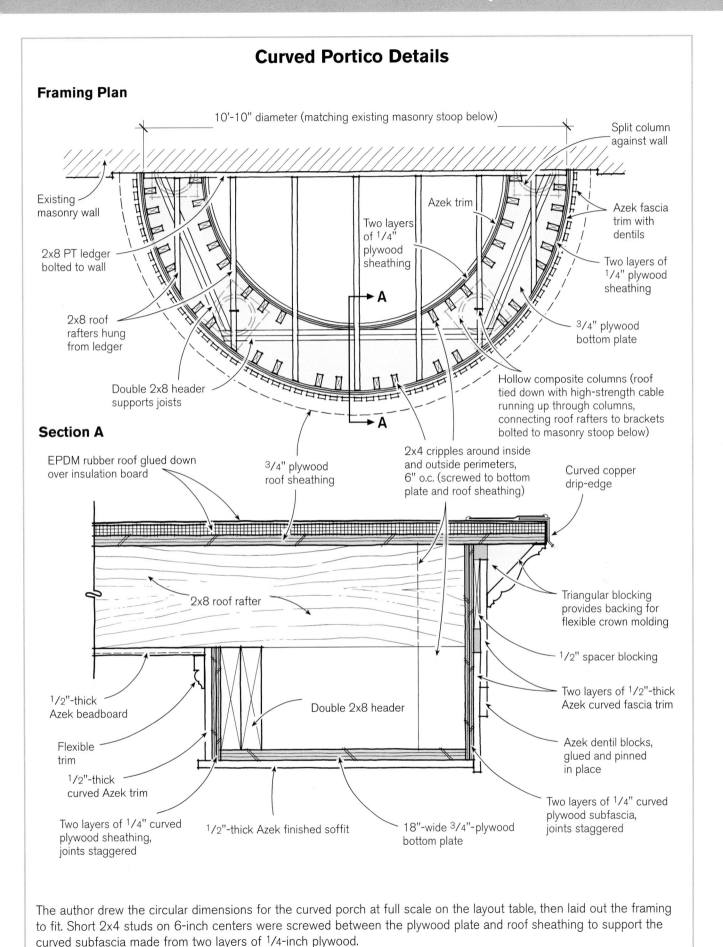

10'-10" diameter (matching existing masonry stoop below)

Split column against wall

Existing masonry wall

Azek trim

Azek fascia trim with dentils

2x8 PT ledger bolted to wall

Two layers of 1/4" plywood sheathing

Two layers of 1/4" plywood sheathing

2x8 roof rafters hung from ledger

3/4" plywood bottom plate

Double 2x8 header supports joists

Hollow composite columns (roof tied down with high-strength cable running up through columns, connecting roof rafters to brackets bolted to masonry stoop below)

**Section A**

EPDM rubber roof glued down over insulation board

3/4" plywood roof sheathing

2x4 cripples around inside and outside perimeters, 6" o.c. (screwed to bottom plate and roof sheathing)

Curved copper drip-edge

2x8 roof rafter

Triangular blocking provides backing for flexible crown molding

1/2" spacer blocking

Two layers of 1/2"-thick Azek curved fascia trim

1/2"-thick Azek beadboard

Double 2x8 header

Azek dentil blocks, glued and pinned in place

Flexible trim

1/2"-thick curved Azek trim

Two layers of 1/4" curved plywood subfascia, joints staggered

Two layers of 1/4" curved plywood sheathing, joints staggered

1/2"-thick Azek finished soffit

18"-wide 3/4"-plywood bottom plate

The author drew the circular dimensions for the curved porch at full scale on the layout table, then laid out the framing to fit. Short 2x4 studs on 6-inch centers were screwed between the plywood plate and roof sheathing to support the curved subfascia made from two layers of 1/4-inch plywood.

**Figure 16.** With the plate temporarily supported by 2x4 posts and the precut framing assembled, the roof sheathing was installed as a single piece (left). To provide backing for the two staggered layers of curved plywood sheathing, the author will install 2x4 cripples 6 inches o.c. (not shown) between the bottom plate and the roof sheathing (right).

bit of our router to cut ¹/₄ inch deep; a few successive passes, each one ¹/₄ inch deeper, got us through the plywood in about three or four swings of the tool.

Next, we cut the base of the structure, the 18-inch-wide curved plywood plate — or "subsoffit" — that would support the rafter framing and be supported by the decorative columns. The tricky part here was to back off the correct distance from the perimeter of the roof to allow for the thickness of our sheathing, trim

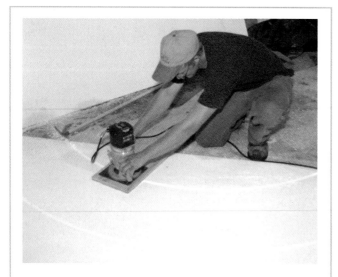

**Figure 17.** Cut from a 4x8-foot sheet of ¹/₂-inch Azek PVC stock, this two-piece matching base cap will be installed under the plywood plate to create a finished soffit.

base, and dentil blocks as well as our crown molding. By previously drawing the location of each element on the layout table, we could see exactly where we needed to make our circular cuts (**Figure 15**, page 188).

The plate was cut out of two rippings of ³/₄-inch plywood wide enough to cover the inner and outer arcs that we had drawn on the layout table. (Note: It's easy to confuse the measurements on the trammel. If the cut is on the outside of the circle, take the measurement from the pivot to the inside of the bit; for inside cuts, measure from the pivot to the far side of the bit.) Using a radius drawn from the center of the circle, we also plotted the angle cuts for the plywood where the two sections would meet.

Once the plate sections were cut to size, we screwed them down into position on the layout table, then laid out the framing so that it would fit inside the curve of the portico. That made it easy to snap header, ledger, and rafter locations on the plywood. Now it was just a matter of measuring each piece, cutting it to length, and fitting it to form the structure; no math involved here, just simple measurements. We could even plot the column locations on the plate while working in the garage.

## Assembling the Parts

After bolting a 2x8 ACQ ledger to the masonry to support the upper end of the rafters, we used temporary 2x4 posts and a few screws to support the plywood base plate (**Figure 16**). With the layout already marked on the plate and ledger and all the framing cut to length, the parts went together quickly. We

**Figure 18.** Two layers of PVC trim cover a double layer of 1/4-inch curved plywood subfascia. The upper layer of fascia trim hides the stainless steel screws fastening the lower layer and provides a ground for the PVC dentil molding.

joined the three roof sheathing sections together by screwing plywood scabs across the seams, then lifted and installed them in one piece.

To build the vertical structure between the bottom plate and the roof sheathing, we laid out and installed 2x4 cripples. Fastened 6 inches on-center around both the inside and outside perimeters, these short studs support the two layers of 1/4-inch A/C plywood sheathing that we used to wrap the structure. Because we layered the plywood and staggered the seams, the curve faired out nicely, providing a smooth base for the fascia trim.

## Cellular PVC Trim

With the trammel already set up to cut the plywood plate, we cut the matching base cap from 1/2-inch-thick Azek PVC material (Azek, www.azek.com). The base cap would be attached later to the underside of the plate to create a finished soffit (**Figure 17**). Because Azek is available in 4x8-foot (and longer) sheets, we were able

to make the base cap from only two pieces of material.

PVC trim has limited compressive strength, but on this small porch the loads wouldn't exceed 1,000 pounds per column. To minimize point-loading, we cut and fit the columns carefully and belt-sanded the tops smooth for full bearing where they would support the soffit. On a larger, heavier structure, we'd have cut the Azek to fit around the bearing points.

In addition to being durable, Azek is easy to work with, and I felt we'd be able to bend this thin 1/2-inch stock to fit the curves around the inside and outside fascia. However, wrapping the fascia with Azek proved to be a challenge in chilly weather. While PVC trim is fairly flexible, we found that Azek's cellular structure does not react well to impacts when the temperature approaches freezing and the material is under pressure. When we flexed a piece and shot a nail into the center of the flex, the piece snapped.

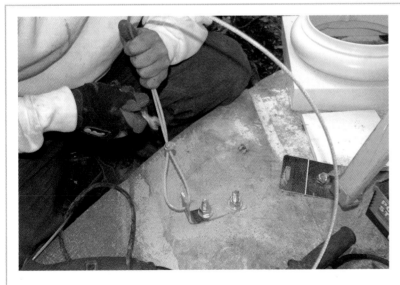

**Figure 19.** To meet local building-code requirements for wind loads, the author attached brackets (left) to the concrete porch; they will be hidden by the hollow composite columns supporting the portico (right). High-strength aircraft cable running up through the columns connects the brackets to the rafters overhead.

So we started in the middle of the lower fascia board and worked toward the ends, screwing with stainless trim screws along the top edge where it would be covered by the overlapping fascia above. Then we carefully clamped and nailed the bottom edge as we slowly wrapped the boards around the outside radius (**Figure 18**, previous page).

After wrapping the fascia, we made and applied matching Azek dentil blocks. First, we glued the back of each block with Azek's proprietary glue, which is similar to plumber's PVC cement but with a lot more working time; then, to temporarily hold the blocks in place while the glue dried, we pinned them with a Senco micropinner. This tool leaves such a small hole you can't see it, even up close.

Next, we installed two columns to support our structure, with split columns against the wall just for show. Besides having to reinforce the masonry stoop with piers below frost level and fudging the stoop's slightly irregular shape, the only hitch we ran into here was meeting the new wind-load regulations. Since we chose to use hollow composite columns, I had to figure out a way to securely tie the roof to the masonry stoop below. So we bolted brackets to the concrete, attached aircraft cable to them, fished the cable up through each column, and bolted the cable to the rafters above after setting each column (**Figure 19**, previous page).

As we finished the interior vertical surface of the fascia, we wedged the top edge of the trim boards against the framing, slowly bent each board into position, then held it there with bar clamps instead of screws or nails (**Figure 20**). When we cut the last piece and snapped it in place, friction held everything tightly so that we didn't need to use fasteners — which would have snapped the Azek in two at such a tight radius.

To finish off the ceiling, we used Azek beadboard, centering the middle board on the centerline and then working toward each corner. We used a cutoff (from the cap trim) as a template to scribe the cut line where each board met the inner curve, positioning the template with two measurements — the long

**Figure 20.** To avoid fracturing the curved interior trim with fasteners, the author coaxed the pieces into position with clamps, allowing friction to hold everything in place (left). He used a base-cap offcut to scribe the beadboard ceiling planks to fit (below left), starting with the longest board in the middle and working toward the two corners (below).

## Working in Circles

Getting accurate measurements when doing circular work can be a little bit tricky. To calculate an order or rough-cut a piece, the key measurement is the circumference of a circle, which is easy enough to calculate (circumference = π x diameter). When the formulas get more cumbersome, I use my Construction Master Pro calculator, which has many built-in circular functions. For example, I can determine the length of a wrapped piece (an arc length) if I know the radius of the circle and take a straight line measurement (a chord length); or I can figure it out by measuring the chord length and the rise (see illustration).

It's also possible to physically measure small pieces of trim along a curve, though it's difficult with a standard steel-tape measure. Instead, use either a tailor's fabric tape or FastCap's ProCarpenter FlatBack tape (www.fastcap.com); either will lie flat and wrap around a curved surface without distorting (see photo). — *M.S.*

Using a few geometric formulas, it's possible to calculate most of the lengths needed for circular work. Many construction calculators automate these functions while working in inches and feet, making calculations faster and more accurate.

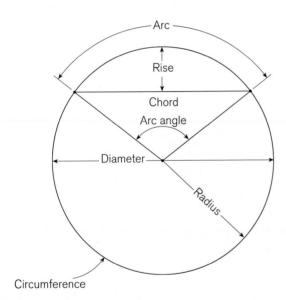

Circumference = π x diameter
(Note: π = approximately $3^1/_7$ or 3.14)

Arc length = arc angle (in degrees) x (π/180) x radius

$$\text{Radius} = \frac{\text{rise}}{2} + \frac{\text{chord}^2}{8\,(\text{rise})}$$

*The FlatBack tape measure's straight blade allows it to lie flat along a curved surface.*

point and short point — which we determined by measuring off the previously installed ceiling board. Since the joint along the fascia would be covered by trim, we didn't need to finesse the scribing.

## Flexible Crown Molding

Finally, we built a base for the flexible 45-degree crown molding that would finish off the top of the fascia. Made of polyester resin and available from several manufacturers, flexible crown must be special-ordered for the specific radius you plan to wrap. Because we needed enough to wrap half of a circle measuring approximately 10 feet in diameter (with a circumference of 31.4 feet), I had ordered two 12-foot-long pieces, the shortest length available (see "Working in Circles," above).

To provide nailing for the crown, we cut triangular blocks out of 2x4s, set them into construction adhesive, and pinned them to the bottom of the roof

**Figure 21.** Triangular blocks cut from 2x4s and installed with construction adhesive were pinned to the roof sheathing (above left); they provide backing for the flexible crown molding used to finish the portico (above right). To place the joints in a less visible position, the author and his helper installed the longest section in the middle, then the two sides (left).

sheathing (**Figure 21**). Then we wrapped a full 12-foot length of crown around the middle section of the fascia so there would be two offset joints at the sides instead of one more visible joint along the center. At first we tried scarf joints to join the two shorter side sections, but we weren't happy with the results. So we simply cut butt joints, backed the joints with small wood shims, and used Marine-Tex FlexSet (ITW Philadelphia Resins, www.marinetex. com) flexible epoxy adhesive as both an adhesive and a filler. Like Bondo, this two-part epoxy can be sanded to a fine finish, but it has a longer working time and is white when it dries, so we used it with the Azek, too.

The portico's EPDM rubber roof was glued down over insulation board. First, though, the roofer dressed up the edge of the roof with a curved copper cap, then flashed the wall with a matching copper flashing tucked into the brickwork. The electrician installed the client's light fixture, and later we returned to put in a new fiberglass entry door.

Our client loved the look of the porch trim so much that we ended up replacing all of the home's exterior millwork with cellular PVC. And while I've recommended that 100 percent acrylic paint be applied over the new trim, it seems that they like it just the way it is.

*Mike Sloggatt is a remodeling contractor in Levittown, N.Y.*

# Chapter 11: Wood & Composite Sidings

- **Working With Preprimed Wood Siding**
- **Installing Fiber-Cement Siding**

# Working With Preprimed Wood Siding

by Marie Tupot Stock

Although wood siding has lost market share to vinyl and fiber-cement in recent years, sales of wood siding remain strong in many parts of the country, especially in the northern half of the U.S. Increasingly, when wood siding is chosen, it's being installed preprimed or prefinished.

Machine priming of siding was first developed in the 1940s, but the use of preprimed siding didn't take off until recently. Today, a wide selection of wood siding, as well as some fiber-cement and composite siding, is readily available preprimed or prefinished.

## Bracing for the Elements

Although wood siding has been installed unpainted for hundreds of years, there are several disadvantages to doing it the old-fashioned way. The unpainted siding can pick up moisture while being transported or stored on site, meaning paint is less likely to adhere. Moreover, when unpainted siding is exposed to the sun, it loses its paint-holding ability and can begin to cup. "We used to buy hemlock, fir, or spruce. Within two days in the sun, it warped," says Jesse Head of Head Construction in Middletown, Calif. "It's not worth bringing on the job." Head, who builds two or three homes a year, hasn't put up a bare piece of siding in more than five years.

According to Mark Knaebe, wood surface chemist at the USDA Forest Products Laboratory in Madison, Wis., sunlight destroys the lignin near the surface of unpainted wood. Lignin is the glue that holds the cellulose fibers together. "When the sun destroys the lignin, the fibers are still sitting there, but they are not glued very well to the wood anymore," explains Knaebe. "If you paint the siding after a couple of weeks of exposure, you're painting over those loose fibers." In controlled tests, wood exposed to the sun for four weeks before painting failed five years earlier than wood painted immediately. Most experts recommend that wood siding be primed within two weeks of installation.

## Factory Priming

Factory-primed siding is produced by passing the siding through a machine coater, which floods the wood with paint. As the board leaves the machine, it passes through a roller or set of brushes designed to remove excess paint (**Figure 1**). Some prefinishers use a vacuum coating machine, which sucks the excess primer off of a board that has been flooded with coating. After emerging from the machine coater, the primed wood is dried. Latex primer can be dried

**Preprimed or prefinished siding can be installed any time of year, since proper painting conditions are not a concern.**

under controlled conditions in 15 to 30 minutes — much faster than oil-based primer, which spends 12 to 24 hours in special drying rooms (**Figure 2**).

## Prepriming Advantages

One advantage of using preprimed siding is that there is no need to wait for good weather to get a protective coat of primer on the boards. Fans of preprimed siding tout other advantages as well: the siding's moisture content can be controlled, all four sides of a board can be coated, and the coating can be applied at a consistent thickness.

*Moisture content.* At a job site, the moisture content of unprimed siding varies. Especially in areas with frequent spells of cool, damp weather, painters are often tempted to work in less-than-ideal conditions. "We have to be careful. We have days when in the morning it's 45 degrees outside, and it can be 110 by the end of the day," notes contractor Jesse Head. "At least with prepriming, it's been done under controlled conditions."

When siding is factory primed by a reputable company, the siding is usually tested for moisture content. For example, Cape Cod Siding in Nova Scotia

Figure 1. As a piece of siding is pulled through a machine coater, it is flooded with paint (far left). On the other side of the machine, rollers or brushes remove the excess paint (left).

kiln-dries its siding to a moisture content of 12% to 14% before priming. However, smaller companies may not be so careful. For example, one factory finisher reported only "occasionally" checking for moisture content in siding before machine priming.

*Priming all four sides.* If siding is nailed up unfinished, then only the front face of the siding can be coated with paint. The unpainted back face of the siding will readily pick up moisture coming either from the building's interior or from wind-driven rain.

Factory-primed siding is encapsulated on four sides — at least until the first cut is made. When installing preprimed siding, a can of paint and a brush should always be on hand. "Unfortunately, a majority of the time this isn't done," says Scott Babbitt, of the Olympic Factory Finish Group. "Unsealed cuts tend

Figure 2. After leaving the machine coater, the siding is placed on racks to dry.

to absorb moisture. That can lead to tannin bleed and premature failure of the siding."

Manufacturers of fiber-cement siding point out that unlike wood siding, fiber-cement doesn't need to be encapsulated, so back-priming is not required.

*Coating consistency and coating thickness.* Advocates of factory priming also cite the evenness of machine application as an advantage. However, not all factory finishers are scrupulous, and less reputable finishers have been known to thin the primer. "There is a tendency on the part of the preprimer to choose a paint that goes through the machine easiest and dries the quickest," says John Lahey, president of Fine Paints of Europe.

Mark Knaebe at the Forest Products Laboratory agrees. "I've seen some lousy stuff coming out," he notes. "Some of it has only half a mil of primer. It should be a minimum of one and a half mils." For adequate priming, according to Knaebe, none of the wood grain should be visible through the primer, which should form a hard film with no noticeable chalkiness. Most experts recommend that 6 mils of wet primer be applied to achieve a dry film thickness of 1.5 to 2 mils.

## Who's Doing the Prepriming?

When you buy preprimed siding at the lumberyard, it isn't always clear whether it was primed by the siding manufacturer or by a so-called "prestaining" company. Some brand-name siding is factory primed by the siding manufacturer (for example, lodgepole pine siding from Cape Cod Siding in Nova Scotia, or StepSaver cedar siding from Skookum Lumber Co. in Olympia, Wash.). These larger companies are likely to have well-established quality-control programs.

However, many lumberyards purchase unprimed siding and contract with a local priming company. Sometimes this is done in large lots, for inventory.

## Prepriming on Site

Instead of buying factory-primed siding, some builders prefer to buy unfinished siding, and to prime the siding on site before installation. That way, they have more control over the process and can be sure the primer is applied thick enough. The work is best done under a roof.

Bob Lipovsky, president of Kingston Construction in Fairfax Station, Va., likes to back-prime the siding on site. "First, we prime everything that's not going to be visible — the back, the ends. Then, when we get it installed, we prime the front," explains Lipovsky. He has found from experience that if the front of the siding is preprimed, then handling it gets messy.

According to Mark Knaebe, from the USDA Forest Products Laboratory in Madison, Wis., "Ideally, you should back-prime with a water repellent, such as Dap

*A site-built drying rack is a necessary for prefinishing on the job.*

Woodlife." He says that research has shown that a water repellent is better at resisting water entry than an acrylic primer and less likely to trap moisture in the siding than oil-based primer.

Dominick Lubrano of DPL Custom Builders in Williamsburg, Va., likes to prime both sides of the siding before installation, sometimes putting two coats back and front if the customer wants the best job possible. But it's certainly not an easy way to go. Lubrano watches the weather for ideal painting temperature — 45 to 50 degrees — and pays attention to the cleanliness of the workplace. Storing the primed siding becomes a major issue. "We had to build drying racks for 8,000 linear feet of siding to store the lumber between coats."

Lipovsky agrees that drying setups take up a lot of space (see photo). He recommends spacing the boards just enough so they're not touching but air can still get to them. At a new home site, says Lipovsky, it's sometimes possible to rig drying racks on tarps in a basement, but it's rare to find enough indoor drying room on a remodeling job.

Wayne Whitelock of Calais, Vt., prefinished the red cedar clapboards for his own house by dipping each board in a site-built trough filled with oil-based stain and then drying the siding on indoor racks. He says the system worked well. The only problem was that he ran short of prefinished siding and had to install a small portion of the siding undipped. That section received a coat of brush-applied stain after installation. Eight years later, the builder can spot the difference. "The siding we dipped is absolutely flawless, but the hand-painted siding is starting to lose its color. Dipping it really does make a difference." — M.S.

Some lumberyards can arrange for custom priming to meet a builder's needs. The turnaround time for a custom order varies — from about three weeks to as much as eight weeks in parts of the country where construction is booming.

### Cost

If you are considering factory priming, the next question is cost. The cost varies, of course, depending on the species, profile, and grade of siding. In most cases, however, a factory can prime siding for considerably less than you can. Also you don't get the problem of sunlight deteriorating the surface, says USDA's Mark Knaebe.

### Top Coat Available, Too

Some siding manufacturers or distributors offer siding that is not only preprimed, but is also prefinished with a top coat. "Seven years ago, we expanded our business to include two-coat work," says Fred Churchill of Churchill Coatings in Grafton, Mass. "We can put on one primer and one finish coat. The extra coat only adds about $400 for 3,000 square feet of siding, compared to an $800 first coat."

Prefinishing saves contractors from weather problems in the Northwest, the Northeast, and the Midwest, the strongest markets for manufacturers of preprimed siding. "The demand is great in the winter," says Churchill. "When you buy a preprimed product and put it up, you have to get that finish coat up in 60 days. When you buy preprimed and finished siding, you can wait until next spring [for touch-up or an additional top coat]."

Several manufacturers, including Maibec Industries in Quebec, offer factory-stained cedar shingles. Each kiln-dried shingle is dipped in an acrylic stain, dried, and boxed for shipment. The use of stained shingles has doubled every year over the last three years, according to Maibec, which now ships a third of their products either stained or bleached.

Some manufacturers of prefinished siding offer paint warranties. For example, Cape Cod Siding guarantees the coating for 15 years. If the coating fails within the first five years, the company supplies the labor and materials to fix it; after that, they supply materials only.

New Jersey builder Matt Porraro usually buys siding preprimed and prefinished. "I know when it's shipped, it's protected," he says. Through his local lumberyard, he requests two coats, and tops the boards with a third coat after installation. He has a simple solution when customers don't think their siding needs prefinishing: he won't guarantee the finish.

Not every builder who has tried prefinished siding is a fan. Bob Lipovsky, president of Kingston Construction in Fairfax Station, Va., sticks with pre-primed siding rather than prefinished. "You end up putting nails into it and you end up painting it anyway," he explains.

Scott Babbitt of Olympic notes that some contractors have unrealistic expectations for prefinished siding. "It's a problem — the perception that prefinished siding can be nailed up and you can walk away," he says. In most cases, prefinished siding will need a third coat of paint after installation, if only to cover caulk and nail heads. A third coat is especially needed with light colors, partly a result of handling and dust on the job site.

## Ordering Preprimed Siding

If you're ready to try preprimed or prefinished siding, make sure it's done right. Ask your supplier to identify who does the priming. Get assurances that the finisher checks the moisture content of the siding before running it through the machine, uses a quality paint, and can verify a minimum dry film thickness of 1.5 mils. For siding that is both primed and finished, look for a reputable company that backs up its work with a written guarantee.

*Marie Tupot Stock is a New York City–based construction and design writer.*

# Installing Fiber-Cement Siding

## by Tim Uhler

The company I work for builds seven to ten spec and custom homes per year on the Kitsap Peninsula, just west of Seattle.

Our crew frames and does most of the siding and exterior finish work. Wood siding is popular in this area, but it's too expensive for spec houses. We used to side with L-P's Inner-Seal, an engineered wood product with an OSB-like substrate. We switched to fiber-cement in 1996, when Inner-Seal became the subject of a class-action lawsuit. Although improved versions of engineered-wood sidings are available, we now side almost exclusively with fiber-cement. Our customers like it because it looks like wood, and they are reassured by the fact that it comes with a 50-year warranty. We happen to use James Hardie's lap siding, HardiPlank (www.jameshardie.com), but I've talked with carpenters who use other brands and hear they have similar results.

It wasn't easy switching to fiber-cement. We had gotten used to engineered siding, which is light, cuts like wood, and comes in 16-foot lengths. Fiber-cement, on the other hand, is heavy and creates a lot of noxious dust when you cut it with a saw (for tips on cutting, see "Cutting Fiber-Cement," page 204). It also takes more pieces to cover a building because it only comes in 12-foot lengths.

## Cutting

There are a number of ways to cut fiber-cement siding, but the most common ones are with electric shears or circular saws equipped with fiber-cement blades. Regular carbide blades will cut fiber-cement, but they dull quickly and overheat and warp when you gang-cut. We also tried diamond abrasive blades; they lasted longer than carbide but put a real strain on our saw. Lately, we've been using Hitachi's Hardiblade (www.hitachi.com/powertools). It's a four-tooth polycrystalline diamond-tipped blade that's designed specifically for fiber-cement. These

Figure 3. The author's crew gang-cuts as many as seven pieces at a time using a wormdrive saw (far left). In contrast with a regular carbide blade, which would be dull after a single day of cutting, this dedicated fiber-cement blade from James Hardie (left) has cut the siding for five 2,500-square-foot houses.

blades are expensive — about $70 per kit. But they'll last for five or six 2,500-square-foot houses. They make smooth cuts, don't strain the saw, and can gang-cut seven pieces of siding at a time (**Figure 3**).

We also use a set of Snapper Shears, basically an electric drill motor with a special cutter head attached (Pacific International Tool & Shear, www.snappershear.com). The shears cut fiber-cement the same way double-action metal shears cut sheet metal. A narrow strip of waste curls up between the knives as the shears make their way through the material. We cut most of our siding with shears. It's slower than using a saw, but it's worth the time because the shears don't produce dust (**Figure 4**).

I've heard of crews using miter saws to cut fiber-cement, but I can't see doing that to an expensive

saw. The dust is very abrasive, which is why we set aside our oldest worm drive for cutting the material. Also, circular saws work better for gang-cutting because you can cut the siding right on the pile rather than having to position the heavy material on the miter saw bed.

***Dust.*** Dust is a big problem when you cut fiber-cement with a saw. The dust contains silica, which can cause silicosis or lung cancer if you breathe too much of it. The manufacturers tell you to wear a dust mask or respirator and to cut outdoors or use some kind of mechanical ventilation.

We've tried wearing dust masks, but they're uncomfortable to wear all day, especially when it's hot. We've also tried setting up fans to blow the dust away and have even held our breath while cutting,

Figure 4. Electric shears, like this Snapper model, will cut fiber-cement without producing dust. The downside is that they're slower than a circular saw and can cut only one piece at a time.

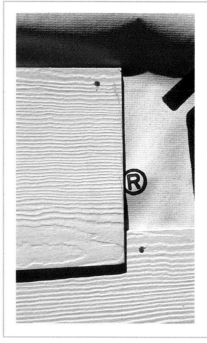

Figure 5. Blind-nailing is common with fiber-cement siding; the standard lap is 1 1/4 inches.

**Figure 6.** The author typically uses a roofing nailer because it fits easily under the eaves and in tight spots. Also, the large nail heads are hard to overdrive — and hold siding flatter than nails with smaller heads.

but neither method works that well. The best solution we've found is to avoid making dust in the first place by using electric shears.

Makita makes a saw (5057KB) that's specifically designed to cut fiber-cement (www.makitatools.com). It has a built-in dust collection container and can also be connected to a shop vac. We've used this saw, and it does a pretty good job of capturing dust. We didn't stick with it because we're die-hard left-blade users, and it's awkward for us to switch to a saw with the blade on the right. We'd probably use this saw if there were a model with the blade on the left.

## Fastening

When fiber-cement first hit the market, Hardie recommended fastening it with roofing nails. You're

also permitted to use certain types of common nails, siding nails, and screws.

According to Hardie, hot-dipped galvanized and stainless steel fasteners are preferred, but electro-plated fasteners are permitted. Be sure to read the installation instructions, because each manufacturer has its own list of approved fasteners. You'll void the warranty if you use the wrong ones.

We still prefer roofing nails. It sounds kind of strange until you realize that most people blind-nail this kind of siding. When blind-nailing, you nail only the top edge, so the heads are hidden by the course above. Check with your local inspector before you do this, because blind-nailing is not permitted for every siding pattern or in every wind or exposure zone. In some cases, you may be required to fasten the bottom edge. Wherever you nail, you have to hit the studs (**Figure 5**).

Another reason we like roofing nails is that the nailers are shorter and more compact than stick nailers, so it's easier to fit them under the eaves. We have two Bostitch roofing guns (www.bostitch.com). Anywhere they don't fit we drive nails with a hammer or palm nailer (**Figure 6**). We use 2-inch galvanized roofing nails for any hand nailing. On a few occasions, we've fastened siding with 8-penny galvanized nails. The siding came out fine, but we prefer to use roofing nails because they seem to hold the siding flatter and are less likely to be overdriven. You don't want to overdrive fasteners; doing so will void the warranty.

A problem with blind-nailing is that it doesn't always pull the siding snug to the house at the bottom edge. If there's a bow in the framing, that can leave a gap between the bottom edge of one piece of siding and the face of the piece below. We have two ways to deal with this. If the gap is less than 1/8 inch wide, we'll caulk it. For larger gaps, we bottom-nail at that location. If the gap is well above eye level, we might use a roofing nail to fasten the bottom edge; if it's lower, we'll use a smaller-head nail (**Figure 7**).

**Figure 7.** Wherever a butt joint doesn't lie flush because of irregular framing, the head of a single nail will close the gap and pull the pieces snug. This is less obtrusive than putting a nail in the corner of each piece.

**Figure 8.** Have fiber-cement siding delivered to a spot where it's out of the way and won't have to be moved. This load weighed more than 4,000 pounds.

## Handling

Fiber-cement siding is a lot more difficult to handle than other siding materials. For one thing, it's very heavy. A 12-foot piece of Hardie's 8¹/₄-inch lap siding weighs 19 pounds. Wider material weighs more. Fiber-cement is also so floppy that you need to carry lap siding on edge. It's liable to break if you carry it on the flat or throw it over your shoulder, like you're used to doing with other materials. It's important to tarp the pile, because fiber-cement is more prone to break when it's wet.

I'm a pretty strong guy, and I won't carry more than three 12-foot lengths of fiber-cement at one time. I used to carry three or four pieces in the crook of my arm but ended up with bruises where the siding rested.

When you take delivery, make sure they drop it close to where you'll be working but out of the way (**Figure 8**). Depending on the product, a unit of lap siding can contain 13 to 18 squares of material and weigh somewhere around 5,000 pounds. You don't want to move it any farther or handle it any more than necessary.

Our company recently bought a used all-terrain forklift, which has been invaluable on siding jobs. It allows us to drive a pallet of material around the job and lift material to carpenters who are siding the second story.

## Layout

Layout and installation are about the same as for any kind of manufactured lap siding. It's great when the siding runs full length, but you're going to have joints if the wall is more than 12 feet long. Because the siding is all the same length, we have the cutman start by cutting random lengths of siding in 32- and 48-inch increments to avoid creating a pattern. The installers combine the shorts with full-length pieces to produce a random joint pattern.

## Coursing

Hardiplank isn't beveled and is designed for a standard 1¹/₄-inch overlap. Layout is easy because you can't really cheat the coursing. We typically use 8¹/₄-inch-wide material, so we end up with a 7-inch reveal. We start at the mudsill and use the same coursing all the way up the building. We hook the tape on the mudsill and mark 7 inches, 14 inches, 21 inches, and so on all the way to the frieze. We're usually framing 8-foot walls, so the top piece of siding is a 4- or 5-inch rip. Since the siding isn't beveled, you have to shim behind narrow rips. If you don't, the top tips in too far, leaving a big gap under the lap. We avoid this by nailing short scraps to the wall above the last full course of siding.

**Figure 9.** Because of its weight, fiber-cement siding is trickier to install than wood clapboards when working alone. Site-made or manufactured jigs, like the panel gauges shown here, are helpful. The gauges catch the upper edge of the previous course and hold the next piece in place while the carpenter nails it off.

## Jigs

Given its weight, you'll need some kind of installation jig if you want to install fiber-cement by yourself. One of our carpenters made a sheet-metal jig to support the far end of the material. His jig hooks over one course of siding and has a lip to support the next course up. The problem is, the jig attaches to the existing siding, so you have to walk down the wall to put it on and then back to lift up the siding.

We recently tried out an inexpensive (about $30) ready-made jig called the Labor Saver from Indian Valley Innovation (www.thelaborsaver.com). It consists of a pair of metal clips that attach to the bottom edge of the piece you're about to install. The clips catch the top edge of the course below and support the siding while you nail it off. There's no need to do layout for every course of siding because the jig automatically gives you a 1¹/₄-inch lap. Malco (www.malcotools.com) makes a similar device called a fiber-cement siding panel gauge (**Figure 9**). When there's no one there to support the other end of the piece, either of these jigs would make it much easier to install siding.

## Raw, Primed, or Prefinished

Fiber-cement siding is available raw, primed, or prefinished. We used to side with raw material but switched to primed when our lumberyard started stocking it. This was definitely a change for the better: I've compared houses we built in the past, and the paint jobs on the ones sided with primed material look better. We've chosen not to use prefinished siding, because it limits color selection, and I can't imagine being able to install it without scratching the finish.

Now that we're used to siding with fiber-cement, we can install it faster than OSB siding. This is partly because we don't have to prime the cut ends of fiber-cement, which you're required to do with OSB material. This makes the work go much faster, and you don't have to worry about getting paint all over everything.

## Joints and Caulking

According to Hardie, end joints can be lightly butted or left ¹/₈ inch open and caulked. We leave a gap at

**Figure 10.** The author's crew always caulk as they go, so they won't have to clean the siding if it gets splattered with mud. Here, a carpenter uses a foam shipping block from a window to smooth the caulking at a butt.

every butt and wherever the siding hits window trim, door trim, or corner boards. We apply caulk as we go, because it rains a lot around here and mud gets splattered on the lower courses. It's a lot easier to apply sealant while the siding is still clean (**Figure 10**).

We save the 1x1 foam squares that manufacturers stick on the corners of windows to protect them during transport. We use them to smear caulking over face nails and butt joints. They do a good job smoothing out the caulk, and it makes the paint job look better.

The installation instructions say you should use paintable caulk that complies with ASTM C 834 or ASTM C 920 — basically, a paintable caulk that remains permanently flexible. If you're not sure about a particular caulk, check the label; the ASTM rating should be on it. It's so rainy here in the Pacific Northwest that we can't use acrylics like Dynaflex or Big Stretch because they'll wash off before they have time to set. We've had good success with OSI Quad, which is one of the recommended brands on Hardie's website.

*Tim Uhler is a lead framer and exterior trim carpenter for Pioneer Builders in Port Orchard, Wash.*

## Cutting Fiber-Cement

### by Rodney Proctor

I've been working with fiber-cement siding and trim for the last several years and have seen it become increasingly popular. Although fiber-cement is a super product, until recently there weren't a lot of choices for cutting it. The regular carbide blade in a circular saw makes a great cut, but the resulting dust is horrible for the customers, the workers, and their tools. Fortunately, as the popularity of these materials has grown, a wide variety of specialized tools and accessories has emerged.

### Cutting With Shears

I plugged along with a regular 7 1/4-inch circular saw with a carbide blade for years until, luckily, I discovered fiber-cement shears (or as they're called around here, "nippers"). I wouldn't recommend them as the only tool, but they are a must-have for anyone installing fiber-cement siding on a regular basis.

The Snapper Shear Steelhead SS404 110V (from Pacific International Tool & Shear, www.snappershear.com) is my personal favorite. This handy tool is a dust-free fiber-cement cutting whiz. It will cruise through miles of cement siding before wearing out the blades (**Figure A**).

The blades can be changed out quickly and inexpensively, at about $70 for a complete kit. It's easy to use, lightweight, quiet, and gives a smooth cut. I use it primarily for 3/8-inch-by-8-inch lap siding. It's not much good for

Figure B. *The pneumatic shear is a real convenience when you're up on the scaffold.*

4x8 sheets, though, and doesn't have the capacity to cut 3/4-inch trim material.

I have also used the Snapper Shear pneumatic SS402 WindShear Steelhead cutters (Pacific International Tool & Shear). These little beauties are great for trimming miscuts. Up on a scaffold you can slip it right in your nailbag. Then it's no problem to unplug your nail gun, slap the nippers on the hose, trim a piece of siding, and go right back to nailing without sending the piece back to the cutter (**Figure B**). The only drawback is that they use a lot of air — 10 cfm at 90 psi. This will quickly drain the compressor, so I don't use them for multiple cuts at the sawhorses.

Another nipper I like to use is the SS414 curve-cutting electric shear (Pacific International Tool & Shear). This is the absolute best tool I've found for cutting curves. It is lightweight and cuts smoothly, without dust. I use it not only for lap siding but also for 4x8 sheets where an arch or even a hole is required. These shears won't cut 3/4-inch material, though, so don't throw away the circular saw yet (**Figure C**).

The 24-inch SS210M Manual Shear (Pacific International Tool & Shear) is a good tool for smaller jobs. It cuts an almost flawless line for butting siding to trim and is especially good at rake cuts or on gable ends, where running cuts are needed (**Figure D**). It's somewhat difficult to push down through the material, though, and multiple cuts are tiring. This tool is also rather bulky

Figure A. *The SS404 Snapper Shear will cruise through miles of siding between blade changes, and it's dust-free.*

Figure C. *The SS414 curve-cutting shear is the best tool I've found for cutting curves.*

Figure D. *The SS210M Manual Shear takes some effort, but it's great for rake cuts up to 21 inches long — no electric power needed.*

and heavy. Although it is strenuous for the user, it's handy for those times when electricity is not available.

## Improved Cutting With Saws

The one drawback shared by all of the shears is the inability to cut more than one piece at a time or to cut 3/4-inch Harditrim. So I always keep a circular saw ready for action.

Makita has come out with a unique line of dust-collecting saws for fiber-cement. The dust collector doesn't completely eliminate the dust, but does cut it down significantly (**Figure E**). By connecting these saws to a shop vacuum, however, they become almost dust-free. I like the Makita XSV10 type 4, heavy-duty (2 peak HP) wet/dry industrial vacuum (from Makita U.S.A, www.makitatools.com). It has a 10-gallon stainless steel tank with a crushproof 12-foot-by-1¹/₂-inch hose and a 14-inch metal-master nozzle. The dust collectors on these saws do hamper your view of the blade while cutting, but the guide on the shoe allows for accurate cuts.

Figure E. *By themselves, the dust collectors on these saws don't completely eliminate the dust, but they do cut it down. If you hook up a vacuum, however, they are just about dust-free.*

**Figure F.** *If you had to choose just one tool, the Makita 5057KB 110VAC, 7¹/₄-inch circular saw with dust collector (left) would be the one. The Makita 5044KB 4-inch circular saw with dust collector (right) is a compact saw that's as solid as the larger Makita, and will cut two pieces at once quite effectively.*

The Makita 5057KB 110-volt 7¹/₄-inch saw with dust collector is excellent for production fiber-cement siding work. It's solidly built and lightweight and cuts any type or size of fiber-cement material available. If you had to choose just one tool, this would be the one. It will make very smooth cuts through five pieces of siding at once (**Figure F**). With a cement-cutting diamond-tipped blade, it cuts smoothly and leaves the stock virtually flawless.

Another option from Makita is the 4-inch 5044KB with dust collector. This practical little saw is compact and great for tight spots. It won't cut as many pieces at a time as the larger model, but it's much more portable. I've used this one 25 feet up on a scaffold with no problem.

**Blades**

I tried blades made by American Tool, DeWalt, Hitachi, Magna, and the stock Makita blades that came with the saw. The blades all worked about the same, which was very well. I've been using some of these blades for almost eight months, and they are not even close to worn out. Typically, these blades have either four or six teeth. Those with more teeth cut smoother, but the blades with fewer teeth definitely last longer.

**What to Buy**

I'd advise anyone who installs cement siding with any frequency to invest in at least one set of nippers and one good dust-collecting circular saw with cement-cutting diamond-tip blades. For the contractor who only occasionally works with cement siding, or for the one-time installation, it's possible to get by with the old reliable circular saw using a diamond-tipped fiber-cement blade.

*Rodney Proctor is a general contractor in Cedar Park, Texas.*

# Chapter 12: Vinyl Siding

ED LADOUCEUR

# Durable Details for Vinyl Siding

by George Schambach

**Allowing for expansion and contraction is the key to a trouble-free installation.**

inyl siding is the highest-volume siding product on the residential market today. The material is relatively inexpensive, readily available, and requires few specialty tools to install. Yet despite the short learning curve, I'm constantly surprised by the number of installers who just can't seem to "get it right."

When our company receives a complaint from a customer, I'm one of the reps who goes out and inspects the work. Often, the customer will point out buckled fascia, loose siding panels, or wavy siding. Over 90% of these problems are because of fastening methods that do not allow the vinyl and aluminum products to expand and contract freely. I'll explain the methods contractors should use to avoid callbacks.

## Level the Playing Field

In most cases, siding should be installed level. On new homes, this is seldom a problem — you just snap a level line around the house by measuring off the foundation sill plate. But older homes can present a challenge. The foundation may have settled, or an addition may be seriously out of level.

Start laying out courses at the lowest spot on the structure, and use a transit, water level, or line level to establish ground zero. Measure up from this low point, and make a mark that represents the top of the first course of siding. Carry this mark around the entire

house, and use a chalk line to connect the points.

Foundations that crowd too far up into the siding can present problems when it's time to apply the siding starter strip. If the foundation wanders away from the siding plane (a stone foundation, for example), a plywood nailing band can be installed to extend a nailing base below the top of the foundation (**Figure 1**). To find the foundation high points, measure down from the level layout line.

## Starting Out Level

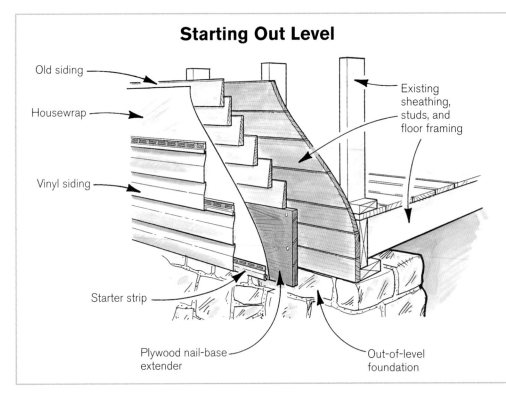

Old siding

Housewrap

Vinyl siding

Starter strip

Plywood nail-base extender

Existing sheathing, studs, and floor framing

Out-of-level foundation

**Figure 1.** Siding should be installed level. When foundations are out of level, extend the nail base with a piece of plywood that matches the thickness of the existing siding.

## Aluminum Soffit and Fascia Details

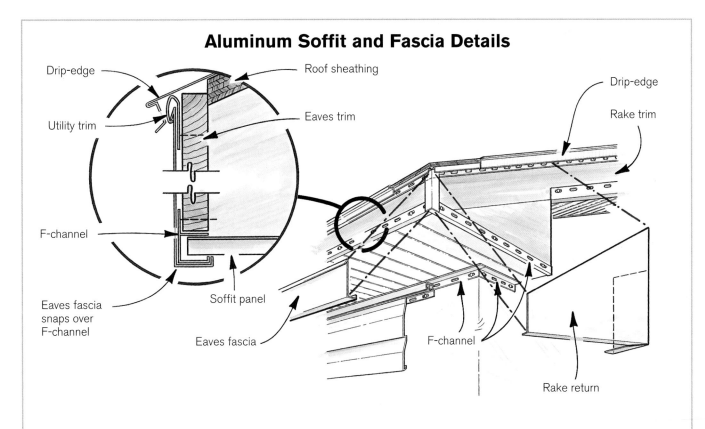

Drip-edge
Utility trim
F-channel
Eaves fascia snaps over F-channel
Roof sheathing
Eaves trim
Soffit panel
Eaves fascia
Drip-edge
Rake trim
F-channel
Rake return

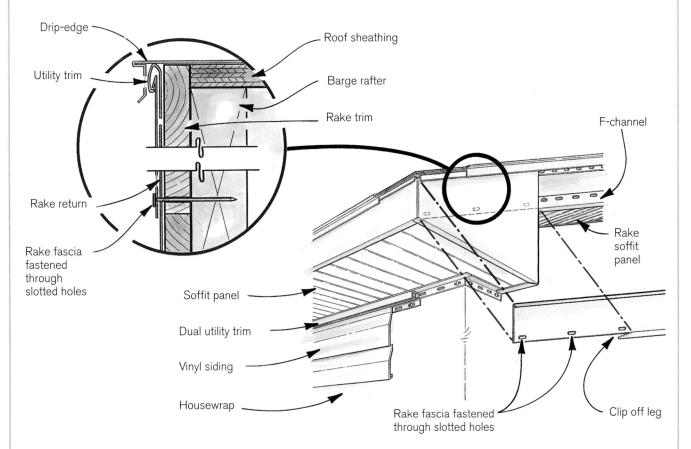

Drip-edge
Utility trim
Rake return
Rake fascia fastened through slotted holes
Roof sheathing
Barge rafter
Rake trim
Soffit panel
Dual utility trim
Vinyl siding
Housewrap
Rake fascia fastened through slotted holes
F-channel
Rake soffit panel
Clip off leg

**Figure 2.** The author prefers aluminum fascia, because it can be site-bent to trim out different rake and soffit configurations. Although small pieces of aluminum (such as the corner insert or the triangular return piece) may be nailed tight, the long lengths of fascia are held in place with trim strips or nails in slotted holes, which allow for movement.

**Figure 3.** Specialty tools are required for a quality vinyl job. Use a snap-lock punch to make tabs in the top edge of preformed metal fascia (far left). These tabs prevent the fascia from pulling out of the utility trim without restricting movement. A slot punch (left) makes the elongated nail holes that allow for movement under a nail head.

## Behind-the-Scenes Protection

Think of vinyl siding as more of a weather screen than a weather barrier. Wind-driven rain will make its way behind this screen. In new work, it's important that you carefully apply housewrap or felt paper before installing the siding. Make sure all seams are overlapped and taped, and that door and window openings are detailed properly.

When an older home is being resided, the vinyl is often installed over the existing siding. In these situations, it's important to "tighten up" the original siding. This usually involves fastening loose boards and recaulking around windows, doors, and other penetrations. Cosmetics aren't important — the goal is to provide a second line of defense for any moisture that finds its way past the vinyl siding.

## Fascia and Soffits

It's a good idea to complete the soffit and fascia work before installing the siding. Soffit material may be either vinyl or aluminum, but for fascia I prefer aluminum coil stock. It's thinner than vinyl, so joints

## Room to Move

It's essential that vinyl and aluminum products be allowed to expand and contract freely. The photos illustrate what happens if movement is restricted. To reduce the chance of problems, follow these guidelines:

- Think of vinyl and aluminum products as being hung, not fastened, in place. To prevent nails from restricting panel movement, installation literature specifies a 1/32-inch clearance between the nail head and the siding panel. I like to tell installation rookies that they should be able to slip the hook end of their tape measure between the nail head and the siding panel. All it takes is one overdriven nail to create problems.
- Adjust the recommended gapping (typically 1/4 inch) to allow for current temperatures. In extremely cold weather, use a slightly larger gap, since cold panels will be on the short side of the expansion and contraction cycle. Conversely, it doesn't hurt to tighten up the gaps in very hot weather.
- Be sure to place all nails in the center of the nailing slot. A nail shank that bottoms out in the nail slot of an expanding or contracting panel will restrict movement.

*A sliding panel that is not pulled up snug in the locking flange may come loose when warm temperatures cause the panel to expand (left). A panel installed in hot weather with the nails driven too tightly will tear when cold weather causes the panel to contract (right).*

- Pull each panel up snug against the locking hem of the previous panel, but do not overtighten. Panels that are pulled too tight can tear when they contract, just as loosely fit panels can pop loose as they expand.
- Fascia runs should never turn the corner. Stop all runs at inside and outside corners and slip a small corner insert behind the fascia to mask the subfascia. — *G.S.*

## Window Details

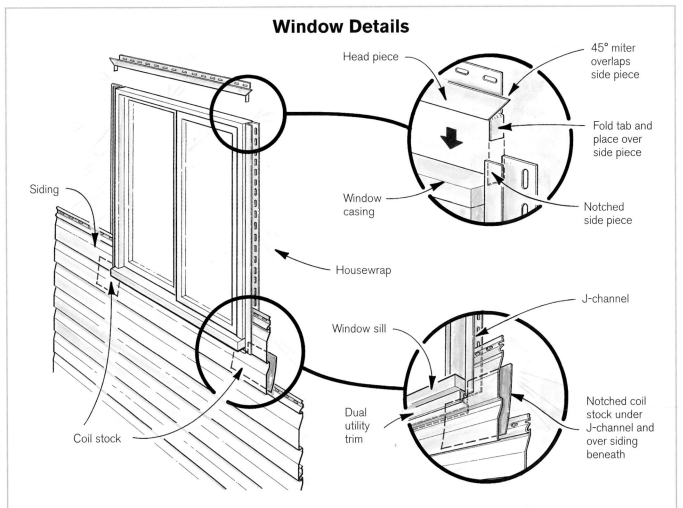

Head piece

45° miter overlaps side piece

Fold tab and place over side piece

Window casing

Notched side piece

Siding

Housewrap

J-channel

Window sill

Notched coil stock under J-channel and over siding beneath

Coil stock

Dual utility trim

**Figure 4.** When trimming a window, first run J-channel around all four sides, detailing the head piece as shown. Place a notched piece of coil stock at each corner of the sill to help direct water running down the J-channel over the top of the siding beneath.

are less apparent, and it can also be site-formed for a variety of eaves conditions.

Never use nails to fasten fascia. Instead, snap the fascia over the F-channel at the bottom of the subfascia and insert the top in a strip of vinyl utility trim under the roof drip-edge (**Figure 2**, page 209). The fascia material will be held firmly in place, but will still be able to expand and contract.

Punch locking tabs in the top edge of preformed fascia with a snap-lock punch (**Figure 3**). These tabs prevent the fascia from pulling out of the utility trim without restricting movement caused by changes in temperature. Fascia that is formed on site from thinner coil stock should have a continuous locking hem formed on the top edge. In addition to locking the open edge of the fascia in place, the hem adds stiffness and helps prevent buckling.

The lower edge of rake fascia should be fastened to the subfascia with aluminum trim nails driven through slot-punched holes. These slots permit the fascia to expand without buckling.

Many installers mistakenly "turn the corner" by

bending the fascia material at a 90-degree angle. Instead, stop fascia runs at inside and outside corners, and tuck a corner insert behind the fascia at these points. The insert provides a "background cover" that prevents the wooden subfascia from showing at the joint.

Soffit panels are held in place by the F-channel at the subfascia and a matching F-channel that's fastened to the wall. Slip the soffit panels into the F-channel slots, and snap the ends together using the locking hem formed into the panels.

### Hanging the Corners

Install vinyl corner posts at all inside and outside corners. To allow for expansion and contraction, the corner post is hung by placing a nail in the top of the uppermost nailing slot. The balance of the nailing should be in the center of the slots, 6 to 12 inches on-center. This allows expansion and contraction to occur at the bottom of the corner post. Hanging the corner post also makes installation easier. I've watched more

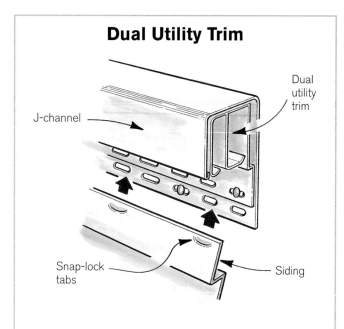

**Dual Utility Trim**

J-channel

Dual utility trim

Snap-lock tabs

Siding

**Figure 5.** Dual utility trim is used to secure panels that have been notched around openings. Use the outer channel if the notch ends at the thicker portion of the panel profile; use the inner channel when the notch ends at the thinner panel profile.

up tighter than the other. Don't do this: over-tensioned panels can tear when they contract. On the other hand, if the fit is too loose, the panel may work free from the locking hem as it expands.

Consider this scenario: It's 10°F outside and you just finished installing a 10-foot length of fascia on the west end of a house. Next summer, when the temperatures hit the high 90s and the sun-baked surface of the fascia reaches 120°F, that 10-foot length will have grown over 1/2 inch. If it can't expand freely, buckling will result.

If the scenario is reversed, and you've installed a 12-foot vinyl siding panel on the hottest day of the year, that panel can shrink a full 1/2 inch when temperatures drop to 10°F. The panel can tear apart if the shrinkage movement is restricted.

If it were up to me, I would require every vinyl siding crew to spend five minutes at the beginning of each day chanting the words: "expansion and contraction, expansion and contraction, expansion and contraction ...." This issue is responsible for more than 80% of the complaints I investigate.

## Door and Window Detailing

Use J-channel around windows and doors to receive the siding panels (**Figure 4**, previous page). The side pieces run long at window or door heads and are notched around the bottom of the sill. Miter the free flange of the head piece, and fold the remaining tab over the side piece to serve as a cap flashing. I recommend caulking around windows and doors before installing the J-channel.

When panels are notched to fit under windows or mounting blocks, the slotted nailing flange is removed. Secure these "flangeless" portions of the panel by fastening a piece of dual utility trim in the J-channel or mounting block, and slip the notched

than one contractor fight with a flopping corner post as they struggled to nail it from the bottom up.

Corner posts are available in 10- and 20-foot lengths. I always recommend using a one-piece corner post. Splices are unsightly, and if designed incorrectly may allow rain to enter.

After the corner posts are installed, measure down from the chalk line snapped earlier, and snap another line that represents the top edge of the starter strip. The starter strip layout line is typically 2 inches above the bottom edge of the first siding course, but the distance will vary depending on the manufacturer. When installing the starter strip, leave 1/4-inch gaps between butting ends and at corner posts.

## Running the Siding

Snap the first course of siding panels into the starter strip and fasten the panels along the top flange with nails driven through the center of the nailing slots. To allow for expansion and contraction, draw the nails up just short of snug (see "Room to Move," page 210). Use corrosion-resistant nails, with heads at least 5/16 inch in diameter (roofing nails, for example). Stagger the end laps and check alignment every five or six courses.

Always overlap panels so the exposed ends face away from main entrances and high-traffic areas. The lap joints will be much less noticeable as people approach the building.

Some installers will try to adjust the panel to an out-of-level condition by pulling one side of a panel

**Figure 6.** Subcontractors can create problems when they fasten exterior fixtures directly through the siding panels, preventing the panels from expanding and contracting freely. To avoid callbacks, use mounting blocks for all surface-mounted fixtures.

portion of the panel into one of the two receiving channels of the utility trim (**Figure 5**).

Use a snap-lock punch to punch barbs along the notched panel edge before inserting it into the utility trim. The barbs will hold the panel in place but allow the panel to expand and contract. Use this detail to secure the cut edge of panels at the soffit as well.

## Subtrade Sabotage

Surface-mounted exterior fixtures (electrical meter bases, shutters, dryer vents, hose bibs, etc.) should always be fastened to mounting blocks (**Figure 6**). The rationale is simple: any item that is fastened directly through a siding panel will lock the panel in place, short-circuiting the nailing slots that allow the panel to expand and contract.

Most suppliers keep a number of prefabricated mounting blocks in stock. Larger items (meter bases, for example) can be mounted on a 1 1/2-inch-thick piece of treated lumber.

No matter how careful you are when allowing for expansion and contraction, another trade can undo the best-laid plans of a quality siding installation in less than ten minutes. Plumbers, electricians, and the phone company installers should mount all of their devices or equipment on mounting blocks.

The general contractor is typically responsible for providing the siding installer with the type and location of required mounting blocks, but in many cases, the problems are created long after the project is completed. It's always a good idea to explain to both the general contractor and the homeowner what can happen if items are fastened directly through the siding. It may not always prevent problems, but at least you'll be able to say, "I told you so."

*Former siding contractor George Schambach, of Deposit, N.Y., owns Catskill Inspections.*

# Aluminum Trim for Vinyl Siding

by Blaine Miller

When it comes to vinyl siding, the hard part is getting the trim right. Fancy vinyl accessories are okay for new work, but they're too expensive for most retrofits, and they don't always work. Plus, trimming old, out-of-whack openings and covering the eaves will quickly eat up your profit.

After working on hundreds of siding jobs with my Dad and my brothers, we've figured out how to produce durable aluminum trim details using the fewest possible steps. The trick is getting everything on the house as uniform as possible before bending any metal. That way, you can mass-produce the bulk of the trim and install it all at once.

## Working With Coil Stock

Aluminum coil stock is one of the most versatile exterior covering materials available. It comes in a variety of colors to match or complement vinyl siding colors, with either a smooth painted surface or a textured vinyl coating. The vinyl-coated stock is a little more expensive ($80 per roll vs. $55 to $60) and is not reversible, but the color options may more closely match some siding accessories.

Narrower rolls are available, but we always buy the standard 24-inch-by-50-foot rolls and fabricate what we need on site using a 12-foot Tapco siding and trim brake (Tapco Integrated Tool Systems, www.tapcotools.com). We use a special holder that mounts on the rear of the brake and loads an entire roll of coil stock. The holder makes it easy to pull coil stock through and cut off whatever length is needed.

Trim wrapped in metal can look good or terrible, depending on how it is handled during fabrication and installation. Here are a few tips:

*Keep everything clean.* A metal shaving stuck in the brake can scratch the surface, and dirty tools and hands can make smudge marks that can't be cleaned off.

*Handle as little as possible.* The more fiddling you have to do with each piece, the greater the chances for damage. Get it made, and install it right away.

*Use hand seamers.* Everybody knows you need a brake to make a long bend, but some installers insist on using a block of wood and a hammer to make the smaller return bends. No wonder a lot of aluminum trim looks like someone pounded a coffee can over a board. Whenever the metal is going to be exposed, use a good set of hand seamers. We like to use seamers made by Malco (www.malcointl.com), which come in widths up to 9 inches.

*Prevent buckling.* Coil stock expands and contracts, so it can get wavy in the sun. To minimize buckling, we always create a 1-inch fold or hem on the edges of flat pieces. We also avoid putting nails through the face, and instead nail sparingly on the narrower sides or bottom.

**Figure 7.** To create a uniform base for the new siding, the author first cuts off window sill horns, then covers the existing siding and trim with a 3/8-inch-thick folding foam board (far left). Next, a layer of housewrap is carefully cut and folded into openings and fastened with roofing nails or staples (left).

## Prepping the Openings

When we start a new siding job, I dress out the window and door openings for trim while my brothers work on the fascia and soffit. This division of labor keeps us out of one another's way, and we each do what we're best at.

Nine times out of ten, the house we're working on will have old wooden windows with flat 1-by trim. As long as the original window frame and stops don't have to be replaced, we can trim out the openings with aluminum. Sash repairs or even vinyl replacement units can be added later. If the windows will be replaced with totally new units, then that work has to be done before we do any siding.

*Squaring up.* I start the job by "squaring up" the openings, using a small handsaw and a pry bar to cut off any sill returns and remove any other projections that will be hard to cover. Some people might complain that we're removing the details, but trying to duplicate moldings with tin will look more "fake" than just keeping nice clean lines. I also nail down any loose siding that might be sticking up, and prep any electrical outlets or water or fuel lines that might be in the way. This is also the time to do any last-minute caulking and sealing of the existing siding.

*Leveling the wall.* We use a 3/8-inch foam-core leveling board to completely cover the existing house (**Figure 7**). We float the leveling board right over any corner boards and existing window trim that are 1/2 inch or less proud of the wall. This trick makes the next steps easier, because it establishes a common surface for everything else to build on, and with vinyl siding those minor variations will not be noticeable.

Next, we wrap the building with Tyvek, to help reduce air infiltration and to establish a good drainage plane behind the vinyl siding and trim. I carefully cut the housewrap into the window opening and secure it with a few roofing nails or staples.

*Wood trim.* Once the surfaces have been prepped and leveled, I apply new wood trim to the window and door openings (**Figure 8**). We usually use 1x4 pine, but it depends on the job and the finished look the customer wants. The wood all gets covered, so No. 2 is good enough, but it does need to be straight and true. To avoid rattling the window, I use galvanized screws to attach these pieces.

**Figure 8.** New 1x4 wood trim is screwed through the foam into the existing casings. Less expensive No. 2 pine is adequate because it will be covered by metal, but the lumber needs to be straight.

## Bending Metal

Once the prep work is done on the entire house, I make and install the aluminum trim pieces. If the prep work was successful, I'll be able to bend most of the aluminum to the same specs, then fit the pieces to the openings by scribing and trimming to final size.

*Using the brake.* I start by cutting the coil stock to rough length and laying out my bends. To rip the

**Figure 9.** The author begins at the sill, scribing the brake-bent metal to finish length (above left), then cutting returns with tin snips (above right). Trim is never nailed through the face. Instead, fasteners are driven through the flanges and tabs (left), which are planned carefully so that joints drain properly without relying on caulk.

coil stock to width, I use a utility knife to deeply score one side while the material is locked in the brake. A couple of quick bends up and down and the piece snaps off cleanly.

To make a bend, I first mark the dimensions on the coil stock, then lock the jaws of the brake down on the marks and pull up on the lower jaw of the hinged brake. It's not rocket science, but it takes some experience to avoid over- or underbending. It's also important to have the brake adjusted for even tension along its length, so the stock doesn't slide as it's bent.

The brake only bends one way — up — so complicated profiles must be bent in the proper sequence, turning and flipping the stock as necessary. Some flat pieces, such as fascia covering, also need to be folded back on themselves, or "hemmed," to prevent buckling. To make a hem, I start by bending 1 inch from the edge as far as the brake will go, then pull the piece out and crimp it flat using the back of the bending handle against the top of the jaw — a fea-

ture built into the Tapco brake. If you're using a rented brake without this feature, you can make this crimp with a wide pair of hand seamers.

## Trimming a Window

Installation starts at the sill, which is the most complicated piece because it must extend completely under the window sash. I scribe (not measure) the rough pieces to final length, then make my final cuts with sharp tin snips (**Figure 9**). I make the final bends for returns and overlaps using a pair of hand seamers. It's important to plan the bends and tabs so that once installed, the aluminum covering acts like a flashing system to shed water without relying on caulks or sealants, which won't last long on the expanding aluminum.

If the sill trim stops short of the window sash (a mistake many installers make), water can run under the aluminum covering and rot out the sash. On this house I got lucky: I was able to loosen up the interior stop enough to slide the sill trim underneath. Other

**Figure 10.** The casing trim makes a clean corner where it meets and overlaps the sill (top left). At the top, the casing is square cut, then overlapped by the head trim, which is mitered and hemmed (right, top and above right). The final step is to install vinyl J-channel at the perimeter (above left).

times, I might have to cut a groove in the old sill with a handsaw, or finish the edge of the sill covering with a hem. If we're reusing the window sash, I also install new weatherstripping.

The side pieces go on next so they'll drain onto the sill, and the header trim comes last, lapping the side pieces and serving as a cap flashing for the vinyl siding (**Figure 10**). All of the trim is fastened through the tabs into the wall with roofing nails; returns are fastened to the edge of the wood casing with colored trim nails. Coil trim nails are available in aluminum and stainless steel, painted to match the coil stock. I predrill for all nails to minimize bending and buckling, and I keep nails out of the face of the stock whenever possible. The final step before moving on is to apply a vinyl J-channel around the unit to accept the vinyl siding.

## Fascia Covering

While I'm working on windows and doors, one of my brothers is prepping the eaves for fascia and soffit, and the other is cutting vinyl soffit and siding. When he is ready to nail up the soffit, I bend the fascia covering. The house shown in **Figure 11** had open-tail rafters, so we had to install a rough pine fascia on all the overhangs. The vinyl soffit floats in an F-channel against the house and is loosely nailed to the underside of the new fascia board. The aluminum covering then floats up under the metal drip-edge, or can be clipped into a vinyl trim channel if there is no drip-edge.

Aluminum fascia is simpler than the window and door trim, but there are still a few tricks. With a double fascia — a 1x4 over a 1x8, for instance — the bend in the covering will keep the aluminum from

**Figure 11.** To prevent buckling, the hemmed upper edge of the fascia trim metal is tucked under the existing drip-edge and nailed up from the bottom through the soffit (left). Similarly, the trim is allowed to "float" when covering old fascia molding (see illustration). To cover two-piece fascia, or when the roofline dips and sags, use two-piece trim nailed up from the bottom only.

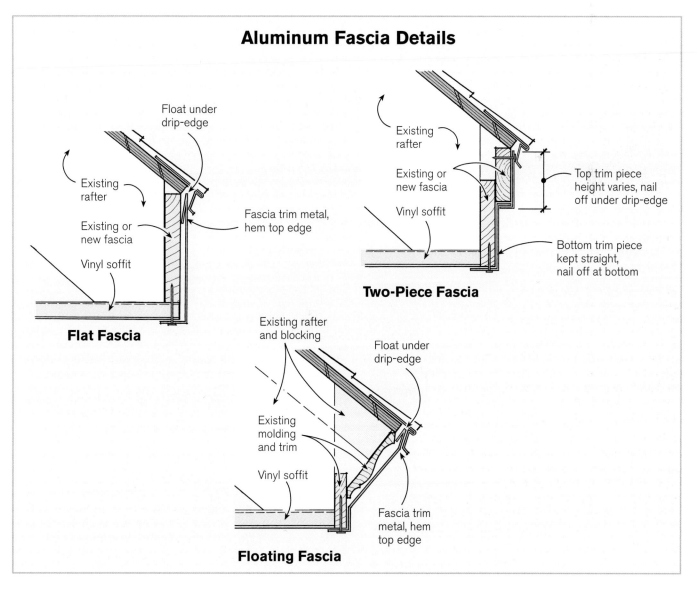

## Aluminum Fascia Details

**Flat Fascia**

- Float under drip-edge
- Existing rafter
- Existing or new fascia
- Fascia trim metal, hem top edge
- Vinyl soffit

**Two-Piece Fascia**

- Existing rafter
- Existing or new fascia
- Vinyl soffit
- Top trim piece height varies, nail off under drip-edge
- Bottom trim piece kept straight, nail off at bottom

**Floating Fascia**

- Existing rafter and blocking
- Float under drip-edge
- Existing molding and trim
- Vinyl soffit
- Fascia trim metal, hem top edge

# J-Less Doors and Windows

## by Ed Ladouceur

Although we use vinyl corner trim, we make most of our other trim from site-bent .019 aluminum coil stock. We buy prepainted aluminum from Alcoa because it comes in a wide range of colors that match perfectly with the Alcoa vinyl siding we most often use. We also use colored stainless steel nails and tinted caulk from Alcoa.

I don't like the look of J-channel around door and window casings, so we use a method that makes it unnecessary. Our "J-less" trim has an integral channel to receive the siding (see photos).

Not all portable brakes have the ability to make the tight reverse bends required; we use the Pro-III Port-O-Bender from Tapco (www.tapcotools.com). Another big advantage to our method is that we're not limited by the width or style of available vinyl trim. We can bend up whatever we need for any application.

Site-bent aluminum is ideal for rake and eaves trim on older houses, because it can be customized to compensate for out-of-square or out-of-level conditions. As with doors and windows, minimizing the use of J-channel goes a long way toward maintaining a convincingly woodlike appearance.

*Ed Ladouceur is president of the Storm Tite Company in Warwick, R.I.*

*The vertical leg of this site-bent window casing stock is designed to be fastened to the wall with stainless steel nails that are concealed by the siding. Mitered corners where the side and head casing meet are secured with a single stainless steel face nail. The lower horizontal leg is dimensioned to wrap around the window casing and be caulked in place (left). The base of the side casing is caulked to the aluminum-clad sill to provide a clean-looking "J-less" window surround (right).*

buckling (**Figure 11**, previous page). Where the fascia is flat, however, you can minimize buckling by putting a hem on the top edge. Fascia covering should "float" over existing molding profiles, and like the vinyl siding, it should be lapped away from the line of sight. If the roof line dips and dives more than the drip-edge can cover, the fascia can be installed in two pieces, keeping the bottom straight.

The same techniques we use for window and door trim and fascia coverings can be applied to other areas, such as frieze coverings and base trim, but we don't overdo it. Items like wide exterior columns almost never look good when covered with coil stock.

*Blaine Miller is part of a family roofing and siding business in Nelson, Pa.*

# Detail: Wood Trim for Vinyl Siding

by John Connor

We install vinyl siding on many of the custom homes we build. It provides the traditional look of clapboards while satisfying our customers' desires for a low-maintenance cladding. As an alternative to the standard J-mold trim at doors and windows, we've created a detail using 5/4 pine with a 5/8-by-5/8-inch rabbet that conceals the ends of the siding while maintaining the appearance of traditional wood trim.

The rabbet begins at the ends of the head trim, travels down the outside of the casing, then turns and runs along the bottom side of the sill trim (**Figure 12**). All of the edge milling is done ahead of time using a table saw on full-length 5/4 pine; the trim is also back-beveled so it sits flat over window and door flanges. After the trim is cut to finish length, we rout the ends of window and door casings as necessary to match the edge rabbets, then prime all sides and edges. Before we hang the trim, we also wrap the perimeter of the opening with a bituminous membrane or an extra layer of felt paper. For added protection against water, we set window flanges in a bead of silicone caulk.

The only place we use J-mold is at the head trim, because it serves to divert water away from the window (**Figure 13**, next page). We run the J-mold long, then turn the edges down so that water draining off the siding above is directed toward the rabbeted casing. We also use 5/4 wood trim under the sill casing to hold the top of the vinyl siding in place.

We use a similar rabbet detail at corner boards to conceal the siding. Since we also like to run corner boards through the skirtboard, the rabbet prevents moisture from building up in the vertical joint (**Figure 14**, next page). Occasionally, we'll use built-up trim at corner boards. Instead of rabbeting heavier stock, we'll lay 3/4-inch pine boards against the sheathing, then overlay another piece of 3/4-inch pine, creating an overhang at the edges to conceal the vinyl.

*John Connor and his brothers are partners in Connor Contracting, a general contracting company with offices in Berlin and St. Albans, Vt.*

**Figure 12.** To avoid exposed J-mold, the author conceals the ends of vinyl siding behind a rabbet cut into the outside edges of 5/4 pine trim. To protect against moisture, the window flanges are set in silicone caulk over a layer of bituminous membrane or felt that rims the opening.

# EXTERIORS

## Head Casing and Sill

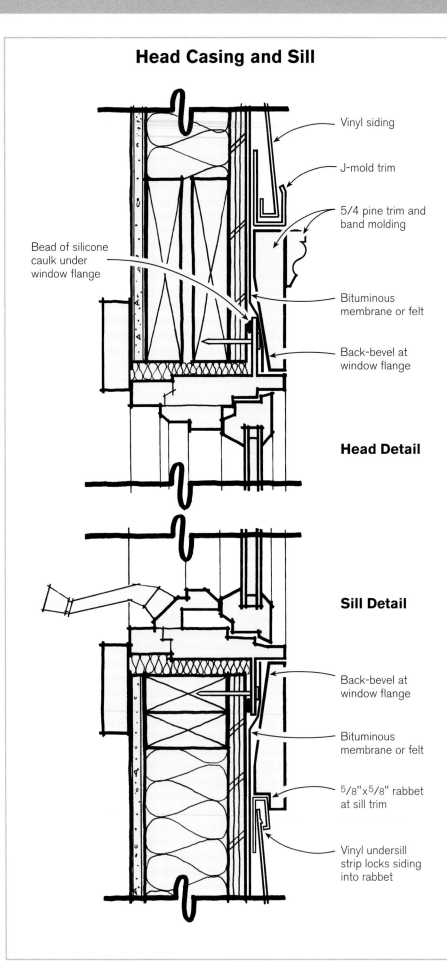

Bead of silicone caulk under window flange

Vinyl siding

J-mold trim

5/4 pine trim and band molding

Bituminous membrane or felt

Back-bevel at window flange

**Head Detail**

**Sill Detail**

Back-bevel at window flange

Bituminous membrane or felt

5/8"x5/8" rabbet at sill trim

Vinyl undersill strip locks siding into rabbet

**Figure 13.** J-mold is exposed only above the head trim (photo above). The molding is cut long and the ends are turned down to direct runoff into the rabbet. At the sill trim, a piece of vinyl undersill trim holds the vinyl siding in place (illustration, left).

**Figure 14.** At corners, the rabbet conceals the ends of the vinyl siding and provides good drainage at the vertical joint where the corner trim passes by the skirtboard (top). At built-up corner boards, 1-by stock applied over spacers achieves the same clean look (above).

# Chapter 13:
# Decks & Porches

- ■ **Fast, Stylish Custom Porches**

- ■ **Efficient Production of Premium Decks**

- ■ **Durable Deck Details**

# Fast, Stylish Custom Porches

by Jim Craig

My company specializes in decks and porches. We keep 10 two- to three-person crews in the field and build more than 90 screened porches every year. To compete against the many superb craftsmen in my area, we've had to develop methods and construction details that enable us to work efficiently and make a profit but still produce a porch that says quality.

## Premium Materials

For starters, I always use top-quality materials, for a couple of reasons. First, using premium materials reduces the risk of callbacks and warranty issues. Second, it tells my customers that I'm concerned about the longevity of my product. And because the materials cost more and have a reputation for quality, the markup yields a greater profit percentage than more conventional materials would.

***Kiln-dried PT.*** We use Madison Wood Preservers' (www.madwood.com) pressure-treated southern pine for all of the structural floor and enclosure framing, as well as for the newel posts and railing systems. Madison includes a water repellent in the treatment process to retard moisture absorption and to resist the effects of weathering.

***Primed trim.*** We use preprimed pine for all of our painted trim. This lumber is coated on all sides with an oil-based primer, and all minor defects and knots are filled and sealed with an exterior-grade filler to prevent sap streaking and bleeding. We apply two top coats of latex trim paint in the field.

**With high-quality materials and standardized methods, you can create custom screened porches at production speeds.**

***Trex.*** We use this wood-plastic composite lumber for the deck surfaces outside our screened porches, as well as for rail caps. It's good looking, machines easily, and cuts down on maintenance chores. Trex decking (www.trex.com) is available in 5/4 and 2-by profiles; we prefer the more substantial look of the 2-by stock.

**Figure 1.** The author installs 2x6 pressure-treated T&G decking to prevent insects from entering between the floorboards of a screened porch. The decking is blind-nailed through the tongue to conceal the fasteners.

**Figure 2.** Two-by blocking, installed on the flat between joists, supports the transition between the diagonally installed porch and Trex sundeck surfaces.

## Flooring to Keep Bugs Out

Many builders screen the underside of the porch deck or install a screened skirt panel around the porch perimeter to keep insects out. We prefer to use Madison's C-select 2x6 tongue-and-groove boards for a solid, gap-free porch floor (**Figure 1**). The product we use is kiln dried after treatment, which eliminates the warping, twisting, and splitting common with ordinary wet PT lumber.

The boards are reversible, with a square-edge finish on one side and a V-groove edge on the other. We typically install the boards diagonally across the joists, V-groove up, and blind-nail the boards through the tongue to conceal the fasteners.

There's a good reason I run my decking diagonally. Whenever you run decking perpendicular to the joists, you end up with scattered butt joints, which degrade the deck's appearance. By running the decking in opposing diagonals from a central point, you can cover a large surface with no end-butts. It's a clean, stylish look.

If a sundeck surrounds the porch, the two structures will share a common floor frame. I use gapped 2x6 Trex decking for the outside portion. To back the seam where the Trex meets the T&G decking, we install 2x6 PT blocking on the flat between joists, flush with the top edge (**Figure 2**).

*Floor framing.* Whether we're building a deck or a porch, we run the floor framing on 12-inch centers. Considering that we always use 2-by decking, that may seem like overkill when 16-inch, or even 24-inch, spacing would be acceptable. But 12-inch centers provide a stiffer platform to build the porch on, particularly if the porch structure is set in from the perimeter of the overall deck framing by several feet. I'd rather not have a cluttered-looking forest of posts and pilings below the deck to support the structure.

The added weight of the 2-by surface material — up to double the dead load of 1-by or 5/4 decking — also makes it advisable to beef up the framing. I run my Trex decking on the diagonal and screw it down at alternating edges to reduce the frequency and appearance of surface fasteners. The closer joist spacing keeps the screw pattern tight. Diagonal decking increases the distance that the board must span between joists, so, again, the closer spacing offsets this effect. And although 16-inch spacing may satisfy the code and my customers might not notice the difference, my floor systems are stiff and rugged — no one has ever complained to me about a springy-feeling deck.

## Framing the Enclosure

We assemble the pressure-treated porch enclosure system on the deck, using 4x4 uprights to define the openings, a 2x4 bottom plate, and a 1x4 top plate. Our stock black aluminum screening comes in 5-by-100-foot rolls, so I design the porch with 5-foot maximum spacing between the upright centerlines.

We have a standard 2'-8" x 6'-9" wooden screen door that we use on nearly every porch. To keep all of the openings at a uniform height around the enclosure, we cut all the uprights equal to the finished height of the door, plus swing clearance. Including the bottom plate, the resulting opening height is 6 feet 11 inches. A 2x4 stretcher at the head of the door opening compensates for the height gain of the bottom plate and provides a backer for the finish trim.

On top of the 1x4 top plate, we build a continuous box beam, using a pair of 2x6s flush with the outside of

## Screen Porch Section

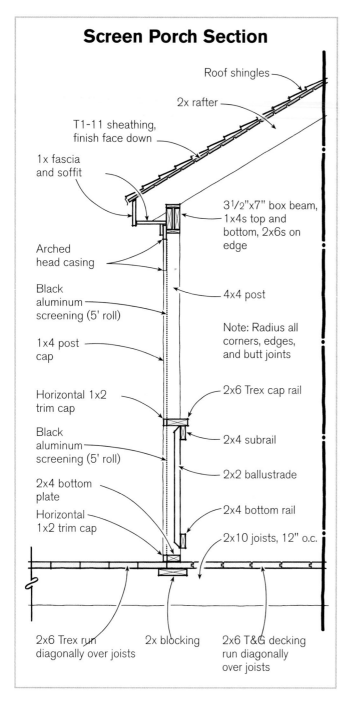

Roof shingles

2x rafter

T1-11 sheathing, finish face down

1x fascia and soffit

Arched head casing

Black aluminum screening (5' roll)

1x4 post cap

Horizontal 1x2 trim cap

Black aluminum screening (5' roll)

2x4 bottom plate

Horizontal 1x2 trim cap

3¹/2"x7" box beam, 1x4s top and bottom, 2x6s on edge

4x4 post

Note: Radius all corners, edges, and butt joints

2x6 Trex cap rail

2x4 subrail

2x2 ballustrade

2x4 bottom rail

2x10 joists, 12" o.c.

2x6 Trex run diagonally over joists

2x blocking

2x6 T&G decking run diagonally over joists

**Figure 3.** A box beam lintel consisting of 1x4 plates and 2x6 sides caps the 4x4 posts and runs the entire perimeter of the porch enclosure.

**Figure 4.** The author's signature "flying gable" roof helps keep windblown rain out of the porch.

the 3¹/2-inch-wide plate and capped with another 1x4 (**Figure 3**). We shoot all of these components together in place with 12-penny galvanized nails. There tends to be some discrepancy between the width of a 4x4 and the width of a 1x4. Because the screening and trim boards will be applied to the exterior face, we're careful to keep all of the framing flush to this plane.

## Building the Roof

The roof configuration depends on the porch design, which is keyed to the style of the home we're working on. One detail that we use on a straight gable roof has become something of a signature for us. We build what I call a flying gable, which, aside from being

attractive, has an important function (**Figure 4**). Water will penetrate only about a foot or so into the porch along the eaves during a rain, but it can penetrate much deeper through a high screened gable. The projecting "prow" of our flying gable provides a deep overhang that keeps the interior space drier.

We use treated lumber to frame the roof, too. The rafters rest directly on the 2x6 box beam. If the rafters are to remain exposed on the interior side, we use ⁵/8-inch T1-11 plywood channel siding, finish face down, to sheathe the roof. The siding provides a finished appearance inside and an adequate nail base for the roofing (it's thick enough to prevent ³/4-inch roofing fasteners from penetrating through to the

**Figure 5.** Surface-installed rails and balusters simplify construction and protect the screening from damage by children and pets. Because the screening doesn't contact the railing or balusters, they are barely visible from outside.

**Figure 6.** Asphalt roofing staples hold the screening tight, and are less tiring to install than conventional screen staples. Sagging screen is pulled tight between staples and secured to ensure a drum-tight fabric installation. One-by post caps and trim caps (left) conceal all staples and provide clean lines on the exterior.

interior). For a more formal interior, we'll frame a flat ceiling and finish it with clear fir T&G edge-and-center-bead paneling. We give the fir three coats of clear urethane finish, or prime and paint it to match the trim of the existing home — either way, it makes a beautiful ceiling.

*Roofing.* We generally use asphalt shingles on the roof, though occasionally we hire a metal roof specialist to install a standing-seam prefinished metal roof.

## Railings

Our typical porch railing system consists of a 2x4 sub- and top-rail with 2x2 square balusters. The balusters are beveled at each end and screwed to the wide face of the 2x4s on 4-inch centers. The 2x4 rails are nailed to the inside face of the 4x4 posts, mitered at inside corners. The balusters thus finish up 2 inches inside the outer face of the enclosure (**Figure 5**). We cap the subrail with a Trex 2x6, notching it fully around the 4x4 uprights. The outer edge of the rail cap ends up flush with the exterior post face. Wider than the 4x4 posts by 2 inches, the 2x6 cap rail overhangs the 2x4 subrail by 1/2 inch on the interior side of the enclosure.

An upgrade rail system consists of a colonial profile pressure-treated top- and shoe-rail, installed on-center between posts. The balusters fit into dadoed grooves in the rails.

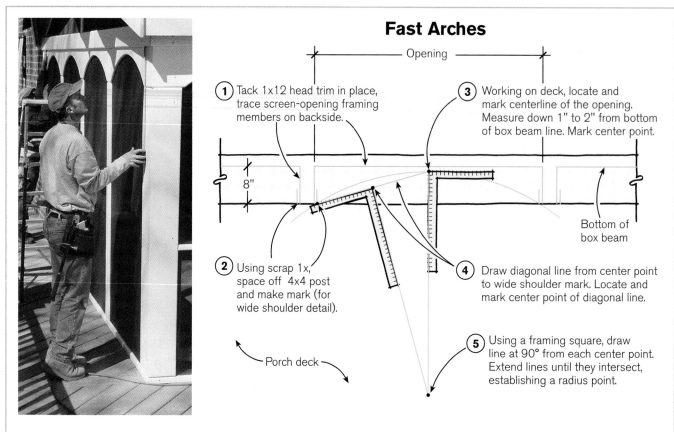

**Fast Arches**

Opening

1. Tack 1x12 head trim in place, trace screen-opening framing members on backside.

2. Using scrap 1x, space off 4x4 post and make mark (for wide shoulder detail).

3. Working on deck, locate and mark centerline of the opening. Measure down 1" to 2" from bottom of box beam line. Mark center point.

4. Draw diagonal line from center point to wide shoulder mark. Locate and mark center point of diagonal line.

5. Using a framing square, draw line at 90° from each center point. Extend lines until they intersect, establishing a radius point.

8"

Bottom of box beam

Porch deck

**Figure 7.** The author uses a simple method for producing custom arches in the continuous, dropped head casing that accents the individual screen openings. After establishing the radius point of the arch, he uses a site-made trammel stick to draw it directly on the 1x12 stock. The resulting arch, cut with a jigsaw, is perfectly matched to each opening.

## Screened Openings

Many builders rely on removable screen panels to complete the porch enclosure. Custom wood frames, aluminum frames with vinyl splines, or a combination of the two will certainly do the job, but they also add a lot of labor and unnecessary cost to the job.

My system is much faster to install, completely effective, and equally good looking. Once the framing is complete, it doesn't take long to screen the openings. We unroll and cut a length of screening sufficient to cover the opening from top to bottom. A couple of 3/4-by-1-inch-wide pneumatic roofing staples tack the screen at the top while we staple down one side, taking care not to pull and distort the screen (**Figure 6**, previous page). Then we staple the opposite side. If the staples are widely spaced initially, the installer can tug at the screen between fasteners to remove ripples and sags. After the bottom and top edges are tacked and the screen is drumtight, infill stapling completes the job. Any excess screening is trimmed away with a utility knife.

The use of roofing staples may seem unusual, but the heavier wire penetrates the hard pine more effectively than lightweight screening staples. Pneumatic stapling is also quicker and much less tiring than squeezing off an equal number of conventional screening staples.

## Arched Trim

Most of our porches feature painted trim that matches the existing house trim. Before installation, we paint the edges and one face of all the primed stock with two coats of premium exterior latex. Whenever possible, instead of measuring, we tack-fit and mark all of the trim in place for speed and accuracy. The first trim board to be fitted is the arched head casing above the openings (**Figure 7**), which is made from a single 1x12 with its lower edge dropped 8 inches below the box beam.

We trace all of the upright locations and the bottom edge of the box beam onto the backside of the head casing for layout and cutting. We hold a scrap of 1-by material alongside the top of the 4x4 posts to create a wide shoulder detail at the arches' spring lines.

Working on the deck, we use a quick layout method to establish the radius for the arches, then cut them out with a jig saw. We touch up the cut with a belt sander, then round over the edges with a 1/2-inch-radius router bit.

***Fast dimensions.*** Before we take the head casing back down for cutouts, we map out the rest of the trim. We temporarily cap the bottom plate with a continuous 1x2 base molding. This makes it easy to

**Figure 8.** Simple, router-rolled corners finish nearly every edge and joint in the system, giving an appearance of heightened detail while concealing small deviations in plane and material thickness.

mark all of the vertical 1x4 post trim in place by standing it on the base mold and marking it for cutting where it meets the head casing.

We cover the edge of the Trex rail cap with a piece of 1x2 horizontal trim. After dry fitting, we label all the pieces for location and take them down for cutting, edge routing, and painting. We prime all of the cuts with an oil-based primer, then coat the weather side of the trim with two coats of latex.

*Fussy details.* The routed rollover edge is another of our signature details (**Figure 8**). Every last finished edge, notch, and joint in my system receives the rollover treatment. The final appearance is not only

attractive, but also subtly informs my customers that every piece of the porch has been "fussed over." Rolling the edges also eliminates the need to shim joints for precise alignment — joints where the boards may be slightly out of plane or of unequal thickness.

When the paint is mostly dry, we install the trim in the same sequence as it was originally laid out: head casing, base mold, post caps, and frieze board. The frieze board closes the gap between the top of the head casing and the roof soffit. We fasten all of the trim with flush-set, stainless, hex-head finish screws. They're easy to reverse if you forget a step or need to make an adjustment.

*Finishing.* Although the trim goes up primed and painted, there's always a need for touch-ups. With all of the jobs I have going, I can keep a subcontracted paint crew pretty busy. To reinforce the water repellent in the treated lumber and keep it looking good, we always apply a semitransparent finish to the floor, American Building Restoration Products' (www.abrp.com) X-100 Natural Seal in Cedar Tone Gold shade. We use the same product in white for all of the railings and balusters. My customers receive a product brochure at the first sales call. I make sure that the supplier has stamped his business address and phone number on the brochure so customers know where to get their materials when it's time to stain or touch up again.

In my experience, the first stain job lasts only about three years on pressure-treated lumber. I tell the homeowner to expect this, but that the follow-up stain job should perform for seven years or more.

*Jim Craig is the owner of Craig Sundecks and Porches in Manassas, Va.*

# Efficient Production of Premium Decks

## by Jim Craig

My company has been building custom sun decks and porches in northern Virginia for more than 20 years. In that time, we've developed uniform production methods and selected premium materials that enable us to sell more than 120 projects every year.

Details and custom options not only sell decks but also provide opportunities for increased profit — typically 15% to 50% higher than for our basic specs. We offer many levels of sophistication, from basic railing systems to enclosed gazebos, decorative pergolas, hot tubs, built-in storage and planter boxes, and more. Nearly every option can be quickly estimated

by the square or linear foot, enabling us to value-engineer the project during the sales process. I have the unit prices memorized, which encourages the homeowner to come to a quick decision and speeds the process of getting a signed contract.

Whether we're subcontracting for a builder or working directly with the homeowner, I always consider how the deck will complement the home's appearance and function, as well as how it will unite the house with the landscape. Many homeowners have trouble visualizing an unbuilt project from sketches or plans, so I've developed a digital presentation portfolio for my laptop that contains images

For greater profits, use premium materials, production building methods, and a menu of custom touches.

of over 500 of our projects. This approach seems to work well — our closing rate in this region's high-end market is better than 50%.

## Materials Matter

Composite decking is our standard surface, and of all the options Trex is our favorite product. Because composites are perceived as a vast improvement over common pressure-treated decking, this choice sets up the basic expectation that we offer a better-quality product than other deck builders in our area. Specifying premium materials also allows us to increase our markup per square foot. For framing material, we use .40 pressure-treated No. 2 lumber, including double 2x10 or 2x12 girders, 6x6 structural posts, and 2x10 joists.

Self-cutting ceramic-coated screws speed assembly of railing systems and trim pieces. The reversibility of the screws allows us to fit many of the components, then disassemble them for painting.

I save a lot of money by purchasing all of our standard hardware in bulk — including nails, screws, bolts, joist hangers, and post bases — and maintaining a steady inventory. We buy our millwork, post caps, lighting fixtures, screen doors, stain, paint, and even skylights the same way. At the beginning of each week, our eight field crews stock up on supplies at our warehouse before heading off to their sites. That way, there's no time wasted on long trips to the lumberyard for small but essential items.

## The Right Size

To be truly functional, an outdoor deck should be no smaller than 450 square feet, with a minimum dimension of 12 feet deep. We try to keep lumber waste to a minimum by sizing our decks in even 2-foot increments, but we don't hesitate to deviate from that if it will result in a better-proportioned space (see "Deck Design Guidelines," page 231, for more design tips).

## Construction Details

Before we break ground for the footings, we assemble the deck framing on temporary support posts (**Figure 9**). This allows us to use a plumb bob to accurately position the anchor bolts for the permanent posts, which are supported by 18-inch-diameter concrete piers.

The piers themselves are poured directly into hand-dug holes that have been widened at the bottom to increase the bearing surface. (The rocky, clay-bound soil in our region provides the only form needed.) The piers are filled flush with the ground surface, making them inconspicuous. Although the code allows buried lumber posts on concrete pads placed below the frost line, I've seen plenty of rotted posts pulled from the ground — even pressure-treated posts — after only 15 years in service.

*Framing.* Whenever decking boards deflect underfoot, a deck can seem unpleasantly flimsy. To ensure a solid feel, we usually frame our decks with 2x10 joists on 12-inch centers. We typically run our decking diagonally. Trex is a dense, flexible material. Although you can special-order it in virtually any length, it becomes impractical to handle in lengths over 20 feet. Butt joints in decking are ugly, so I purposely break the deck surface into pattern sections limited by the maximum plank length and separated by inlet strips — full-width 2x6s that all the planks in an area die into (**Figure 10**).

A 2x10 finish band wraps the perimeter of the deck framing and conceals the joist end-nails.

*Working with Trex.* Because Trex doesn't have the warping tendency of solid lumber, heavy fastening isn't needed. Originally, our specs called for the decking to be screw-fastened on alternating sides of each board, one screw per joist, to minimize the pattern of the fasteners. But several years ago, our building department started requiring double fastening at every joist, so that's now our standard method.

A Quik Drive screw gun automatically sets proprietary square-drive, ceramic-coated trim-head screws below the surface (**Figure 11**, page 230). This leaves a little eruption of material, or "mushrooming," around the hole. While one worker screws the decking, another follows behind and hammers the mushrooms flush, effectively concealing the screw heads. To create a more finished appearance, we also use a router to radius the edges of all butt joints and any place where the decking changes direction.

**Figure 9.** The basic frame of the deck is assembled on temporary posts placed where they won't interfere with the permanent posts (above). The site for each footing is determined with a plumb bob, and the holes are dug by hand (top right). Once the concrete piers have been finished flush with the grade and drilled to accept an expansion bolt, the posts are fastened to post anchors with a palm nailer (above right).

**Figure 10.** Running the deck boards diagonally eliminates unsightly butt joints. The layout is planned so that no individual board will be longer than 20 feet (left). Joists are spaced on 1-foot centers to provide a stiff surface underfoot. Where adjacent diagonal runs meet, an inlet strip, fastened to blocking between joists (right), provides a pleasing transition.

**Figure 12.** Tropical hardwood decking is fastened with the Eb-Ty connector system, which uses a slot-mounted plastic biscuit. Rather than cutting individual slots with a biscuit jointer, the author increases productivity by ordering deck boards with premilled grooves.

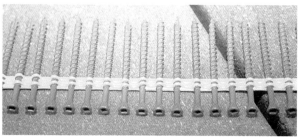

**Figure 11.** The decking is fastened with trim-head screws, which are buried slightly below the surface of the composite decking. Each screw creates a small "mushroom" that is hammered flat to conceal the screw head.

**Solid wood decking.** We offer solid-wood decking as a higher-priced upgrade. On those jobs, we use ipe, a tropical hardwood, and fasten it with Eb-Ty concealed connectors (Eb-Ty, www.ebty.com). The Eb-Ty connector is an oval-shaped plastic wafer designed to fit in a standard biscuit slot cut into the edge of the plank. We save significant time by ordering the 5/4x6 ipe planks premilled with a running groove on both edges, replacing the biscuit cutter entirely (**Figure 12**). But installing ipe still takes longer, because each connector must be individually screwed to the joist beneath.

**Railing posts.** We make most of our rail posts from 4x4 cedar, because pressure-treated posts tend to split and check as the lumber dries out. We occasionally use pressure-treated posts as a budget concession but only after warning the customer to expect those types of flaws. To locate the posts along the deck's perimeter, we divide each side of the deck into equal seg-

ments of 5 feet or less.

To make post installation as efficient as possible, we cut the 4x4s to a standard 45 1/2-inch length before squaring a line across each at the level of the deck surface. We then drive a hanger nail partway into the post, just above the line (**Figure 13**, page 232). This nail helps hold the post at the proper height while it's plumbed and temporarily toe-nailed in place. Once all the posts have been positioned in this way, each one is drilled for a pair of 1/2-inch carriage bolts spaced on either side of the centerline and as far apart vertically as the joist depth will allow.

We place a full post at either side of every corner and transitional angle, leaving a gap between them approximately as wide as the maximum 4-inch gap between balusters. This is structurally stronger than relying on a single post, and it gives a distinctive and substantial look to the railing system.

**Railing assembly.** We like to limit railing sections to maximum 5-foot lengths. Longer segments allow too much lateral deflection under loading and may also require awkward-looking intermediate support between deck and subrail to prevent sagging. After bolting the posts in place, we measure between sections and assemble a section of railing to fit. Our most popular railing systems include a top and bottom railing separated by the balusters.

Kids like to climb up on the horizontal subrail of a baluster railing to peer over the top. But all that hopping up and down soon separates the subrail from the balusters. To counteract that, we screw the center and end balusters through the top and bottom rails. That's much more effective than hoping kids won't be kids. The remaining balusters are secured with finish nails, which leave smaller, easily filled holes.

We always fill all fastener holes and sand and stain the railing systems. If the customer elects to use pres-

## Deck Design Guidelines

*Principal activities*. In planning a deck, we consider the three activities that decks are most often used for — socializing, barbecuing, and eating — and provide a distinct area for each. The socializing area should comfortably accommodate a few chairs, a lounger or two, and maybe an umbrella table. The minimum area I allow for this is 12-by-12 feet. An eating area, which will include a larger table and at least four chairs, also requires a minimum of 12-by-12 feet (**Figure A**). The grill area requires at least 50 square feet. Anything smaller compromises the comfortable enjoyment of the space.

*Let it flow.* It's important to place the deck stairs where traffic between the house and yard won't pass directly through any of those three areas. Placing stairs at an outside deck corner will usually create a diagonal flow across the deck, resulting in an awkward division of space. It's best to keep steps as close to the entry door as possible. If elements of the house or landscape make that impractical, I center the steps on the deck. A nominal 4-foot-wide walkway across the middle of a 16-by-28-foot deck will still provide comfortable 12-by-16-foot areas to either side.

*Location, location, location.* An attached deck built in the wrong place is destined to go unused. Placing the deck up against the home's breakfast and family areas makes it appealing and easy to use. Ideally, the location will allow indoor and outdoor activity and entertaining to flow seamlessly together.

*Not always on the sunny side*. The best side of the house for a deck isn't always the sunniest side, and sun isn't always the owner's objective. Mature trees can be a nice source of shade, but they also have some draw-

**Figure A.** *The three primary uses of a deck are socializing, cooking, and eating. Each activity should have its own space. Comfortable socializing and dining areas require at least 150 square feet each.*

**Figure B.** *Enclosing the base of a deck with paneling or lattice provides a ground-hugging look and prevents it from appearing spindly. Where an elevated deck is located above a walkout basement, substantial support posts help provide a solid feel.*

backs. A tree-shaded deck soon gets a stained and tired appearance as sap and pollen deposits take their toll. Where this is likely to be a problem, I recommend a darker decking color to help conceal any discoloration and reduce cleaning maintenance.

On the other hand, a dark surface on a sunny deck can become uncomfortably warm underfoot. In that case, I recommend a lighter-colored surface. Composite decking lumber is available in various shades to help accommodate those situations.

*Hugging the ground*. Because leggy decks with exposed posts tend to look unfinished and less secure, we keep our decks as low to the ground as possible. If the landscape falls away from the building, forcing an elevated deck, a skirt enclosure or latticework helps to visually anchor the deck. If the deck will be located above a walkout basement — especially one that provides finished living space — we sometimes extend the outdoor living space on both levels by installing a stone patio or ground-level platform below the main deck level, and connect the levels by steps and walkways (**Figure B**). The goal is for the deck to integrate the house and landscape.

*Paint and stain.* The average deck is built of pressure-treated lumber and simply left to weather. Meanwhile, the house to which it's attached has painted trim, siding, and other architectural embellishments. From the start, the deck looks like a crude alien growth. Extending the house trim color to the deck's perimeter, step risers, and railing system helps to integrate deck and house, creating a more refined look. We apply two coats of oil-based stain to all exposed wood surfaces. Few builders enjoy painting, and it certainly complicates the building schedule, but it adds to our profit, and it generates referrals because it really sets our decks apart. — *J.C.*

**Figure 13.** A temporary "hanger nail" driven into a precut post at the level of the deck surface provides temporary support while the post is tack-nailed in place before bolting (left). To provide a simpler, stronger installation, posts are paired at either side of angle transitions and corners. The 4-inch gap between posts corresponds to the standard baluster spacing (right).

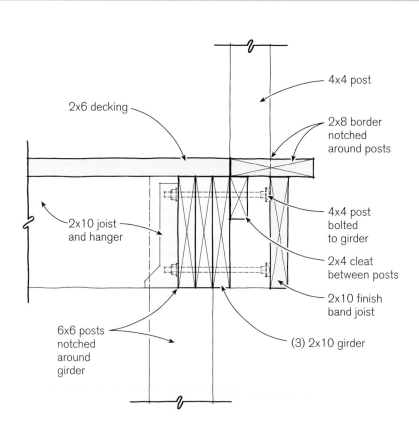

2x6 decking

4x4 post

2x8 border notched around posts

2x10 joist and hanger

4x4 post bolted to girder

2x4 cleat between posts

2x10 finish band joist

6x6 posts notched around girder

(3) 2x10 girder

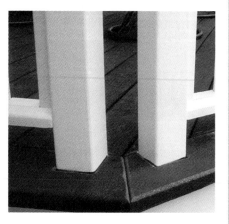

**Figure 14.** In an optional upgrade to the standard post system, the deck boards are cut flush with the girder, and 2x4 cleats are nailed between the posts (top right). A 2x10 finish band joist is then fastened to the faces of the posts, followed by a 2x8 laid flat and notched around the posts (illustration above). The embedded posts have a strong visual connection with the deck, while the overhang at the band joist creates an attractive shadow line (above right). The double posts at each corner and angle are stronger than a single post, and give the railing system a distinctive and substantial look.

**Figure 15.** The author's base-priced deck uses a square-baluster-and-rail system, but a broad range of additional styles are available for a variable upcharge, which is calculated by the linear foot. The ornate Chippendale railing (left) is a premium-priced option, while the Madison Colonial (right) is a more modest upgrade.

**Figure 16.** Built-in lighting adds after-dark atmosphere and improves safety. Low-voltage sconces are installed in the deck posts (far left), and step lights in the stair risers illuminate the treads (left).

sure-treated railing components, I recommend a darker finish color to better conceal the inevitable cracks and checks in the lumber. Lighter colors only highlight the defects.

## Upgrades

Details sell decks and increase our profits, so I charge for the details as separate line items.

*Decorative railings.* For example, the posts in our standard railing system are visibly bolted to the exposed face of the band joist, but we also offer an optional post detail that embeds their bases in the deck surface (**Figure 14**). The square-foot cost of our basic deck is based on the externally mounted posts. If the customer wants to upgrade to the embedded posts, we charge an additional $20 per linear foot of railing. If the customer selects our 6x6 cedar post option, which includes a decorative finial cap, chamfered corners, and a base molding, we charge $180 per post.

We also offer a broad range of railing options, from the upscale Chippendale style to the relatively modest Madison Colonial version (**Figure 15**). The latter isn't much more difficult to assemble than the base-priced square-baluster-and-rail system, but it provides a higher profit opportunity. If your average markup is, say, 35%, adding such higher-priced options can easily bump it to 50% or more.

*Outdoor lighting.* In recent years, local building departments have begun to require safety lighting for exterior stairs. This hasn't posed any problem for us, because we've always offered and recommended a lighting option (**Figure 16**). We use low-voltage Hadco sconce and step lights (Hadco, www.hadcolighting.com) that we build into the stair risers and mount on the rail posts. This makes the deck a much more pleasant place to be after dark, and it's a big selling point for us as well as an important source of added profit.

*Jim Craig is the owner of Craig Sundecks and Porches, in Manassas, Va.*

# Durable Deck Details

## by Ron Hamilton

The key to building decks profitably is quality. With so many low-end decks being built, durable and attractive decks built with premium materials act as advertising for future jobs — 80% of my jobs come through referrals and repeat business. Over the many years I've had my deck business, I've come up with some solid guidelines for each stage of construction.

### Design and Materials

First, I avoid low-end jobs and clients shopping for the absolute lowest price. In general when I design a deck, I avoid the simple square and rectangular designs that flood the market. Instead, I try to incorporate angles and I usually lay the decking at 45 degrees or with a combination of straight and angled sections.

I use only premium materials. One of the reasons so few contractors last in the deck market is that expensive callbacks eat into their profits, their reputations, and their time. I have very few callbacks, and some of my oldest decks still look great and continue to bring me referrals. Overall, premium materials are more than worth the added cost. They last longer and age with fewer problems.

Ninety percent of my work is with treated southern pine. Other naturally rot-resistant softwoods, like cedar, tend to be too soft and susceptible to surface wear. I use a premium-grade decking pretreated with a water repellant, such as GP's Southern Gold Plus decking (Georgia-Pacific, www.gp.com/build).

For fasteners, I use only screws and bolts. I avoid simple galvanized products and instead use other

**Figure 17.** Galvanized post anchors make for a secure attachment to concrete pier footings and help prevent decay at the bottom of the post.

coated products such as Dec-King Screws and RSS Lag Screws. Dec-King Screws (ITW Buildex, www.itwbuildex.com) have an electro-zinc base coat covered with a tough epoxy paint. RSS Lag Screws (GRK Canada, www.grkfasteners.com) are a thin-shank, high shear-strength fastener with a protective coating. I use these screws instead of traditional thick-shank lag screws because they have built-in washers and don't require predrilling.

Although using only bolts and screws takes more time, this makes a big difference in quality. Screws will not pull out over time as the lumber expands and contracts with temperature changes. Their stronger holding power also minimizes warping of the lumber.

### Deck Support

I usually use pier foundations built with foundation-grade 6x6 posts. Typically, one of my decks might project 16 feet out from the house wall. In that scenario, I

**Figure 18.** The author notches carrier beams into the 6x6 support posts (far left). The ends of the beams are clipped for a nicer appearance (left).

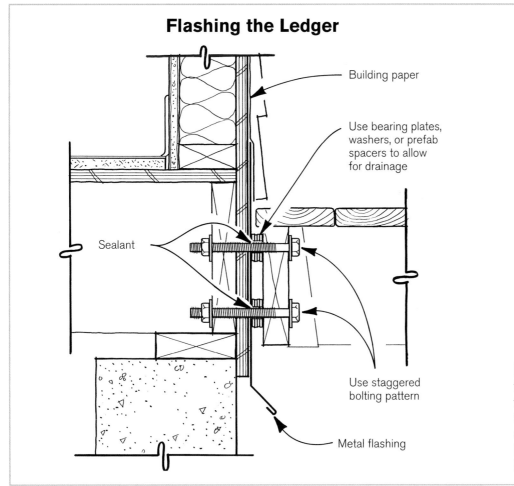

## Flashing the Ledger

Building paper

Use bearing plates, washers, or prefab spacers to allow for drainage

Sealant

Use staggered bolting pattern

Metal flashing

**Figure 19.** Properly flashing the ledger ensures that no water can get to the house framing and cause decay. The detail shown here allows water to drain behind the ledger.

place carrier beams at 7 and 14 feet. The 2-foot canti-lever allows for easy pier layout because the carrier beams do not have to be positioned exactly.

I set the posts on concrete pier footings placed 4 to 6 feet apart. These footings are 3 to 4 feet deep to protect against frost heaves. Recently I've begun using Simpson galvanized bases (www.strongtie.com) that anchor the posts to the concrete footings (**Figure 17**).

Next, I look to my framing layout to determine the overall height of the posts. The height of the finished decking is 3 inches below the door entry sill. On mul-tilevel decks, I plan finished decking heights to match my standard 7 1/2-inch stair-riser height. I use a water level to mark, then cut the posts to height. I notch the post tops to accept the carrier beams (**Figure 18**), which I attach with through-bolts. I also clip the visi-ble corners of the carrier beams for aesthetic reasons.

## Flashing the Ledger

I through-bolt the ledger to solid framing and use a flashing detail that prevents water from reaching the house framing (**Figure 19**). Although the ledger is pressure-treated, the sheathing and band joist are not. Any water trapped between the ledger and the sheathing can lead to rot, which threatens the struc-tural integrity of the ledger.

## Deck Framing

I usually use 2x8 joists 16 inches on-center. I have found that the best way to hang joists is to first screw them to the ledger to set them and then go back and install the joist hangers. Because I often install the decking at a 45-degree angle, I need to plan where the seams will fall while laying out the joists. Joists positioned at seams are raised to the level of the fin-ish decking (**Figure 20**, next page). I then install 2x6 ledgers on either side of the raised joists to support the ends of the decking. This detail visually breaks up the overall decking surface.

With the floor joists installed, I check the rim joists with a string line to avoid reproducing the bow of a house wall along the outer edge of the deck. Also, if the deck is not exactly square, the angled miter cuts of the decking will run off-line at the seams.

After making sure the deck joists are straight and square and trimming any long floor joists, I attach the outer rim joists with screws. I miter the rim joist cuts and pull the joints tight with five screws. I slightly overcut these miters to ensure a snug, clean joint line.

Then, before the decking goes down, I install block-ing for securing the railing posts (**Figure 21**, page 237). I make sure each post rests in a corner so it can be lag-screwed or bolted in two directions.

**Figure 20.** The author uses a raised joist with 2x6 cleats on both sides to catch the ends of angled or straight-run decking boards. This detail breaks up the decking into smaller areas and avoids the use of splices in the deck boards.

## Decking and Rails

I always order 15% more decking than I need for a job so I can pick only straight, unwarped pieces. I use 5/4x6 decking on most jobs. I install all decking heart side up and avoid seams by running mitered decking cuts into the raised joists I mentioned earlier.

Using a Makita (model 6832) autofeed screw gun, the decking goes down solid and will not loosen with time and weathering. Since the decking shrinks as it dries, I lay successive courses tight. This results in a gap of 1/8 to 1/4 inch after a few weeks. Spacing the deck boards during installation would result in gaps that are too wide.

## Dressing Up a Deck

*Decorative railings.* Liven up the railing by breaking up the monotony of the regular baluster pattern. I sometime use a sunrise pattern, for instance (see photo, below), with baluster "rays" sandwiched between arcs cut out of 2x12s. This pattern works well in a 5-foot length.

*Benches and planters.* Deck furniture often clogs up the middle floor space of a deck, while built-in benches encourage people to use the perimeter space. I build benches with 2x4 frames and 5/4x6 decking for seat and back. I make the seats 18 inches wide and recline the backs at 70 degrees.

*Routing.* As a finishing touch, round over all visible edges, including railing caps, stair treads, and any uncaptured edges of the decking.

*Glue.* Use a water-resistant treated-wood glue to ensure that miter joints remain tight over time.

*Water seal.* Apply immediately upon completion of deck. I use Wolman RainCoat (www.wolman.com).

— R.H.

*The sunrise pattern and built-in benches are two of the details the author uses to set his decks apart.*

**Figure 21.** Secure blocking below the deck provides a snug corner for bolting the bottom of rail posts.

Railings need to be strong for obvious safety reasons. I use a finish railing height of 36 inches for residential jobs, with railing posts every 4 to 6 feet. The 4x4 railing posts extend down through the decking and are lag-bolted into solid blocking. To attach balusters, I run 2x4s on the outer sides of the posts at the top and at deck level. I run the bottom 2x4s either flush to the decking or 3 inches up. Running them flush covers

any end checking that occurs as the decking dries out. Running the 2x4s 3 inches above allows a space for sweeping and snow removal. I cap the top with a 2x6, edge-routed for a more finished appearance.

## Stairways

I build stairs with a 7½-inch rise and either 2x10 or double 2x6 treads. I use a 2x8 riser to close the back of my stairs, which adds both cosmetic value and strength. When laying stairs out, I bring my first step off level with the deck floor. This allows me to lag-screw the stringer from the back of the rim joist. At grade, I either dig in solid 4-inch concrete blocks or pour a concrete pad.

## Pricing Jobs

On average, materials account for about 50% of the total cost of a job. I have set unit costs for standard extras such as benches and planters.

A typical 600-square-foot deck takes me and my small crew around four days: a day to dig and pour pier foundation footings, a day to frame, a day to install decking, and a day for steps and rails. Extra time is needed for options such as benches and planters. I bid nonstandard extras on a time and materials basis.

*Ron Hamilton, of Saylorsburg, Pa., owns Hamilton General Contracting.*

# Chapter 14:
# Interior Prep Work

■ **Running a Production Trim Business**

■ **Fine-Tuning the Frame for Finish**

# Running a Production Trim Business

by Keith Kelly

In the Charlotte, N.C., area, where my business partner and I work as interior trim carpenters, the landscape is dotted with countless new home developments. Capitalizing on the influx of people into the Sunbelt, many large national builders have set up operations here.

We decided to specialize in servicing the needs of these large national builders, so we've had to develop systems to cope with the large volume they require. In a sense, we've created subspecialties within the already specialized trade of interior trim carpentry. Our current methods allow us to produce a high-quality interior finish for our customers while working quickly and efficiently. I'll focus here on the three major subspecialties that enable us to trim hundreds of houses a year with surprisingly few people.

## Rough Trim Crew

We start with the "rough" trim crew; this is the group that trims what I call the meat-and-potatoes of a house. To guarantee that this crew can work as efficiently as possible, we first make sure that all the material is stacked in the garage or the house. By doing that, we avoid an unnecessary trip or a lost day.

Next, my partner or I make sure that all the appropriate door swings are clearly marked on the door-jamb rough openings (**Figure 1**). If the house has been primed or the drywall has been splatter-textured, it may be necessary to remark the door swings. This step is important, because it enables the carpenters to start spreading the doors throughout the house right away without having to consult the blueprints.

All the termination points of specialty trim such as crown, chair rail, wainscot, and so forth are next marked on the drywall in the appropriate rooms. Although we specialize in tract housing, a number of builders we work with are now offering semicustom homes, so marking out the specialty trim accurately is crucial.

Trim upgrades are clearly defined for us by the builder's sales center, which typically posts an option sheet on site for us to consult (**Figure 2**). This careful communication helps to ensure that customers get the upgrades they are paying for. It also helps to create uniformity in the builder's houses, so a customer can get the same finished product as a model home she visited in a different neighborhood.

Once these tasks are complete, the rough crew is prepared to work with few impediments. On occasion, a slight problem may arise — a door rough opening that is too large or a bowed stud in a wall, for example. Minor problems like these are commu-

**Figure 1.** Stocking the site with the complete trim package and marking door swings and special trim locations ahead of time (above) allow AMK's carpenters to do what they do best — work competently and efficiently.

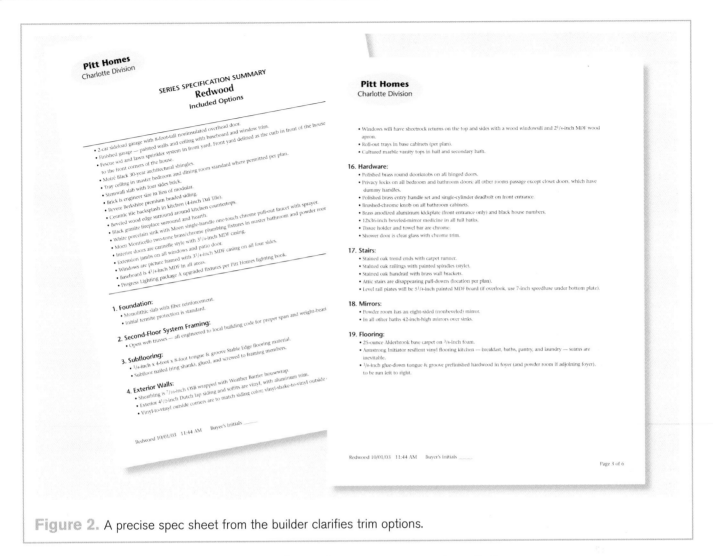

**Figure 2.** A precise spec sheet from the builder clarifies trim options.

nicated directly to the building superintendent, who then makes the necessary repair.

As a matter of good recordkeeping, as well as to limit the potential blame game, we note any such problems, whether minor or major, on our company's two-part carbon forms (**Figure 3**, next page). We record the date, subdivision name, lot number, and the supervisors of both our crew and the builder. If there's a need for extra material, for example, the quantity ordered is recorded and both the builder and our office get a copy. This serves two purposes. The first is that it prevents the inevitable confrontation that would happen when we needed the material to finish the house and no one remembered whether it was ordered. The second is that it allows us and the builder to track trends. If, for example, both our office and the superintendent notice that a particular floor plan is always short of base molding, then a revision can be made for all future takeoffs. This is especially helpful when a new home plan is developed. Using this method in some of the larger subdivisions, we have gotten material takeoffs so accurate that we've eliminated returns and saved the builder the cost of leftover material or restocking.

## Stair and Rail Crew

Assuming everything goes as planned, the house is then ready for our next subspecialty, the stair and railing crew. Although we call them our stair and rail crew, they concentrate mainly on railings. In our area of the country, most stairways are prebuilt in a factory and set in the field by either the frame carpenter or the stair maker. Nevertheless, our crew is able to site-build stairs when it's needed.

Although the stairs are prebuilt, the railing systems are not. Depending on what the customer selects or the style of the home, our crew might encounter post-to-post railings, volutes, pin-top easings and goosenecks, or occasionally wrought iron. We supply the stair crew with a well-appointed van equipped with any tools they might need — the usual trim equipment such as miter saws, finish guns, and table saws, as well as routers, a biscuit joiner, an assortment of clamps and glues, and, for the occasional blocking installation, a framing gun.

Blocking is critical for a secure, sturdy rail connection when the rail and rosette intersect with a wall. Unfortunately, the needed block is often overlooked by the rough carpenters. Our first reaction

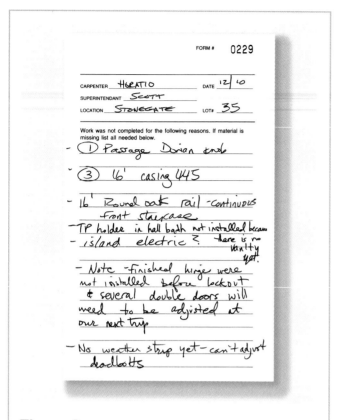

FORM # 0229

CARPENTER HORATIO   DATE 12/10
SUPERINTENDANT Scott
LOCATION Stonegate   LOT# 35

Work was not completed for the following reasons. If material is missing list all needed below.

- ① Passage Dorian knob
- ③ 16' casing 445
- 16' Round oak rail -continuous Front staircase.
- TP holder in hall bath not installed because
- island electric? there is no vanity yet.
- Note -finished hinge were not installed before lockout & several double doors will need to be adjusted at our next trip
- No weather strip yet - can't adjust deadbolts

**Figure 3.** A two-part carbon form records missing items before they get to be a big problem.

we screw the drywall patch back to the studs and mark it clearly with an X so the touchup crews won't miss it.

In addition to the necessary tools, we also stock a large assortment of fasteners, wood plugs, and extra rail fittings such as goosenecks and easings, just in case of the rare mistake. Our stair crew requires little supervision; they're seasoned veterans and are more than capable of spotting potential problems. Instead, at this stage, my partner or I take the time to make a trim punch list. If we notice anything that's missing or not up to our standards, we'll have the rail crew complete the punch-out before they leave.

Victims of their own efficiency, our rail crew is rarely unable to complete at least one house's rail system in a day. Rather than have them unpack all their tools and start a second house, we typically use their time to catch loose ends. Sometimes the "extra" time can be used to build specialty items such as bookshelves, art niches, or mantels.

Although there are local competitors who specialize only in the fabrication and installation of stairs and railings, our system is both efficient and cost effective for our customers. Because we eliminate the need to bring in another subcontractor, we avoid the scheduling conflicts that might arise. For example, when our company installs both the trim and the railings, we're clear on who's running the base cap on the stringers, and how the various baseboard termination details will get built. Although items like these may seem trivial, we aim to finish the house as close to 100% as possible before the painters are scheduled to begin. We learned long ago that a return trip into a production house is neither cost effective nor good for our reputation.

used to be to rip open the wall and nail a block in from the front side, but we've learned that it's far less obtrusive to cut the drywall on the back of the wall. After locating the stud bay where the blocking is to be installed, we cut the drywall very carefully so that the same piece can be reinstalled for a perfect patch (**Figure 4**). After the block is nailed off,

**Figure 4.** The crew opens up the back of the wall to add missing blocking for a stair-rail rosette. The drywall is cut carefully and reinstralled, producing an invisible patch.

**Figure 5.** Lockout crews install door and other hardware and fine-tune the finished job.

## Lockout Crew

Our first phase is typically finished when the rail system is complete and the house is completely trimmed. Later, after the painting is done and the finish floors are installed, we bring in our "lockout" crews. In our area of the Southeast, lockout entails installing all the interior doorknobs, exterior locks and deadbolts, house numbers, and kickplates, and running any shoe moldings on hardwood, tile, and vinyl floors (**Figure 5**). Depending on the scope of work, it might also include installation of bath accessories such as toiler paper holders, towels bars, and medicine cabinets.

Early on, we couldn't rationalize how these functions fell under our scope of work, but we've since come to use the lockout as a fine-tuning process. Any doors that need to be adjusted or trimmed are done at this stage. Exterior doors, which are almost always set by the framers, are given a final adjustment so that they operate easily for the new owners. Plus, we have one last opportunity to correct any small mistakes or to finish any task left hanging. For example, the lockout crew sometimes has to patch in small sections of base molding that we may have been unable to complete during the first trim — for example, next to base cabinets that were not yet set. Lockout gives us a chance to catch these things. Upon completion of lock, the house should be totally finished, according to our scope of work.

An added benefit of our lockout process is that it creates a great opportunity for us to try out potential carpenters before throwing them into the faster-paced rough crews. It's become a sort of minor league for our company. We feel it provides a great advantage for a new carpenter to see what we expect in the finished house.

By creating a familiarity with the final process, we also believe it leads to greater efficiency when trimming new houses. Nothing can be more counterproductive than having to explain every detail of what we expect a finished house to look like or having the carpenter feel that he has to ask lots of questions before installing trim. Many of our long-term carpenters started out on our lockout crews and still fill in there when needed.

## Uniformity and Flexibility

In conjunction with this informal training process, we also try to keep the same group of carpenters working in the same product line when possible. One of the biggest demands that our national builder clients make is for a uniform finished product. One builder told us that they like to enter a house and not know what area of the country they're in. Needless to say, that sort of uniformity doesn't happen overnight, so it's crucial for us to maintain a stable group of employees. Fortunately for my partner and me, our carpenter turnover has been very low. In fact, nearly two-thirds of the carpenters on our jobs have been working with us for at least three years. This stability has helped eliminate what I call the "A-team, B-team mentality" — what you get when you hire some really good carpenters and some not-so-good carpenters. Instead, we like to employ exceptional carpenters and excellent carpenters.

We realized a long time ago that things will not always go as planned. People call in sick, trucks break down, and houses are not always ready when a builder says they will be. By accounting for the many variables of completing a house quickly and efficiently, we've created a system of redundancy that allows everyone to settle into their own routine, performing the tasks they enjoy most and reaping the satisfaction of great productivity and a job well done. At the same time, there's just enough flexibility to prevent anyone from getting bored. Because our carpenters are versatile, if we need someone to change gears and pitch in to finish a job on time, it's not a problem.

The result is a system that allows us to trim several homes a day without having to compromise our quality, while providing a satisfying work environment for our carpenters.

*Keith Kelly runs AMK Construction in Charlotte, N.C., along with his partner, Wally Ackerson.*

# Fine-Tuning the Frame for Finish

by Frank Caputo

A s an interior trim contractor, I know my work won't look good if the framers are sloppy. That's why I always carefully inspect the walls before my crew shows up — hopefully before the drywall is hung.

Sometimes, when it's my first time working for a GC, the drywall's installed before I even see the site. I'll still do the inspection, but if I encounter surfaces that are lumpy, bowed, or out of plumb, I make it clear that unless the builder tears off the drywall and fixes the frame, the trim won't look right. The builder has to do this only once to realize that it's cheaper and easier to inspect and fix the frame before the drywall or plaster goes up (see "Plaster Tricks," facing page).

**Figure 6.** The author checks rough openings for width (above left), height (above), and plumb in both directions (far left). He marks obvious problems with paint, or writes notes on tape if the problem is less obvious (left).

## Plaster Tricks

### by David Frane

On walls that will be finished with a skim coat of plaster, you'll get a neater trim job by borrowing a technique from the days of wood lath and three-coat plaster: the plaster ground (see illustration). Plaster grounds are wood strips that are installed where they will be covered by interior trim and that serve as trowel guides during plastering. When properly shimmed to create a uniform plane, plaster grounds keep wall surfaces uniform where they need to be. Doors go in quicker, and casings lay flat against the plaster without the need to chop plaster, taper jambs, or plane the backs of casings.

It takes time to install grounds, so use them only where you have to meet exacting tolerances or where the grounds will pay for themselves by speeding up the finish work. Grounds don't make the plasterer's job any harder, but they make extra work for the drywall hanger, who will have to cut the blueboard to fit around them.

We often install plaster grounds just below the tops of baseboards and along both edges of crown moldings. Exterior window and door jambs can be used as grounds, too, since they go in before the drywall. For interior doors that get installed after the plaster, we sometimes nail 1/4-inch-thick lauan strips around the edges of rough openings, letting them project the same distance past the face of the blueboard as the door jamb will.

*David Frane is a senior editor at* JLC *and a former builder.*

### Using Plastic Grounds

Plaster grounds

Crown molding

Moisture-resistant drywall for skim-coat plaster

Chair rail

Plaster grounds

Baseboard

**Flat walls.** *On walls that will receive a plaster skim coat, the author uses plaster grounds — wood strips that serve as trowel guides during plastering and that are later hidden by trim. This ensures a flat wall surface behind running trim.*

---

The builders I regularly work for pay me to inspect the framing because they know that I'll not only look for problems that will affect trim, but also point out other defects that may reduce the quality of the finished home. When I find a problem, I mark the area with spray paint and maybe write a note on the stud. The builder then has the framer — or another sub — fix the problems, and I inspect one more time.

When the repairs pass muster, the builder has drywall installed.

## Door Openings

I begin by checking every door opening for height, width, plumb, and swing (**Figure 6**). I also check to make sure the jack studs align with the kings and that all studs align with headers and plates. This sounds pretty basic, and you'd think the framers would be able to get it right, but I constantly find errors.

*Out-of-plane framing.* Say the header projects 1/8 inch beyond the jack on one side of the wall, and the king stud projects 1/8 inch beyond on the other; now

you've got a wall that's 1/4 inch too thick (**Figure 7**, next page). If this weren't fixed, I'd have to beat and chop the drywall to get the casings to lie flat. So I mark the problem area, and the framers fix it either by hammering the framing into line or by shaving it flush with a power planer.

*Check the R.O.s.* A couple of years ago I was working for a new builder on a large house and didn't have the opportunity to check the frame before drywall. The first passage door header I measured was 97 inches off the floor, and I needed a minimum of 98 inches for the custom doors, which were already on site. Going around the house, I found that every door opening was an inch too short. To get the doors to fit we had to cut out the bottoms of the headers — an all-day project that made a terrible mess.

The site supervisor had assumed the framer would get it right, and the sales rep for the door company didn't measure the R.O.s. It was a costly mistake that had been overlooked by three different people; someone should have checked those openings before the drywall went up.

**Figure 7.** This header (left) and rough sill (center) will have to be beat or planed flush to the jacks. At right, spray paint indicates doubled studs that need to be planed flush to one another.

**Figure 8.** This electrical box was originally installed tight to the king stud, but later was blocked to provide clearance between the cover plate and casing.

*Blocking.* It's important to know in advance the width of the casings. Back when 1⅝-inch and 2¼-inch casings were the norm, electrical boxes and baseboards could be fastened to the king studs. But with wider casings, you have to block electrical boxes off the studs; otherwise the cover plate won't clear the casing (**Figure 8**). When the casing is wider than the door trimmers, I recommend putting a block at the floor, too, to catch the top end of the baseboard. This may sound like Framing 101, but oversights happen and it's nice to catch them before drywall.

## Windows and Exterior Doors

Next, I inspect the windows, to make sure that each one operates freely and, when opened slightly, leaves an even gap between sash and jamb. If the gap tapers, it means the window was installed out of

**Figure 9.** The author sights the gap between this slider and its jamb to make sure the unit is installed square (far left). The green arrow indicates that shims are missing at the lock. When window or door units are not installed properly, a note tells the framers to reset or adjust the units (left).

Figure 10. Low spots in the framing (far left) can be padded out with drywall shims, dense strips of a cardboard sold by drywall suppliers (left). The shims come in bundles of 50 or 100 and are 3 to 4 feet long, 1½ inches wide, and about 1/16 inch thick.

Figure 11. Although parts of this wall (left) have already been planed, the author checks it again for flatness because it will receive wainscot paneling. The junction between floors is a common problem area in stairwells (center); the overhanging subfloor (right) will have to be trimmed to prevent an obvious bump in the drywall.

square and needs to be reset. I check for the same things on sliders, and that the jamb is shimmed at the lock (Figure 9).

With vinyl windows, it's common to return the drywall into the opening and butt it to the windows. When that's the finish detail, I make sure that the windows are centered in the openings; if they're not, the reveal between the drywall and the jamb will be uneven.

Since resetting windows is not always easy, I may recommend centering a unit by padding out one side of the opening. If the window is getting jamb extensions, the finish carpenter can even the reveals.

I always check the alignment of ganged windows, and between doors and flanking windows or sidelights. If these units are to be connected by casings, then the heads need to be perfectly aligned. If they are off by more than ⅛ inch, I'll ask the contractor to reset them.

### Walls

After that I check all the walls for flatness, using an 8-foot level as a straightedge and looking for gaps or bumps that exceed ⅛ inch. I examine the wall at several elevations and mark trouble spots with paint. The framers will plane the high spots and shim the low ones (Figure 10). It's often easier just to replace

**Figure 12.** In the bathroom, the author checks the height of the blocking for the toilet-paper holder (left) and leaves a note for the contractor indicating that blocking is needed for linen-closet shelves (right).

any badly bowed studs. The goal is to make the wall as flat and straight as possible before covering it with drywall.

Certain walls are critical. For example, a bowed stud behind a vanity may prevent the wall mirror from lying flat. A bump in a wall behind a planned run of cabinets may also need to be addressed: while it may not show at the cabinets — which get shimmed straight — it will show up at the backsplash.

I also carefully check any wall that's receiving wainscot paneling or horizontal trim like chair rail or crown (**Figure 11**, previous page). Dips and bumps that aren't noticeable in a vast expanse of drywall will suddenly become visible when you cover them with trim.

For instance, I once installed a chair rail in a dining room where a 3-foot section of wall was badly bowed; I had told the builder he needed to fix it and he'd said, "It's okay the way it is, just do the best you can." Of course the bow looked even worse once the trim was on. The builder didn't like what he saw, and he had to demo the drywall, plane the studs, repair the drywall, and install the trim a second time.

*Backing.* I also look for backing for fixtures like toilet-paper holders, towel bars, vanity sinks, handrails, and bar tops (**Figure 12**). And I make sure there's proper backing for beamed ceilings.

On cabinet walls, I compare the framing with the layout from the cabinet shop (**Figure 13**). I want to make sure that all the electrical outlets and plumbing and gas stub-outs are where they're supposed to be. I also check the heating vents to verify that they are blocked, secured, and not so high that they interfere with the crown.

**Figure 13.** The author gives special attention to kitchens, checking to see that the walls are flat at the backsplash and that all rough-ins are in their correct locations.

**Figure 14.** Soffits must be plumb (far left) and level (left). Low joist hangers (below left) also have to be fixed.

*Ceilings.* Ceilings should be flat, and details like soffits and coffers should be straight, plumb, level, and aligned where they meet (**Figure 14**). We install a lot of crown around soffits and coffers, and it doesn't look right if the vertical framing is out of plumb. I also check to see that any nailing blocks that have been installed are flush to the face of the joist or stud. If the blocking stands proud, I mark it so that the framer knows to plane it or beat it back.

Although checking an entire house may sound like a lot of trouble, the effort is worthwhile. It usually takes me most of a day to inspect a typical 5,000-square-foot home, and another couple of hours to inspect the repairs. And the builders don't complain about paying me, because they know that the cost of repairing any problems after the drywall's up would far exceed the price of my inspection.

For my part, I know that if the frame is right, I can produce the kind of topnotch finish work both the builder and I will be proud of.

*Frank Caputo is a finish carpentry contractor in Cool, Calif.*

# Flattening Walls for Paneling

## by Rick Castillo

I work as a finish carpenter in the Santa Barbara, Calif., area. Although some of my finish work has included installing the cheap, faux-walnut panels, I've also had the pleasure of working with intricate hardwood paneling and ornate frame-and-panel wainscoting. I use a couple of tricks to prepare the out-of-true walls to receive the paneling.

## Spot Check

It's crucial to thoroughly check the floor, walls, and ceiling of the room for level, plumb, and square. I start at the floor and use a builder's level or water level to locate the highest point in the flooring. Because I've been caught before, I also make sure the other trades have properly nailed off all of their work. If the floor framing has been exposed to the elements for any length of time, it's quite possible that some nails have worked loose and the subfloor has moved. Also, loose drywall will throw off your measurements, especially in the corners.

**Benchmark.** The first step is to locate and mark the high point in the floor; this will be the benchmark for all vertical measurements. Too often an inexperienced carpenter will start to install paneling at the low point of the room and discover on rounding the corner that the bottom rail of the frame-and-panel assembly has to be tapered for the tops to meet at the corner.

The next step is to confirm that all of the door and window jam heights are uniform and are at the same elevation from the benchmark. If the doors and windows are all in the proper relationship to one another, paneling around them will flow much faster and look much better. Again, the builder's level works best for this job.

I then use a tape to compare horizontal distances between sets of doors and pairs of windows to make sure they are also uniform.

**Crowns and valleys.** I examine the walls for crowned studs and bows using a 6-foot level held horizontally on edge. By sliding the level across the studs, you can quickly locate the high spots and find any large curves in the wall. As I move around the room, I power-plane any protruding studs to bring them back into plane with adjacent studs. Finally, I check the ceiling to find the lowest point.

## Box Within a Box

The most serious defect, whether it's the uneven floor, bowed wall framing, misaligned doors or windows, or a low ceiling corner, determines the next step. The goal is to establish a new plane for the paneling. In essence, I am laying out and creating (with the aid of shims) a surface that forms a perfectly flat and square box just touching the inside points of the actual out-of-square, out-of-plumb, curved-and-skewed existing room.

Once I establish the new planes, I mark the floor with a chalk line, then transfer the line up to the walls using shims nailed to the studs. For instance, if two of the four walls are leaning inward and a third has a bow in it that curves away from the center of the room, I have three new "margins," as I call them, marked on the floor. I then transfer the lines up the walls by shimming out portions of the wall to these new planes. Once I've established the new "box," I can figure out an accurate layout for the paneling.

## Grounding on Two Screws

Furring the walls to the new margin lines is time-consuming and tedious. To speed the process, I use partially driven drywall screws as a ground for my 6-foot level to create straight and plumb walls. First, I drive a drywall screw near the sole plate and adjust it out to the chalk line. I then drive another screw at a point on the stud 5 feet or so above the first screw and make minor adjustments in or out so my level is plumb when pushed against both of the screws. The goal is to transfer a perfectly plumb line from the control line on the floor up the face of the wall. It then becomes a matter of simply filling in the space between the level and the wall with shims. The furring can be done much faster because you are working to the edge of the level instead of a plumb line. I simply insert two shims from opposite sides until they touch the level, remove the level, and shoot them with a nail gun.

**More screw tricks.** The drywall screw technique is also useful when installing a coffered ceiling. The approach is the same as with a vertical wall except you are dealing with a horizontal plane. You can also use the same trick to true up a twisted structural post when wrapping it with finished lumber.

*Rick Castillo is a finish contractor working in southern California.*

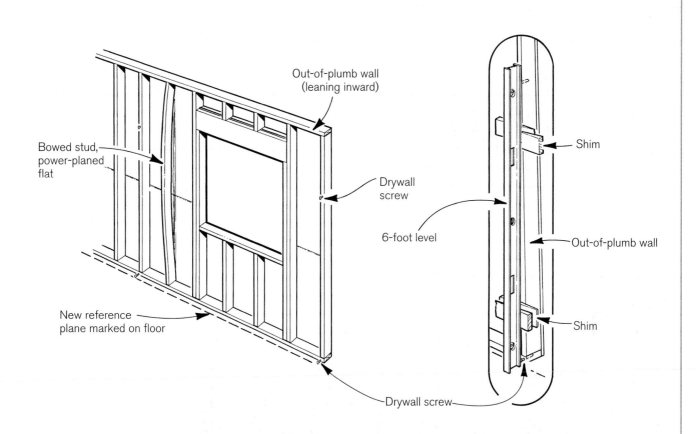

Out-of-plumb wall
(leaning inward)

Bowed stud,
power-planed
flat

Drywall
screw

6-foot level

Shim

Out-of-plumb wall

New reference
plane marked on floor

Shim

Drywall screw

*To determine whether a wall is flat, the author uses a 6-foot level as a straightedge (left photo). He trims protruding studs with a power plane. He then snaps a reference line on the floor representing the new wall plane (illustration). He drives a drywall screw into the sole plate, stopping the head even with the reference line on the floor. A second screw higher on the same stud is adjusted until the 6-foot level reads plumb as it rests against the two screws (center photo). Then, using the level as a straightedge, he slips shims behind it and nails them off (right photo). This transfers the reference plane up each stud, creating a perfectly flat and plumb backing for finish panels.*

# Chapter 15: Windows & Doors

- **Production Prehungs and Window Trim**

- **Fast, Accurate Door Hanging and Trim**

- **Hanging a Custom Door**

- **Trouble-Free Pocket Doors**

- **Production Jamb Extensions**

- **Quick Jamb Extensions for Vinyl Windows**

MIKE RAND

# Production Prehungs and Window Trim

by Ross Welsh

I'm a trim carpentry subcontractor in Sacramento, where my company specializes in large subdivisions. Before we start a new group of homes, I make a three-ring binder for each house, filled with mini-plans that show door swings and sizes, shelving arrangements, and the heights and locations of easily forgotten items like towel bars and paper holders.

In the morning, two of the carpenters start spreading doors and casing, while the third sets up the compressor, hoses, and a miter-saw work station. It's important for one carpenter to start hanging doors within the first half hour, because most of the trim can't be installed until after the doors are in place.

## Prehung Door Installation

Prehung door installation is best thought of as an assembly process. I keep shims, a white mallet, a pry bar, and a drywall saw in my tool bucket. We place the bucket near the latch side of the door opening and hang my nailer on the bucket by its belt hook. The bucket should be out of the way but within easy reach. We place the prehung door assembly near the hinge side of the opening, with the hinges facing into the room (**Figure 1**). We lean the precut casing against the wall just one more step away, for easy access later. Strategically spreading the material and positioning the tools this way make a huge difference in installation time. If you find yourself moving the door or casing out of the way when you walk into the room, it was put in the wrong place when the room was stocked.

*Floating jambs.* I start by cutting back drywall from the rough opening with the drywall saw and removing the shipping nails from the door unit with

**Figure 1.** The author's tool bucket and the materials to install and trim a door are perfectly placed to reduce needless effort. One carpenter will install the door, and another will follow to install the trim package.

a hammer. After slipping the prehung unit into the opening, I open the door 90 degrees; it should stand on its own. If it's being installed in a room with carpeting, we block the jamb up about ½ inch to allow the carpet to be tucked underneath. Next, I hold the door jamb close to the upper hinge and shoot two nails through the jamb near the top, making sure the jamb is about 1/8 inch away from the trimmer stud (**Figure 2**). My goal at this point is to "float" the assembly in the rough opening, as close to its final position as possible. I continue tacking with two nails near the bottom hinge and four nails spread top to bottom along the latch side. At this point the jamb should be floating in the rough opening and not touching the floor or the trimmer studs.

Keeping the jamb away from the rough opening at first allows me to move it in any direction later, as I manipulate the jamb and check its relationship to the door and the wall. I usually start by shimming at the bottom hinge and continue around the frame. The pry bar can quickly close a margin or raise a jamb leg, and the mallet can bring a jamb leg into the plane of the opening. The process is a gradual series of shimming, nailing, and adjusting. As a general rule, I try not to nail too much too soon.

*To plumb or not to plumb.* I adjust cross-legged jambs at the bottom, where the casing can be rolled in or out, while keeping the head jamb flush with the wall so the casing will have nice tight miters. When I have to choose between actually plumbing a door and installing it to appear plumb with adjacent walls, I take the latter approach. Hiding other people's mistakes is part of the job, and making the door and casing parallel with an adjacent corner is usually more important than hanging it plumb.

After the door is thoroughly shimmed and nailed and is working well, I reach for the drywall saw and cut off the shims. Next, I grab a head casing and hold it in position on the head jamb. The head casing's length determines my reveal and leads the way for positioning the legs. I usually slam the door a couple of times while I'm casing, just to make sure the installation is correct. Doorknobs will be installed later.

## Window Stool and Apron

The standard window trim in our area is a simple stool and apron installed below an aluminum or vinyl window. The stool is notched to leave ears on each end and is trimmed with a small apron underneath, usually with 30-degree angled ends.

*Window sticks.* Cutting and fitting window trim efficiently calls for a pair of "window sticks," which

**Figure 2.** The first step in installing an interior door is to shoot a couple of nails into the top of the hinge side of the jamb. Leaving space between the jamb and the framing at this stage makes it easy to drive shims into place later (A). After the shims are in place, the door should open and close freely without hitting the jamb or binding at the hinge (B). Adjustments are simple to make if the jamb is allowed to float until everything lines up correctly. A soft rubber mallet helps to bring the jamb into alignment with the opening without marring or denting the material (C). The head-jamb reveal is easily adjusted with a flat bar after the jamb is tacked in position (D).

**Figure 3.** With the stool supported by aluminum window sticks, the blade of a combination square is aligned with the window return to transfer the required cut to the stool (A). The depth of the notch cut is then picked up with the square (B) and scribed onto the stool (C) before the notch is cut out with a cordless jigsaw.

are 2-foot lengths of ¼-by-1½-inch aluminum bar stock with a blunt chisel-like edge ground on one end. After we've used the chisel end of a stick to scrape any excess drywall mud away from the stool area, we tap the sticks into the gap between the window frame and the rough framing to create work supports that are used to lay out and cut the stool and apron (**Figure 3**). Aside from the window sticks, only a cordless jigsaw, a combination square, an angled template for the apron, and a pencil are needed.

With the stool supported in position by the sticks, I transfer the width of the opening to the stool with a combination square. I hold the square on the stool with the blade extended toward the window. I'm careful to hold everything steady. This method transfers the exact shape of the stool to the stock, whether it's square or not. Next, I pull the stock away from the window and put the head of the square on the wall and slide the blade until it hits the window frame. This shows me the depth of the notch. I lock the square and transfer the depth to the stool by sliding the head of the square along the inside edge of the stool with a pencil riding in the notch at the end of the blade. Finally, I trim the ears to 1½ inches long and start on the apron.

The apron is the same length as the stool, so we simply transfer the length from the stool. We mark the angles on the back of the apron with a template made from the same material. For clean-looking cuts, the apron is then cut face down with a jigsaw and the stool is cut face up. We often notch many window stools at once and fasten them while the baseboard is installed.

*Other trim options.* Full window trim is not common in the production homes in our area, but when the plans call for it, we use a table saw to rip extension jambs to width. The only information I need for each window is height, width, and jamb width. The cutting list I generate goes from long to short and shows a destination for each piece. I get this information well ahead of our usual trim date because it lets me precut all my window pieces in the more controlled environment of my shop.

After cutting the jamb stock to manageable lengths using a stop system on the miter saw, I rip it to the correct widths. The completed jamb extensions are bundled together with heavy rubber bands. This makes it easy to assemble them into frames on the job site, just before they're installed on the windows.

*Ross Welsh is a finish carpentry subcontractor in Sacramento, Calif.*

# Fast, Accurate Door Hanging and Trim

## by Byron Beck

I run a company that does nothing but finish work. Our crews trim everything from commercial buildings to high-end residences. We're constantly looking for ways to simplify procedures so we can cut labor costs. It's a tribute to the skill and organization of our carpenters that we can compete over such a wide range of projects. As a subcontractor, the success of my business also depends on forming relationships with builders. Fortunately, I've worked with many of the same contractors for years. I try to touch base with them before they order trim, because starting out with the right materials on hand increases our chances of making money.

### Hanging Doors

We rarely use prehung door units, preferring instead to hang the doors ourselves (**Figure 4**). Factory prehung units are cheap and easy to get, but the quality is just not there. Mortises are often poorly cut, and you're stuck with someone else's idea of what the margins should be. Many door-hanging companies also

**Figure 4.** The author's crew use special workbenches to assemble jambs and hang doors on site. The benches hold door panels on edge at a convenient working height and are equipped with all the tools and jigs needed to hang doors and install hardware.

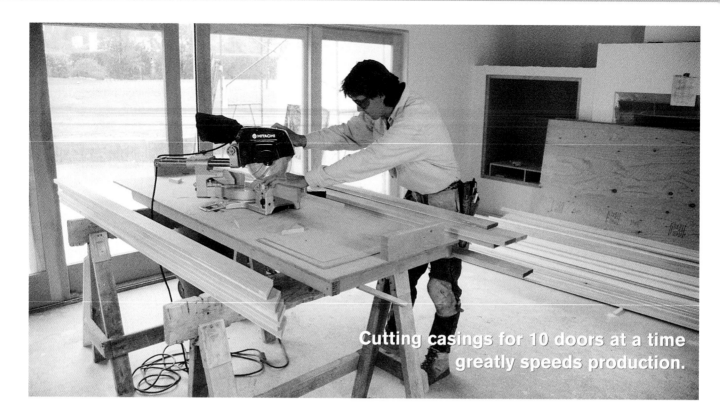

Cutting casings for 10 doors at a time greatly speeds production.

clip hinge screws so the units will fit into rough openings, but there's always the chance hinges will work loose when they're secured by fasteners that haven't got much bite. As for shop-hung doors, even though many of the houses we trim have custom-made doors, little is gained by letting shop guys put them in jambs. There's not much cost savings, and it delays delivery of the doors. By hanging the doors ourselves, we can also determine the number of hinges to use. Standard-height doors get three hinges; those that are taller than 6 feet 8 inches get four hinges.

*Jamb details.* The single best way to ensure that door casings go on quickly is to put them on jambs that are the right width. Mathematically, 2x4 walls with ⅝-inch drywall should be 4¾ inches thick. But walls always end up thicker than they're supposed to be, so I ask the GC to supply jambs that are ⅛ inch wider than the wall. That way, we don't have to chop drywall to get casing miters to lay flat. This is a minor point on real production jobs, but something you can't afford to overlook when trim has to be just so.

Around here in southern California, Mediterranean-style houses are very popular. Most are detailed without interior casings — the drywall laps right onto the jambs, and reveal lines are created by L-bead or bull-nose-bead around the openings. This means that door and window jambs are narrower than usual because they land flush with the edge of the studs instead of projecting ½ inch. It's also important to remember that in these buildings, all windows and doors must be installed before drywall.

The GC usually gives us knockdown jamb units, which we assemble by gluing and screwing the heads into rabbets in the side jambs. We've hung plenty of doors on jambs made from 4/4 stock, but we prefer 5/4 jambs because they're stiffer and there's more landing area for casings. The extra-wide edge is especially important on Mediterranean-style houses because we cut shallow kerfs along the edges of the jambs to ensure that the drywall reveals come out even (**Figure 5**). When the rocker applies beads around the opening, he tucks one leg of the bead into this slot. The buildings we work on usually get ½-inch drywall, so we make ⅛-inch-deep kerfs and instruct the rocker to use ⅝-inch bead. It's important to mill the right size kerf; if it's too deep the bead will flop around because it doesn't bottom out.

*Fitting hinges.* We use a router and a Bosch hinge mortising jig to cut in hinges. One carpenter routs while his partner drills screw holes and attaches hinges. If there's a large centrally located area to work in and the building is compact, we machine all the doors and jambs at once. But if there are a lot of doors (say 50 or more) and they are spread out over a large area, there's a good chance someone will get confused about which way some of them swing. So we find we make fewer mistakes when we hang doors five or ten at a time. Working with smaller batches also reduces the chances that a single error will ruin all of the doors.

## Installing Jambs and Doors

After a jamb is assembled, we put it in the opening and plumb the hinge side, both side to side and front to back. Next, we level the head by squaring off the hinge

## Trimless Detail

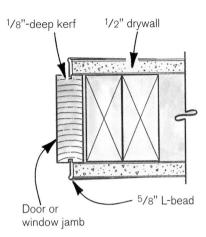

1/8"-deep kerf

1/2" drywall

Door or window jamb

5/8" L-bead

**Figure 5.** The author uses either L-bead or bullnose corner bead (photo) for a trimless, Mediterranean look. To ensure a clean reveal, he cuts a shallow kerf in the edges of the jambs, into which one leg of the bead is inserted (illustration).

jamb with a framing square and fasten it in place. Then we tack the strike side so it's roughly parallel to the hinge jamb. Finally, we hang the door, shimming the strike side till the margins are straight and even all around. This is easy to do by eye. On stain-grade work, we aim for margins the thickness of a dime; for painted trim, gaps are the thickness of a nickel, ensuring that the door still fits after a few coats of paint.

We use 15-gauge pneumatic-driven nails (most of the guys on the crew use Senco models; www.senco.com) to hold jambs in place. Typically, we use five pairs of 2 1/2-inch nails per side. The strike side gets them high, low, then evenly spaced between; we nail the hinge side high, low, and at each hinge. To keep heavy doors from sagging, we shoot a couple of long screws through the jamb behind the upper hinge. If we can find long screws that match the hardware finish, we'll send them through the hinge itself.

## Installing Jambs Without Doors

I prefer to install jambs and doors at the same time, but if the door delivery is delayed, I put the jambs in without them rather than bring the whole project to a grinding halt. And in a Mediterranean-style house, it's impossible to drywall until the jambs are in.

One problem with installing jambs before you have doors is that it's hard to know exactly what size to make the finish openings. An oversize door can always be planed to fit, but if the door is slightly undersized, you have three equally undesirable choices: You can hope no one notices the oversized strike-side margin; you can split the difference by shimming behind the hinges; or you can remove, cut down, and reinstall the jamb unit. If the doors aren't on site, we avoid the problem altogether by making jamb openings slightly undersized. That way, we're covered if the blanks are a little small.

*Cross-stringing.* Even if you haven't got the doors, it's not hard to install jambs so they're straight and plumb. But few walls are perfectly flat, so setting jambs parallel to the studs doesn't guarantee doors will lie flush when closed. One technique we use to ensure that jamb components are in the same plane is called "cross-stringing." Here's how it works (**Figure 6**, page 262):

Fasten the hinge and head jambs in the usual way, but don't fasten the strike-side jamb yet. Tack 4-penny finish nails high and low into the edges of the side jambs. Working from the hinge side of the opening, stretch a dry line from nail to nail diagonally across the opening, making sure the string touches the jamb at all four locations. The strings should barely touch where they cross each other. If they're in contact, move the lower edge of the strike jamb in or out of the opening, then move the jamb back until the strings just touch. At this point, the strike side is in the correct position relative to the face of the hinge jamb. Plumb and straighten the strike jamb, then double-check it using the string to make sure you didn't move it out of plane.

*Cross-sighting.* Stringing jambs is foolproof, but it does take some time. Cross-sighting is faster and does just as good a job. Begin by plumbing and leveling the hinge and head jambs. Plumb the strike side, but don't drive the nails home. Now move to a position where you can sight diagonally across the opening — you should be about 5 feet back from the nearest jamb and fairly close to the wall. You're in the right spot when you can sight the edges of the near and far jamb at the same time. Since you know that the hinge jamb is plumb, the strike side is good, too, when it sights parallel. If the edge of the strike-side jamb is not parallel to the edge of the hinge-side jamb, adjust it until it aligns. Double-check by sighting from the other side of the opening. I know it sounds complicated, but once you understand what cross-sighting is all about, it's very easy to do. And you'd be surprised at how accurate it is.

# Prehanging Your Own Doors

**by David Frane**

As a former carpentry foreman for a custom home-building company, I spent most of my time supervising finish carpenters. We worked on expensive custom homes, where fine interior finish work is one thing that separates the homes from average construction.

We approached our work systematically, since careful planning lets us control costs and devote more time and money to the unusual parts of the job. It's always best to group like tasks. An inefficient carpenter will hang and case a door, then case a window, then install a few pieces of baseboard, then do another door, and so on. An efficient carpenter will hang all of the doors, then case all of the doors and windows, then run the base.

## Installing Doors

Interior finish work usually starts with hanging and casing doors. Prehung, precased doors are fairly common these days, and when using stock doors with standard jambs, they're probably the way to go.

However, we tended to have a mix of stock and custom doors and a variety of jamb widths, so we prehung and precased our own doors. This gave us more control over the quality and scheduling of the work. Last-minute changes to details such as door swings are less disruptive with our own carpenters doing the work. When the carpenters who

prehang the doors are the same ones who install them, it's less likely that defective doors, jambs, or hardware will slip by unnoticed. Doing the prehanging ourselves also gave us a wider choice of casing profiles to choose from.

It's faster to case doors on a waist-high workbench than to case them on the wall. The work area must be well lit and have plenty of electrical outlets. You can waste lots of time hunting for blown breakers or tripping over the tangle of cords. And what passes for fine craftsmanship in a dim work area often looks like a hack job when the lights are turned on.

**Bevel.** Doors should have a 3-degree clearance bevel on the latch side. If the blanks aren't prebeveled, you'll have to get out the power plane and bevel them yourself. Determine which side to bevel by siting down the edge. If it's bowed, be sure to set the concave face toward the door stops.

**Assembly.** After the side jambs have been dadoed and cut to length, but before they've been assembled, cut the hinge mortises (**Figure A**). When hanging more than a few doors at a time, it's best to use a router and a hinge mortising jig. We used a Bosch three-hinge jig that will accept an extension to mortise a fourth hinge on oversized doors. Mortise the jambs and doors, drill holes for the hinge screws, then install the hinges on the jambs and doors.

The next step is to assemble the jamb unit and put the door inside it. Insert a couple of 3/32-inch spacers between the strike edge of the door and the side jamb, placing one high and one low. Then hold the unit together by nailing through the side jambs and spacers into the door with finish nails. Don't drive these nails home; you'll need to remove them before hanging the door. (I've seen more than one carpenter scratching his head wondering why the prehung unit he just installed wouldn't open.) A scrap wood spacer between the bottom edges of the jambs is a good idea if you have to transport the doors.

**Door casings.** Next, precase the latch side of the jamb unit. Cut the miters with a chop saw, compound miter saw, or a radial arm saw. It doesn't matter what you use, as long as the saw is large enough, is well calibrated, and has a sharp blade. This is also a good time to precut the casings for the other side of the door, as well as for the windows.

Whenever possible, we secured our miters with biscuits. (This is nothing new, by the way — I once took casings out of a 1920s house that had football-shaped splines in the miter joints.) Most carpenters use a portable plate joiner for cutting the slots, but when doing pro-

**Figure A.** *Prehanging doors: Even on high-end custom jobs, the author kept costs in check by production-line preparation in the shop. Here, workers mortise a run of doors for a new house with a router and mortising jig.*

**Figure B.** ***Precasing doors*** *in the shop makes installation go quickly at the site. A table-mounted router with a slot cutter for biscuits (1) and a pneumatic finish nailer (2) speed the work. Two biscuits at each miter (3) produce tight-fitting, stable joints (4).*

duction work it's often faster to use a router table with a properly sized slotting bit (**Figure B**).

To assemble the casings, glue the miters, insert the biscuits, and screw the joint shut with long drywall screws, screwing from above so that the plug won't show.

***Installing the door.*** There are lots of ways to hang doors, and I've tried most of them. My preference is to install the jamb with the door hanging in it (**Figure C**). You know it's right if the head jamb is level, the hinge jamb is plumb, the margins are an even 3/32 inch, and the face of the door is flush with the jambs.

To install the door, nail through the casing just as you would with a precased window. You still have to shim and nail the jamb, but the door will stay put while you're doing it. Align the unit in the opening, then fasten the side jambs. Nail at the top and bottom, as well as at hinges and strikes, using 12-penny or 16-penny finish nails. I've seen jambs nailed with finish guns, but I don't trust the narrow-gauge gun nails to hold things where they belong. Remember to solidly back the jambs with shims wherever you nail. (One disadvantage to using precased doors is that you can't slide the shims all the way through like you can with uncased doors).

I always try to use dry shims, since they won't shrink and cause the doors to sag. A few days before installing the door units, I would break open the bundle of shim shingles and spread them out somewhere warm to dry. It's easier to work with shims that are all the same width, so I also ripped the shingles to around 1 1/2 inches.

As an added precaution against sagging doors, I screw the jamb to the jack stud at the top hinge. One way to do this is to put a long drywall screw through the jamb behind the hinge. A slick alternative is to replace one of the short screws in the top hinge with a 2 1/2-inch version, which will penetrate the jack stud by at least 1 inch. If you always replace the same screw, it's easy to come back later and tweak sagging doors by lifting the door and tightening the long screw.

*David Frane is a senior editor at JLC and a former building contractor.*

**Figure C.**

***Installation:*** *The author prefers to install the jamb precased, with the door installed. If the head jamb is level and the hinge jamb plumb, it's easy to align the strike jamb for a perfect fit.*

## Installing Jambs Without Doors

### Cross-Stringing

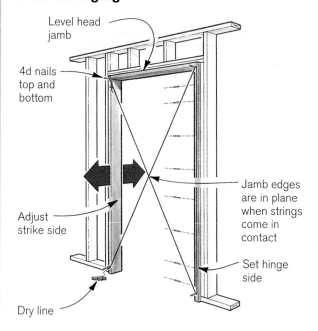

Level head jamb

4d nails top and bottom

Adjust strike side

Dry line

Jamb edges are in plane when strings come in contact

Set hinge side

### Cross-Sighting

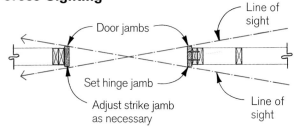

Line of sight

Door jambs

Set hinge jamb

Adjust strike jamb as necessary

Line of sight

**Figure 6.** After fastening the hinge-side and top jambs, stretch strings diagonally across the opening (top). Adjust the bottom of the strike-side jamb in or out until the strings just touch. To check the jambs by eye (above), move about 5 feet diagonally away from the doorway and sight along the edge of the hinge jamb through the opening to the far side of the strike jamb. Adjust the strike jamb as necessary. When the edges align, the strike jamb is in plane with the hinge jamb.

## Casing Doors and Windows

We like to cut all of the door casings at one time. The job is often split between a journeyman, who measures and cuts, and an apprentice, who installs. Start by marking the reveal line on the jamb using a pencil and an adjustable square. Make a mark at the corners where casings meet, and every foot or so along the jambs.

To determine the length of side casings, measure the distance from subfloor to horizontal reveal line; this is the distance from the short point of the miter to the square cut at the floor. (We usually cut casings about 1/4 inch short because the finish floor, which is

**Figure 7.** To speed installation of extension jambs, pre-assemble them on a workbench, then shim and nail to the jack studs just like a door jamb.

usually installed after we've put up the trim, will cover the gap.) To find the length of the head casing, measure horizontally between your marks in the corners of the head and side jambs; this is the short-point-to-short-point dimension of the head casing. You need to measure only once for the side casings, because they will fit either side.

**Windows.** We use a similar procedure to measure window casings. For picture-framed trim, measure from reveal to reveal all the way around; for windows with stools, measure stool to reveal for side casings, and reveal to reveal for heads.

The jambs on the windows we case are rarely the full thickness of the wall, so we have to extend them. We make frames out of 4/4 stock and install them as units. They're held in position the same way door jambs are, with shims and finish nails (**Figure 7**).

This method works well for both production and high-end work. Just make sure you keep track of which casings go on which doors and windows. I can't overstress the importance of this, especially when the guy who installs casings isn't the one who measured them. To avoid confusion, write a number on the back of each casing that matches the number of the door or window it goes with. Stack the parts for each unit and tape them together so they won't get mixed up. We use painter's masking tape, because it doesn't leave any residue and it's easy to break open the bundle. The installer takes it from there.

Measuring and cutting a large amount of trim at one time can really increase efficiency. You'll eliminate repetitive measuring and spend a lot less time walking back and forth to your saw.

*Byron Beck is a woodworker and finish subcontractor in Santa Barbara, Calif.*

# Hanging a Custom Door

by Tom O'Brien

**With a router, a hinge template, and a few other specialized tools, custom doors are almost as easy to fit as prehungs.**

One of the classic tests that distinguish a skilled carpenter from a wannabe is the ability to hang a door the old-fashioned way: assemble a jamb set, fit the door blank, mortise the hinges, and put all the pieces together.

Hanging a door from scratch is way more time-consuming than installing a prehung, but it's an extremely flexible process. If I need to hang a door in a hurry and can't wait for the lumberyard to order a particular prehung, it's a safe bet that the jamb material and door blank I need are in stock.

More often, if I'm remodeling an older home and need to fit a door to a nonstandard rough opening — or if I want to recycle a salvaged door panel — the solution is to build a custom-sized jamb set and trim the door to fit.

## Assembling a Jamb Set

Years ago, before prehung doors became as popular as they are now, you could buy ready-to-assemble jamb packages for popular door sizes that simply needed to be nailed together. These days, the suppliers in my area keep only 7-foot lengths in stock, so even a standard door frame has to be cut to size.

If I'm fitting the jamb to an existing door blank, I measure the door and add 3/16 inch to the width and

about 1/2 inch to the height. These measurements represent the inside dimensions of the jamb.

For strength — as well as appearance — I rabbet the tops of the side jambs to receive the head jamb (**Figure 8**, next page). It's possible to use a trim saw and a chisel to plow out the rabbets, but a router does the job faster and better.

Before cutting the head to length, remember to add 1/2 inch to account for the 1/4-inch depth of each rabbet.

*Routing the rabbet.* After scribing the thickness of the head jamb on the end of each side jamb, I make another pencil mark that represents the width of the router's base plate (measured from the inside edge of the bit) and clamp a straightedge at that point.

I make a test cut on a piece of scrap to verify that my measurements are accurate and that the router's depth setting is spot-on, then I rabbet all of the side jambs one after another.

I fasten the parts together with carpenter's glue and 2-inch drywall screws.

If the door stops are on the job at this time, I'll tack them in place using a method shown in Figure 15 on page 268.

## Setting the Jambs

A solid-core door panel can weigh 100 pounds or more. To support this much weight, the jambs have to be securely fastened — but they must also rest solidly on the floor. Otherwise, over time, gravity and centrifugal force will take their toll.

I always check the floor with a level to determine whether one side of the rough opening is higher than the other (**Figure 9**, next page). If the jambs will rest directly on a subfloor, I simply place a shim underneath the low side. If the jambs are set directly on top of a finished floor, as they were on the job shown in the photos, I scribe the high-side jamb and cut it to fit.

I roughly center the jamb in the opening, using a homemade spreader to keep the width at the bottom the same as at the top (**Figure 10**, page 265). I then slip a pair of shims behind the bottom hinge and pin the jamb by driving a pair of 2½-inch nails underneath them.

I plumb the face of the jamb with a 6-foot level, then shim and pin the top hinge following the same procedure. I don't secure the latch-side jamb until after the door is completely hung.

## Test-Fitting the Door Blank

In the bad old days, a door blank was truly a "blank." Cut square on all four sides, it had to be trimmed —

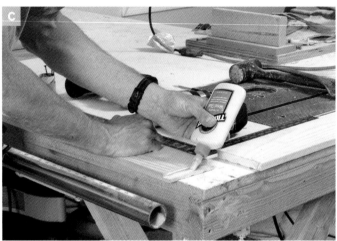

**Figure 8.** A square-cut scrap of jamb stock (A) acts as a straightedge for routing a ¼-inch-deep rabbet into the top end of each side jamb (B). Carpenter's glue (C) and 2-inch screws (D) ensure that the jambs stick together for the long haul. To prevent splitting the narrow jamb material, all of the screws are countersunk.

**Figure 9.** Before putting in the door jamb, the author checks the floor with a level to determine whether one side is higher than the other (A). Since this jamb is resting on top of finished flooring, the high side must be scribed (B) and trimmed, or the head jamb won't sit level. A fine-toothed Japanese pull saw is more accurate than a power saw and cuts almost as quickly (C).

**Figure 10.** After the jamb is placed inside the rough opening, a spreader keeps the bottom square with the top, while a straightedge ensures that the assembly stays in plane with the wall (A). With the jamb centered in the rough opening, the bottom hinge is shimmed and tacked, with nails driven beneath the shims to permit adjustment (B). Then the top hinge gets the same treatment (C). Note that although the author is using a prehung door jamb in this photo sequence, installation of a site-assembled jamb set is exactly the same.

and the latch side beveled — on site to fit the opening. Still available, but often only by special order, this type of door is called "full and square."

These days, "prefit" door blanks are more common; they're beveled on both sides and slightly undersized, so a 3'-0" door blank should fit perfectly inside a 3-foot jamb opening.

Before making any cuts, I like to prop each door blank inside the designated jamb, shim it tight against the head, and check the fit on all sides. If the jamb was installed without stops, I tack a short length of scrap to the head jamb to prevent the door from falling backward.

It's particularly important to make sure that the latch-side edge of the door is beveled, and that the bevel faces inward. To prevent a costly mistake, I put a mark on the top corner of the door that reminds me where the hinges will go (**Figure 11**, next page).

On those occasions when I'm installing a "full and square" door, I hold the latch side jamb tight against it; then I open my scribers to 3/16 inch and scribe the door. I keep an older Porter-Cable 9118 planer (www.deltaportercable.com) permanently — well, almost permanently — set on a 3-degree bevel, and I always work from the same side of the door, so it's a simple matter to put the right bevel in the right place.

Before I take the door out of the opening, I set my scribers to the proper width and mark the cut for the bottom of the door. In most cases, I like to see a ½-inch gap between the bottom of a door and the finish floor; I usually leave 1 inch of space beneath

bathroom doors to allow for ventilation.

For years I cut door bottoms the tedious, old-fashioned way, using a straightedge to guide a standard circular saw. Last winter I started using the Festool plunge-cut saw and guide-rail system (www.festoolusa.com). With this tool there's no need to measure for an offset — or to knife-cut the grain to prevent splintering. Instead, you just clamp the base on the cut line and the rest is gravy.

Like all Festool products, the saw is hideously expensive, but it's well worth the cost if you hang a lot of doors or need a first-rate dust-collection system.

## Mortising Hinges

If I'm hanging just one door, I mortise the hinges freehand with a laminate trimmer and a chisel; for more than one door, I use a full-size hinge template (**Figure 12**, next page).

Manufactured hinge templates come in a variety of styles. Fixed units, such as those from Templaco (www.templaco.com), are inexpensive and easy to set up, but you need a different one for each size hinge, and they take up valuable storage space.

I use a Bosch adjustable hinge template (www.boschtools.com). It's a bit of a hassle to set up but extremely versatile — and when I'm done, the whole contraption fits into a case that's not much bigger than a lunchbox.

After assembling the template and setting up the router, I practice on a 2x4 to make sure that the location of the hinges and depth-of-cut are correct. I

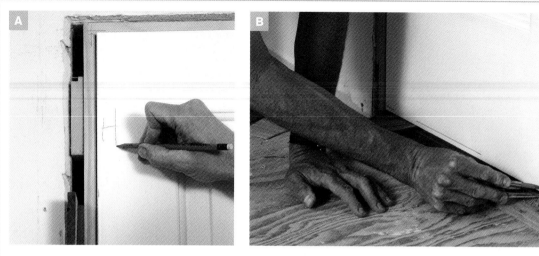

**Figure 11.** The author marks the top corner of the door (A) to designate both the hinge side and the edge that should get fully mortised. Before taking the door down for mortising, he scribes the bottom to fit the floor (B). Although they're expensive, specialized cutting tools like Festool's plunge-cut saw (C) and Porter-Cable's 9118 planer (D) make trimming and beveling edges error- and splinter-free. A simple door buck, assembled from scrap 2x4s, holds the door steady.

**Figure 12.** Before setting the pins that fasten a hinge-mortising template, the author makes sure that the stops underneath and at the top fit tightly against the door (A). To work with a template, he fits the router with a 1/2-inch mortising bit encircled by a 5/8-inch template guide (B). This setup leaves rounded corners that are easily squared up with a soft tap on a corner chisel (C). A self-centering Vix bit ensures that the hinge screws lay flat (D).

**Figure 13.** To cut the hinge mortises for the jamb, the author butts the template's end stop gauge tight to the head jamb, then makes sure before he sets the pins that the two thickness stops on either side of each hinge section are tight to the frame (far left). He follows the same procedure for cutting the mortises as for cutting the door (left).

**Figure 14.** Although it's designed for drywall, a board lifter is an ideal tool for finessing a solid-core door onto its hinges. Unlike a pry bar, this tool has a built-in fulcrum as well as a stirrup, so you never need a third hand to reach down and reposition it.

secure the panel on its edge in a door buck, then fasten the template to the door using the pins provided.

To prevent chipping, I rout the top and bottom edges of the hinge mortise first; then I plow back and forth across the grain before making a final pass around the perimeter of the template to make sure the edges are crisp and smooth.

After the template is removed, a corner chisel makes quick work of the radius corners left behind by the router bit. I check the fit of each hinge, then use a self-centering Vix bit to drill for the screws. To allow wiggle room when hanging the door, I put only two screws in each hinge at this time and leave the screws loose.

The jamb gets mortised in place, following the same procedure as for the door (**Figure 13**). Then I separate the hinges, fasten the loose hinge leaves to the jamb, and go back for the door.

## Hanging the Door

I set the door panel in front of the opening and lever the hinges into position (**Figure 14**) using a foot-operated board lifter that I bought from a drywall supplier (www.marshalltown.com). After the hinge pins are in place, I tighten the screws.

Now I'm ready to fasten the latch side jamb. With the door closed, I shim the jamb at the top and the bottom, making sure that the reveal is the same on the side as it is on the top of the door.

Then I open the door and pin the jamb by driving a pair of nails underneath each set of shims. I use a combination square as a straightedge to align the jambs with the drywall.

When I'm satisfied that the reveal is consistent and

**Figure 15.** When it's time for door stops, the author scribes a pencil line the same thickness as the door on the face of the jamb (far left). To prevent the door from binding, he leaves the line showing, except for at the point where the strike plate will go (left).

— most important — that the door swings freely, I nail through the shims to make sure they can't slip loose. The jamb also gets shimmed and nailed behind the latch.

## Applying Stops

If I didn't tack on the stops when I assembled the jambs, I usually hold off until I'm set up to run casing and baseboards.

To lay out the stops, I mark a point on the face of the jamb that corresponds with the inner edge of the door, then scribe a line with a combination square (**Figure 15**). To prevent the door from binding, I leave the pencil line showing everywhere except for the point where the strike plate will be located — usually 3 feet above the door.

Until the lockset goes in, I pin the stops with just three or four brads each. Once I'm satisfied with the operation of the door — when I hear that subtle, reassuring thunk as it shuts smoothly, with no bounceback — I'll nail the stops home.

*Tom O'Brien is a renovation contractor in New Milford, Conn.*

# Trouble-Free Pocket Doors

by Gary Katz

At first glance, installing a pocket-door kit might seem like a pretty simple task. But the truth is, messing one up is pretty simple, too. I'm going to share some of the lessons I've learned — the hard way — about pocket-door kits, along with some tips for improving their function and feel.

Pocket-door kits come in two types: good and bad. Inexpensive kits with light-duty track and carriage wheels (sometimes called "trucks") are the bane of door-hangers and homeowners. Not only are they difficult to install, but in no time at all the track bends or the wheel bearings wear out. And everyone knows fixing a pocket door isn't easy or cheap.

So whatever kind of door you're using, invest in heavy-duty track and high-quality carriage wheels. Several makers have good kits, including Johnson (www.johnsonhardware.com) and Hager (www.hagerhinge.com). The kit shown in this article is from Pemko (www.pemko.com).

In addition to the split studs and track, which is

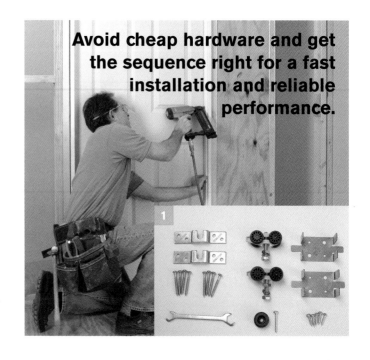

Avoid cheap hardware and get the sequence right for a fast installation and reliable performance.

mounted to the header frame, most pocket-door kits come with pretty much the same hardware (**Photo 1**): two door hangers, two roller carriages, two floor brackets, a rubber bumper, and a wrench.

## Resizing the Header Frame

The first step when you're installing one of these kits is to check the size of the rough opening (**2**) and, since the kits are supplied for 36-inch doors, to cut down the head frame if the door is narrower. The width of the rough opening should measure two times the width of the door plus 1 inch. For Pemko's Husky Heavy Door kit, the height of the rough opening should measure the door height plus 5 inches, though most other models require an additional 4 inches in header height.

For doors narrower than 36 inches, you have to do a little math. Start by doubling the difference between your door and a 3'-0" door. For example, a 2'-8" (32-inch) door is 4 inches smaller than a 3'-0" door; 4 x 2 = 8 inches. Subtract that amount from the header-frame top cleat (**3**, **4**) and from the aluminum track (**5**), but don't cut anything just yet. A piece of masking tape makes it easier to see the mark on the aluminum frame.

When it comes to the two pieces of wood that cover the sides of the track, which are half as long as the header piece, you want to cut off only the differ-ence between your door and a 3'-0" door — 4 inches in this example (**6**). I use a jigsaw to cut the wood (**7**) and a hacksaw to cut the track (**8**), then reinstall the end plate (**9**).

## Installing the Frame

Cut out any bottom plate and snap lines on both sides of the opening (**10**). For 6'-8" doors, measure up from the floor 81¼ inches on the jack (**11**) and partially drive in a screw, centered on the stud (**12**). Don't use a nail for this; it's easy to relocate a screw if need be.

With 80-inch-tall doors, 81¼ allows ½-inch clearance from the floor and automatically aligns the head jamb with existing prehung jambs so that the casings will line up around the room. Nothing looks worse or more unprofessional than a pocket door with casing that's an inch taller than that of surrounding prehung doors. Site conditions vary considerably, so be sure to check your door and the jambs on your job before mounting the head track. For odd-size doors, locate the mounting screw by adding 1¼ inches to the door height.

Next, slip the header-frame end plates over the screws (**13**), check that the track is perfectly level (**14**), then snug up the end-plate screws and install the remaining screws.

Once the head is secure and level, insert one of the split-stud mounting plates into the bottom of a split

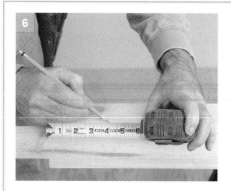

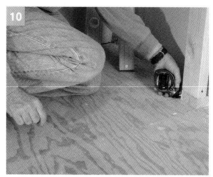

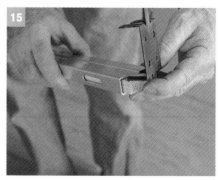

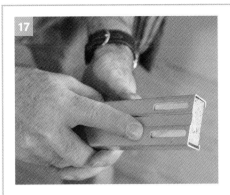

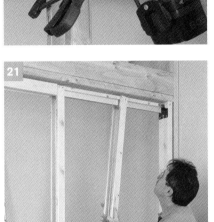

stud (**15**), then insert the bottom of a second split stud on the other side of the plate (**16**). Note that the top of the split stud has two notches in the aluminum frame so that you can run screws through the face of the stud into the head frame (**17**).

Temporarily clamp the tops of the split studs to the header frame, then fasten with 1½-inch screws (**18**). Plumb the split-stud pair to the floor (**19**), then fasten the plate, centered between the snap lines (**20**). Use Tapcons or anchors on concrete.

Install the second split-stud pair the same way. If possible, be kind to the drywallers and try to align the split studs with the cripple studs above (**21**). On a remodel, I'll just center the second split-stud pair. Attach each stud to the head with screws, then plumb the bottom, making sure the studs are centered on the two snap lines.

It's important, when drywall is installed before the door is hung, to stiffen the split-stud wall with a temporary brace (**22**). Otherwise, the drywall installers might bend the inner split studs and pinch the door. (If you hang your doors before drywall and leave them in the pocket, good luck!)

***Plywood stiffener.*** A great way to reinforce the split-stud wall is to install a ripped piece of ¾-inch plywood between the studs.

First, fasten the top of the plywood to the header frame (**23**). Then drill ⅛-inch pilot holes through split-stud slots and fasten the split studs to the plywood with 2½-inch screws (**24**).

It's a good idea to position these holes near the top or the bottom of the slot, so as to leave as much room as possible for fastening the split jamb to the split stud later. When using a plywood stiffener, I install the second (midspan) split-stud pair after the plywood is attached to the first split stud (**25**); I secure the second split stud to the header, then to the plywood, then to the floor.

## Hanging the Door

Cut the bottom of the door to clear carpet or other flooring. To measure the necessary door height, install the carriages in the track, suspend a carriage hanger from one carriage, then measure from the bottom of the hanger to the floor. Subtract for carpet or other finish flooring, plus allow at least ¼-inch clearance.

This is one case where cutting a little too much off the door is better than not cutting enough: if you don't cut enough, you may have to remove the door after all the trim is painted. We've all had to do that at least once. What's even worse, though, is if a tile floor is installed, you may not be able to get the door out of the pocket. (Don't ask how I know this.)

Center the carriage hanger on the door, approximately 3½ inches from the edge. It's best to avoid mounting hanger screws into the end grain of door stiles, but on narrow doors there's little choice. When I'm working with a heavy door and have to install hanger screws into end grain, I mortise out a section of the top stile with a plunge router and a template jig, then glue a solid block of wood into the mortise.

Always predrill pilot holes for every screw you put into a door (**26**). Fasten the hangers with 1½-inch mounting screws. It helps a lot if on the first try you position the hangers with the bolt slots facing the front of the door (**27**). If you haven't done so already, insert the carriages into the track (**28**).

Hanging heavy doors alone isn't hard. Start by angling the back of the door into the frame opening, then tip it up on the front edge and slip the rear hanger plate over the carriage-wheel bolt (**29**). Slide the door into the pocket a little bit, then raise the front edge of the door and slip the front hanger over the front carriage-wheel bolt (**30**). Don't bother adjusting the height of the hangers until the strike jamb is installed.

## Installing the Trim

Install the strike jamb, plumb and straight (**31**), and fasten it securely to the trimmer (**32**). Then adjust the carriage-wheel bolts to align the door parallel with the strike jamb (**33**).

I always attach split jambs with screws, locating the screws in the split-jamb legs so they center on the cutouts in the aluminum frames (**34**). To position the split jambs properly, use a spacer the same thickness as the drywall or other finish wall material (**35**).

Attach the split-jamb heads last. To make life easier for the next carpenter to work on the door, I use screws in both jambs, because replacing the door sometimes requires the removal of both of the top split jambs. Remember that the door stop will cover all the screws.

I install the door guide next. Holding the guide near the bottom of the door, I center the door in the pocket opening, then drive a nail partially into the slots on each side of the guide (**36**). I adjust the guide up or down while sliding the door in and out of the pocket, checking that the bottom of the door isn't rubbing.

To make sure it's centered, I open and close the door several times; once I'm positive everything is sweet, I stand up and double-check the whole thing

one more time, then kneel down and drive two more nails into the holes on each side of the guide plate.

There are several types of door guides available; for custom doors, I prefer a floor-mounted guide. I cut a kerf in the bottom of the door with a router and slot-cutter, wax the kerf with a candle, then mount the guide to the floor, centered in the pocket opening.

I install the door stop using as few 1-inch brad nails as possible (**37**). To allow for seasonal movement, as well as for a latch, I make the gap between the door stop and the door about 3/16 inch.

Nail door stop on the legs of the split jambs, too, covering the door-guide plate (**38**). I accommodate the thickness of the plate by carving out the back of the door stop slightly. Again, you should use as few nails as possible so the stop can be removed easily if the door ever needs adjustment. And if you can help it, don't caulk the door stop to the split jambs! Also, I don't install stop on the strike jamb unless the client insists; it looks silly and gets scarred every time the door is closed.

Finally, install the rubber bumper on the rear jack stud. If you're not hanging the door before drywall, don't forget to get that bumper in while the cavity is still open. Use a properly sized spacer block to ensure that the front edge of the door is flush with the door stop at the face of the split jambs when the door is fully retracted into the pocket (**39**). (Make sure to allow for the thickness of both the split jambs and the stop.)

Now wait for the drywallers to finish the wall, then install the casing (**40**). One last note of advice: Use 1¼-inch nails to fasten the casing to the pocket wall. Do the same for the baseboard.

*Gary Katz is a finish carpenter in Resada, Calif.*

# Production Jamb Extensions

by Gary Katz

**Take all dimensions at once and preassemble frames for fast and accurate window jambs.**

## Common Jamb–Extension Profiles

### Square-Edge

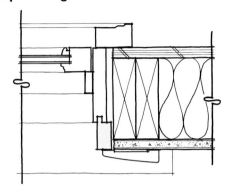

### Tongue & Groove

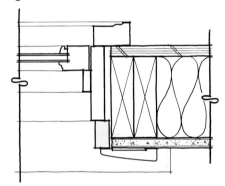

### Back-Rabbet

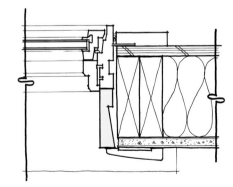

**Figure 16.** Jamb extension profiles differ, depending on the shape of the window jamb and the width of the wall. A square edge works well on a plain window jamb when the extension is narrow, while some extensions must be milled with a tongue to fit a corresponding groove in the jamb. For wide walls, a back-rabbet reduces the length of the screw needed to attach the extension.

W indow extension jambs are a fact of life for trim carpenters. In new construction, sometimes the wall thickness hasn't been determined when the windows are ordered; in a remodel, the wall may gain thickness — from rigid foam insulation, for example, or the addition of furring and paneling. But often, we just plain forget to order wider window jambs, which is unfortunate because most window companies manufacture windows with either custom-sized jambs or factory-installed extensions at little or no additional cost.

A Marvin window, for instance, should rarely need extensions because the company builds jambs to almost any width. Upcharges for wider jambs are modest. Similar nominal charges apply to manufacturers who ship windows with factory-installed extensions.

Andersen casement windows, on the other hand, always need extensions because the jambs are only $2^7/8$ inches wide. The extensions, which are shipped loose, come in three sizes, but they're reasonably priced.

## Three Types of Jamb Extensions

Depending on the design and width of the window jamb, the profile of the extensions takes one of three shapes (**Figure 16**). The simplest extension is a piece

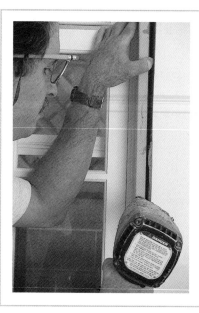

**Figure 17.** MDF is not a good material to use for extension jambs. While it mills easily and takes paints well, it tends to split when screwed or nailed through the edge.

jamb extensions. Fastening through the face of MDF material works well, but nails or screws driven into the edge without predrilling cause flaking and splitting (**Figure 17**). Since jamb extensions are all about endgrain — extensions are fastened to the jamb through the edge, then the casing is fastened to the extension by nailing into the same edge — it's best to use real wood. If the job is being stained, pick material that matches the grain pattern of the window jambs.

***Milling jamb extensions.*** I prefer to mill extensions in my small shop because it's easier and faster, though I often cut them on site, too. Either way, to increase productivity and save installation time, I measure all window and door extensions before I'm called to install the finish work so that all the material is on the job the first day of work. I purchase stock in widths and lengths that result in the least amount of waste, though I try to avoid ripping more than two extensions from one piece of stock. This reduces milling time and eliminates the need for a surface planer, because I can use the factory edge on the room side. A table saw equipped with a fine-tooth carbide blade makes a smooth enough cut for the inside edge, which is butted against the window jamb. If the extensions are thin, however, I often rip more than two out of a single piece of stock, then pass them through my portable surface planer. I also ease the exposed corner of all extensions with a table-mounted router or hand-held laminate trimmer using a 3/16-inch roundover bit. If you don't own all those tools, buy the narrowest stock you can find and anticipate a little more waste.

Tongues and back-rabbets can be milled quickly with only a table saw. The tongue for an Andersen

of square-cut stock that butts against a square jamb edge. Another type of extension has a tongue that mates neatly into a corresponding dado in the jamb, such as you'll find on Andersen jambs. A third type, called a back-rabbet, is standard for manufacturers like Eagle. A back-rabbet is especially useful for wide extensions where you want to avoid having to drill a deep countersink.

***Site-built extensions.*** Either because of job-site complications or forgetfulness, I often mill my own extensions from S4S stock. For paint-grade windows, I use finger-jointed pine. While it's tempting to use MDF because it's readily available, mills easily, and paints beautifully, I think MDF is the wrong material for

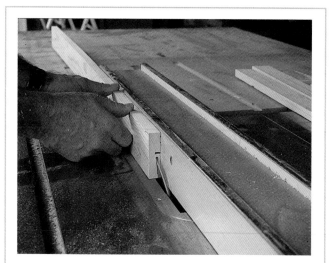

**Figure 18.** A back-rabbeted extension can be milled on site in two passes with a table saw. The bevel cut begins at the corner of the stock and meets the shoulder cut about 1 inch from the window-side edge. Back-rabbeted extensions can be fastened with a nail gun before the window is installed.

**Figure 19.** The author preassembles picture-framed extensions in his shop. All four corners are screwed to the keep the joints tight.

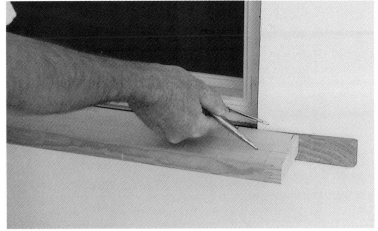
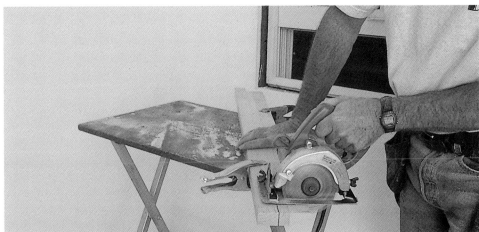

**Figure 20.** On windows trimmed with a stool and apron, the stool horns must be long enough to catch the casings (above left). If the horns need to be scribed for a tight fit against the wall (above right), the author creates a slight back-cut using a panel saw (left).

extension requires several passes, though I often eliminate the tongue for thin extensions, and apply them flat, directly on top of the dado. Back-rabbets can be made in two passes (**Figure 18**). The shoulder cut for a back-rabbet should be made about 1 inch from the window-side edge of the stock; the bevel cut begins at the corner and angles to meet the shoulder cut. If the extension can be applied before the window is installed, using a nail gun to fasten the extensions is faster than screws.

## Picture-Frame Extensions

Most of the jamb extensions I apply are less than 1 inch wide to make up for the thickness of shear paneling that was forgotten when the windows were ordered. For narrow extensions, I measure all the windows on the job, precut the pieces to length using a repetitive stop on my chop saw, and pin-nail them to the jambs. To find the width of the extensions, I hold a block of wood or a square flat against the wall and measure from the window jamb, then I add 1/16 inch to make it easier to install the casing. I take several measurements on each window, especially at the head and sill, where drywall tends to thicken, then I average the measurements. If the dif-

ference is more than 3/16 inch, I make custom rips.

When extensions are wider than 1 inch, however, I preassemble them in my shop, where I can work faster on a large waist-high work surface with all the necessary tools in easy reach. I fasten the corners with screws (adding glue won't hurt, but it's slower), just like the head and legs of a jamb, so that the joints will never spread (**Figure 19**).

I approach picture-frame windows differently from windows with stool and apron. Because I preassemble the frames in my shop, I measure for picture-frame jamb extensions while I'm figuring the material takeoff. It's faster than it sounds, because no matter how many windows a house has, most are the same size. Measure the inside dimension of the jamb and add twice the reveal — 3/8 inch for a 3/16-inch reveal, 1/2 inch for a 1/4-inch reveal. Sometimes, the extension frame has to slip over window stops that are proud of the jamb. In that case, measure outside to outside between stops and add 1/16 inch for clearance.

My extension jamb takeoff is usually a short list of window sizes with slash marks for each frame I'll need. Occasionally, a window size will be listed twice, with different extension widths.

**Figure 21.** After fastening the back-rabbeted extension jambs to the stool with drywall screws, the author drills pilot holes in the shoulder using a tapered countersink bit (left). He also countersinks the stool so the screws won't interfere with the apron (right).

## Stool and Apron Extensions

Window stool is applied directly to the jamb and serves as the jamb extension as well as the sill, so it must be cut to fit before the extension legs and head can be installed. This work must be done on site, but production techniques can speed installation.

As with every piece of repetitive door and window trim, first measure and cut all the stool to width and length, then scatter the pieces to every window, along with precut extension legs and heads. Next, scribe and cut each piece of stool, and test the fit. After all of the stool is cut, fasten the extension jambs to the stool, then attach the complete frame to the window. This method minimizes the number of times I change tools and dramatically speeds an otherwise slow and expensive process.

The stool has to be long enough to catch the ends of the casings, but finding the dimension is easy arithmetic. First, double the width of the casing; then add twice the casing reveal on the jamb plus twice the casing reveal at the end of the stool. Now add that total to the inside dimension of the window jamb. For example, a $3^1/_2$-inch-wide casing with $1/_4$-inch reveals at both the jamb and stool requires a piece of stool that is 8 inches longer than the inside jamb measurement.

Scribing the stool to fit isn't too difficult, either. After cutting the stool to length, measure in at each end and make a mark at the width of the casing plus the jamb and stool reveals (4 inches for $3^1/_2$-inch casing with $1/_4$-inch reveals). Then hold the stool against the finished wall and align the marks with the inside edges of the window jamb (**Figure 20**, previous page). While still holding the stool in place, get ready to scribe the horns so they'll fit tightly against the walls and the window jamb. First, take a quick

measurement to verify that the stool and jamb are parallel. If they're not, slip a small shim behind one end of the stool to correct the problem. Then spread your scribes the distance between the stool and the jamb, and scribe the horns from the finished wall. This scribing technique works well for bullnosed returns, too, and always results in a tight fit.

I use a small panel saw to cut scribes because the combination of high rpm and a small blade help in making fine, slightly curved cuts. I keep the blade square to the stock at the start of the cut, so the end of the stool will meet the wall square, but I back-bevel the inner portion of the notch so that the piece will fit tightly against the wall without any struggle. I finish the inside corner of the cut with a back saw, also back-beveling slightly.

***Installation.*** Wide, back-rabbeted extension jambs should always be firmly attached to each other and to the stool. Only then should they be installed on the jamb. The joint between the extension jamb and the stool is especially weak and can spread if it isn't properly secured.

On large job sites, I like to assemble the frames on a worktable, which I carry into each major room. I have an old Ryobi chop-saw stand, but a set of sawhorses or a Workmate and a sheet of plywood work well, too. For large windows and small rooms, the floor makes a good worktable, with one wall used as a brace. I bring along two cordless drills, one with a long Phillips driver and one for drilling pilot holes. I use a tapered drill bit and countersink for pilot holes, and $1^1/_2$-inch drywall screws to fasten the legs to the heads and to the stool (**Figure 21**).

While the extension frame is still lying flat on the floor or worktable, I use a $9/_{64}$-inch bit to drill pilot

## Cutting Your Own Shims

Although using screws eliminates the need for shims, on especially wide extension jambs, shims are still a good way to prevent the jambs from splaying and the joints from spreading. It's good practice to place a shim on both sides of each corner, and at the center of the opening on all sides. Also, while everything is open, it only takes a second to stick a couple of shims between the sill and the stool to support the weight of exploring children.

I don't like the spongy quality of packaged shims, so I make my own. Wide MDF shims are easy to cut on a chop saw, and they chisel off easily. But for most applications, I use a sled on my table saw to crosscut scraps of 2x6 into endgrain shims. The sled is an 8-by-12-inch scrap of 3/8- or 1/2-inch plywood with an angled notch cut into one end. The shoulder of the notch is 5/16 inch deep, and sets the thickness of the butt end of the shim. The angled cut is 53/8 inches long, just shy of the width of a 2x6. A large block of wood screwed to the back of the sled serves as a handle to keep my hand far away from the blade.

To cut shims, slide the saw fence over until the sled is just beside the blade. Then, hold a short length of 2x6 in the sled's notch and push both through the table saw blade. When the shim falls off onto the sled or behind the blade, slide the sled back for the next cut. I cut shims until the angle on the 2x6 gets too steep, then I turn the piece of 2x6 around and cut in the other direction. — G.K.

*The author prefers to make his own endgrain shims, which are strong but easy to snap off. He crosscuts 2x6 scraps using a sled made out of plywood with a tapered notch cut along one side. When the angle on the 2x6 gets too steep, he turns it around and cuts from the other end.*

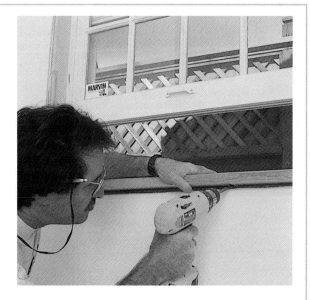

**Figure 22.** After positioning the preassembled frame against the window jambs (left), screw the extensions through the back-rabbets (center), and fasten the stool through the countersunk pilot holes (right).

**Figure 23.** To achieve a consistent reveal when installing stacked extension frames, the author uses a wood block milled on all four edges.

**Figure 24.** When the window is out of plane with the wall, paint-grade extensions can be individually scribed (top), then ripped with a panel saw and sanded (above). For stain-grade extensions, however, the author prefers to measure both ends of each piece to make sure the ends mate perfectly.

holes completely through the back-rabbet for the mounting screws. The pilot holes are large enough so that the screws slip through the extension. Angle the holes slightly to make it easier to reach the screw with a driver. But don't angle the holes too much or the tip of the screw might penetrate the face of the jamb.

Though the stool isn't back-rabbeted, I still drill a few "pocket" holes through the bottom. I start the holes with a 3/8-inch bit, drilling perpendicular to the stool about 2 inches from the edge of the frame. Then I slowly raise the drill, bring the bit almost vertical, and bury the tip in the stool. Finish the hole with a long 1/8-inch bit. With a pocket hole, the screw heads are countersunk and never interfere later when it's time to install the apron.

Next, position the frame against the jamb. I use a long Phillips driver in a magnetic bit holder to drive 1 1/2-inch drywall screws (**Figure 22**, previous page). One screw about every 1 1/2 feet is more than sufficient. If the drywall is already installed and cut close to the window opening, a quick hammer blow will clear a path to the pilot hole. Also clear the drywall from the pilot holes beneath the stool and screw the stool to the jamb.

## Stacking Jamb Extensions

Doubling up jamb extensions is another way to trim thick walls. Double extension frames, or stacked extensions, can be faster than wide, one-piece extensions because double frames are easy to preassemble from square-cut stock, and they can be installed in stacks, one after the other, using a nail gun.

For double extensions, use smaller reveals, which allow more wood for fastening. Measure for the first frame just as for any other window, then add 3/8 inch for the second layer, which leaves a 3/16-inch reveal. To speed up installation, I use a

reveal block — a 3/4-by-3-inch square piece of wood with a 3/16-inch-deep rabbet all the way around — which can be positioned quickly in each corner, in any direction (**Figure 23**). I cut and assemble the frames in my shop, then fasten them to the window jamb, one on top of the other. If the second extension is 1 inch thick or less, I attach the pieces one at a time.

## Scribing for Irregular Walls

Framing isn't always plumb, and occasionally a window or door jamb can't be set parallel or in plane with a wall. Some trim carpenters install extensions proud of the wall, then use a portable power plane to cut them almost flush to the wall. If the drywall is installed, a 1/16-inch-thick spacer taped to bottom of the plane prevents planing the drywall and ruining the blades.

But extensions can also be scribed. I use two methods: one is fast and crude; the other, slow but perfect. For apartments and tract housing, I position each piece of the frame against the jamb, then lay my pencil against the drywall and scribe a line on the back of the extension (**Figure 24**). I use my panel saw to cut along the scribed line, then sand the edge near the reveal line and ease it with my laminate trimmer and a roundover bit.

I take a little more time in custom homes, particularly with stain-grade material. Before assembling the frame, I measure and find the widest point of the jamb extension. Starting from that corner of the jamb, I mark and then measure both ends of each extension, so that the mating ends are exactly the same dimension. I rip the pieces with my panel saw, or freehand on a table saw, then sand and ease the edges before assembling the frame.

With either method, always apply the apron under the stool last. That final detail is the easiest and yet the most gratifying part of the whole job.

*Gary Katz is a finish carpenter in Reseda, Calif.*

# Quick Jamb Extensions for Vinyl Windows

by Frank Caputo

Here in California, most new homes have vinyl windows. Since these units are only a few inches deep, the drywaller or finish carpenter must bridge the gap between the window and the inside face of the wall. On moderately priced homes, this is done by returning drywall into the rough opening and butting it to the window. But on the high-end homes I trim, it means installing wood jamb extensions and then casings.

Early in my career as a finish carpenter, I used wood shims to align jamb extensions with the window. But I stopped using them after learning a trick from an older finish carpenter. At the time, we were installing rabbeted stools across the bottom of window openings that were to be finished top and sides with drywall returns.

## Drywall Screws Instead of Shims

Rather than supporting the stools with shims, the carpenter I was working with installed them over the heads of drywall screws sunk partway into the rough sill in a straight, level row. His method of preshimming stools was much faster than using shims. The method I use now to shim jamb extensions is based on that stool shimming trick — the difference being that I have to preshim all four sides with screws. To do this, I set screws around the inside perimeter of the rough opening so that the heads are in line with the outer edges of the window.

The photos shown are from a house containing vinyl windows with 1¼-inch-wide jambs. The extensions are made from ¾-inch fir. We build the jamb extensions to the same outside dimensions as the windows so there will be a ½-inch reveal where they butt to the vinyl.

We don't trim anything one at a time; we measure all the windows and then prebuild all the jamb extensions. On this job we picture-framed the casings, so the extensions were four-sided frames butted and screwed at the corners.

While one carpenter measures windows and builds jamb extensions, the other preshims all the rough openings with drywall screws.

## Aligning Screws

We set screws so their heads are in line with the outside edge of the window jamb. The idea is to put them as close as possible to the window but still get them in straight. The width of the screw gun prevents us from putting them much closer than 1½ inches away; we can't get them nearer without putting them in at an angle. I don't worry about shimming the opposite edge of the extension because it will be secured by a casing.

We start by sinking a row of screws along all four sides of the opening — one screw at each end, one in the middle, and enough in between so no two are more than 12 inches apart (**Photo 1**). Using a square-cut block of wood as a measuring device, I align the bottom screws first. I put the edge of the block against the jamb and land the end of it on the screw (**2**). If the screw is installed correctly, the end of the block will be flush to the edge of the jamb. If the block is too high, I drive the screw deeper; if it's too low, I

back the screw out. A screw gun works well for the initial installation, but a screwdriver is better for fine adjustments.

Once the heads of the end screws are aligned with the jambs, I place a straightedge (in this case a level) on top of them. I then raise or lower the rest of the screws (**3**) so that their heads just touch the bottom of the straightedge. The screw heads now form a straight line that is aligned with the edge of the window. It's great if the line turns out to be perfectly level, but more important that it be parallel to the jamb. If the screws read badly out of plumb or level, I know the window was poorly installed. If the window is seriously out of whack, the framer needs to come back and reset it so it's plumb, level, and square.

The next step is to repeat this process up one side of the window (**4**). This window was too tall for a 4-foot level to work as the straightedge, so we used a straight piece of wood instead (**5**).

If the window was installed correctly, the level will read plumb when placed against the straightedge (**6**).

## Spacing Across

Although it's possible to set the remaining screws to the other two edges of the jamb, it's faster and more accurate to set them by "measuring" off the screws that are already in. We don't actually measure; we use spacers that are exactly as long as the extension is wide and high. The spacers are made from off-rips of the jamb stock; since most houses contain multiples of the same windows, we can often use the same spacers over and over.

To set the spacing, we put one end of the spacer against a screw that has already been aligned and run it across to the screw on the opposite side of the opening (**7**). The spacer should just barely slip

between the screw heads (**8**). If it doesn't, then we have to run the screw on the side that has not been aligned in or out until the spacer fits.

We repeat this process all the way up the side of the opening. When we're done, the screws on the second side will be perfectly parallel to those on the first side and exactly as far apart as the extension unit is wide.

We adjust the screws at the top of the opening by spacing off the screws along the bottom. A quick and easy way to make the adjustment is to place the bottom end of the spacer on a bottom screw and swing the top end of the spacer off to the side of the protruding screw above. It's a simple matter to run that screw in or out by hand (**9**) until the spacer just slips by (**10**).

Once this has been done with all the screws at the top of the opening, the jambs are ready to be installed.

## Installing the Jambs

At this point, the screw heads around the opening form straight lines that are aligned with the outside edges of the window jamb. To install the jamb extension, we simply fit it between the screw heads (**11**).

If the jamb stock is straight, the jamb unit will slip right in and there will be no slop between it and the screw heads. If the jamb stock is bowed, we might have to tap the unit into position.

Usually it's a perfect fit, but if a screw is high the jamb extension will encroach on the ½-inch reveal. We fix this by putting a block over the high spot and hitting it with a hammer, slightly burying the screw head in the back of the extension.

Our last step is nailing off the jamb extension. Since we want to nail near the screw heads, we mark their locations in pencil on the jamb. That way, we won't accidentally nail where there is no "shim."

## Quick and Simple

Shimming with drywall screws may sound complicated, but it's actually quite simple. In the time it takes to read this story, I could preshim a jamb extension.

The process takes about 20 minutes per window, which is less time than it used to take me to install jamb extensions over wood shims. It's nice not having to buy or haul around a bunch of shims of questionable dryness. All I need are a straightedge, a block of wood, a screw gun, a screwdriver, and some 1¼-inch and 2-inch drywall screws in my pouch.

This same basic method can be used with wood windows, though in most cases those units come with the jamb extensions already attached. One thing you will have to adjust for is butting to a narrower jamb. The screw heads might have to be set deeper to obtain the desired reveal.

## Laser Method

Sometimes we set the screw heads to a laser line rather than to a block. With single windows, using a laser is no faster than using a block; but with clustered (ganged) windows, it's a significant time-saver.

Although clustered windows are rarely installed in perfectly straight lines, the jamb extensions on these units must be perfectly aligned; if they're not, variations will show up in the casing reveal. Since the laser beam can span multiple windows at the same time, we use it to align adjoining jamb extensions.

To begin, we set up the laser so that the horizontal beam lands on — or just clips — the bottom edge of a jamb. The beam represents the top of the screw head and the back of the jamb extension. If the windows are not perfectly level or aligned, the beam will be high in some places and low in others. We adjust its height until we have a compromise that works for all the windows. Then we set screw heads to this line across the bottom of the openings — much as we do when we use a block, except now we're gauging the height of the heads with a laser.

The trick is to make sure that the beam always has something to land on; otherwise it won't be visible. For example, if the screw head is below the beam and the window jamb is above it, the beam will disappear into the gap below the window. When that happens, we hold a piece of paper — in this case a window label — behind the screw so that we can see the beam.

We then raise or lower the screw head until it splits the beam (**12**). The lower half of the beam will hit the screw head and the upper half will be visible on the paper. We repeat this process up the side of the window (**13**).

*Frank Caputo is a finish-carpentry contractor in Cool, Calif. Special thanks to John Bynes for help with the photography.*

# Chapter 16: Running Trim

■ **Finish Carpentry, Production Style**

■ **Installing Crown Molding**

■ **Working With Polymer Moldings**

■ **Installing Flexible Trim**

# Finish Carpentry, Production Style

by Ross Welsh

I'm a trim carpentry subcontractor in Sacramento, where my company specializes in large subdivisions. Many of our jobs involve trimming out more than 100 homes at a time. While some carpenters might expect the work to be dull and repetitive, I've found that doing it well is a challenge and calls for a special set of skills.

We're careful to vary the work so people don't get bored. A carpenter might install doors for most of the day, then later notch 45 window stools. The next day, he might do shelving or baseboard. Organization and overall efficiency are critical. A production trim carpenter has to do accurate work, because materials are so tightly estimated that there's little extra stock available to fix mistakes. Trimming out an entire 2,800-square-foot house usually yields only a couple of handfuls of scrap.

## Getting Ready

Although all the homes in a given development are similar, most builders offer a variety of options, such as crown molding, upgraded trim, and premium entry doors. The best GCs will post a list of the buyer's selections on a window or garage wall early, so we know in advance what options are included (**Figure 1**).

*Plans and FAQs.* Before we start a new group of homes, I spend some time going over the plans with my foreman, the framer, and the suppliers on the job. This allows us to make corrections early so they don't eat up valuable time and materials. I then make a three-ring binder for each house filled with mini-plans that I generate from the simplified floor

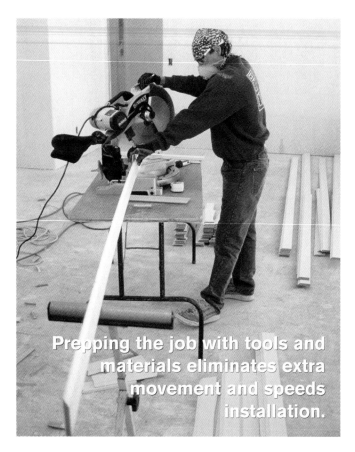

Prepping the job with tools and materials eliminates extra movement and speeds installation.

plans included in the builder's sales brochures. My mini-plans show door swings and sizes, shelving arrangements, and the heights and locations of easily forgotten items like towel bars and paper holders.

The binder also contains a set of our installation guidelines for the particular subdivision we're working on, which lay out the basic ground rules for the project (see facing page). These two documents contain the answers to most everyday questions and save the carpenters from having to track me down or bother a supervisor for the information. I give the binder to the crew leader, who makes it available to the carpenters on the job.

## Stocking Material

A few days before we start a job, the builder arranges for delivery of the trim package. When we get the trim package, it's been partially prepared by the supplier. The casing is precut, and the shelving comes as a package of components that includes the shelves, poles, hook strip, pole supports, and sockets. Window stools and aprons are cut to within 1/2 inch of the size needed, and baseboard and crown molding are delivered in 16-foot lengths (**Figure 2**, page 288).

One popular design in our area is a 2,800-square-

**Figure 1.**
Builder option lists show all products and details that deviate from the standard spec. Good builders post them in the home to spell out the options that the homeowner has chosen, allowing the author's crew to confirm that the correct materials package has been delivered.

## Installation Guidelines for XYZ Communities

XYZ Communities posts a floor plan and features list in the rear window (first floor) of each house they build. Please review these lists each time you work on a house to familiarize yourself with the options that affect your work. For instance, look for changes in door swings, upgraded hardware, etc. XYZ offers many options to their buyers, so please don't assume that any specific plan is always built the same.

- Mirrored bipass wardrobe doors are standard in master bedrooms. But mirrored doors go in other bedrooms as an upgrade option in many houses. Please review the features lists to be sure you're installing the appropriate bump jamb.
- Bump jambs are set back $3/4$" from the bipass opening. The back of the wardrobe track for wood doors is set to the back edge of the bump jamb, and the valance lies over the opening by $1 1/2$" each side and 1" up on to the header. The material is $3 1/4$" wide, so it covers the track by $2 1/4$".
- Be prepared to fully adjust exterior doors at interior trim stage. Do not case until door operates properly.
- Window stool apron is cut at 30 degrees.
- Follow shelving layouts on mini-plans. Standard heights are as follows:
  - 5 stacks behind a door measure from floor to top of cleat: 16", 30", 44", 58", 72". This is typical for reach-in pantries.
  - 4-plus-1 stacks measure from floor to top of cleat: 24", 38", 52", 66", 80". This is typically used in master wardrobes with 16"-deep partitions, four 16"-deep lower shelves, and one 12" top shelf at 80". The shelf at 80" often ties in with a shelf and pole at 80". Master 5 stacks have the same heights as 4-plus-1 stacks.
  - Face frame 5 stacks measure from underside of header to top of cleat: 14", 28", 48", 62", 78". The shelves must come flush to the front of the opening.
  - Standard single shelf and pole height is 66" to top of hook strip.

- Pole supports are spaced no farther apart than 32". Do not install any rosettes, poles, or pole supports unless all the pole supports are installed. This is known as our all-or-none rule.
- Trim all interior attic access holes with door stop to support drywall lid.
- Garage attic access doors must be installed with at least two 3" screws in each jamb. Install passage knob at time of door installation.
- Case all patio doors.
- Install 2"-by-2" support at all thresholds.
- Standard towel bar height is 48" above finished floor. Wall-mounted paper holders are 24" above finished floor and 24" from back wall. Cabinet-mounted paper holders are 4" to 6" below countertop. Follow mini-plans for bar, ring, and paper holder locations. If you have any questions, ask Ross or the lead carpenter on the job.
- Standard installation of spring bumps is at the bottom of the door so it hits baseboard.
- On exterior doors, install two 3" screws at each hinge and two at each strike plate.
- Install shower poles above tile.
- Check hardware packages against the features list to confirm you are installing the correct package. Don't assume the package on site is correct. Also, inspect all hardware for dents and scratches as you're installing it. Don't install damaged hardware. Put it back in the box and give the box and a shortage list to the superintendent or his assistant.
- Please scrap out each house when you're finished each day.

Finally, XYZ strictly prohibits eating in the houses, parking on the driveways, or interfering with the erosion-control materials. Doing any of these things can result in heavy penalties. Please abide by these rules at all times.
  Thank you in advance for reviewing these guidelines and following them.

A critical element in the planning process includes generating a set of installation guidelines meant to answer carpenters' frequently asked questions so that they don't have to bother a site supervisor or track down the boss. This extra effort at the beginning saves time and reduces mistakes. — *R.W.*

**Figure 2.** The partially prepared trim package is delivered to each house, where the first task of the trim carpenters is to break it down and distribute the material from room to room.

foot, two-story model with 15 interior doors, 15 windows, 28 shelves, baseboards with radiused corners, and lots of decorative columns and pop-outs. If we assign three carpenters to such a job, we can finish it in one day. If all goes well, one carpenter will have a couple of hours at the end of the day to start spreading material or hanging exterior doors in the next house.

*Spread out.* Before we can start making sawdust, the material package needs to be spread throughout the house. The idea is to place the materials within easy reach of where they'll be needed but out of the way of other operations in the same area. Spreading the material properly also confirms that the package is complete.

In the morning, two of the carpenters start spreading doors and casing, while the third sets up the compressor, hoses, and a miter-saw workstation. It's important for one carpenter to start installing doors within the first half hour, because most of the trim can't be installed until after the doors are in place. One of the spreaders soon begins cutting and building wardrobe and pantry shelving, leaving the third to make sure the others have the tools and materials they need to keep moving ahead.

## Prehung Door Installation

We work primarily with prehung doors. Prehung door installation is best thought of as an assembly process. Our procedures for doors and door and window trim are covered in "Production Prehungs and Window Trim," page 254.

## Baseboard

The first step in baseboard installation is to study the option list to determine which areas will be carpeted. We install the baseboard in those areas first, leaving the remaining base for the final base-over trip (see "Running Baseboard," facing page). To ensure accurate measurements, we use a garden scraper with a long handle to clean up the drywall at corners and knock away blobs of joint compound.

*Recording measurements.* Baseboard measurements are taken behind the door installer. Each of us uses a slightly different notation for recording our measurements, but they all involve writing down the length with notations to indicate the type of cut for each end. (To avoid confusion, each crewmember cuts only his own material.) For example, a back slash to the right of a number means inside miter to me. That same slash to the left means an outside miter, and the addition of a "2" means 22$\frac{1}{2}$ degrees. Measuring needs to proceed systematically; personally, I work from left to right.

*Miter-saw tips.* Accurate measuring and efficient handling of material at the saw are vital to working productively. We use miter saws mounted on folding tables and roller stands to support our work. That equipment is very portable, yet sturdy enough for the job.

The flow of material should go from one side to the other, with the material within easy reach to keep it oriented consistently. I like it face up with the top away from me. I pull stock from my right and first make the left cut, which becomes the zero end for my tape. After I've cut the right side, the material continues its flow to the left and is stacked in order room by room.

Because I'm right-handed, I try to keep the saw swung right whenever possible for better visibility, flipping the material as needed (**Figure 3**, page 290). As the stacks of baseboard accumulate, we distribute them to the appropriate rooms and stand the material in position, ready for installation.

*Longs and shorts.* In general, we try to cut the material in order of installation. Sometimes we will cut a few long pieces first to create medium and short offcuts for economical use of material, but shorts are plentiful later so we're careful not to overdo it. While we're cutting base, we make a bunch of little pieces to follow the rounded shape of the bullnose outside corners that are common in our area. Unlike a typical 90-degree corner, they require a third corner piece cut at 22$\frac{1}{2}$ degrees on both ends. With the saw set at 22$\frac{1}{2}$ degrees, we make the first cut, then flip the material, slide to a standard mark, and make the second cut. Keeping the saw in the same position, we flip the stock back over for another first cut and repeat until we have enough. We carry a few undersized and oversized corner pieces with us to give us some flexibility when we're fitting and nailing.

*Tacking and nailing.* When nailing, we carry a mini pry bar and a pneumatic finish nailer; plus, we keep a hammer and nail set nearby. To nail off, I tack

## Running Baseboard

### by Byron Beck

My first job on a finish crew was doing baseboard. The older guys didn't want to spend all day on their knees, plus they probably figured I couldn't do much damage down at floor level. For weeks at a time, I did nothing but baseboard. After a while, I began to look for ways to speed production. One of the techniques I came up with was measuring and cutting all the base in a room at the same time.

*Planning and layout.* Start by deciding in what order you're going to install pieces. The order of installation determines which ends get coped and which butt the wall. In general, right-handers work counterclockwise around rooms, because the copes are easier to cut that way; left-handers go the other way. Then take a short scrap of base, hold it where the butt end goes, and trace its outline on the adjacent wall (see photos). Do this at every corner where a coped joint occurs.

*Measuring.* Now measure the distance from the unmarked end of the wall to the trace mark at the far corner. The mark represents the short point of the miter we use to guide the cope cut. Measure every wall in the room and write the dimensions on a sketch of the floor plan. Measurements of long walls that require scarf joints will be more accurate if you hook your tape on a nail driven into the trace line and measure back the other way.

Baseboard stock is usually 12 to 16 feet long, which means we can usually do walls in one or two pieces. As long as there's only one scarf joint per wall, we're comfortable cutting everything at once. But if there's more than one scarf joint in a run of trim, install the coped end first, then any pieces in the middle, and save the piece that butts into the corner till last.

*Cutting and installing.* Once you have a complete list of dimensions, go to the saw and cut all the base. You'll be surprised how little time it takes to make copes when you do them one after another. Our carpenters rarely use their coping saws; instead, they cope with Bosch D-handle jigsaws. It's much faster than hand coping, and what they can't get with the jigsaw they remove with a small Makita angle grinder. As with casings, the cut man bundles pieces for his partner to install.

We can cut and install all the base in a 20-by-20-foot

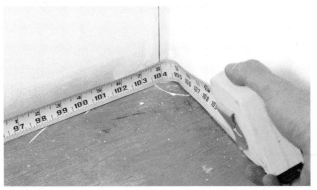

*Precutting all baseboard speeds installation. To get accurate dimensions, trace the outline of the base molding on the wall (top) and measure to your mark (above). This is the short point of the miter that will guide the coped corner cut.*

room in 30 minutes, about half the time it takes doing it one piece at a time. Normally, we do all the trim before hardwood floors go down, and use shoe molding to cover the gap between base and flooring. We set the height of the base by inserting spacers between the molding and the subfloor. But if the wall is to be paneled, the base has to be dead level. In that case, we use a laser to shoot reference lines.

Mediterranean-style houses typically have some rooms with stone floors. Since no one wants to see shoe molding or continuous grout joints at the base, we can't install base till after the stone is in. There's no way around having to scribe the base to the floor, but we can still cut all of it at the same time. We'll cut the base to length when we do the rest of the trim, then scribe and install it later on.

*Byron Beck is a woodworker and finish subcontractor in Santa Barbara, Calif.*

**Figure 3.** When mitering baseboard for an inside corner at each end, the left miter is cut first, with the saw tilted right and the material right side up (far left). The material is slid to the left and marked to length on the back-bottom corner. To make the right-hand cut, the baseboard is turned upside down on the fence, leaving the mark facing up and clearly visible (left).

the baseboard in place while holding it up 3/8 inch with my mini pry bar, so carpet can be tucked under it later (**Figure 4**). I tack in the same direction I measure and cut — that is, from left to right, since I'm right-handed. If everything fits, I backtrack and finish nailing. Walking backward, I keep my left side to the wall and sight down each stud, bringing the nail gun in with my right hand.

Any miscut pieces noticed when tacking should immediately be set aside with a note written on the piece describing the mistake. At this point, we don't go back to the saw, because trips to the saw waste time. If we need a break from the repetitive task of fastening and have a few corrections to make, we do a group of recuts all at once, saving some time.

***Handling small pieces.*** Decorative arch pop-outs, especially those with bull-nosed drywall corners, can have as many cuts as an entire bedroom. Holding all the tiny pieces and fastening them safely present a

real challenge. If a house we're working on has a lot of areas like that, we use a hot-melt glue gun to temporarily hold the pieces in position. We've found that once the gun is thoroughly heated up, the glue will remain fluid for about five minutes after it's unplugged, making it into a sort of low-tech cordless tool. We glue the tricky little pieces to the wall before we nail them, which allows us to keep our hands out of harm's way (**Figure 5**).

## Shelving

Shelving requires moving the most tools, but it can still be done by making one trip to a bedroom with your arms full. We carry a nail gun, a cordless circular saw, a cordless drill, and if the shelving is elaborate, a 4-foot level. The hand tools in your toolbelt should include a 12-inch speed square, torpedo level, 12-ounce hammer, nail set, mini pry bar, #2.5 pencil,

**Figure 4.** In areas that will be carpeted later, the base is held 3/8 inch above the floor with a mini pry bar as it's tacked in place.

**Figure 5.** The small filler pieces needed to wrap bull-nosed corners are tough to nail safely, so they're temporarily held in place with hot-melt glue.

small handheld elementary-school-type pencil sharpener (Staedtler #51027), a good 16-foot tape measure, and a supply of 2-inch screws and 1 1/2-inch pneumatic nails. My belt also contains a holster for the cordless drill.

The material kit for the closet should be ready and waiting. Material up to 6 feet long should be leaning against a wall away from other work areas, but longer material works best positioned strategically on the floor.

***Closet basics.*** To install a shelf and pole, I mark the back wall of the closet 66 inches up from the floor. Then I measure the width of the closet and, with the tape measure still in hand, transfer that measurement to the back hook strip (back cleat) and shelf. After checking for square, I cut the hook slightly short with the cordless circ saw, using my

## Custom Millwork: Planning and Layout

**by David Frane**

Most of our projects are big enough to justify custom milling of almost all trim, even when the architects specify stock profiles.

**Custom milling.** Custom milling has a number of advantages. One advantage is that if the trim will be painted we can have it milled in poplar. Poplar is cheaper than pine and produces crisper profiles. And though I miss the smell of pine trim on our jobs, I don't miss the way it dents and loses edges. Another advantage with custom millwork is that cornices and casings that are usually built up from two or more stock moldings can be milled as one piece. It's almost always easier to install one large molding than two smaller ones. It also makes for a better job.

Most two-piece baseboards consist of a piece of 3/4-inch-thick flat stock capped with a small molding. The lower part of the base spans small hollows in the wall, while the cap bends right into them. This can look pretty bad; the reveal between the top edge of the base and the molding profile should be uniform.

Of course, one-piece trim isn't always a blessing. At inside corners, single-piece baseboards have the shortcoming of requiring you to cope the entire width, rather than just the molding. A compromise solution is to mill everything so that the cap fits into a groove on top of the base (see photo). This not only keeps the cap running parallel to the base; it also ensures that if the base shrinks a bit, a crack won't open up between it and the cap.

**Layout.** Careful planning is the most important part of any job. It's always best to group like tasks. After the doors have been hung and cased, it's time to do the running trim. This includes baseboard, chair rail, and crown molding.

The first step is to snap level lines on the wall to represent the top edges of baseboards and chair rails, and the bottom edges of crown moldings. Some carpenters just let the baseboard follow the floor, but long pieces of baseboard aren't always straight and floors aren't

*With two-piece baseboard, the author uses a custom-milled base cap that interlocks with the baseboard. This leaves a consistent reveal at the front edge of the cap and prevents cracks from appearing at the joint if the base shrinks.*

always flat or level. Baseboard that's parallel to an out-of-level floor is more noticeable than baseboard that is level but not parallel to the floor. In small rooms you can make these lines with a water level or an accurate 6-foot level. In large rooms, it's easier to use a transit or builders level.

**Installation sequence.** You should also spend some time planning the installation sequence. For instance, if the baseboard or crown molding in a room has scarf joints but the last piece has to be coped on both ends, you're doing something wrong. Why try to fit a piece with two coped ends when you can finish with one that has been coped on one end and scarfed on the other?

It should go without saying that joints should fit tight and lay flush. Stock that is dented, bowed, or otherwise defective belongs in the dumpster, not on the building. The nails holding trim to the wall should penetrate a good inch into the framing and there should be enough of them to hold the trim in place: one nail per stud for crown molding, two nails per stud for baseboard. The inside corners of molded trim should be coped and the running joints scarfed. To keep scarf joints from telegraphing through the paint, we glue them with yellow glue. Nail in a regular pattern and in such a way that you don't destroy the details of the trim.

*David Frane is a senior editor at JLC and a former builder.*

foot for support. While holding it up to my mark on the back wall, I level it with my torpedo level and nail it off into studs, which is easy at this stage because the walls aren't painted yet.

Next, I measure, cut, and install the side hook strips (cleats), which cover any small gaps at the ends of the hook strip. Inside corners are often out of square, so before I cut the shelf, I check them with a 12-inch speed square. I then eyeball the needed adjustment and transfer it to the shelf.

Most of the simple closets we trim call for bypass doors with a track, valance, and bump jambs. I measure for those items while I have my tape out and cut them while I still have the cordless circular saw in my hand. The metal tracks are supplied slightly short, so they just screw into place. When I have my cordless drill in hand, I do all the screw work at once, including the pole supports, pole sockets, and track. The last step is to measure and cut the poles. I never try estimating or precutting poles before this point.

*Walk-in closets.* Most of today's master closets are really large — some are larger than my college studio apartment. When trimming those, we add a 4-foot level and a 3-foot ladder to our arsenal of tools. We precut as much material as possible at the miter saw, but a large, complicated closet is usually a series of small projects, where one step must precede another to get accurate measurements. The design for those complicated closets is spelled out in our mini-plans.

## Crown Molding

We prefer to install crown molding after the mess from the standard trim package has been cleaned up. Although the speed and reliability of pneumatic finish nailers makes them our first choice for most trim work, this is one area where we opt for the hose-free convenience of cordless nailers instead.

We usually cut the material in position on a large miter saw, using a workstation setup similar to the one we use for baseboard. The material is positioned upside down, with the fence representing the wall and the table representing the ceiling. This gives us the needed compound cut by moving just the miter table, without time-wasting bevel adjustments.

*Around the room.* Measuring for crown molding starts with the long walls. After two carpenters have pulled those measurements, one carpenter starts to cut the long pieces, while the other measures the shorter walls and lays out reference marks on the walls with a gauge block. When the molding has been cut to length, the carpenters position themselves on ladders at opposite ends of it. Once they've confirmed that the length is correct, the crown is tacked in position.

One carpenter then sets up at the end of the next piece and hands the material to the carpenter who has stayed in place. Continuing around the room this way ensures that only one carpenter moves at a time. While one is setting up for the next piece, the other is fastening. With one room complete, the cutting carpenter returns to the saw, while the remaining carpenter finishes nailing and sets up in the next room.

## Base-Over

Our last scheduled task, called "base-over," is to install door hardware and the remaining baseboard over vinyl, tile, and hardwood flooring. This also involves a quality check of all our work and can take one carpenter up to a full day. A few days before the base-over, I check the house and get together with the superintendent to make sure we don't forget any loose ends. Our goal is to be 100% complete at this point. Making additional trips to finish up odds and ends after the final base-over is a time-waster that can put a big dent in overall productivity.

*Ross Welsh is a finish carpentry subcontractor in Sacramento, Calif.*

# Installing Crown Molding

by Gary Katz

I've heard it said that cutting crown molding is a test of a finish carpenter's skill. But I think that cutting crown molding can be just as easy as cutting baseboard, a lot more fun, and you don't have to wear out your knees. Here I'll show you the techniques I use to maintain productivity and precision while installing crown molding. The first step is always careful layout and measurement.

## Layout and Measurement

If crown isn't installed in a straight line, the molding will wiggle and wobble between the ceiling and walls, and tight margins between the crown and tall door and window casings will be hideously unequal. So I always snap lines before applying the molding.

To determine where the bottom edge of the crown will sit on the wall, place a piece of the molding in a

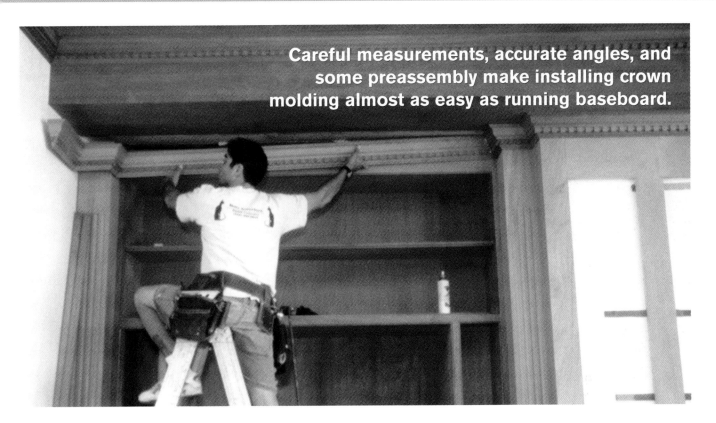

Careful measurements, accurate angles, and some preassembly make installing crown molding almost as easy as running baseboard.

framing square, just as it will sit on the wall — with the bottom edge of the molding on one leg of the square and the top edge against the other leg. To help visualize the position of the molding on the wall, hold the square in the air and pretend that the top leg is the ceiling. Rock the crown until both "feet" lie flat against the square, then check the measurement at the bottom of the crown (**Figure 6**). That measurement is called the rise — the distance from the bottom of the crown to the ceiling.

If I'm trimming only one room, I measure the rise

of the molding, mark the bottom edge of the crown at each corner in the room, then snap chalk lines across all the walls. (If the walls have already been painted, I use a dry line and pencil in small marks every 6 or 8 feet along each wall.) Whenever I'm installing crown in more than one room, especially on large jobs, I transfer the rise measurement to several small blocks of scrap material. Each carpenter working on the job can then carry the same gauge block so that all the crown will be installed at the same elevation (**Figure 7**).

**Figure 6.** With the top of the square as the ceiling, the rise of the crown molding is measured to the bottom of the crown.

**Figure 7.** A gauge block the size of the rise simplifies layout.

**Figure 8.** Install a stop along the length of your saw base to stabilize crown molding when cutting in position.

To avoid unnecessary steps up a ladder, I measure the length of each piece while I'm snapping lines on the walls. The measurements are always taken right along the chalk line — not at the ceiling. I write those measurements, in large numbers, just above the line on each wall.

To minimize trips to the saw, I make a cut list for each room. When measuring pieces over 8 to 10 feet long, I add 1/16 to 1/8 inch and spring them into place so that corner joints are tight. For pieces under 8 to 10 feet long, I measure precisely to within 1/32 inch.

I use typical carpenter notations to identify the cuts: Inside corners are noted with a "V"; outside corners are marked "OC"; and self-returns are "SR." So for a piece that's 64 inches long, with an inside corner on the left and an outside corner on the right, I write on the cut list: "V 64 OC." If the angle is 90 degrees, I don't make a notation; but for other angles — like a 22 1/2 — I make a note next to the type of cut (see "Finding the Right Angles," page 297, for more about this).

## Cutting in Position

Crown molding can be cut "in position" or "on the flat." Each method has a specific use, and clever carpenters should become proficient at both. For each method, I've developed simple routines and techniques that increase efficiency and accuracy.

The most efficient way to cut crown molding is in position — with the molding standing upside down and leaning against the miter-saw fence. Cutting in position means that the material is always in the same position on the fence and never has to be flipped end for end; the bevel of the saw is never changed from 90 degrees; and aligning the blade so that it enters the material exactly on the measurement mark is just as easy as cutting baseboard.

Everyone in the trade refers to this method as the mysterious "upside-down-and-backwards" position. No further examination of the enigma seems ever to be required. But carpenters might better imagine that the crown molding isn't really upside down and backwards — the saw is. The base of the saw is the ceiling.

Whenever I cut crown in position, I always start by placing a short piece of the molding on my saw (upside down). I trace a pencil line across the crown along the fence and along the base, then set a straight piece of scrap material, about 3 or 4 feet long, at the bottom line and fasten it with screws to my extension wings, where it acts as a stop (**Figure 8**). With the stop attached, the molding is held securely in position, the bevel is cut exactly the same way every time, and long lengths of material are easy to handle.

Visualizing the correct direction of a cut is also easier if we imagine that the fence is the wall and the base of the saw is the ceiling. For inside corners, the long point of the miter and the bevel is always on the wall or fence (just like with baseboard); for outside corners, the short point of the miter and the bevel is always on the wall or fence (just like with baseboard). That rule never changes (**Figure 9**).

As with baseboard, if the piece has an inside corner (most have at least one), I cut that end first, then hook my tape on the long point and reach across the

**Figure 9.** The long point of an inside corner is always against the wall or fence (far left). The short point of an outside corner is always against the wall or fence (left).

**Figure 10.** Measure an inside corner by hooking the tape over the long point.

**Figure 11.** Measure an outside corner by aligning the short point with the edge of the saw fence and hooking the tape over the fence.

crown to measure the opposite end (**Figure 10**). If the piece has two inside corners, I prefer to cut the right-hand corner first — that way I pull my tape from my left side and the numbers are right side up. With the stop in place, the molding never moves while I'm measuring.

For pieces that have two outside corners, I cut one

end and align the short point of the miter with the edge of the fence, then hook my tape on the fence and measure to the opposite end of the molding (**Figure 11**). For long lengths, I align the short point with the end of my extension wing, then hook my tape over the extension wing and measure to the opposite end of the molding.

## Using the Bosch Angle Finder

The Bosch Angle Finder (about $120) is a must for cutting crown molding on the flat, and it's easy to use. When cutting crown on the flat, I read every corner, not just the 22½-degree oddball corners. That way, every joint comes together perfectly tight the first time.

Start by spreading the arms on the BAF until the LED reads the exact spring angle of the crown molding you're installing (refer to **Figure 14**, page 297), then press the black bevel/miter (BV/MT) button. The spring angle will be entered into memory — confirmed by the appearance of "SPR" in a black box at the lower left corner. (Unfortunately, the BAF doesn't have a permanent memory, so you must enter the spring angle of the crown for every corner. I'm hoping Bosch adds a keypad in the future so the spring angle can be entered more quickly and accurately.)

Next, place the BAF in the corner of the walls and open it until both arms are flat against each wall, then press the BV/MT button again. The abbreviation "CNR" will appear in the LED, confirming that the corner angle has been entered.

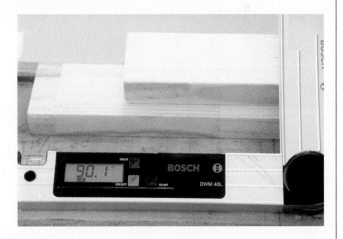

*After entering the spring angle of the crown molding, measure the angle of the corner and press the BV/MT button again — "CNR" will appear in the display.*

Press the BV/MT button a third time, and the miter angle will come up in the display, along with the abbreviation "MTR." Finally, press the BV/MT button one last time, and the bevel angle will be displayed, along with the abbreviation "BVL." It's that simple. — G.K.

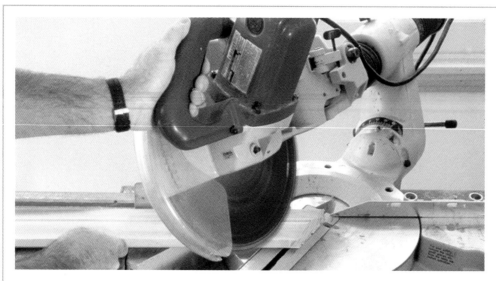

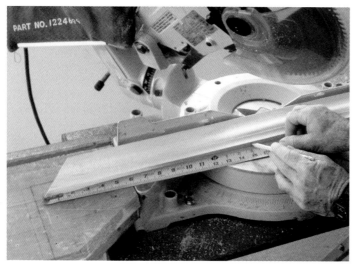

**Figure 12.** To cut LH inside corners and RH outside corners, the bottom edge must be against the fence and nearly hidden from view, so cut those corners first (left). Then flip the material, hook your tape on the long point, and make your measurement mark on the bottom edge of the molding (below left). That way you can control exactly where the blade meets the measurement mark (below).

Also as with baseboard, I first cut any end with a self-return, then hook my tape over the long point of the self-return and measure to the opposite end of the molding.

## Cutting on the Flat

Crown molding with a rise of over 4³/4 inches can't be cut in position on most miter saws. (The DeWalt 706 12-inch and the Hitachi 15-inch miter saws will cut crown in position with a rise up to 6 inches.) I prefer to cut in position whenever possible, especially on jobs with any real volume, because cutting in position is much faster than cutting on the flat. But extremely large crown moldings are becoming more popular, and they must be cut on the flat with a sliding compound miter saw.

Most carpenters find that cutting on the flat isn't nearly as straightforward as cutting in position. I follow a few simple rules that make the job less confusing and more efficient.

*Flip the material, not the saw.* Though my Makita 12-inch saw (LS1211) bevels in both directions, I try

not to change the bevel angle if I can help it. I find it's faster to flip the molding end for end — that is, unless I'm cutting in a small room or hallway. Then I have no choice and have to flip the bevel (more on that in a moment).

*Keep the bottom edge measurement in sight.* Crown molding measurements are almost always marked on the bottom edge and never on the top of the molding. That's one reason cutting crown in position is easier — the bottom edge of the molding is always up, so all measurement marks are clearly visible, and aligning the saw blade with the measurement mark is not difficult.

Cutting crown on the flat (with the bevel tilted only toward the left) isn't quite so simple because the bottom edge isn't always in view. But by thinking ahead, I'm always able to have the bottom edge of the molding away from the fence just when I need to, so that I can easily align the saw blade with the measurement mark.

*Cut LH inside corners and RH outside corners first.* To cut left-hand (LH) inside corners and right-

**Figure 13.** Some pieces are too long to spin around, necessitating flipping the bevel angle on the saw two ways instead.

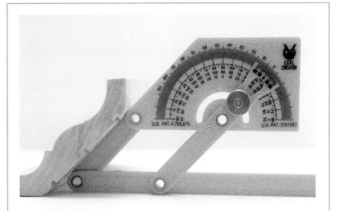

**Figure 14.** An inexpensive low-tech protractor is all you need to find the spring angle of crown molding. Hold the crown against a wall or flat surface, with the bottom edge down in the same position in which it will be installed at the ceiling. Then spread the protractor open between the wall and the back of the crown.

hand (RH) outside corners, the bottom edge of the molding must be against the fence and nearly hidden from view. When the bottom edge is against the fence, accurately aligning the saw blade with the measurement mark is difficult and time consuming. So I cut those corners first, then flip the molding end for end and hook my tape on the long point of the miter-bevel to mark the opposite end. Cutting the RH corner is easy because the bottom of the molding is away from the fence, and I can quickly and accurately align the saw blade with the mark (**Figure 12**).

For pieces with LH inside corners and RH outside corners, pieces with two outside corners, and long lengths that I don't have enough room to spin in the air (**Figure 13**), I flip the motor to the opposite bevel. There's simply no other way to cut these pieces with the bottom edge and the measurement mark away from the fence.

Clearly, a double-bevel saw has several advantages over a single-bevel saw, because with a double-bevel saw long material rarely has to be flipped or moved. Cuts can be made quickly and accurately with the bottom edge of the molding always positioned away from the fence, and inside corners can always be cut first, which makes it easier to hook a tape measure. The only disadvantage is that the saw bevel must be flipped, which requires one more step and a little more time.

## Finding the Right Angles

With crown molding, there are four important angles to consider: the corner angle (the angle where the walls meet), the spring angle (between the back face of the crown and the wall), the bevel angle (the angle to be cut, measured from the back

face of the crown), and the miter angle (the angle to be cut, measured from the bottom edge of the crown).

In order to determine the bevel and miter angles, you first have to determine the spring angle (**Figure 14**). Bevel and miter angle charts are available for cutting crown moldings with 45- and 38-degree spring angles. But not all patterns of crown molding are milled with a spring angle of 45 degrees or 38 degrees.

Even the best SCM saw in the world won't be of any help if you can't find the right bevel and miter angles. When I first started using these saws and ran into oddly angled corners or a crown pattern I couldn't cut using the standard settings marked on my saw, I always tried to cut the crown in position first, and then determine the right bevel and miter setting from the pieces I'd cut. These days I don't worry about such nonsense because I use a Bosch Angle Finder (BAF) and read the angle of every corner (even the 90-degree corners, because they're rarely 90 degrees) before cutting any crown (see "Using the Bosch Angle Finder," page 295).

## Coping Inside Corners

Coping inside corners has long been the best method of joinery, and for wood crown molding that rule still stands. For MDF and urethane moldings, however, coped joints are not always the best choice. MDF moldings don't cope well because when the material is compressed, the sharp coped edge folds back like thick skin. Urethane-molding manufacturers, on the other hand, insist that all joints be fastened with proprietary adhesive — which isn't possible with a coped joint.

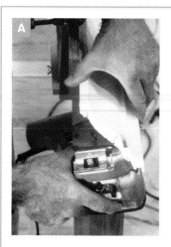

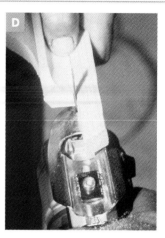

**Figure 15.** Begin coping with the Collins Coping Foot by cutting a series of relief cuts (A). Cut down through the S-curve (B). Cut back up toward the cove relief (C). To finish the cut, use a small piece of stock to back up the fragile bottom edge, so that the sliver-thin miter overlap won't snap off (D).

I still do my coping the same way I originally learned, by cutting an inside-corner miter first. Occasionally, I use a coping saw, too. But for today's large hardwood moldings, I rely most often on a Collins Coping Foot (Collins Tool Company, www.collinstool.com).

*Using a coping foot.* A jigsaw, equipped with a Collins Coping Foot, makes quick work out of both softwood and hardwood crown molding. The best person to demonstrate the technique is the inventor of the foot, Dave Collins.

Dave starts coping by making a series of relief cuts along each step in the profile. He also cuts a relief at the deepest point in the S curve. Next, he slices down the S curve and uses the angle of the coping foot to simultaneously push and leverage the jigsaw blade perfectly along the line of the profile. Turning the saw around, he then eases the blade up toward

the top of the crown and terminates the cut neatly into a relief cut. The bottom of the crown is cut last, first by cutting up through the cove, then by cutting parallel with the grain, leaving a final sliver of wood to form the appearance of a miter (**Figure 15**).

## Installing Crown

Before lifting crown into position, I mark the stud layout on the wall, just beneath the snap line. I mark the joist layout in the ceiling, too, just outside the footprint of the molding. If the joists aren't running perpendicular to the wall, I cross-nail the molding to the ceiling: Every 18 inches I drive two nails about 2 inches apart, angling the nails toward each other at 45 degrees. If the joists are running perpendicular to the molding, I try to hit every one. Occasionally, I use a stud finder, though I tend to rely more on a simple magnet (Tot-Lok Key, available from Woodworker's

**Figure 16.** A magnetic Tot-Lok Key on the ceiling identifies the position of a joist.

**Figure 17.** Use a piece of scrap, cut with inside-to-inside corners (at right in photo), to ensure proper positioning of the first piece of a corner joint.

**Figure 18.** Use a softwood block to drive the corner together, tapping the top of both pieces toward the wall to close a gap at the top of the miter, or tapping up on the bottom edge of the molding to close a gap at the bottom of the miter.

Supply, www.woodworker.com) (**Figure 16**).

*Don't nail the corners.* I usually begin installation with the first piece I measured, especially if I've coped any joints. But I also try to install exceptionally small pieces first, just like baseboard, so that longer pieces can be sprung into position.

With a typical two-person crew, molding must be applied to the wall one piece at a time; fastening ends and corner joints must often wait until the next piece is installed. To position the first piece on the wall properly, I carry two short scraps, cut with inside and outside angles. The scraps help ensure that the corners will line up once the final piece is applied (**Figure 17**). But until that piece is installed, I never nail near the ends or corners — I always fasten the molding only near the center of the wall. Once two adjoining pieces are applied, I work the corner until it's perfectly aligned and tightly closed.

*Tap up or down.* Working a corner joint together sometimes requires a little patience. Walls and ceilings are never perfectly straight. Miter saws may cut moldings at perfect angles, but a slight bow in a wall or a belly in a ceiling will throw a curve into a corner. I carry a block of soft wood so that I never have to hammer directly on the crown. First I tap the bottom edges of both pieces until they're aligned (**Figure 18**). If the top of the corner is open, I tap the top of both pieces toward the wall. As they slide down the wall, the top corner will usually close up. If the bottom of the corner is open, I tap the bottom of the pieces toward the ceiling.

*Shim bad walls and ceilings.* Wall and ceiling corners are notoriously bad in modern homes. I often

have to shim the molding slightly to close up a joint. For that purpose, I cut shims from scraps of MDF (**Figure 19**). These shims need be only 3 or 4 inches long, and 1/4 inch thick at the heel. Once installed, they snap off easily just flush or even behind the face of the molding. I try to keep the molding as straight as possible. On paint-grade jobs, the shims and the gaps flanking the shims can be covered with caulk; on stain-grade jobs, the walls often must be floated by the drywall crew after the crown is installed.

## Preassembling Crown Molding

If all walls and ceilings were framed perfectly straight and flat, installing crown molding would be a lot easier — compound mitered joints would pop together just right every time. But the fact is, finish carpenters must perform perfect joinery in an imperfect world. Preassembling crown molding is one way to cope with imperfect walls and ceilings, speed production, and improve the quality of mitered corners.

*Inside and outside corners.* For most short runs of crown molding — especially coffered ceilings, around bookshelves, mantelpieces, and even in vestibules — I prefer to preassemble as much of the crown as possible. Of course, preassembled pieces must be measured perfectly, or labor and material will be lost to runs that fail the fit test. So I measure all pieces carefully: I measure short pieces with outside corners exactly; for short pieces with inside corners, I often subtract 1/32 inch; for long pieces, I add a little, maybe 1/16 inch in 8 feet. I miter all corners and fasten them with glue and nails. The finished assembly must fit tightly but not too tightly (**Figure 20**, page 301).

*Miter clamps.* Miter clamps are essential hand tools. They ensure tight-fitting miters in casing, crown, and panel molding, and for preassembling

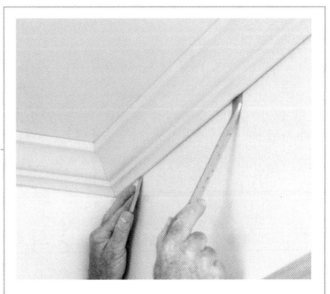

**Figure 19.** MDF shims are often necessary to close up a joint.

## Rounding a Corner

Cutting a three-piece corner takes a little more time than a caulked 90-degree corner, but I prefer the look because it adds drama to the molding and the corner. As with three-piece baseboard corners, I start by making a corner mockup, then use that to mark every outside corner in a room (right). Most often, the small center piece is 3/4 to 7/8 inch wide, from short point to short point, with both ends cut at 22 1/2-degree angles.

Three-piece bullnose corners should be preassembled whenever possible, so that small pieces don't have to be held and nailed in place. Miter clamps are the best tool to draw the joints tight (below left) and hold them that way while they're cross nailed. Once the corner has been assembled and the glue allowed to dry, installing the three-piece assembly is simple and painless (below right). — G.K.

*Before any measurements can be taken, bullnose corners must be laid out with a three-piece mockup.*

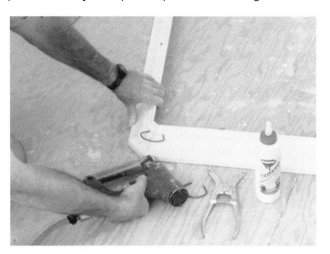

*Wherever possible, preassemble complete corners.*

*Preassembled corners are easy to install, and the joints are sure to be snug.*

crown molding, they are a must.

I use two types of miter clamps (**Figure 21**). Ulmia clamps are available from several catalogs such as Garrett Wade (www.garrettwade.com). A lighter-duty set of spring clamps is also manufactured by the Collins Tool Company. The Ulmia clamps come in two sizes and are manufactured from heavy spring steel. These heavy-duty pinchers, with sharp chisel-cut points, grab ferociously and leave a like-size mark. There are times when I need these aggressive clamps, especially when I install large MDF crown moldings. But for most work, the lighter-duty and easier-to-use Collins clamps are more suitable. And because they have sharp needle points, those clamps leave only small marks. I use the miter clamps to squeeze the glued-up corners closed, then I secure the miters with brad nails. I allow the glue to dry a little before installing the assembled section of crown. At first all this special care may seem

to take longer, but installation is amazingly quick and joinery is precise. These miter clamps are indispensable for making three-piece bullnose corners (see "Rounding a Corner," above).

## Preassembling Splices

Whenever possible, I prefer to preassemble splices in crown molding, whether the material is stain grade or paint grade. I make up all splices before beginning the installation, which allows time for the glue to dry before cutting each piece for length. Of course, preassembling splices in runs longer than 30 feet sometimes requires more than a three-person crew, but I find that scaring up a few additional hands for a long lift is always worth it — these splices are nearly invisible.

I used to use the thickest backing that I could behind a spliced joint because it's easier to secure 3/4-

Figure 20. Preassembly guarantees tight-fitting miters, especially with difficult-to-cope dentil crown (above left; also see photo at top of page 293). Temporarily secure the corners with miter clamps, then fasten with glue and brad nails (above right). Small hallway and bathroom rectangles should always be preassembled because they can be installed in just minutes (left).

inch backing to the molding with brads or staples than it is to fasten 1/4-inch backing. But these days I fasten the backing with a polyurethane hot-glue gun, so the size of the backing is limited only by the size of the crown. Of course, the backing can't be so thick that it interferes with the crown seating properly against the wall and the ceiling. On smaller crown profiles, there's often enough room only for thin plywood.

I start by attaching the backing to the back of the crown — always the piece cut with the inside miter — using a Titebond HiPurformer hot-glue gun (www.titebond.com) and staples for extra security (**Figure 22**, next page). Next, I turn the crown over, so I can see the joint, then apply hot glue to the joint and the backing before pressing the two pieces together (**Figure 23**, next page). You can also use carpenter's glue on the joint and hot glue only on the backing. Thirty-second hot glue doesn't take long to set. Then I turn the splice over again, and, for safety's sake, I fill it full of staples.

Figure 21. For preassembling crown, casing, and panel moldings, miter clamps are the secret. Ulmia clamps are on the left, Collins clamps on the right.

**Figure 22.** Preassembling splices is faster and guarantees tight field joints. First, fasten the backing to the piece with the inside miter.

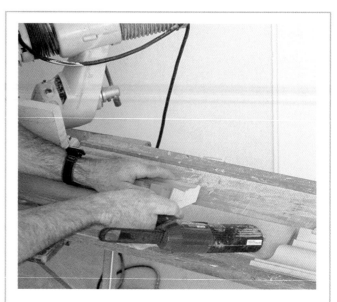

**Figure 23.** Polyurethane hot glue speeds up the task and guarantees flush-fitting, trouble-free splices. If you're a skeptic, apply yellow glue to the joint first.

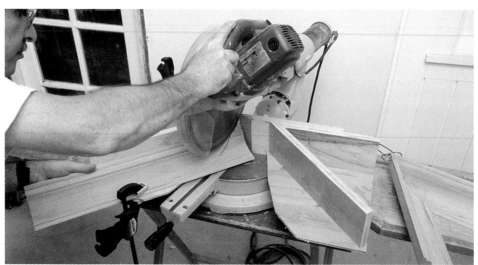

**Figure 24.** The author used two scraps of 3/4-inch plywood about a foot long by 4 inches wide for the accessory fence, both cut with 45-degree miters on the ends (above left). The fence is attached to a 3/8-inch plywood base, which hangs about 4 inches past the fence to provide a base for moldings (above right). For safety and tight joinery, be sure to clamp the fence to the saw and the material to the fence before cutting (left).

## Cutting Acute Angles

I've spent hours trying to get the right-sized block stuck in the right spot between the back of the crown and the fence on my saw, just so I could cut an angle sharper than my miter saw would permit. But cutting acute angles doesn't have to be a nightmare. With the right jig, these sharply pointed miters can be measured and cut as easily as any standard corner.

I prefer to cut crown in position, rather than lying flat, as I've said, and these angles are no exception. So I've made two accessory fences that clamp to the extension wings on my sliding compound miter saw. I built the fences 4³/₈ inches tall because that's the maximum depth of cut on my Makita 12-inch saw. Each accessory fence is at a 45-degree angle to the metal fence on my saw. I use plywood scraps for the accessory fence (**Figure 24**).

When using this fence, you must use clamps to secure the workpiece! Cutting sharp miters is easy with this fence, but it's also easy to cut your hand off, so don't be stupid. Clamp the fence securely to the miter saw, and clamp the workpiece securely to the fence. Don't try to hold the material with your hand, because the cut won't be precise — and a miter saw, especially a sliding saw, will grab the wood and pull it right into the blade, along with your hand.

## Finding the Miter Angle

Cutting a sharp miter is easy with an accessory fence, but figuring out the right miter angle can be a little confusing, no thanks to that guy (whoever he was) who designed the first miter scale on a chop saw.

Remember, when your miter saw is set at zero, it's actually making a 90-degree cut. So the only accurate mark on most chop saws is 45 degrees, and all those marks between 0 (90 degrees) and 45 are larger than 45, not smaller: the 22¹/₂ mark is really 67¹/₂ degrees. Mark the real angles on your saw with an indelible marker. Find the angle of the corner with a simple protractor; then split that angle and dial in your chop saw to the exact miter.

To set the saw at the correct miter angle using an accessory fence, I simply subtract the miter angle that I want to cut from the angle of the accessory fence (45 degrees), then swivel the saw that sum from the 0 mark. In other words, if I'm working on a 40-degree acute angle and I want 20-degree miters, I subtract 20 degrees from 45 degrees (the angle of the accessory fence). The result, 25 degrees, is the amount that I swivel the saw. Now those marks on the miter saw scale are actually helpful.

*Cutting acute angles on the flat.* Cutting on the flat is almost easier, because SCMs can bevel up to 45 degrees, and many can miter up to 60 degrees, well within the angles needed even for a sharp 45-degree corner (56-degree miter and 46.7-degree bevel for crown molding with a 38-degree spring line).

Unfortunately, the Bosch Angle Finder isn't (yet) programmed to determine bevel and miter angles for corners that are much tighter than 60 degrees, so for most octagons, the BAF is useful only for reading the angle of the corner. To get the miter and bevel angles for acute angles, refer to a good crown chart, one that goes below 60 degrees (most do not).

*Gary Katz is a finish carpenter in Reseda, Calif.*

# Working With Polymer Moldings

## by Peter Schrader

Contractors are used to working with wood, so when they first hear the term "polymer moldings," they're often skeptical. But my company has been selling and installing polymer moldings for many years. We've found the material to be easy to work with and reliable.

Polymer moldings are manufactured from a high-density polyurethane foam that is cast in a silicone-lined mold. As the castings cure, a smooth outer skin forms. The cured molding receives two coats of factory-applied latex primer. The final product has an impact resistance similar to that of white pine, but is much lighter in weight, with a density ranging from 12 to 20 pounds per cubic foot. The moldings can be used for interior and exterior applications and are available in nearly 100 profiles of running trim. Door and window pediments, decorative brackets, louvered vents, decorative panels, wall niches, and ceiling medallions are also available, depending on the manufacturer.

## Better Than Wood?

Polymer moldings offer certain advantages over wood. They won't rot, and changes in humidity do not cause the swelling and shrinkage that often creates the most visible problems with wood trim.

Using polymer moldings also saves on labor when installing complex profiles. Unlike ornate wood moldings, which are often built up using smaller

**Figure 25.** One-piece polymer molding offers substantial labor savings over ornate plaster or built-up wood trim.

pieces of trim, polymer trim is manufactured as one piece. The installer needs to cut, fit, and fasten only one piece of trim instead of many. When the installed cost of polymer molding is compared with carved wooden moldings or ornamental plaster trim, there's just no contest — polymer molding can be installed at a significantly lower cost (**Figure 25**). Depending on the situation and the complexity of the molding profile, the savings can range between 10% and 50%.

## Choosing a Supplier

There are a number of manufacturers of polymer moldings, and while there is little difference in their respective manufacturing processes, lead times and reliability can vary widely from one supplier to the next. For running trim, we've had good success using Focal Point (see "Sources of Supply," facing page). We seldom have to wait more than a week to ten days for an order to be delivered, and our distributor keeps a wide range of molding profiles in stock.

For us, deciding what lengths of trim to use is easy, since the majority of the moldings we use are only available in 12-foot lengths. Some profiles are also available in 8-foot and 10-foot lengths, and a few are available in 16-foot lengths.

To calculate quantities of running trim, I make a sketch of the areas to be trimmed, and note the required length for each run of trim. By combining appropriate lengths, I can optimize the yield from a 12-foot length of molding. Depending on the width and pattern of the molding, I'll add 6 to 12 inches to the noted lengths for each miter cut or pattern-matching butt joint. The moldings can vary up to 2 inches in length, so we're careful not to rely on every piece being a full 12 feet long.

## Working With Polymer Moldings

Working with polymer molding isn't at all difficult, but it is a little different from working with wood. We use the same tools as when we work with wood moldings. The molding can be cut using a fine-toothed handsaw, but we prefer to use a 15-inch Makita chop saw equipped with a standard trim blade (**Figure 26**). To save time, we fasten the trim using pneumatic finish nailers, but a hammer and finish nails can also be used.

*No grain, no pain.* We use a hand plane to quickly remove material from the edges of the molding or fine-tune a miter cut. The first time carpenters take a plane to the polyurethane core, they're surprised to find that the feel is similar to wood (although it requires much less effort to remove material). Since there is no grain, the molding can be planed from any direction.

Power planes and jointers can also be used to work the trim, and we often use a belt sander to remove material when scribing a piece of trim to an irregular surface or adjusting a miter cut. The 80-grit belts we use take an aggressive bite, though, so the belt sander must be fed into the workpiece carefully.

*Joints and attachments.* The most significant difference in working with polymer molding is the way the pieces are joined together and fastened to the wall. Adhesive, not nails, is used to bond splices and miters together, and to secure the molding to walls, ceilings, and soffits. Most manufacturers supply a proprietary adhesive for this purpose that is applied with a caulking gun. The Focal Point adhesive that we use is about the same consistency as any cartridge adhesive, but it has such good bonding characteristics that our installers have been using it for most other applications where a general-purpose adhesive is needed.

It's important to spread a generous bead of adhesive over the entire mating surface of both parts. There should be ample squeeze-out as the joint is drawn together; excess adhesive can be removed with a putty

**Figure 26.** Polymer moldings cut easily with a handsaw, though the author prefers a 15-inch chop saw.

**Figure 27.** One-piece moldings are mitered, not coped, at inside corners. Nail and screw holes are filled with a spackling or glazing compound. Properly finished joints are invisible after painting.

FOCAL POINT

let it cure overnight), we fill any gaps, hammer dents, or imperfections with either DAP vinyl spackling compound or joint compound. The smooth texture of joint compound is ideal for filling shallow depressions and small gaps. We use spackling compound for large gaps or areas that need to be built up, and we also apply a coating of spackling compound to any areas of the foam core that become exposed during tooling.

DAP glazing compound (www.dap.com) works best for filling nail holes — the material doesn't shrink, and the filled holes don't require sanding or spot-priming before painting. We use a good-quality paintable latex caulk to fill any gaps at walls, ceilings, or soffits.

## Painting and Staining

The polymer molding is primed at the factory with a vinyl primer that will accept latex or oil-based finish coats. The factory prime coat is first-rate and can easily be mistaken for a finish coat of paint. We spot-prime all joints and any areas where spackle has been applied to ensure that the finish coat will dry evenly and display a uniform sheen.

A simulated wood grain finish can be produced by applying stain over a beige primer coat (factory-applied beige primer can be specified at no extra cost). Proper staining technique requires a little practice, but can be picked up quickly by a painter with average skill. Some molding styles can be ordered with a factory-applied wood grain finish.

A dramatic faux marble finish is also possible, but you'll need to find a finisher experienced in this technique. Each painter will have his or her own marblizing style, and preparing a few sample pieces for the customer to approve is always a good idea.

*Peter Schrader is president of Schrader and Company in Burnt Hills, N.Y. Peter and his shop manager, Robert Page, have been installing polymer moldings since 1985.*

knife before it cures. The surface cleans up with mineral spirits. A small amount of adhesive will continue to squeeze out of the joint after assembly, and it's often necessary to double-back with the mineral spirits.

The adhesive cures in 24 hours at room temperature and it can be used at temperatures as low as 10°F. Below room temperature curing slows, and it may take three days or more to reach full strength.

Just before installing a piece of molding, we apply a bead of adhesive along both edges of the molding where it will come into contact with the wall, ceiling, or soffit. We press the molding in place, and use our finish nailers to fasten the molding along both edges. It's the adhesive that we rely on for the long-term connection, however: after the adhesive cures, the nails are just along for the ride. We also use the finish nailer to pull and hold outside miters together as the adhesive cures.

## No Need to Cope

When working with wood moldings, inside corners are generally coped, and long runs of trim are spliced using scarf joints. With polymer moldings, however, we use a butt joint to splice running trim, and all inside corners are mitered, not coped (**Figure 27**). (The smooth outer "skin" that forms over the urethane foam core does not lend itself well to feathered edges.) We cut our running trim 1/8 to 1/4 inch long and "spring" it into place. This ensures that ample pressure is applied at the joints as the adhesive sets. Joints that are assembled properly will not open up over time. In fact, I've returned to many past jobs and have not been able to locate any seams.

*Filling gaps.* After the adhesive has set (we usually

<table>
<tr><td colspan="2">**Sources of Supply**</td></tr>
<tr><td>**Flex Trim**<br>www.flextrim.com</td><td>**Nu-Wood**<br>www.nu-wood.com</td></tr>
<tr><td>**Focal Point**<br>www.focalpointap.com</td><td>**Outwater Plastics**<br>www.outwater.com</td></tr>
<tr><td>**Fypon, Inc.**<br>www.fypon.com</td><td>**RAS Industries**<br>www.rasindustries.com</td></tr>
</table>

# Installing Flexible Trim

by Ross Welsh

As a finish carpentry subcontractor, I've been thrown a lot of curves lately by the builders in my area. Curved walls, turret entries, and oval hallway soffits are becoming the norm. A few years ago, our crew might have used flexible baseboard a couple of times a year, but now we see curves and use all types of flexible moldings on about half the houses we trim.

When I first used flexible baseboard about 17 years ago, on a cold day it was about as pliable as a frozen garden hose. It had to be warmed up before installation on a cold job site, and even then it was difficult to nail and would sometimes crack. Though it's still stiffer in the cold and more flexible in a warmer environment, the material now available is much better.

## Ordering Flexible Trim

There are three major manufacturers of flexible polyester-resin moldings similar to what I use: ResinArt, Flex Trim, and Flex Moulding (see "Sources of Supply," page 310). All three supply molding profiles in a large variety of patterns and sizes to match common wood moldings. In general, I think of flexible molding as a generic product and order it through my regular millwork suppliers. Flexible baseboard can be ordered stock and bent on site, while most casings and crown moldings must be custom-made for the desired curve (**Figure 28**). Most of my experience has been with ResinArt because it has the shortest lead time at my supplier.

***Stain grade available.*** So far, I've worked only with

**Figure 28.** Flexible baseboard is easily site-bent to almost any required curve, but most crown molding and casing must be custom made to fit the situation.

paint-grade flexible molding, but grain-embossed stain-grade material is also available. Most makers offer a single style of grain-embossed material, but DuraFlex offers a choice of smooth, oak, and pine surfaces.

According to the manufacturers, staining requires a heavily pigmented gel-type stain and a protective topcoat with a clear finish. Unlike the process with wood molding, finishing must take place after installation; otherwise, the finish will peel and distort as the material is handled.

Manufacturers also offer accessories like simulated carvings, capitals, medallions, and other appliqués. My work is strictly indoors, but these flexible products can also be used outside. I haven't seen any claims made about UV resistance, but manufacturers say they are insect-proof, moisture-proof, and resistant to extreme heat and cold.

When I'm ordering flexible moldings, I always tell my supplier whether I'll be matching MDF or finger-jointed trim. The MDF trim is a hair thicker, and, because the flexible moldings are made to order, the manufacturer can account for that. This means I can avoid a lot of laborious sanding or shimming on site to get the profiles to match.

Flex Moulding offers Superflex, a very supple material for tight bends, though we've found that it bends too easily for most applications. In situations where the framing or drywall work is irregular, it actually conforms to dips and bumps. The standard-flex products bridge such inconsistencies, producing a more uniform curve along the wall. Although the standard products we use all have similar flexibility, temperature can affect how easy they are to work with. On cool mornings, I'll place the stiff material in the sunny driveway for a couple of hours to soften it up.

## Cutting, Finishing, and Fastening

Flexible molding cuts easily with regular woodworking equipment, but positioning and handling the material can be a challenge. It takes a little time to get used to, but we've found a few techniques that help. Basically, it comes down to extra support, sometimes in the form of continuous support at your miter-saw station or provided by a jig.

When it comes to installation, the consensus among the various manufacturers is that gluing is the way to go and that nails and screws should be kept to a minimum. To prevent distortion along the material's edge caused by fasteners, manufacturers suggest using super-type glues with a set time of about two minutes and even a spray accelerator. So far, I've had good luck with construction adhesive and pneumatic finish nails and brads. It's important to nail carefully, however. Nailing too close to an edge can cause a bump along the edge, and hitting the hollow of the crown can collapse the material.

After establishing the proper nailing pattern, I rely heavily on pneumatic fasteners and use construction adhesive only at joints. I haven't tried hand nailing, but it seems like it would require a lot of predrilling and patience. I suppose the fast-setting glues would help a lot if you don't have access to air tools.

## Baseboard and Chair Rail

Flexible baseboard is an off-the-shelf material at most dedicated millwork suppliers, but you probably won't find it at the home center or standard lumberyard. My supplier carries it in three styles for matching the most common baseboard profiles in my area. My supplier also stocks chair rail, which we find useful for many trim details, in two or three styles. One of our projects used flexible chair rail for simulated wainscoting with arch-topped panels. But chair rail like that requires a special order, because the molding is curved on the wider, flat side, like casing.

Flexible baseboard is the simplest product to use. Because it's no more than 3/4 inch thick, it can bend to all the wall contours we routinely see, down to inside and outside radii of less than a foot. Although Flex Trim claims it can provide endless lengths by special order, the boxes we get from ResinArt contain rolls from about 7 feet to 12 feet long; I think anything longer would be too unwieldy.

*Square cuts and miters.* A square cut on baseboard can be made by simply laying it flat on your miter saw and letting the far end fall where it may. You can cut miters in the same position using the bevel feature of a compound saw, but we usually cut baseboard miters in the normal upright position with the flexible material sandwiched between two pieces of scrap similar in height. The scrap prevents saw pressure from collapsing or distorting the material as it's cut. Odd angles are the norm when working with curves, so test fitting and recuts are part of the routine. Once I've cut one end, I hold the piece in place and mark the next cut. Trying to measure along a curve is generally awkward and inaccurate.

*Curves and straight runs.* Of course, flexible baseboard can also make a straight run, so we sometimes avoid a splice by continuing the material along a straight section to the next curve. Flex costs nearly ten times the price of the MDF trim material we commonly use, so we try to limit this practice. Most inside-radius situations allow me to snap a slightly long, square-cut flex piece into place between the two square cuts at each end for a tight fit. Most outside-radius situations require using more traditional scarf joints, but we like 30-degree joints instead of 45 degrees. The more acute angle matches up better.

Unlike crown, where we use brads, on baseboard we use heavier, 15-gauge finish nails. The sturdier nails hold better, and baseboard doesn't have the delicate edges of crown molding. But we still keep nails

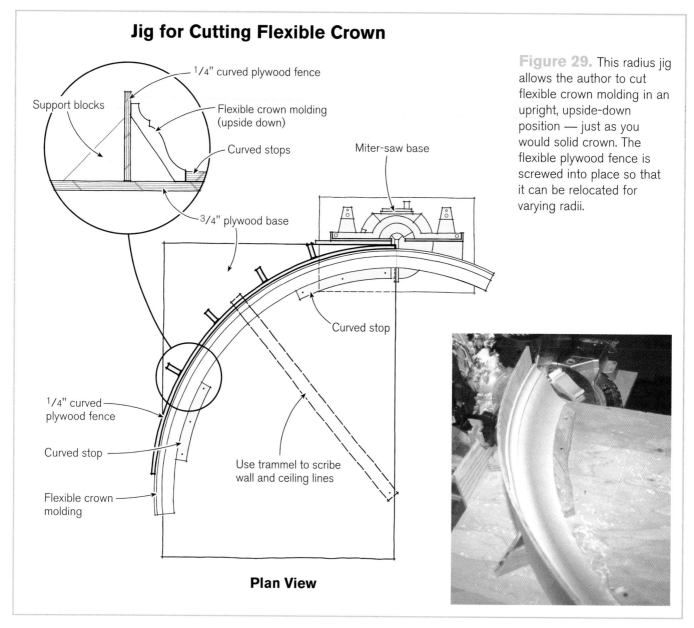

## Jig for Cutting Flexible Crown

1/4" curved plywood fence

Support blocks

Flexible crown molding (upside down)

Curved stops

Miter-saw base

3/4" plywood base

Curved stop

1/4" curved plywood fence

Curved stop

Use trammel to scribe wall and ceiling lines

Flexible crown molding

**Plan View**

**Figure 29.** This radius jig allows the author to cut flexible crown molding in an upright, upside-down position — just as you would solid crown. The flexible plywood fence is screwed into place so that it can be relocated for varying radii.

away from the edges, and nail top and bottom for adequate holding.

## Casing

Because curved casings for doors and windows are bent on the wider flat side, they are typically made to order. We order our flexible moldings through our millwork supplier, who can usually get custom orders in about a week.

*Custom curves.* Ordering flexible casing in a quarter, half, or full circle is a fairly straightforward process. The Flex Trim website gives information on ordering and also explains how much a curved molding can deviate from its designed radius. Wider patterns and smaller radii are less forgiving than narrower patterns and larger radii. What I find interesting are the possibilities with ovals, ellipses, and other irregular radii. If you can describe your project

with a good drawing or template, it can be made to order.

*Fitting curved casings.* Installing a half-circle of casing over an arched opening is fairly simple because the side casing is cut square at the top. To start, I lay out the inside line of the arch from leg to leg with a set of trammel points. Along that line I then set a series of finish nails on which the flexible casing can rest. With the casing hanging from the nails and draped over the side casings, I mark its length. The first cut is laid out by simply marking where the flex and rigid casing meet on the inside and outside edges. I usually make the first cut with a handsaw or small circular saw. When I'm happy with the first cut, and have the material back in position, I mark the second cut. Thinking slightly long is good in a situation like this. Although most of our jobs use MDF casing, we use the same process for stain-grade material.

**Figure 30.** Finish nails help hold the crown in place and free a hand for operating a nail gun. Because the author uses MDF moldings, inside corners are mitered, not coped.

## Crown

It's a good thing I like working with crown, because installing crown molding on curved surfaces has proven to be a big challenge. I recently finished a small task where the framer didn't follow the plans and the millwork salesman's measurement of the subsequent "custom" work — an oval ceiling soffit — was off just enough to create a problem. It turned out that I was trying to work with material made to a radius of 1 1/2 inches less than I needed. As I attempted to position the crown along the wall, the top edge would pull away from the ceiling. By the time the new material arrived, installation seemed easy. The lesson is that flexible crown is not very forgiving and must be ordered accurately. Because we work in production housing, ordering in advance from the plans is a necessary part of the process. As long as everyone builds to the plans, there's no need to field-measure, but double-checking can prevent time-consuming and expensive mistakes.

The radii on the plans we get are called out as a rough measure, so we compensate for drywall thickness to make our orders more accurate. The drywallers in our area bend two layers of 1/4-inch gypsum board to make the curves, so adjusting the radius 1/2 inch makes the pieces fit better. It's important to remember that you subtract 1/2 inch for inside curves, but add 1/2 inch for outside curves.

Flexible crown molding can be manufactured with an irregular radius (as in ovals and ellipses, for example), and the profile can be oriented upside down from standard if desired. But irregular radii will require a template or drawing, and upside-down profiles require special instructions on the supplier's order sheet.

*Cutting floppy crown.* I cut crown in position whenever possible, using a curved jig to hold the material upside down (**Figure 29**).

It takes a little while to make the jig, but once you've made it, you can reuse it for other radii. I usually make the fence 4 feet long, but the curved support can be as short as a foot or so. Orienting the plywood's grain vertically makes bending it easier.

Once I determine the miter angle with a Bosch Miter Finder, I place the jig with the cut line, which I call the "diameter line," at 90 degrees to the fence and close to the blade. On most saws, you have to set the miter angle first, then position the jig. After I make the first cut, I hold the molding on the wall and mark the second cut. A series of nails along the wall and ceiling can help support this unruly material (**Figure 30**). In most situations, I cut inside miters long and snap them into place.

*Backer blocks.* I highly recommend putting backing behind crown joints. When you push on the face of flexible crown, it collapses and may not spring back. So I carry triangular backing blocks, just like the ones I use on the cutting jig, to support the void at the joints and serve as a gusset for splices (**Figure 31**). These blocks don't necessarily have to be attached to the wall. If there's a slight difference in the thickness of the two materials, I'll use shims to raise the thinner piece into place (**Figure 32**, next page).

Fastening crown requires greater care than fastening other types of flexible molding because nails easily damage the crown's thin edges. Using 18-gauge brads prevents bumps and damage along the edge, and the thinner wire size also allows some tweaking for tight joints and miters.

Like curved casing, flexible crown made for a fixed

**Figure 31.** Triangular blocks keep the crown from bowing in, provide nailing at joints, and make transitions to regular crown molding easier.

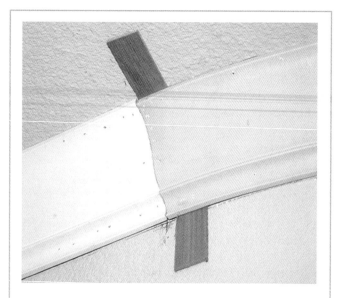

**Figure 32.** MDF is often thicker than flexible molding, so shims placed behind the flexible molding smooth the transition.

**Figure 33.** Crown molding can't be bent in place like baseboard, and there's little room for error when ordering. Manufacturers require a specific radius or template, and, although the material fits in a small box when shipped, it won't fit around a curve with a different radius.

radius cannot be straightened (**Figure 33**). That means finding the transition point between the curve and a straight run is critical. Using a straight-edge, I check to see where an outside-radius wall falls away from the straight run, or where an inside radius lifts the straightedge. I join those transition points with square butt joints backed with the triangular blocks. It's a little easier with an inside-radius piece, because the material can be cut slightly long on the jig and snapped into place. I cut outside-radius pieces as square as I can with a circular saw, then carefully fit the rigid molding, relying on a slight back cut, some whittling, and patience.

*Ross Welsh is a finish carpentry subcontractor in Sacramento, Calif.*

## Sources of Supply

**Flex Moulding, Inc.**
www.flexiblemoulding.com

**Flex Trim**
www.flextrim.com

**ResinArt**
www.resinart.com

# Chapter 17: Cabinets & Shelving

- **Fast Closets With Melamine**
- **Installing Framed Cabinets**

# Fast Closets With Melamine

by Chas Bridge

I've been using white melamine to finish closets for years. Readily available in 12-, 16-, and 24-inch widths and in 8-, 10-, and 12-foot lengths, edge-banded melamine is perfect for building attractive, durable, and economical shelving that can be adapted to many different closet layouts.

Recently, I've been purchasing my melamine from a local cabinet shop rather than through a lumberyard. This saves me about 25% compared with the price for basic white lumberyard melamine and allows me to offer my customers a broader selection of colors and patterns. Once homeowners see how many options are available, they rarely choose plain white melamine, even though colored and special-order melamine can cost more (**Figure 1**).

Another benefit is that my cabinetmaker is willing to rip melamine to width and run it through his edge-banding machine. Although I'm limited to 8-foot lengths (the cabinetmaker buys 49-by-97-inch sheets), I can get any width I like. The shorter length isn't a problem, because closet rods need to be supported every 3 or 4 feet anyway; I can land shelf joints on brackets that carry the rod.

This also means that I now use shelf cleats made out of melamine instead of MDF. While I could make the melamine cleats myself, I don't want to edge-band that much material on site — it's just too slow — and the lumberyard doesn't sell edge-banded material in narrow widths. As for MDF, it would need to be puttied, caulked, and painted, an especially time-consuming job if the shelves are tightly spaced. When you factor in the labor, MDF cleats can be much more expensive than the shelves themselves.

## Design and Layout

It seems that when people design a custom home, they decide how big the closets should be and then move on to the thousands of other decisions they have to make. In most cases, the next time they think about the closets is when the wall paint is dry and they can finally see the space. This is about the time I arrive on site. So the first thing I do is talk to the customers about what they want and describe to them solutions that have worked for my previous customers.

*A layout stick simplifies planning.* To save time during this process, I use an 84-inch-long layout stick instead of a measuring tape. Because it contains all of my favorite measurements, I can hold the layout stick against the closet wall and quickly show my clients where everything might go. These locations are just suggestions; the homeowners can have any layout they want. To make it easier for them to visualize the layout, I mark shelf locations by placing blue painter's tape on the walls. If there are any doubts, I leave the tape up for a few days and let the owners move the "shelves" around till they're happy (**Figure 2**, page 314).

Once the layout has been determined, I mark the cleat locations on the wall. Since the walls are already painted, I always measure to the top of a cleat so that the shelf will hide my marks. At the same time that I'm laying out shelves, I mark stud centers so I know where to nail through the cleats.

## Recommended Details

Closet shelving systems vary in accordance with the size of the closet and the clients' storage needs. A

**Figure 1.** The author buys the entire closet package from a cabinetmaker who rips melamine into shelves and cleats before banding them with a matching edge (far left). This nearly eliminates ripping and edging material in the field and allows customers to get highly customized shelving in virtually any color or pattern they want.

# Typical Details for Closet Shelving Systems

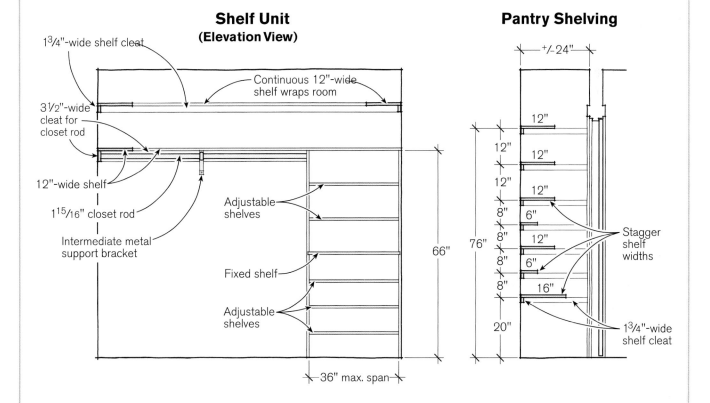

## Clothes Closet

### Single

+/–24"

3½"-wide cleat

12"-wide shelf

Door casing

Install closet rod in front of shelf for easier access to hangers

Cleats run full depth of closet; attach to corner studs at either end and any intermediate studs

66" (measured to top of cleat, typical)

### Double

+/–24"

12"-wide shelf

Door casing

Double closet rods

12"-wide shelf

84"

42"

3½"-wide cleat

## Linen Closet

+/–24"

12"-wide shelf

16" to full-width shelf

Full-width shelves

1¾"-wide shelf cleat

12"
12"
12"
16"
20"

72"

## Shelf Unit
### (Elevation View)

1¾"-wide shelf cleat

Continuous 12"-wide shelf wraps room

3½"-wide cleat for closet rod

12"-wide shelf

1¹⁵/₁₆" closet rod

Intermediate metal support bracket

Adjustable shelves

Fixed shelf

Adjustable shelves

66"

36" max. span

## Pantry Shelving

+/–24"

12"
12"
12"
12"
12"
12"
8"   6"
8"   12"
8"   6"
8"   16"
20"

76"

Stagger shelf widths

1¾"-wide shelf cleat

The author has installed a lot of closets, so he has a pretty good idea of what does and doesn't work. Clients can have whatever configuration they want, but if they do not have a particular layout in mind, he recommends using the ones shown above.

Figure 2. To help his clients visualize shelving options, the author uses a layout stick premarked with standard shelf measurements. Blue painter's tape indicates potential shelf and support locations.

basic layout might consist of a single shelf and either a single or double closet rod, while a larger closet might also have room for a stack of fixed or adjustable shelves. Another, more costly, option is to include a bank or two of drawers. If the room has an otherwise empty wall, we could install a fully edged cleat with Shaker pegs or coat hooks on it (**Figure 3**).

I use a full 3¹/₂-inch-wide cleat for shelves with closet rods but only a 1³/₄-inch-wide cleat for shelves without. A typical cleat height for a single rod is 66 inches above the floor; for double rods, the cleats are typically 42 inches and 84 inches up (measurements are always to the top edge of the cleat).

When I build a stack of shelves, I like to make them 84 inches high — the same height as the cleat for an upper shelf rod. Each closet wall might have a different layout, but if they all terminate at a wraparound shelf at 84 inches, they will integrate cleanly.

*Banks of shelving.* Double closet rods are popular, which means that there often is a lack of shoe storage space. The solution is to build a separate stack of shelves and use the lower portion of it to store shoes. I usually install fixed shelves spaced 6 inches apart, but if the customer wants adjustable shelves, I'll drill a series of shelf-support holes spaced 2 inches on-center. To prevent the sides from bowing out, I'll install a fixed shelf halfway up the stack.

Another easy option is to install adjustable shelves between two stacks of fixed shelves. It's simply a

matter of drilling holes for the shelf supports in the sides of the fixed shelf units and installing them as far apart as the adjustable shelves are long.

*Varied width and spacing.* In a linen closet, I put the first shelf 20 inches up from the floor and the second 16 inches above the first; from there, I install shelves 12 inches on-center up to a height of 6 feet. For pantry shelving, I like to stagger the depth and height. I'll start with a 16-inch-deep shelf, then place a 6-inch shelf 8 inches higher, then put a 12-inch shelf 8 inches above that. This arrangement allows single-depth cans to sit behind taller items while staying visible. Any really tall items can sit on the 16-inch shelf and shoot past the 12-inch shelf (see illustration, previous page).

## Ordering Stock

I'm not limited to standard widths when I order stock from a cabinetmaker. Most of the time I order 6-, 12-, 16-, and 24-inch shelves, but there have been plenty of times when I opted for other widths.

I don't order cleats ripped to width because in our humid climate a narrow rip with a band on only one edge would "banana" (bow due to absorbed moisture) pretty quickly. To prevent this from happening, I order the cleats twice as wide as necessary (typically 4 inches for 1³/₄-inch cleats and 7¹/₂ inches for 3¹/₂-inch cleats) and ask the cabinetmaker to band both edges. This seals them up pretty well, and on the day I plan to install them I cut them to width by ripping them in half. They won't bow immediately, so everything is fine as long as I nail them up that day.

Ripping the cleats also gives me a sharp, square edge where the shelf hits the cleat. No caulking is necessary, because there will be a good tight fit. I'm always careful to handle ripped melamine edges carefully, because they're sharp enough to cut a person's hands.

Figure 3. Drilled to accept Shaker-style clothes pegs, this cleat was edged by the cabinetmaker in the shop and then cut to fit on site; only the ends were edged in the field.

**Figure 4.** The author uses peel-and-stick vinyl tape to edge areas where the particleboard core is exposed. Here, he uses a dual-blade trimmer to cut the tape flush to the face of a melamine shelf. This trimmer also works on wood veneer edging.

*Edging in the field.* There are often messy spots where the particleboard core is exposed. This might happen when a piece has to be ripped on site or when a shelf or cleat runs partway across the wall. I handle this by edge-banding the exposed area in the field. Instead of heat-sensitive material that goes on with a heat gun or iron, I use a peel-and-stick edging called Fastedge (FastCap, www.fastcap.com). The back is coated with a pressure-sensitive adhesive, which sticks very well and is much easier to apply than traditional edging materials.

The manufacturer also sells a handy pressure roller for pressing peel-and-stick edging onto the surface, and a dual-blade trimmer for cutting it flush to the edge of the melamine (**Figure 4**). Trimming is necessary because edge bands are wider than the thickness of the material they are designed to edge. These tools make the job so easy to do, there's no reason to ever leave an exposed edge unfinished.

I can buy a 250-foot roll of the maple-pattern Fastedge for approximately 30 cents per foot. Iron-on edging is about a nickel less per foot, but the peel-and-stick is so much easier to use, it trumps any difference in cost.

## Joining Shelves

When shelves go around an inside corner, I butt one to the other and join them with pocket screws — two near the front and one in the middle (**Figure 5**). There's no good way to fill these holes, so I hide them by drilling them where they're hard to see. If the shelves are below eye level, I drill from below; if the shelves are up high, I drill from above. I use an aluminum Kreg jig (Kreg Tool Co., www.kregtool.com) to guide the bit; it's much superior to the newer plastic models (see "Tight Connections With Pocket Screws," next page).

In many closets, the top shelf goes all the way around the room, so if the heights are right, the top of the door casing can act as a cleat.

## Using Dadoes

When building stacks of shelves, I like to dado shelves into the sides. This has a great "wow" factor

**Figure 5.** With pocket screws, the author can make a strong, tight joint with a minimal amount of labor. This shelf (left) is higher than eye level, so the screws go in from above. When the shelf is lower (right), the author hides the holes by installing the screws from below.

# Tight Connections With Pocket Screws

**by Gary Katz**

I first saw the Kreg Pocket-Hole Jig at one of those fast-talking woodworking-show demonstrations. It immediately got my interest. I knew I could use it for joining stile-and-rail work perfectly, as the demonstrator suggested, but I suspected there would be lots of other uses as well. I bought the K2000 ProPack kit for under $150 (replaced by the K3 Master System from Kreg Tool Co., www.kregtool.com). It comes with the jig, two support wings, accessory blocks for drilling pocket holes in 1/2-inch and 11/2-inch material, a 6-inch face clamp, a pocket-hole drill bit and stop collar, two Phillips-head and two square-head extension drivers, and a small assortment of Kreg's pocket-hole screws. It's a pretty complete package, except for the screws. You'll need more (drywall screws work, too). The kit also comes with a Mini Kreg Jig; I've used that tool almost as frequently as the main jig.

I also bought an extra drill bit (you can send the bits to Kreg for sharpening) and a 9-inch face clamp for some of the bigger projects I had in mind. Other than a few set-up tasks, the kit is almost ready to use right from the box. Kreg recommends mounting the jig on a 1x12 board, so that workpieces have better support (**Figure A**). I chose to mount my jig on a 20-inch length of 2x12 planking because I knew I'd be working on bigger material than just 1x4 stiles and rails.

To use the jig, you simply place the workpiece between the clamp and the drill guide and then pull the

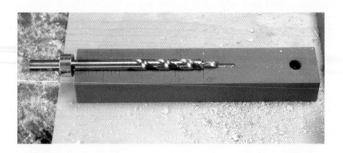

**Figure B.** *The jig's support wings include a handy guide for setting the stop collar on the drill bit.*

toggle. Three bushings in the top of the drill guide are smartly positioned to allow a choice of pocket-hole positions: the two outer bushings — spaced farthest apart — are meant for 1x4 stock, the two bushings on the left are perfect for 2-inch-wide stock, and the two closest bushings on the right are great for material under 2 inches wide.

A guide molded into both of the jig's support wings makes it easy to attach the stop collar at the right position on the drill bit (**Figure B**). The support wings are marked for 1/2-inch, 3/4-inch, and 11/2-inch material. Simply lay the bit in the molded guide, with the shoulder of the bit aligned with the thickness of material, and then tighten the collar on the bit. The collar controls the depth of the pocket hole so that the pocket-hole screw penetrates just far enough without poking out the other side (**Figure C**).

Drilling is easy and fast. The steel pocket-hole bit is sharp and aggressive from the factory. I've used mine to drill hundreds of holes — in softwood, hardwood, and MDF — and it's still sharp. The bit is designed to draw sawdust and shavings quickly out of the hole, and then they're dumped out the side of the jig, without jamming the bit in the bushing. Unlike a spline joint or biscuit joint, only one mating piece needs pocket-hole preparation. This saves time and permits final adjustments.

Kreg urges users to build a simple plywood grid for face-frame assembly (**Figure D**). I already had a pair of glue-up stands, but I built the grid anyway and I'm glad of it. The grid allows easy access to all joints so that glue-up, clamping, and fastening (even for large frames) are quick and easy. Unlike splines and biscuits, pocket-hole assembly can begin at any face-frame joint. Simply apply glue, clamp the two pieces, and drive in the screws.

**Figure A.**
*Mounted on a piece of 2x12 for greater stability, the Kreg jig makes quick work of pocket-hole joints.*

**Figure C.** *The Kreg jig can make joints in material from 1/2 inch to 11/2 inches thick.*

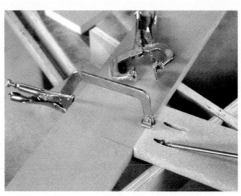

**Figure D.** *A simple plywood work grid makes it easy to manipulate face frames for making joints and for glue cleanup (far left). The vise-grip clamp holds joints secure for screwing (left).*

Kreg's proprietary pan-head screws are definitely better for pocket holes than drywall screws. Kreg's flat-bottomed pan-heads seat in the pocket hole and pull tight, without spreading the wood fibers. Bugle-head drywall screws tend to bury themselves farther in the hole and

**Figure E.** *The Mini Kreg Jig comes in handy for installing cabinets and bookcases, and for joints in hard-to-reach places.*

split the stock, especially in MDF. To save money on screws, I found myself using both types. I used Kreg's screws for composite material and drywall screws for solid wood, especially 11/2-inch stock. But even then, care must be taken when driving pocket screws. Applying too much torque can strip the screw hole, shear the screw, or drive the screw too deep. Using a cordless drill with a sensitive clutch gives me the control I need.

The Mini Kreg Jig, also included in the ProPack, is always in my tool tote (**Figure E**). It's perfect for drilling holes in existing floor joists and fixing squeaking floors, but I've used it for installing bookcases and cabinets and even held it by hand. I've also used it to drill pocket holes in cabinets that I hadn't remembered or couldn't drill before assembly.

I've used pocket holes to assemble large bookshelves built from 11/2-inch material and have even turned to pocket holes for gluing up blanks for wide doors because I didn't have enough clamps and didn't want to wait for the glue to dry. Other applications suggested by the manufacturer include angled joinery, tabletop aprons, edge banding, jamb extensions, and even picture frames.

*Gary Katz is a finish carpenter in Reseda, Calif.*

Figure 6. There are a lot of ways to support fixed shelves, but the author prefers dadoes because they're fast and hide any chipping that occurs when the shelves are cut to length (far left). With the right-size router bit, he can get a tight fit (left).

with clients and is faster than any other shelf-support method you could reasonably do on site.

I could support the shelves with individual cleats, but that would look clunky and there would be all those extra cleats to deal with. A plate joiner might work, but whatever you gain by not cutting a dado, you lose by having to slot both sides of the joint and use glue. One of the nice things about using a dado is that it hides any chipping that occurs when you crosscut shelf pieces.

**Special-size bit.** I use a router to cut the dadoes. Plywood is usually undersized, but the 3/4-inch melamine I use is actually a full 3/4 inch thick. As a result, the dadoes have to be more than 3/4 inch wide or the shelves won't go in. I make 1/4-inch-deep dadoes with a .78-inch straight bit (Woodline). The bit's extra three-hundredths of an inch is just enough for a perfect fit (**Figure 6**).

**Laying out and cutting.** I start by clamping both sides to a bench, aligning the sides, top, and bottom so that both pieces can be laid out and cut at the same time. I mark dado locations by transferring marks from the layout stick, which could be either standard locations or marks that correspond to where the clients put the blue tape on the wall. Even if the layout is slightly off, the sides will still be identical when you use this method.

Because I clamp the sides with their front edges touching, there is minimal chipping where the bit exits one and enters the other. To guide the router square across the face of the stock, I use a Clamp 'N Tool Guide (Griset Industries). Available in 24-, 36-, and 50-inch sizes, this aluminum rail has a built-in clamp that holds it square to the stock. I could do the same thing with a board and a couple of screw clamps, but the purpose-built guide is self-squaring and less likely to vibrate loose.

Figure 7. Thin enough to be covered by the finished flooring or by baseboard, small pieces of flashing nailed to the verticals hold the shelving in place.

Figure 8. Short lengths of edged melamine help support the shelves. The author then overlays a second, continuous strip of melamine, fastening from behind to conceal nail holes.

## Assembly and Installation

The shelf banks are quite heavy, so I assemble them on the floor as close as possible to their final location. I put the shelves into the dadoes without glue and nail them in from each side with four 1⅝-inch 18-gauge brads. To hold the unit against the wall, I fasten 1¾-inch cleats below the top and middle shelves with a 15-gauge finish nailer.

There are a couple of ways to stabilize the sides of the shelving unit where they hit the floor. If I am working on subfloor, I nail a small piece of metal flashing to the bottom of the side, allowing it to project beyond the edge, and nail through it into the floor (**Figure 7**). On hardwood or vinyl floors, I will run a pocket screw through the side and into the floor. When I'm done, I use colored putty to conceal any visible nail holes.

Some of my customers have been asking for banks of drawers. I don't mind installing drawer units, but it is not economically feasible to fabricate them in the field. On one recent job, I ordered knock-down drawer units from CabParts (www.cabparts.com). The company's service and product were excellent, but the freight charge was way over the estimate. Next time, I'll explore a supplier who is closer to home.

To support some inside corners and the front edge of long runs of shelving, I install narrow, edged strips of melamine stacked vertically and wedged between the shelves (**Figure 8**). Overlapping these pieces and nailed from behind, another continuous piece of melamine strengthens and conceals these joints and gives the shelving a finished look.

*Chas Bridge is a finish carpenter in Sequim, Wash.*

# Installing Framed Cabinets

## by Carl Hagstrom

I install about a dozen high-end kitchens a year, and have developed a system that prevents frustrating and costly backtracking. Since no two custom kitchens are the same, I have to tweak my approach to fit each situation, but many tasks I perform remain the same regardless of the kitchen.

### Plumb Walls: An Installer's Best Friend

In my experience, the primary concern of most carpenters when they approach a kitchen installation is to find out if the floor is level. But what about walls that are plumb and square? I've found that in the overall scheme of cabinet installation, the order of importance is: plumb, square, and level.

When walls are plumb, I can make good time. I position the cabinet in place, screw it to the wall, and move on. When walls are not plumb, I'm forced to fuss with shims. Judging the right amount of shim to shove behind a cabinet is a matter of trial and error. I take my best guess, suck the cabinet tight to the wall, check for plumb, and then loosen the screws and adjust the shim until the bubble falls between the lines. It's not difficult, but it is tedious.

Walls that lean away at the top are the most problematic — you have to shim the tops of the uppers, which is a tough reach. When a wall leans in, I can hang the upper from the top rail, then slip shims behind the lower portion of the cabinet.

Save time with careful layout and the right tools.

Base cabinets can be even tougher in this situation. If the wall leans out, the base cabinet is forced out of plumb when it's drawn tight to the wall. You then loosen the screws, the cabinets drop from the line, you moan and groan, and then try and hold the cab-

**Figure 9.** While a helper unloads the truck, the author uses a 4-foot level to check the walls and floor. A level is better than a construction laser for finding bumps and dips in the wall — and plenty accurate for a kitchen installation.

inet to the line while gauging how much shim has to go in behind it. And then there's a gap at the exposed end of the run where the plumb cabinet meets the out-of-plumb wall. This must be covered with a molding or a scribed end panel.

*Square walls.* If a prefabricated laminate countertop is specified and the plan calls for an inside corner, I pay close attention to the squareness of the walls. Prefab counters that are mitered for inside corners install square. If the walls are out of square, there will be a gap where the backsplash meets the wall.

In production work, this gap is closed off with a molding. In higher end work, this is often unacceptable. Prefabricated counters can be special ordered to fit an out-of-square condition, but lead times are long.

*Levelness affects appliances.* When the floor is out of level, I typically start the layout from the highest point. Many appliances won't fit in their opening if the counter is less than 34½ inches above the finished floor. Starting at the high point usually avoids this problem.

# Cabinet Layout Essentials

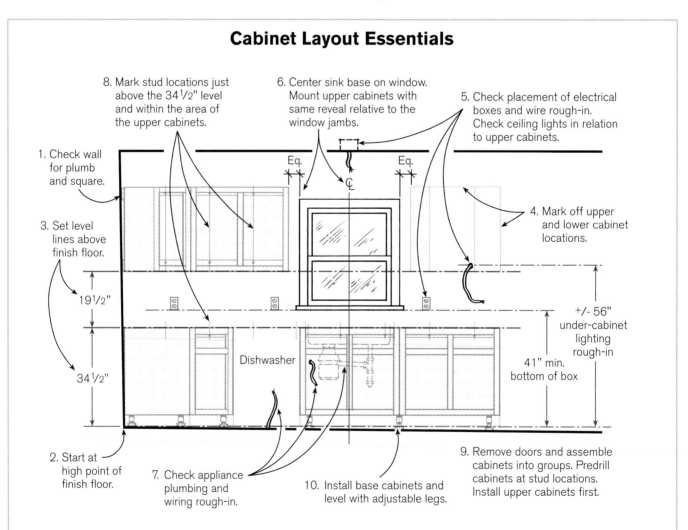

8. Mark stud locations just above the 34½" level and within the area of the upper cabinets.

6. Center sink base on window. Mount upper cabinets with same reveal relative to the window jambs.

5. Check placement of electrical boxes and wire rough-in. Check ceiling lights in relation to upper cabinets.

1. Check wall for plumb and square.

3. Set level lines above finish floor.

Eq. | Eq.

4. Mark off upper and lower cabinet locations.

19½"

34½"

Dishwasher

+/- 56" under-cabinet lighting rough-in

41" min. bottom of box

2. Start at high point of finish floor.

7. Check appliance plumbing and wiring rough-in.

10. Install base cabinets and level with adjustable legs.

9. Remove doors and assemble cabinets into groups. Predrill cabinets at stud locations. Install upper cabinets first.

**Figure 10.** One hour spent laying out the job can save many hours of backtracking later. Check walls for plumb and square, and floors for level. Locations of all cabinets, plumbing, and wiring must be verified, and every cabinet should be checked against the plans — before installation begins.

**Figure 11.** The author assembles the upper cabinets on the floor as a unit, shimming from the back until the fronts are straight and flush. Note the level used as a straightedge.

## Laying Out Cabinet Locations

The first things I check are the walls. I prefer to use a 4-foot level for this process (**Figure 9**). Unlike a construction laser, my bubble stick lets me know right away when there's a hump or bulge in the wall or floor. To those who argue that a 4-foot level isn't accurate enough, I counter that accuracy is relative. A kitchen must be straight and flat — being 1/4 inch out of level overall will seldom affect the job. My goal is to find the high point of the floor and work from there. That way, I know right away if I'll be working late.

After sizing up the walls and floor, I draw a level line on the wall at 34 1/2 inches from the highest spot on the finished floor (**Figure 10**). If the finished floor hasn't been installed, I add its thickness (plus any underlayment) to the 34 1/2-inch dimension. Since most countertops are 1 1/2 inches thick, setting base cabinets to this height results in a finished counter height of 36 inches. Then I measure up 19 1/2 inches from this line, and draw a second line, which represents the bottom of the upper cabinets. If these dimensions seem at all confusing, just remember that finish counter height is 36 inches, and the distance between the counter and the upper cabinets is 18 inches.

Next, I mark out all the upper and lower cabinet locations on the walls. These aren't precise layout marks, but they let me size up the cabinet placement and review the layout for potential problems.

***Electrical placement.*** The most common snafu I encounter is improperly placed or missing outlets and switch boxes. Moving or adding a device box before the cabinets are installed isn't so bad — the "hack tracks" in the drywall can be easily hidden behind the cabinets.

The bottom of a device box should be at least 41 inches from the finished floor, and the run of device boxes should be level. If the electrician measured from an out-of-level subfloor when he set the boxes, they'll need to be relocated. I also check for an outlet where the refrigerator is located, and for a feed wire for the exhaust hood. Unless the joists are open below, the feeds for ranges, ovens, dishwashers, and garbage disposals should be in place as well.

I also check the layout of any ceiling or soffit lighting. These lights are typically placed 16 inches or so from the wall, and they can present a problem if they fall within the area of a 24-inch-deep overhead refrigerator cabinet, wall oven, or pantry.

***Checking for symmetry.*** The majority of kitchens I install have a sink base that's centered on a window. In these situations, I use my layout marks to verify that the cabinet will end up centered, and that the

**Figure 12.** Marking stud locations on the backs of cabinets is easier than marking them inside (far left). The author predrills holes for the mounting screws from the back (left), then finishes up with a countersink bit from the inside.

upper cabinets on either side of the window will show the same reveal relative to the window jambs.

*Proper piping.* I check that drain lines, supply lines, and toe-kick heaters are located properly. Finally, using an electronic stud finder, I mark where all the studs are. I draw vertical stud lines within the area of the upper cabinets, and place a mark just above the 34 1/2-inch base cabinet level line.

The entire layout process takes about an hour, and once completed, allows me to focus on installing. My helper unloads and sets up tools while I do the layout. The last item on my list is verifying that all the cabinets are on site and that they match the plan dimensions.

## The Easy Way to Hang Cabinets

I don't like working any harder than I have to, so I try to do as much work as possible before the cabinets are hung. As soon as the cabinets are unloaded, my helper or I remove the cabinet doors. Many of the doors must be removed for clamping purposes, but more important, it eliminates the risk of a door being damaged as the cabinets are installed.

*Uppers first.* I always install upper cabinets first. They're easier to install when I don't have to reach over installed base cabinets, and there's less chance the base cabinets will be damaged. I lay the uppers

---

## Design Review Catches Problems and Speeds Installation

### by Rob Corbo

We install eight to twelve kitchens a year for a local home center — as a way to stay busy and to grow our small construction company. This program has considerably strengthened our core business by the contacts we've established with homeowners, real estate agents, interior designers, and architects. But working with a home center means dealing with stock cabinetry and designers with varying degrees of experience. To sell our services in this low- to medium-priced renovation market, we needed a set of procedures that would minimize our risk and make our installations more efficient and profitable. To help identify and track potential problems, we've developed a checklist (at right).

### Cabinet Design Review

When a stock-cabinet design for a home center doesn't work out, the installer may be faulted for not identifying the problem early on. So we carefully check the kitchen dimensions used by the designer against those we gathered during our site visit.

First, we verify that the linear inches of cabinets specified by the designer fit into the actual space. We also double-check corner clearances, blind cabinets and sink bases, appliance openings, and cabinet reveals at windows and doors.

Stock cabinets are available in a limited range of sizes, typically in 3-inch increments. Wall cabinets rarely exceed 36 inches in width, while base cabinets are usually less than 45 inches wide. To make everything fit together, we use fillers supplied by the manufacturer.

Available in 3-inch and 6-inch widths, fillers are handy not only for completing cabinet runs but also for solving numerous problems and measuring mistakes. We use them to center sink bases on windows, set blind cabinets, align base and wall cabinets at appliance openings, and provide cabinet-drawer or dishwasher-door clearance with opposite-corner cabinet handles. We always ask the designer to include extra fillers in the order.

*Sink base.* The sink base is usually centered on the window above it. We find the center of the window and plumb down, marking the centerline to the floor to find the sink base's exact location. From the sink base, we measure the cabinet run in both directions to determine if any fillers are needed to align cabinets at appliance openings or to evenly end wall and base cabinet runs.

*Corner clearances.* In L-shaped and U-shaped kitchens, appliances and cabinet drawers and doors on opposing corners must clear each other when they are open. We like to specify at least 2 1/2 inches of face frame or filler at each corner, which allows enough clearance for 3/4-inch-thick overlay doors with 1-inch-deep handles.

Occasionally the door of an appliance — such as a dishwasher, range, or compactor — may need to clear a cabinet handle; it too will need to be installed 2 1/2 or 3 inches off the corner. When necessary, we can add a filler to the face frame to achieve the proper clearance.

*Blind units.* Stock wall or base blind units, which are installed at corners, are often listed as measuring 33 or 45 inches, but they actually measure 31 or 42 inches. This difference allows the installer to adjust the cabinet off the wall enough to attain proper corner cabinet clearance. Any space between the wall and the cabinet will be hidden by the adjoining cabinet (in the case of a wall cabinet) or by the countertop (in the case of a blind base).

*Appliances.* Ranges with microwaves or fans above require that wall and base cabinets line up evenly to create the proper opening. Undercabinet appliances — like dishwashers, compactors, and wine coolers — require only the appropriate width between base cabinets.

on their backs on the floor, and assemble them as a group (**Figure 11**, page 321). I clamp the face frames together, drill pilot holes, and then screw the face frames together. When the entire "block" of cabinets is fastened together, I lay a straightedge on top of the face frames, then shim between the floor and the backs of the cabinets until everything is flat. Then I shim the spaces between the sides of the cabinets and run screws through the sides at the back of the cabinets to lock them together as a unit.

I use Fuller countersink bits (W.L. Fuller, www.wlfuller.com) to drill all the pilot holes. They're inexpensive (around $5 each), use standard twist drill

bits, and are easy to adjust for length. I use square-drive screws (McFeely's, www.mcfeelys.com) for all fastening chores. The square drives have a thicker shank than drywall screws (less chance of snapping them off when working with hardwoods), and the screw heads don't strip out as easily as Phillips head screws.

***Predrilling for stud locations.*** After I've fastened the cabinets together, I stand them up and lay out the studs on the back of the cabinets (**Figure 12**, page 321). I then drill from the back of the cabinet through the hanging rail (at the stud lines), until the drill bit just pokes through to the interior of the cabinet. I finish the pilot holes by countersinking from

We pay particular attention to refrigerators because they vary in both width and height. We've found that designers and homeowners usually get the refrigerator width right but may miss sizing the cabinet height above; the taller the refrigerator, the smaller the cabinet height.

While measuring cabinet runs, the sink-base location, and appliance openings, we also check cabinet distances from all windows and doors. For visual symmetry, cabinets should be an equal distance from door and window open-

ings. Once again, we use fillers to help align cabinets at windows, doors, corners, appliances, and ends of runs.

Sometimes there are situations that can't be addressed with fillers, such as a pipe chase. While a custom cabinet can be built to fit around such irregularities, a stock cabinet must be cut and modified on site to accommodate them.

*Rob Corbo is a building contractor in Elizabeth, N.J.*

### Kitchen Estimate/Installation Checklist

**Cabinets**
- ✓ Measure all runs
- ✓ Check cabinets will fit
- ✓ Check sink base is centered on window
- ✓ Check wall cabinets are symmetrical on both sides of window
- ✓ Check refrigerator width and height to wall cabinet above
- ✓ Check plumbing in existing sink base:
  - ✓ Check condition
  - ✓ Check if water supply is thru wall or floor
  - ✓ Check wastewater alignment
  - ✓ Will refrigerator need a water supply?
- ✓ Check location of range gas feed
- ✓ Check to see if exhaust is vented and how
- ✓ What material will the countertop be?
- ✓ Will any appliances be relocated or added?

**Demolition**
- ✓ How extensive a demolition?
  - Cabinets
  - Appliances
  - Floor
  - Gut

**Electric**
- ✓ Will dedicated lines be needed?
  - Disposal
  - Microwave
  - Refrigerator
  - High hats
  - 220 range
- ✓ Will additional ceiling lighting be added?
- ✓ Will under- and/or overcabinet lighting be added?
- ✓ Are additional countertop receptacles needed?
- ✓ Are there two countertop circuits in place?
- ✓ Kick heater

**Plumbing**
- Sink/faucet hookup
- Disposal
- Range
- Refrig water
- Kick heater
- Relocate radiator

**Floor**
- ✓ Will there be a new floor?
  - Tile
  - Wood
  - Laminate

**Splash**
- ✓ What will the splash be?
  - Tile
  - Full
  - Rock

**Figure 13.** Wires for under-cabinet lights are roughed in at a safe height behind the wall cabinets. The author then slices the drywall to bring the wire down to the correct height at the bottom of the cabinet.

inside the cabinet. This method is much more foolproof than laying the pilot holes out from the interior of the cabinets, since it eliminates the need to deduct for cabinet sides.

My next step is to get the block of cabinets in position on the wall. A number of years ago, I was introduced to an amazing tool: the Gil-Lift (Telpro Inc., www.telproinc.com). This is a dedicated cabinet lift that allows me to lift up to 300 pounds of cabinets single-handedly and roll them into place. The lift mast removes easily from the dolly, which I use to move base cabinets around. Forget the leveling lasers: If you install any kitchens at all, a Gil-Lift is one tool

you shouldn't be without. I figure it took me about four kitchens to recoup the $575 cost of this lift.

If you don't have a cabinet lift, then the size of the block of cabinets you assemble will be determined by the number of people available to help lift the assembly in place. Before I had a lift, I would fasten temporary supporting brackets to the wall. With these brackets, I could fasten the block of cabinets to the wall without the need for an extra pair of hands to hold them up.

***Undercabinet lighting.*** At this stage, if there is any undercabinet lighting, the feed wires must be fed through as the cabinets are positioned. A good electrician will leave a loop of wire 56 inches above the finished floor. It's better to locate this wire too high rather than too low. I cut a trough through the drywall and lower the wire to its proper height (**Figure 13**). If the wire is too low, the wall will have to be patched after the wire is raised. I drill a $5/8$-inch hole in the back of the cabinet just below the bottom shelf and feed the wire through as the cabinets are lifted in place.

## Base Cabinet Basics

When all the uppers are in place, I install the base cabinets. Base cabinets come in two flavors: those with integral bases forming the toe kick and those without.

Base cabinets with integral toe bases are typically moved into position, the face frames are fastened together, and the rear hanging rails are held to the level line and fastened to the studs. Then the cabinets are leveled front to back using shims slipped under the toe bases. If you didn't establish your layout line from the floor's high point, you'll be hacking away at these integral toe bases to adjust

**Figure 14.** Plastic leg levelers (left) speed the task of leveling base cabinets (right). Finished toe kicks attach with metal clips — or can even be screwed directly into the plastic legs.

the cabinet to the rising floor.

Most of the cabinets I install do not have toe bases. Originally, the cabinetmaker I work with supplied plywood base frames that the cabinet boxes would sit on. I would level the toe base frames, set the cabinets on top, and screw the hanging rail to the studs. This made for a lot of work on my knees, and if the cabinet needed to be shifted left or right, the locked-in-place toe frames often had to be relocated. After rethinking the process, I now use adjustable feet called leg levelers. They fasten to the underside of the cabinet, and the threaded portion of the foot is extended or retracted by turning the base of the foot (**Figure 14**). The leg levelers we use cost about $1.50 each. They're made by Camar and are available through kitchen component suppliers.

A typical kitchen might require $50 to $60 worth of leg levelers. The additional cost is more than offset by the elimination of the toe frames, and the labor savings when leveling the cabinets. Finish toe boards attach to the feet with spring clips and can be removed to access wires or piping.

## New Clamp in Town

Aligning and clamping face frames can be tedious. For years, I've used Bessey clamps for this task (Bessey Tools North America, www.besseytools.com). Their smooth action makes for a first-class clamp. I've recently added a new clamp to my bag of tricks, a

**Figure 15.** Pony "Cabinet Claws" are the newest weapon in the author's installation arsenal. They draw the cabinets together and keep the face frames perfectly flush at the same time, acting like an extra pair of hands.

dedicated face-frame clamp called the Cabinet Claw, by Pony (about $50 per pair, from Adjustable Clamp Co., www.adjustableclamp.com). This dual-action clamp simultaneously pulls the face frames together and flushes them up (**Figure 15**). While these clamps can't replace my Bessey clamps for every task, for face-frame work they're well worth the cost.

*Carl Hagstrom is a a builder in Montrose, Pa.*

# Chapter 18:
# Custom Interiors

- ■ **High-End Interiors With MDF**

- ■ **Efficient Frame-and-Panel Trim**

- ■ **Quick Coffered Ceilings**

# High-End Interiors With MDF

by Bill Posey

I've built homes for some 30 years, but for the past decade or so, my design/build firm has focused on the highly competitive new-home market. Most of my homes are in the "move-up" category in desirable neighborhoods. Buyers in that market segment expect some interesting architectural details and a premium trim package. It could be my formal education in accounting, or it could be old-fashioned Yankee ingenuity (or frugality), but I've always prided myself on good-looking trim details that don't cost a fortune. Those details make my homes distinctive

and get people in the door, but it's their impact on the bottom line that's made my business successful.

One of my favorite ways to give my customers something out of the ordinary while saving money is to use MDF trim instead of solid wood. Besides standard trim details like baseboard, casing, and crown, I use it for custom details like wainscot and built-ins. With MDF trim costing less than half of what a similar wood product costs, I can create an attractive high-end look without pushing the selling price into the stratosphere.

**Figure 1.** Using MDF for most of the trim leaves room in the author's budget to use attractive figured hardwoods in high-visibility areas like sills, window seats, and other built-ins.

## Simple Panel Wainscot

**by Trevor Kurz**

Building a room full of true raised-panel wainscot is a lot of work and a heavy drain on most budgets, so we've come up with a simple, straightforward way to create the look of panel wainscot without the extraordinary expense.

We start by striking a level reference line around the perimeter of the room with a rotary laser, marking the desired top of the chair rail. In the room shown here, the chair rail was a continuation of the 5/4 window stool (**Figure A**). Whenever we can, we use full 1-inch stool, which fits with the period detailing we like.

If we're working in a room that already has drywall, we carefully remove the 1/2-inch board below the reference line and clean up the studs. One thing I hate to see is a receptacle in the middle of a wainscot panel or — even worse — cut into a stile. So we also take this opportunity to relocate the wiring in such a way that receptacles can be mounted horizontally on the baseboard, centered between the floor and the base cap (**Figure B**).

Next, we attach the 1/2-inch MDO plywood that serves as the field for our panels and as a nailer for the stiles and panel molding. We spend some time laying out the plywood seams so that they fall behind

### Wainscot Section

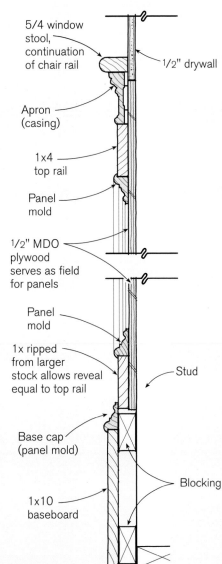

5/4 window stool, continuation of chair rail

1/2" drywall

Apron (casing)

1x4 top rail

Panel mold

1/2" MDO plywood serves as field for panels

Panel mold

1x ripped from larger stock allows reveal equal to top rail

Stud

Base cap (panel mold)

Blocking

1x10 baseboard

**Figure A.** *The chair rail was a continuation of the 5/4 window stool. The panels (inset) were made nearly square on this job to maintain a consistent width, but the author prefers them to be taller than wide.*

**Figure B.** *The 1/2-inch MDO plywood panels, nailed directly to the studs, also serve as nailers for the stiles and panel molding. The panel frames are assembled quickly with biscuits and glue and immediately nailed to the wall.*

the stiles, and we mark them on the walls so we have no excuse for missing.

Here, we made the top rail and stiles from 1x4 poplar, and the bottom rail from wider stock, which allowed us to keep the 3 1/2-inch reveal; the larger stock also served as a nailer for the base cap. We used a 1x10 base with a custom 5/4-by-1 7/8-inch base cap.

Frame assembly is usually quick and easy. We cut all the parts to length on the miter saw, then assemble the frame with biscuits and glue. No clamping is necessary, as we immediately attach the frame to the wall with 2 1/2-inch finish nails, making sure to hit the studs. When you do this, remember to make one corner stile 3/4 inch wider than the overlapping one so the reveals remain the same.

On this job, we ran the base cap around the perimeter of each panel instead of using a different panel mold. We had this profile custom milled; it laps the 3/4-inch material nicely, and you have to look closely to determine whether it's one or two pieces.

We finished up with the installation of the 1x10 baseboard and base cap.

*Trevor Kurz designs and builds custom homes on Cape Cod in Massachusetts. His partner Bob Cifelli also worked on this project.*

I think that cost-effective finish work today is really about knowing how and where to integrate new or nontraditional materials. There was a time when I used only natural wood for all my casings and finish trims. Now I actually choose MDF over wood because it's better for painted trim — with the money I save, I splurge on hardwoods for areas that call for a strong first impression (**Figure 1**, page 328).

## What's Available?

I try to stick with stock profiles because the factory-applied primer makes finishing easier, although I sometimes use custom wainscoting. Some MDF profiles are new designs, but many are based on traditional wood profiles. One of my favorites is Windsor 3$^1$/2-inch casing. This versatile trim can be used for window and door casings, chair rail, or top-rail on wainscoting, or even as a frame for bathroom mirrors. It creates a custom effect with minimal work. Because this trim is so versatile, I never throw anything away — I'm always finding new uses for even the smallest pieces (**Figure 2**).

## Working With MDF

MDF is made from super-compressed paper and glue, so it doesn't have any discernible grain. That's both the most notable benefit and the greatest difficulty in working with it. On the plus side, it can be cut, machined, and filled easily; on the minus side, the lack of grain makes thin sections prone to breakage. As a result, we miter rather than cope inside corners. Another key to successfully working with MDF is using sharp tools — especially sharp saw blades. We use high-quality, 80-tooth blades and sharpen them regularly.

We also glue miters and returns, using MDF 2400 Adhesive from Koetter Woodworking (www.koetterwoodworking.com). This two-part adhesive sets fast, so it's critical to check the fit first. A small bead of adhesive is applied to one side of the joint, and the other side is sprayed with activator. Once the two pieces touch, there's only about five seconds before the bond is set.

Another helpful tip is to use 18-gauge brads instead of 15-gauge finish nails. We've found that the smaller wire reduces "mushrooming" or "puckers" around the nail hole and makes finishing easier. Initially, I had concerns about the smaller nail having enough strength, but we haven't had any problems.

Besides costing less than wood, one of MDF's greatest attributes is its dimensional stability. Seasonal changes in temperature and humidity won't cause swelling, splitting, or opening of joints. That makes it the perfect wainscot material (**Figure 3**). (Also see "Simple Panel Wainscot," previous page).

**Figure 2.** Windsor casing made from MDF costs about half what the same profile costs in wood. But because it's more dimensionally stable than wood, MDF miters don't open with seasonal moisture changes. The author uses a fast-setting adhesive to guarantee tight joints.

**Figure 3.** Using MDF wainscoting in a variety of heights complements standard stool and head casing heights, creating a much livelier interior. The author installs the wainscot with construction adhesive and a few 18-gauge brads to hold it in position while the glue sets — making for fewer nail holes to fill. Windsor casing, rabbeted on the bottom, makes a good cap (left).

## Finishing

When it comes to paint, the primed finish of MDF is obviously easier to cover than bare wood. I use MDF trim with a smooth, baked-on finish, which saves time in sanding and can eliminate a second coat of finish paint. We fill nail holes and imperfections with Dap 222 filler and caulk gaps with a high-quality latex caulk. Once the MDF trim is painted and finished, the final touch is to urethane the bird's-eye or curly maple stools and caps.

I have finally come to the conclusion that not only can MDF be used in place of wood, but it delivers a better result when painted trim is desired. I attribute a lot of our success using MDF to our talented finish carpenters, who put together the custom details that create our unique look and style.

*Bill Posey is the owner of W.E. Posey Design/Build in Shelburne, Vt.*

# Efficient Frame-and-Panel Trim

by Gary Katz

Craftsman-style wood paneling is one of the easiest types to install because the stiles and rails have no sticking profile: they're cut square, which means you don't need cope-and-stick router or shaper bits. And with square-cut stiles and rails, there's no need for fancy panel molding, either. The trick is to preassemble all the stile-and-rail sections and install the panels before fastening anything to the walls or columns.

We recently finished a job where we wrapped structural columns with a frame-and-panel treatment. The columns supported angled arches, which continued the paneled treatment. Fortunately, the owner wanted a collar of crown molding near the top of each column, which provided a good way to hide the joint between the column panels and the angled panels for the archways.

## Careful Layout and Design

I wanted to know exactly what we were up against before we installed anything, so we started with a laser and shot control lines on the OSB substrate of each column. Control lines don't have to represent any specific height or elevation; they just provide a level reference from which all other layout marks can be measured. (I use control lines whenever I'm setting windows and doors, so the jambs and casings will all be aligned.)

Measuring up from the control lines, we quickly discovered that the headers weren't framed level. In one opening the header was crowned down, with a 1/2-inch sag. The floor was out of level, too, as much as 1/2 inch across a single opening. We established the lowest header as our starting point and laid out the paneling for the head jambs from that elevation.

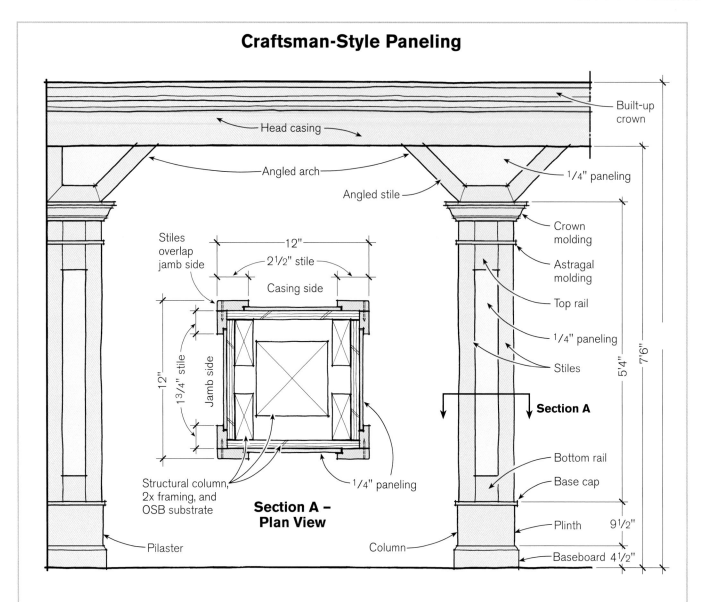

## Craftsman-Style Paneling

**Figure 4.** Rabbeted stiles and rails, joined with pocket screws, and 1/4-inch plywood panels create a production version of an expensive-looking paneling job.

Using the same control lines, we next marked the location for the finished spring lines of each arched opening, so that all the spring lines would match and be perfectly level. The only problem that remained was the floor. I knew there would be two different widths of panels — narrow ones for the inside "jambs" of each opening, and wider panels for the outside "casing" on each opening (**Figure 4**). But I was determined to make the panels all the same height. The best solution for the out-of-level floor was a classical one — I just allowed for a second joint between the shaft of the column and the plinth, the perfect location for a base cap. The base cap mimics a classical column, which has a torus molding above the plinth; scribing the baseboard solved the rest of the problem.

## Story Pole

Before starting any woodwork, we laid out the dimensions of the column panels on a story pole, just to be sure we had it right. We made the top rail wide enough to accept the crown molding and still leave an exposed rail that was wider than the stiles. We also increased the width of the bottom rail so that it would accommodate the additional base cap molding and still be wider than the top rail (columns look best with the heaviest elements at the bottom).

Burma teak is the most popular type of wood used in Craftsman-style homes in the Pasadena area, but the owner of this home chose alder, which is much less expensive and still a good-looking hardwood. I usually use sheet goods for wainscoting, typically hardwood veneer with an MDF core. But for this job,

**Figure 5.** Pocket screws make for tight joints between rails and stiles (A) and allow the frames to be handled while the glue is still wet. In a quick operation, a carpenter rabbets the frame (B), then installs the panel with glue and staples (C, D, E). The panels were cut 1/8 inch smaller than the overall width to allow for seasonal movement.

solid wood was the only choice because there was no molding hiding the inner stiles and rails, and the outer edges were visible, too. Though it added considerably to the board-foot price, I ordered all the solid material S4S from a local supplier to save milling time. For the 1/4-inch paneling and 3/4-inch plinths, I used alder veneer with an MDF core.

## Assembling the Columns

Wrapping the lower section of each column was the easy part of this job. We used the story pole to determine the heights of all the panels, then cut a stack of stiles and rails. The wide top rails had to be glued up because the alder boards didn't come wide enough. Since the backs of all the panels were hidden against the columns, we were able to use pocket holes to

secure the boards and didn't have to wait for the glue joints to set up. We also used pocket holes to secure the stiles to the rails, which allowed us to move along at a pretty good clip (**Figure 5**).

We didn't even wait for the glue to dry before rabbeting the back of each frame for the 1/4-inch panel. We set the panels in a small bead of glue, dropped each panel in place, and then secured it with staples.

Installation went pretty fast, too, at least on the center columns. We eased the edges of every outside corner to emphasize the joinery and provide a little wiggle room: installing flush corners can be much more demanding. Next, we glued up the corners, holding them in place with clamps so we could adjust the fit before securing the corners and the field with finish nails (**Figure 6**, next page).

**Figure 6.** Clamps hold the glued panels in place while a carpenter secures the joints and the field with finish nails.

## Scribing Panels

Four of the columns butted up against walls. Though there were no backs to those columns, we still made all the panels the same size as the columns in the field, which allowed an extra 3/4 inch for scribing the frames tightly to the walls.

We used the same scribing technique we would use to scribe a door casing that butts a wall. We started by installing the jamb panels first (the inner panels that formed the jambs of each archway), then temporarily clamped the "casing" panels in place. Whenever you scribe casing to a wall (or to anything), it doesn't matter how far off the wall you hold the casing. What matters is that the casing be parallel with the jamb. We positioned the inside edge of the casing panels in line with the jamb panels, then spread our scribes the exact distance from the

**Figure 7.** Pilaster columns are scribed to the wall (far left), then trimmed to the line with a Makita panel saw (left), held to cut a slight back-bevel for a tight fit at the wall.

**Figure 8.** The routed inside-corner rabbets on angled panels (far left) were finished by hand (left).

face of the jamb to the edge of the casing (**Figure 7**).

Our 4³/4-inch Makita panel saw (model 4200N) works great for cutting scribes: the little monster spins at 11,000 rpm, fast enough to cut without tear-out, and it's small enough to follow even the wiggliest walls. We always clamp the workpiece to a table before cutting a scribe, so we can concentrate all our attention on the job. Following a scribe line seems a little easier, too, if you tilt the blade slightly and undercut the workpiece. The slight bevel also makes it easier to get a tight joint at the wall.

## Layout for the Arches

Scribing a few panels on the columns caused only a small wrinkle in our production schedule, but my real fear was the arches. I figured they'd slow us to a crawl. Fortunately, clamps and a pocket-hole jig solved that problem (see "Tight Connections With Pocket Screws," page 316). The panels for the head jambs were easy because we assembled them in rectangles, just like the panels around the columns, then we cut the miters at the spring lines with a sliding compound miter saw. The panels that cased the openings went much slower because we had to dry-fit all the pieces in place.

We started by cutting and mitering all the heads together, then secured them in place with clamps. Next we cut and fit the angled stiles, labeling and marking the location of each piece. We took the marked pieces to the bench, where it was easy to fasten them together with glue and screws, using a 9-inch Kreg pocket-hole clamp (Kreg Tool Co., www.kregtool.com). We used the same bearing-guided router bit to let the panels into the frames, cutting the tightly angled corners by hand (**Figure 8**).

**Figure 9.** Some of the columns have miters in two directions, requiring careful dry-fitting (left). Even the ¼-inch panels are mitered (right).

**Figure 10.** Some arches were longer than the length of available alder stock. These sections were preassembled with pocket-screw joints at midspan.

**Figure 11.** The column plinths (far left) were assembled from 3/4-inch alder-veneer plywood. Baseboard followed flooring. The finished paneling is reminiscent of early 20th-century Craftsman-style woodwork (left).

The panels on the entry side of the room posed their own problem, because the 1/4-inch paneling had to be mitered in every corner (**Figure 9**, previous page). We left each panel a little long, then scribed the pairs to fit perfectly. Some of the panels on the hallway side were even more troublesome, because they were longer than the available alder stock (alder isn't available in lengths longer than 10 feet). To ensure a tight-fitting mid-span joint, we used pocket screws to preassemble the entire span in one piece. We used the same technique we'd perfected on the front side, tem-porarily fitting the pieces in place, assembling them on the bench, then installing the completed panels (**Figure 10**, previous page).

The finished result was a Craftsman look on a production schedule, completed in a fraction of the time that would have gone into the old-world handiwork of the original Craftsman style (**Figure 11**). In this case, it took modern tools and good planning.

*Gary Katz is a finish carpenter in Reseda, Calif.*

# Quick Coffered Ceilings

by Gary Katz

As a production finish carpenter, I'm always looking for faster, better ways to get the work done. Recently, my crew and I have developed a method for building coffered ceilings in a fraction of the time it used to take — and with a fraction of the frustration.

In the past, we would try to get onto a new-construction job before the insulation contractor so we could install blocking between the ceiling joists for coffered ceiling beams. On remodels, we had to open up the drywall to install blocking for the runs that were parallel to the ceiling joists. What a mess that was! I also remember bolting full-length dimension lumber beams to more than a few ceilings, because we had been taught that you had to have solid back-ing. The trouble was, it was nearly impossible to get it perfectly straight and a nightmare when it came to wrapping it with finish lumber.

Forget all that nonsense. These days we use lightweight hollow backing that goes up in hours instead of days, without having to install any in-the-ceiling blocking — and every beam is perfectly straight. The approach depends on adhesive instead of bolts, and a continuous diaphragm that's secured directly to the ceiling joists through the crown molding.

Here, I walk through the process as it applies to a paint-grade ceiling we did recently. You'll be able to apply the method to any style of coffered ceiling that you're building.

## HOLLOW BACKING

**1.** It's faster to build all of the hollow backing boxes in the shop, where it's more comfortable to work and all my tools are only an arm's reach away. Figuring out how many supports you need doesn't require an exact drawing, just a sketch. Finger-jointed pine makes the best backing (rather than MDF) because pine doesn't split, no matter which direction you nail into it.

**2.** The center cross-shaped supports take the most time, but with all the pieces precut and stacked close by — and a full glue bottle — the job goes quickly. Form the cross by butting two short pieces of backing into a longer piece, then overlap the three-piece joint with another piece. Use plenty of glue and brads.

**3.** After the base of the cross is made, nail the side backing in place. If all the pieces are cut square on a miter saw, then the inside corners will fasten together tightly and form perfectly square corners, which makes it easy to fit all the moldings.

**4.** For this job, we used three types of hollow backing: the cross-shaped pieces for intersections, U-shaped pieces for ends and mid-span supports, and L-shaped pieces for corner backing.

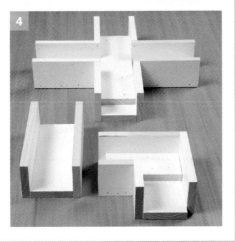

## CAREFUL LAYOUT

**5.** Lay out the ceiling carefully, twice, with pencil lines before snapping any chalk lines. I first make small pencil marks. Once I'm sure those marks are correct, I lengthen the marks into continuous pencil lines, using a straightedge, so I can see the beams before snapping chalk lines. Only when I'm positive that all the beams are centered properly do I reach for a chalk line. I snap lines on both sides of every beam, and on the ceiling and the walls around the perimeter. In this room, we'll be covering up the entire ceiling, so making a mess of the drywall to change lighting layout was not a problem.

**6.** Panel adhesive (Liquid Nails, PL 400, for example) is an inexpensive product that has quietly revolutionized the building trades. We use it frequently for securing material to concrete, stone, wood, and drywall. In this case, we depend on the adhesive for partially supporting the ceiling. Once the crown is installed, the diaphragm can never move.

**7.** Even though the adhesive caulking only partially supports the ceiling, we take the stuff seriously and apply a liberal amount, especially where there's no joist passing above the hollow backing.

**8.** Wherever there's a joist, nail it good. But where there's just drywall, angle the nails in all directions to hold the backing to the ceiling while the adhesive dries.

**9.** With premade components and careful layout lines, installing the backing goes quickly.

## BEAM BOTTOMS

**10.** Allow the adhesive to dry overnight before installing the beam bottoms — adding too much weight too soon might spoil the job. We always start on the perimeter walls, though in some cases, it's best to run the beams first. The design of the ceiling will determine the right procedure.

**11.** Few rooms are square. Use a protractor to gauge the proper miter angles, or just overlap the boards and mark the cuts.

**12.** Use a square to tie the marks together while the board is still in place, just to be sure the miters are aligned in the right directions.

**13.** We use a 1/4-inch slot cutter mounted in a router to make the kerf. A biscuit joiner will work, too, but a biscuit is always a little sloppy and won't register the two pieces perfectly flush, like a spline will.

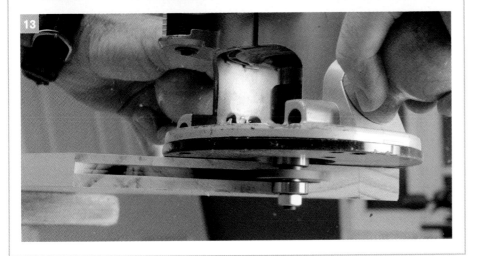

**14.** We cut splines from 1/4-inch MDF because it's exactly the right thickness. Glue the kerf on the installed piece and insert the spline, then apply a liberal amount of glue to all surfaces of the spline and to the shoulders of the miter before installing the second board.

**15.** Install the center beam bottoms next, splining those butt joints to the perimeter soffit. Cut all the pieces a hair long and spring them into place. Run the kerfs long so splines can be slid into place after the pieces are in position. Remember, the long kerfs will be covered by the beam sides.

**16.** Fasten the soffit to each piece of backing, but just tack it with brads so it will be easier to string the beam bottoms straight.

**17.** On this job, we didn't have to make the beams perfectly straight. This built-up cornice has large reveals between each piece of molding, which hides a lot of sins in the ceiling. Using a string and some long shims, we just got them close to the eye — within 3/8 inch. But with some designs, the beams must be installed almost perfectly straight.

## BEAM SIDES

**18.** All of the interior moldings are preassembled. The inside corners are mitered, glued, and cross-nailed, forming tight, long-lasting joints. Start with the fascia boards that form the sides of the beams. On some ceilings, we use baseboard installed upside down for the beam sides.

**19.** Measure the pieces tight, then subtract 1/16 inch so they'll slip easily into place. Since each piece is usually of a slightly different length, we draw a diagram of the ceiling grid, mark the front or back of the room, then label each piece as we measure and cut. We then follow the drawing to assemble the pieces, so each side will be in the correct position.

**20.** Every finish carpenter should carry a block of wood for tapping the sides in place. On WindsorOne's Classical Colonial frieze (www.windsorone.com), which we're using here, the cove at the bottom always points back toward the beam bottom or soffit.

**21.** Brad nails will not pull the moldings together! We carry an assortment of quick-grip clamps to squeeze the pieces tightly together before fastening them.

## THE PANELING

**22.** I use a RotoZip (www.rotozip.com) for all cutouts in 1/4-inch sheet goods. The circle-cutting attachment is easy to use and eliminates the need for a compass and jigsaw. There's a little light in the tool that's especially nice.

**23.** We stained and finished the 1/4-inch oak panels before installing them, simplifying the finisher's job considerably. Because the crown molding goes in next, the panels don't have to be cut tight. Just be sure all the grain runs in the same direction. Before sticking the panels in, we use a magnet or a nail to find the ceiling joists and mark their locations on the frieze boards.

**24.** Liquid nails and a few brads are all that's needed to secure the panels against the ceiling.

## THE CROWN

**25.** Cut and preassemble all of the crown molding, just like the frieze boards. Again, measure the pieces tight, then subtract 1/16 inch so they'll slide into place. Glue the miters, squeeze them together with spring clamps, then lock the miters together with 1-inch 18-gauge brads in both directions.

**26.** The top of the crown will go in easily, but the bottom snugs up tight. If it's a little too tight, plane off one edge just slightly.

**27.** If the ceiling has a deep belly or bow in it, sometimes the crown won't sit flat against the paneling. That's no problem on a paint-grade job — you can just caulk it. But with stain-grade paneling, a bad ceiling can be a nightmare on joinery, especially if you're trying to assemble the crown one piece at a time. Preassembling the crown offers another alternative — attaching the paneling directly to the crown.

**28.** Use a brad nailer to pin the crown to the panel, then flip the panel and bend the brads over. Or you can cut the panel to fit flush on the bottom of the crown, then glue and staple it to the crown from behind.

**29.** Apply another liberal amount of panel adhesive (yes, we buy this stuff by the case), this time in small balls, so the adhesive will act as a shim, filling any void in the ceiling and forcing the paneling against the crown.

**30.** The crown and panel lift into place as a unit.

**31.** Remember to nail off the crown to every joist you can, using 2$^1$/$_2$-inch 15-gauge nails. Once the crown is nailed to the ceiling and to the fascia, and the fascia is nailed to the soffit, it would take a crowbar to remove this coffered ceiling — and most of the drywall would come with it.

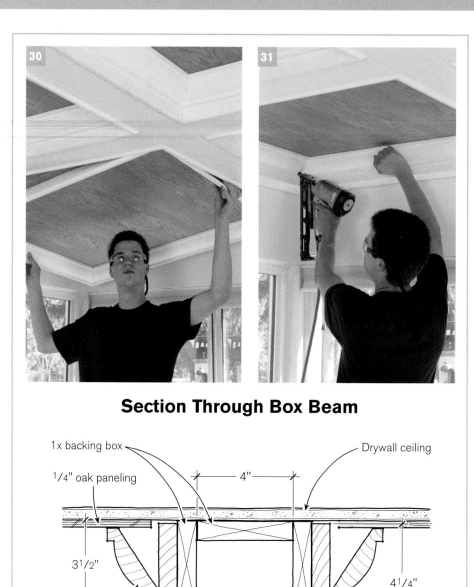

## Section Through Box Beam

1x backing box

$^1$/$_4$" oak paneling

Drywall ceiling

4"

3$^1$/$_2$"

4$^1$/$_4$"

Crown molding

Frieze molding

5$^1$/$_2$"

1x6 soffit

## THE BED MOLDING

**32.** Install the bed molding last. You can cope this molding if that's your style, but we miter the corners. The bed molding shown here, also from WindsorOne's Classical Colonial line, is 1⁵/8 inches thick and has a complicated beaded profile, so it's a tough profile to cope.

**33.** Read the corner with a protractor to figure the right miter. If the miter opens a little, it's usually because there's a belly in the wall. Place a shim between the molding and the wall, and then caulk behind the trim.

*Gary Katz is a finish carpenter in Reseda, Calif.*

# Chapter 19: Stairs

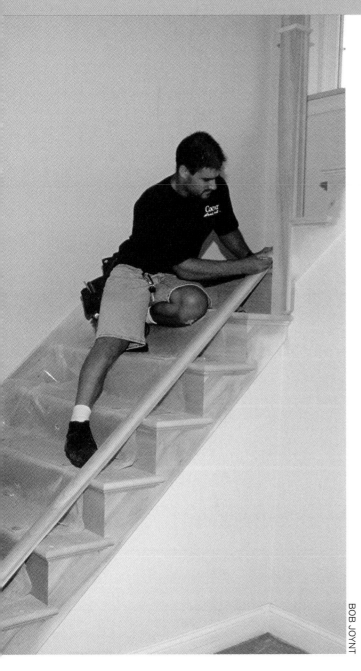

- **Installing Manufactured Stairs**

- **Trimming Out Manufactured Stairs**

- **Simple Site-Built Stairs**

BOB JOYNT

# Installing Manufactured Stairs

by Andrew P. DiGiammo

A prebuilt stair takes two men just an hour or two to install, and it costs the contractor little more than he would pay for the materials alone.

I'm a design/build contractor in the high-end custom market in coastal New England. For every house or remodel I take on, I create a unique design, which includes the staircases.

Like a lot of builders, I used to have my own carpenters build our custom stairs. Then one day, my neighbor invited me to check out his stair-building shop, Cooper Stairworks (www.cooperstairworks.com, now owned by Horner Millwork in Somerset, Mass.).

When I saw the details his shop was using — precision-routed stringers, fully housed risers and treads, glued tongue-and-groove joinery, and so on — I realized that I was doing my customers a disservice by custom-building stairs instead of installing the shop-built product. Then I saw what the shop was charging for a stair package, and I realized that I couldn't beat the price, either — certainly not for stairs of this quality.

I employ excellent finish carpenters, but I can't expect guys who are building a handful of staircases a year to be as efficient or as accurate as professionals who build stairs every day. And a big shop has the volume buyer's advantage: I pay almost as much for the materials to build a stair as the shop charges me for the finished item — and that's before I even look at my labor cost.

Bear in mind that there are lots of stair manufacturers around the country. They sell stairs for every kind of house, from multifamily tracts to million-dollar palaces. I don't suppose my supplier is unique, but I haven't shopped around much — you should check out your local supplier's operation if you're seriously considering manufactured stairs.

## Cost

In my market, prices look something like this (including stairs and railings): for a straight box stair, to be placed between two framed walls with railings attached to the walls, I expect to pay around $900 to $1,000. That's with southern yellow pine risers and oak treads; for basement-grade wood, you could cut that almost in half, but to go up to poplar risers or all oak would add a few hundred to the base price. (Note: All prices in 2000 dollars.)

For a slightly nicer stair, partially open on one side, the base price is a little more, say $1,400. Little extras like a bullnose bottom step and railing volute would add about $300.

If you choose stairs that are partially open on both sides, or completely open on one side, then you're up to around $2,000 (it's the railings that make most of the difference). For this type of stair, poplar risers would add almost $200, oak risers more like $400,

**Figure 1.** Curved stairs are built on a wall mockup that is framed using plates cut from a full-scale CAD pattern. Identical plates are sent to the site so the actual wall will match the shop jig. Railings are test-fitted in the shop before the stair is shipped.

**Figure 2.** Stair builders will quote jobs from plans, but they generally send a field rep to the site to verify measurements before starting work.

and common upgrade options like bullnose steps or volutes bump it up another $400. At this level you'll get a very nice stair for a good-quality upper-middle-market home.

*Curved stairs.* When Cooper Stairworks builds curved stairs, they output a full-scale print of the floor plates for the curved wall from a CAD program, and use that as a template to cut wall plates from plywood. They send an exact duplicate of the wall plate to the site for the framers to use, and then rig up a full-scale replica of the wall itself in their shop (**Figure 1**). They build the stairs right onto the mocked-up wall, so when the finished item arrives on site, it drops right in place.

## Scheduling

Besides cost, another big advantage of manufactured stairs involves scheduling. As a rule of thumb, the longer a job takes, the less money I make. In the case of stairs, a prebuilt installation takes a few hours, while building the stairs on site could tie up my best carpenter for a week or more.

By using a shop-built component, I avoid uncertainty in both schedules and costs. If my carpenter on site runs into a snag on a site-built stair, the whole project stops until he's back on track. A week can easily turn into 10 days. This doesn't just blow my cost estimate for the stair itself: by interrupting the schedule, it also creates other costs that you can't even account for. But when I order prebuilt stairs, it's the supplier's responsibility to deliver them on time and on budget. The stair package is a fixed cost that I can predict on the first day of the job.

## Ordering Stairs

As soon as I have a firm set of plans, I fax a copy to the stair shop with a description of the stairs. They send me back a price for the complete package, including railings, and let me know when they can deliver. They also quote me a price to install the stairs, but it's usually cheaper to use my own crew. I pay for an outside installer only when my own people are tied up on another site. When you do have a manpower problem, though, it's nice to know your supplier can come in and do the job right.

The supplier won't build stairs from plans. After the house is framed, they send a rep to the site to

**Figure 3.** Perfect-fitting tread returns are glued and air-nailed to the treads (left). A tongue on the back of each tread (center) matches a groove routed into the face of each riser. Gluing and nailing these joints, the stair builder makes up a complete set of tread-riser pairs in about 20 minutes (right).

**Figure 4.** Stringers are precision-routed on a computer-controlled machine. The treads are securely wedged (left), glued (center), and screwed (right) in place.

measure the actual dimensions of the opening (**Figure 2**, previous page). It's the rep's responsibility to make sure the stairs are built to fit.

The time for installing the stairs is flexible. We always build rough stairs when we frame the house so the crew and subs don't have to use ladders to get from floor to floor. We tear these out when the manufactured stairs arrive, which can be any time after the roof is on, either before or after drywall.

Damage is an obvious concern. The manufactured stairs come wrapped in protective plastic, with tread protectors tacked on. It's pretty safe to install them early on, but I still like to wait until most of the subs are gone — no point in tempting fate.

On the installation shown here, it worked best to install the stairs after framing and before drywall; railings didn't go on for another month.

**Figure 5.** Glue blocks are stapled and glued to every joint from the underside (far left) to add solidity and prevent squeaks. Next, cove molding is finish-nailed beneath each tread nosing (left).

**Figure 6.**
Kerfed plywood is bent around a pre-made form to make a bullnose riser.

## How the Stairs Are Built

When I saw the way the stairs were put together in the shop, I was impressed with both the efficiency and the quality of the process. With every tool set up for its specific purpose and all the materials on hand, the production process moves right along.

Dedicated tools make first-rate joinery possible. For example, tread returns fit very tightly because the matching pieces are milled on the same router using different jigs.

And although the work goes faster than it ever could on site, the shop uses connection details that few builders employ. Tongue-and-groove tread-riser joints are glued as well as nailed (**Figure 3**, page 349).

Tread and riser ends are fully housed in dadoes in the stringer, and are held snugly in place with wedges, glue, and screws (**Figure 4**). After everything's fastened, the installer adds reinforcing glue blocks on the back sides of all the tread, riser, and stringer joints (**Figure 5**).

The bullnose riser assembly is a good example of the blend of efficiency and quality. The process involves routing and kerfing out a strip of 1-inch finish plywood for the riser, bending it around a radius form, gluing and nailing the whole assembly in place, trimming the butt end to length, and attaching the finished riser to the staircase (**Figure 6**). It probably takes less time for a worker to do this in the shop than it would take a carpenter on site to set up his power tools.

## On-Site Installation

You can figure on two people taking part of a morning to install just the stairs (**Figure 7**). Railings might take the whole afternoon. If you've got a bigger set of stairs, like a full 90-degree radius stair, you'll need some extra labor on hand to help with the lifting. And, of course, expect the fine work to take longer.

By the way, if the stairs are big, remember to leave a way into the building. I forgot that once, and we had to cut a large curved stair in two pieces just to fit it through the door.

Before you place stairs, a last check of openings and of plumb and level is a good idea. On the job shown, the installer was confused for a minute because someone had removed a post under the floor to pour the basement slab. Every time the installer tried to shim up the landing, the floor below

**Figure 7.** Two men can easily carry and place a typical straight staircase (left). For large or complicated staircases, you may need more manpower. The installer pins the lower staircase section in place, using a scrap of landing tread to determine the correct height for the top edge of the riser (right). He places the first screw where cove molding will cover it later.

**Figure 8.** The joint at the landing newel (far left) serves as a focal point for aligning the entire stair assembly. The installer shims and plumbs this location carefully, then screws through the upper stair stringer into the lower stair riser to firmly lock the joint (left). Fasteners at this point will be covered later by the newel post.

dropped instead — until it dawned on him that he needed a temporary post in the basement.

But if the framing is on the money, as it should be, installing a staircase is like installing one cabinet: get it in place, check all your dimensions and spacing, check level and plumb, fasten it, and you're done.

With a two-piece assembly, as soon as the lower run is tacked and clamped in place, you can walk on it (carefully!) while you're putting in the upper section. The joint where the two sections meet has to be dead-on plumb and level, and shimmed flush as needed (**Figure 8**). This location is a good place to put fasteners, because the landing newel-post will cover them up later.

That center joint is the focus for the whole stairs — you get it right and pin it, and then adjust at the top

and bottom of the stairs if you have to. Most of the time in new construction, everything fits right in place, but if there's any planing or shimming needed in a remodel job, do it at the bottom or the top.

The stairs come from the shop with the finish floor height and centerline marked on the lowest riser (**Figure 9**). If you have to trim or shim that, do it so that the change is minor in the center walking path. By code, you have 1/4 inch to play with — more than you'll probably ever need. Coming out of the shop, I've never seen any of the rise or run dimensions on the stairs themselves deviate from dead-on perfect.

At the top, lay a scrap of landing tread on the riser to check the height. The landing tread comes with the stairs and makes the transition from the 1 1/16-inch tread thickness to the 3/4-inch wood floor-

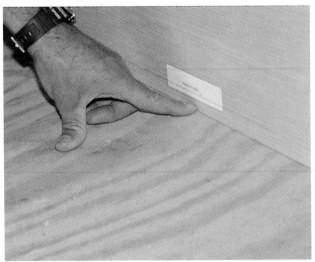

**Figure 9.** The installer uses a piece of landing tread, supplied with the stairs, to check the fit at the top (left). A label on the lowest riser (right) shows the finish floor height and indicates the centerline of the stairs.

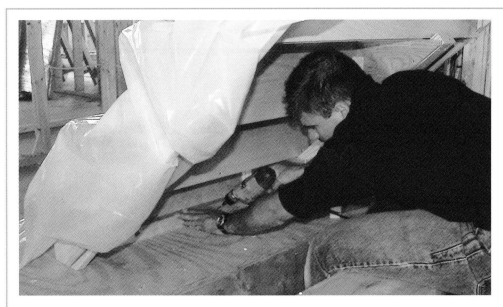

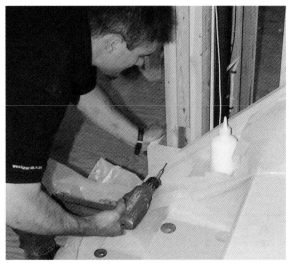

**Figure 10.** A cleat glued and screwed to the deck serves to hold the bottom stringer tight to the floor (left). Screws into the cleat through the face of the stringer will be buried behind flooring and molding. Screws into the studs from underneath are also invisible (below left). Visible fasteners (below right) are countersunk and plugged.

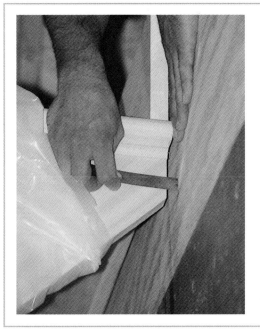

**Figure 11.** A ⁵⁄₈-inch gap is left for installing drywall around the stairs (far left). Precut shims (left) speed this process.

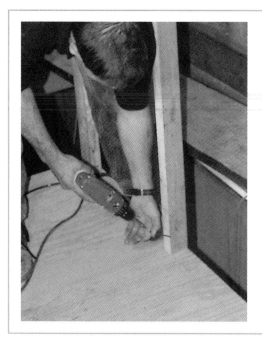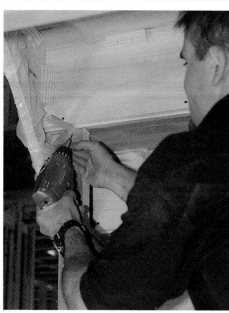

**Figure 12.** Before leaving, the stair installer places temporary braces at midspan in each run of stairs. It's best to build in a crown of perhaps $1/4$ inch to allow for slight settling and framing lumber shrinkage over time.

ing thickness; we install it when we install the floor. The stairs are right when the scrap lies flat on the subfloor and fits just right on the riser.

*Fastening*. The stairs are fastened to the wall studs at the side, under the steps if possible (**Figure 10**, previous page). We also pin them to the landing, and to a cleat screwed into the subfloor behind the bottom riser. Drywall screws seem to work fine for all these locations; when we have to place screws in the stringer above the steps, we countersink them, then plug and sand. Never use nails instead of screws — that's the one thing that is likely to cause squeaking over time.

All around the staircase, we use $5/8$-inch shims at the fastening points to hold the assembly away from the framing (**Figure 11**, previous page). That lets us slide drywall behind the stairs later. The joint between wall and stairs will eventually end up being covered with a cove or quarter-round molding.

*Support*. On the job shown here, the shop's installer put temporary bracing under each run of stairs at midspan (**Figure 12**). If it were one long run, he'd have put in two braces. It's a good idea to shim the supports to create a slight crown, say, $1/4$ inch or

so; as lumber shrinks, everything tends to settle and sag a little.

If my crew were installing, we'd probably frame up the wall right away, just like any other stud wall, with the top plate right up under the stair treads and with a $5/8$-inch gap between the framing and the stringer to accommodate drywall. Again, we'd shim slightly to create that crown.

## Making the Choice

Depending on your situation, you may have good reasons for wanting to build stairs yourself. But the reality of my business is that I have to provide the best quality I can within a limited budget. As a small-volume custom builder in a tight labor market, I have to use my skilled workers as efficiently as possible. I can't afford to keep a finish carpenter on staff just to build stairs. Manufactured stairs give me and my customers the best value available, and I see no reason to go back.

*Andrew P. DiGiammo is a design/build contractor and a partner in an architectural firm in Assonet, Mass.*

# Trimming Out Manufactured Stairs

by Paul Alves

After many years of installing stairs in the field for Cooper Stairworks, I became one of the leaders of the production team in the shop.

I was part of the team of stair builders on the project described in "Installing Manufactured Stairs" (page 348). A couple of weeks later, after the drywall was in, I went back to the site to install the railing system. Here, I describe that process.

Like many other stair builders, Cooper Stairworks (www.cooperstairworks.com, now owned by Horner Millwork in Somerset, Mass.) will send people to the site to install the stairs and railings if the contractor needs that. However, the packages we send out are complete enough that any carpenter can do the on-site work. In fact, even some skilled homeowners have installed their own packages.

We do most of the measuring and fitting in the shop, so the site installation usually takes a day or less, depending on the complexity of the stair system.

## Precut Pieces Simplify Things

Many of the pieces in the railing package are premeasured, precut, and prenotched in the shop, based on the field measurements taken by our site rep. We cut each railing package at the same time as we build the stairs, using the actual stairs to guide us (**Figure 13**). The posts are cut to the appropriate height and notched at the bottom to fit snugly in place. Likewise,

**Prefit railing packages save time and eliminate costly mistakes at the job site.**

BOB JOYNT

the treads on the stair itself are prenotched at the appropriate location to accept the posts. This means it's hard to install the posts anywhere but exactly at the right spot. As long as you've positioned the stairs correctly and are careful to fasten the posts perfectly

TED CUSHMAN

**Figure 13.** The stair shop prefits each railing system to the actual stairs as the stairs are built, so that no complicated layout is needed on site. Here, a shop carpenter test-fits a post to a stair set (left), then checks the plumb cut on a railing (right).

**Figure 14.** Posts and stair treads are prenotched at the shop to ensure the proper post location and height, but the posts are drilled on site.

*TED CUSHMAN*

plumb, everything else should drop nicely into place.

## Step by Step

The job shown here was a straightforward post-to-post design. We had to run posts and rails all the way up the steps, which are open on one side, and also around the landing at the top, which is open to below. As always, I took the installation in phases: first the posts, then the landing treads and fascia under them, then the rails and balusters, then the baseboard at the mid-landing, and finally the necessary cove and cap moldings.

In order to be efficient, I complete each phase before moving on: When I'm setting posts, I set all the posts. When I start to install rails, I do all the rails, and so on. That way I'm not running back and forth between different tools and setups.

***Posts.*** The first task is to set the posts. As I mentioned, the posts come prenotched and precut to height, with the caps and any other trimwork already applied. But we drill the posts in the field because different builders use different methods of attachment (**Figure 14**).

Some builders even use nails to attach the posts. When squeaks do occur, it's usually because the builder has used nails without glue. We prefer wood screws (or long drywall screws) and yellow glue. Screws bring the pieces tightly together, while the glue actually does most of the work.

Unlike the posts that attach to the stair itself, the landing post upstairs attaches through the drywall into the framing (**Figure 15**). The post should be perfectly plumb and square so when you install trim

around it and attach the railings, all the joints can be a simple square cut. Setting these is a little trickier than setting the ones that attach to the stairs themselves, because the built-up drywall mud may cause the angle to be irregular. I always set this post temporarily and check square and plumb. If it's not right, I back the screws out and shim the post or shave it as needed. If the post is in at the top, I can shim behind it, because the fascia will hide the shim; but if it's in at the bottom, I have to grind the top down — shims at the bottom would show. I test-fit everything until it all looks good, then screw it together for the last time.

After all the posts are in, a final check of level is a good idea. If for some reason the floor is out of level, the railings will be too unless you adjust the posts. You could vary the height at which you attach the railings to the post, but it would be noticeable. Instead, if the posts aren't level, I shim up the low ones to even things out (the landing tread will hide the shims).

***Landing tread.*** The landing treads come next in the sequence. They come with the package, but they have to be cut to length and attached.

The landing tread has a profile that matches the stair tread on the front edge and the flooring thickness on the back. It makes the transition from stairs to floor at the mid-landing and top landing. It also serves as edge trim for the flooring around the area that's open to below, providing a visual transition. I predrill and countersink each piece for screws, then glue and screw it to the subfloor, plug the screw holes with matching bungs, and touch-sand them.

Treads are usually finished but not painted, so it's important to match the plugs to the tread. Pick plugs that are the same color and species of wood, and align the grain when you insert them.

The landing tread helps lock the posts in place, and it also hides any shims you might have used to adjust the post heights because of floor variations (**Figure 16**, page 358).

***Fascia.*** The next piece I install is the fascia under the landing tread sections that edge the opening. This piece stabilizes the landing tread itself and also helps lock in the posts. Again, it will hide any shims behind the post where the posts attach to the wall.

I install the landing tread first, then the fascia, so I can make sure that the landing tread is perfectly level all three ways: out from the floor, side to side, and front to back. When the balusters are put in place, if the landing tread is not level, a crack will show at the joint where it meets the baluster.

The landing tread extends $2^1/8$ inches out over the opening, so it could easily sag or rock. So to prevent this, I set a small level on the landing tread, hold the fascia firmly up under it with one hand, and nail the fascia on with 8d finish nails. I don't use glue here because I'm fastening to drywall. The drawing in **Figure 17**, page 358, shows how the landing trim is built up.

**Figure 15.** Corner landing posts may be thrown out of plumb or square by the drywall and tape. The author checks for plumb and square (top, left and right), then shims or grinds as needed before attaching the post permanently (above, left and right).

BOB JOYNT

**Figure 16.** The landing tread helps lock in the newel posts and hides any shims that may have been used to adjust the post (left). The landing tread must be perfectly level so that no cracks appear at the bottom of the balusters. The author attaches the landing tread with 8d finish nails (right).

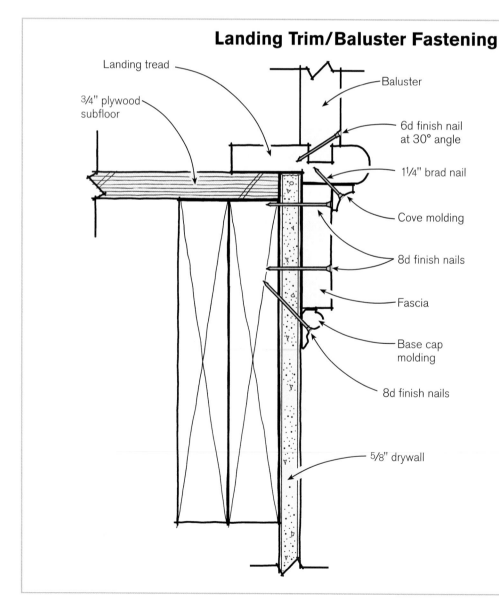

## Landing Trim/Baluster Fastening

Landing tread

3/4" plywood subfloor

Baluster

6d finish nail at 30° angle

1¼" brad nail

Cove molding

8d finish nails

Fascia

Base cap molding

8d finish nails

5/8" drywall

**Figure 17.** Landing tread and fascia are fastened in place before balusters are set. Cove molding and base cap are nailed on last.

**Figure 18.** The author uses glue and screws to fasten the rake rail to the post from below. A block clamped to the post steadies it in place.

BOB JOYNT

The little pieces of cove and cap molding I save for later — for now I move to the rails.

## The Rail Deal

I start with the rake rails (the sloped ones). These have a pitch cut at the bottom that has already been done in the shop. In case of some discrepancy, the other end has been left long. In the field, I set the rail down on the stairs and butt that bottom cut to the bottom post, then mark the top of the rail where it meets the top post (see photo, page 355).

This method is more accurate and quicker than using a tape. I use the same method on the level railings: I take the actual rail (first checking to make sure again that the posts are plumb), cut a square cut on one end, butt that to one post, mark the other end on the next post, then cut at the mark.

In my experience, the more you measure, the more chances you get to mess up. If you take out the tape, measure between posts, and then go down and measure the railing, there is always the chance that you'll cut it an inch short. Marking the piece in place, how can you go wrong? And since some custom railings cost $14 or more per foot, I don't want to make any mistakes.

After cutting the rake rail, it's time to fasten it in place (**Figure 18**). This particular rail is placed in the center of the space between the bead and the cove on the post. I mark the center point; then, measuring across the face of the pitch cut and dividing the measurement in half, I come down that distance and make a mark. I cut a temporary block to fit between that mark and the piece of bead molding below, and clamp the block in place. This gives me a place to rest the rail.

When I set the end of the rail against the post (after applying glue to the face of the cut), the top

end rests against the upper post, and the rail stays in place while I drill it and fasten it with screws.

Again, the rail has not been predrilled for the screws in the shop — that's left to be done on site. That's because some other installer might want to attach the rail some different way; in that case, they wouldn't want the holes. But this is the way we recommend fastening it — screws and glue make a strong joint.

I fasten the top of the rake rail with finish nails, nailing down through the rail into the post. This is a paint-grade installation, with poplar rails — if it were a harder wood intended to get a clear finish, I would generally screw into the face cut from the back side of the post.

You can see in the photos that the rake rail has been predrilled for the balusters. It's hard to lay out and drill those holes on site, so we do it in the shop ahead of time. The level rails, however, are not predrilled; that leaves the customer some flexibility in laying out those balusters.

*Level rails.* From the top of the stairs around the landing opening, we set rails level from post to post. Again, as I set these rails I use a block to support the rail in place.

How we fasten rails to posts depends on the location (**Figure 19**). At corners, we drill and screw

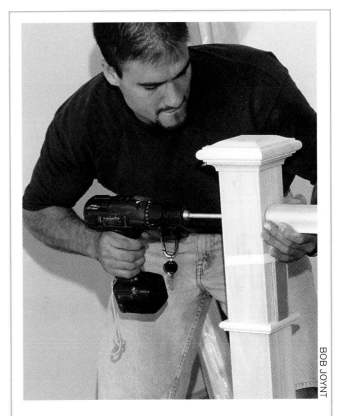

BOB JOYNT

**Figure 19.** For efficiency and accuracy, the author holds the actual rail in place to mark the cut. Using a measured block to support the rail, he fastens it with screws through the back of the post.

**Figure 20.** At the wall, the author uses a rosette to attach the rail. He screws the rosette to the end of the rail, then to the wall.

BOB JOYNT

## Attaching Rails With Rail Bolts

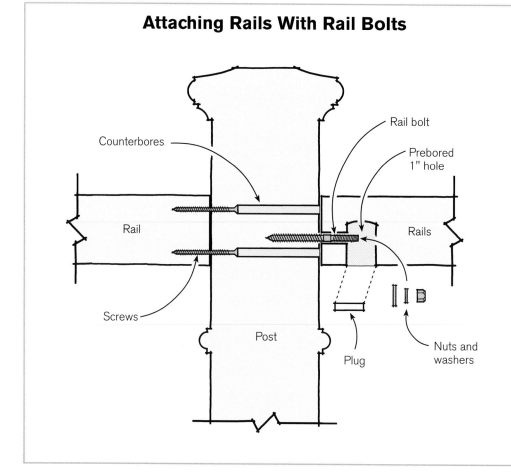

Counterbores

Rail

Screws

Post

Plug

Rail bolt

Prebored 1" hole

Rails

Nuts and washers

**Figure 21.** Where two rails meet at a post, only one side can be screwed. The other side is attached with a rail bolt. One end of the bolt has screw threads for attaching to the post; the other end is machine-threaded to accept a nut. A pilot hole for the bolt in the end of the rail and a 1-inch hole for the nut under the rail are prebored at the shop. In the field, the installer has to drill a pilot hole in the post, attach the bolt, and then tighten the nut from beneath the railing. A plug hides the hole in the rail.

through the post into the butt end of the railing, off-setting the screws slightly so they don't interfere with each other. Where a railing butts to a wall, we apply a rosette to the end of the railing and screw the rosette to the wall (**Figure 20**). At center posts where railings attach on opposite sides, we drill and screw through the post on one side, but on the opposite side we use a rail bolt.

Whoever invented the rail bolt did stair builders a big favor. It's used for blind fastening of rails to posts, and also to join two rail sections together as needed (**Figure 21**). On one end it's a threaded screw, and on the other end it's a bolt. The screw end goes into a predrilled hole on the post or on one railing section; the bolt end goes into a hole in the other rail. But first we predrill a 1-inch hole under the railing, just big enough to get a nut through. We insert the nut from underneath and tighten it onto the bolt to bring the assembly together.

With an over-the-post rail system, we preset all the rail bolts. Where there's a joint, we attach the rail bolt to one railing and predrill the 1-inch hole in the matching piece's butt end. We preassemble the whole railing in the shop to make sure it's right, then dismantle it and ship it. All the installer has to do on site is put it back together and tighten it up.

*Balusters.* The treads and the rail have been predrilled in the shop to receive the balusters. The bases of the balusters are level with the rails, but the upper turnings are rail-oriented — the profile follows the pitch of the railings.

In the field, I install the center baluster first, then sight the railing to make sure it's straight (**Figure 22**). In fact, I like to put a slight crown to it, on the assumption that it might sag over time.

I also double-check the railing height. The rake rail height should be measured plumb from the top of the tread at its tip to the top of the rail (**Figure 23**). Our local code calls for a 34-inch rail height, but that varies from place to place. I marked my level at the 34-inch height so I can make a quick measurement perfectly plumb without having to use my tape.

If the railing is at the correct height, I proceed to install all the rake balusters. I first measure and cut each baluster to length. Then I take the baluster, line it up with the hole in the rake rail, push it up, slip the pin over the hole in the tread (which we have first squeezed a little glue into), then drop the baluster back down (**Figure 24**, next page). At the top, I predrill a hole and put in a 4-penny finish nail. At the bottom, we send in one 6-penny nail to keep the baluster from spinning. The nail goes about 3/8 inch from the top of the tread, on a 30-degree angle going into the baluster, so it goes right through the pin and connects into the tread.

*Level balusters.* Unlike the rake rail and the stair treads, the level rails and the upper landing treads are

**Figure 22.** The author slides a baluster into the predrilled hole in the railing, then lowers the pin into the hole in the tread. He sights the rail: it should have a very slight crown.

## Measuring Railing Height

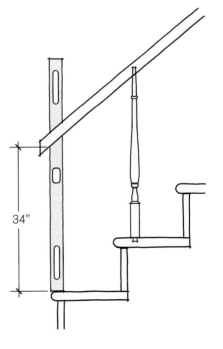

34"

**Figure 23.** Railing height should be measured from the front and top of the step, straight up to the top of the railing. The author uses his level, which is marked for 34 inches, the code-prescribed rail height in his locality.

**Figure 24.** The author fastens the top of the baluster with a 4d finish nail and the bottom with a 6d finish nail.

not drilled in the shop. Again, the contractor on site may have his own preference for laying out and attaching these elements, or a discrepancy on site could affect the spacing between the post and the wall. So before I can install those balusters, I have to mark and drill the landing tread and railings (**Figure 25**).

I use dividers to mark the landing tread, but first I have to figure the spacing. I look first at the spacing of the balusters on the stair treads; I want the landing balusters to be in that vicinity. Say it's 4¹/₂ inches: I measure the distance between the landing posts (which happens to be just under 4 feet) and divide that number by 4¹/₂ inches to see how many spaces I need to mark off. The answer is 10 spaces, so I divide the total distance by 10 to get the interval, which is close to 4¹/₂ inches. I set that distance on my dividers and step it off to mark the centers of the holes.

I drill the bottom holes first, then transfer the centers to a story pole that's cut to the length of the rail. I use the story pole to transfer the marks to the underside of the rail, and then drill the upper holes.

## Finishing Touches

Once the balusters are in, all that's left is a few trim pieces. At the mid-landing, I install a couple of pieces of baseboard. I place the baseboard on two scraps of the actual flooring material to elevate it, so that the flooring contractor can slide his material under there later. Base cap molding goes on above the baseboard.

**Figure 25.** The author marks his hole centers with dividers (left), drills the holes, and transfers the hole centers to a story pole (center), then transfers the same layout onto the underside of the rail (right).

**Figure 26.** Using 8d nails, the author applies base cap molding around the stringers and landing baseboards. He uses the same material flipped upside down below the stringers on the open side of the stairs, and below the fascia around the open landing.

BOB JOYNT

I also apply base cap below the fascia around the upper landing, using 8-penny gun nails. Here, the base cap is flipped upside down (**Figure 26**).

Cove molding covers the joint where the fascia butts up under the landing tread. Cove molding under the stair treads was already applied at the shop in the same way; but on site I still need to place a couple of final pieces of cove under the landing treads at the top of each run of stairs.

To finish up, I plug all the 3/8-inch countersunk screw holes with wood plugs and sand them flush.

*Stair builder Paul Alves was formerly a production coordinator at Cooper Stairworks in Somerset, Mass.*

# Simple Site-Built Stairs

by Jed Dixon

I've been building stairs full-time for the past 25 years in high-end homes in the Boston and New York City areas. Most of these stairways are complex, with curves and spirals. But when it comes to straightforward stairs, I've developed a technique that can easily be followed by any decent site carpenter, even without access to a millwork shop. Here, I'll walk you through the way I would go about trimming out a fairly simple, but elegant, staircase made entirely out of stock parts — something you might put in a high-end spec house, for example.

Obviously, before trimming a staircase, you've got to design and build the structural undercarriage. I use several framing details that lead right into my trim-out technique (**Figure 27**, next page). If I'm not building the undercarriage, I try to get the framers to incorporate the key features of my system.

## Newels Are Key

The first step in trimming out a stairway is to set the newel posts. I'll be focusing on turned newel posts

**Careful layout is the key to a custom look using stock stair parts.**

with a block at the top — where the handrails are cut to fit between the starting and landing newels (post-to-post). Because the newels bear the strain that goes on the rail, they need to be locked in tight. I put the newel posts in first and fit all the other trim to them.

Locating newel posts is a straightforward procedure that works off the centerline of the handrail and balustrade.

**Bottom newel.** I like to place the bottom newel on the second step, just above the starter step. If you put the newel on the front of the bottom tread, you end up with a very narrow stair. It looks like a cattle chute and doesn't feel very welcoming. Also, when the newel is placed slightly up on the stairs, it's much easier to put your hand out and step on the first tread from the side, so you actually turn as you begin going up. The curved bullnose tread and starter step that I often use make this common sideways approach comfortable.

To locate the bottom newel front to back, I set it where it will catch the front overhang of the second

tread, plus a slight reveal. To find the side-to-side location, I work off the centerline of the handrail (**Figure 28**).

The rail centerline is determined by the width of the balusters and by an arbitrary decision as to where the balusters are placed. I think that balusters always look better when their edges line up with the skirt-board below. I also prefer the first baluster on each tread to sit right on the corner so that its front edge lines up with the riser below. The balusters seem to grow more naturally out of the stairs that way.

**Where nosing meets newel.** Traditionally, the tread nosing dies into the newel posts. For this to work out, the newel posts must be wide enough to catch the nosing. To calculate the minimum newel width, add half the baluster width to the tread overhang, plus the reveal where the tread dies into the newel — then double it. For a $1\frac{1}{4}$-inch baluster (minimum standard size), a $1\frac{1}{8}$-inch overhang, and a $\frac{1}{8}$-inch reveal, you need at least a $3\frac{3}{4}$-inch newel. That's bigger than most readily available commercial newel

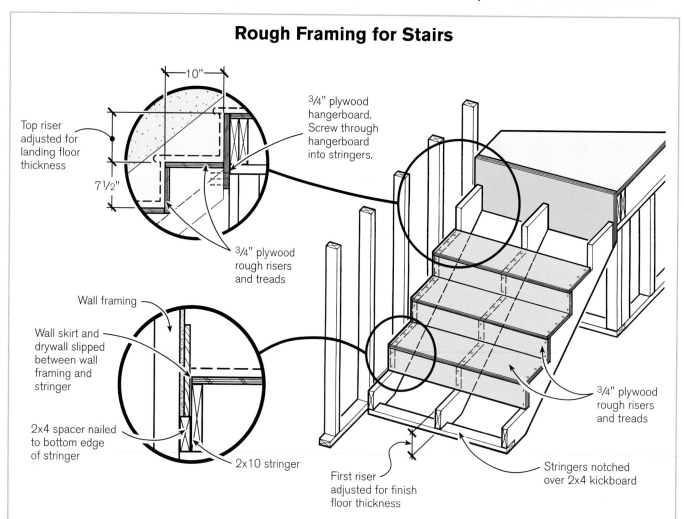

**Rough Framing for Stairs**

10"

Top riser adjusted for landing floor thickness

7½"

3/4" plywood hangerboard. Screw through hangerboard into stringers.

3/4" plywood rough risers and treads

Wall framing

Wall skirt and drywall slipped between wall framing and stringer

2x4 spacer nailed to bottom edge of stringer

2x10 stringer

First riser adjusted for finish floor thickness

3/4" plywood rough risers and treads

Stringers notched over 2x4 kickboard

**Figure 27.** The author spaces the stair undercarriage out from the wall framing with a 2x4 along the lower edge of the inside stringer to leave room for the drywall and the wall skirt. To strengthen the entire carriage system, he installs ³/4-inch plywood sub-treads and sub-risers — glued and screwed.

posts, which may be 3 inches square or even smaller.

If you use a wider 1¾-inch baluster, you're going to need at least a 4¼-inch newel post. Any other solution will cause design problems. You'll have to make a little return on the nosing where it extends past the newel post, or worse, put the centerline of the handrail in so far that you create a weak newel attachment.

*Cutting newels to length.* When laying out a newel post, I first determine the best side and lightly mark it with an "F" for "face." Next, I cut the newels to length at a dimension determined by the handrail height and how far the newels extend below the sub-tread (see "Laying Out Newel Cuts," next page). I put the landing rails at a height of 36 inches above the finish floor, and the rake rail at 32 inches above the tread noses.

*Notching the bottom newel.* After a newel is cut to length, it's time to figure out how it will be notched. The bottom newel needs a pocket notch that lets the tread of the first step slide underneath while the newel face continues down over the drywall. Newel

posts are expensive, so the cuts for pocket notches have to be figured carefully. Work your layout from the centerline of the handrail and from the face of the subriser. Remember, the notch dimensions are determined by the dimensions of the baluster, drywall, face skirt, and reveal. When marking the notch cut, make sure that it accurately accounts for the riser height as well as the thickness of the stair tread and finish flooring. I still scratch my head over these things, even after building stairs for years. Drawing the whole scenario out on the post and looking at it while holding the post in position is essential to avoid costly mistakes.

*Landing newel.* The landing newel is longer than the bottom newel because it catches the landing rail at 36 inches above the finish floor and then runs below the tread far enough to catch the face skirt and scotia molding. All that said, a typical landing newel would be cut about 55 inches down from the top of the newel block. The newel will appear to extend down below the landing and will need to be finished

## Laying Out the Bottom Newel

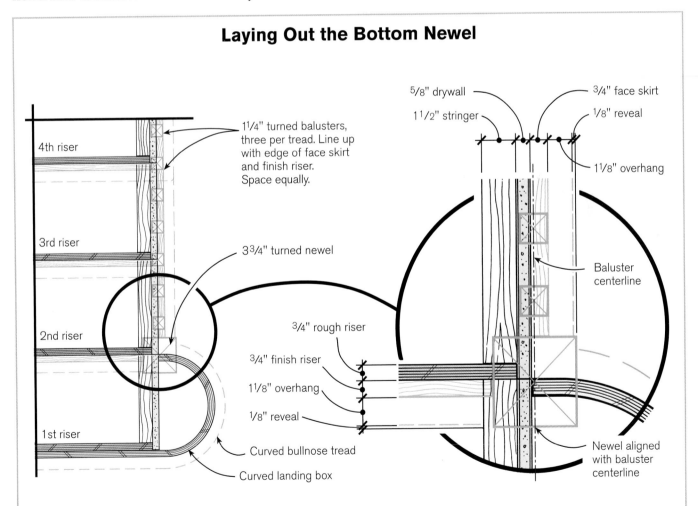

**Figure 28.** If the baluster edges line up with the face skirt edge, the centerline of a handrail is going to be half of one baluster in from the face of a face skirt. The treads are typically cut to overhang 1⅛ inches. The minimum width of newels equals half of the baluster width plus the tread overhang plus an optional reveal — times two. Because many readily available newel posts are not wide enough to notch solidly into position, the author always specs wider newel post styles.

## Laying Out Newel Cuts

When post-to-post newels are turned on the lathe, blocks are left at the bottom for attaching the newel to the carriage and at the top where the handrails attach. Rails are typically attached to newel posts one inch below the edge of the top blocks.

**Newel lengths.** To determine the length of a bottom newel, you have to carry the line of the top of the handrail across to the front side of the newel to a point exactly over the nose of the second tread (slightly in from the newel edge, to allow the nosing to die into the newel with a slight reveal). This requires knowing the angle, or pitch, of the staircase. Although you can estimate the angle with a sliding T-bevel, I like to use a calculator for added precision. The angle equals the inverse tangent of the rise/run. On a scientific calculator enter **Rise ÷ Run = Inv Tan**. Or

with a Construction Master calculator, enter the rise per tread and the run per tread and push **Pitch**. With a rise of 7.5 and a run of 10, it's 36.9 degrees.

From this point, measure down 32 inches to where the level of the finish tread nose will be. Because the finish tread slides under the bottom newel, this line becomes the top of the pocket notch. To create as strong a connection as possible, I extend the bottom newel all the way down to the subfloor so that the flooring sub can lock the post in place with his flooring. If I don't beat the flooring sub to the job, I've got to give up on this detail and scribe it to the finish floor.

The landing newel is a little bit different — it has a longer top block that allows it to pick up both the landing rail at a height of 36 inches and the rake rail at 32. Leaving a 1-inch

## Bottom Newel

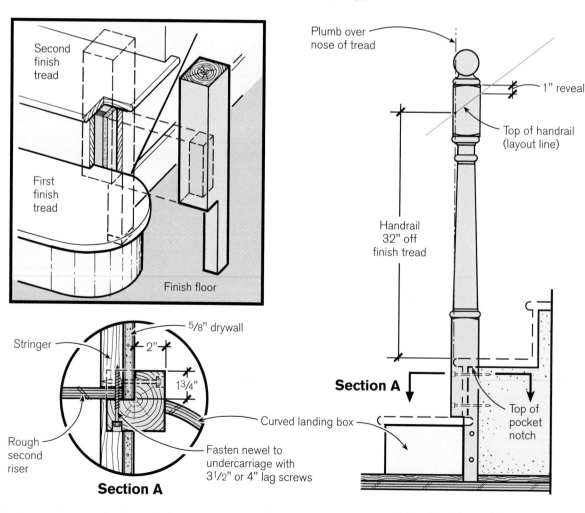

reveal above the landing rail, the top edge of the newel block has to be 37 inches over the finish floor. The bottom end of the landing newel should extend below the face skirtboard. Typically, you also have an apron on the landing. If the stair turns and rises up the next run, the next face skirt will also butt into the landing newel. In either case, it's common to run base cap upside-down on the apron, or under the face skirts, and your newel has to be long enough to catch everything. I always draw it out full-size (either on the wall or on paper) to determine what that length is. Typically it's around 17 inches if you use a 1x10 for your skirtboard.

***Pocket notches.*** Newel pocket notches need to position a newel front to back so that the tread or landing overhang dies into the newel, and side to side so that the newel is centered on the handrail/balustrade centerline. Front to back, we

know that there's a 1¹/8-inch overhang plus a ³/4-inch riser plus a ¹/8-inch reveal. That's 2 inches, which brings us to where the bottom portion of the cut is made. Side-to-side in our example (with 1¹/4-inch balusters, ⁵/8-inch drywall, 1x10-inch skirtboard, ¹/8-inch reveal), the side of the notch cut ends up being ¹/8-inch beyond the center of the newel.

Beyond this, layout differs for bottom and top newels. For the bottom newel, the lower section must be cut to fit around the curved riser box used for the first step. In addition, the pocket needs to make way for the tread to slide underneath. And over the tread, the notch positions the newel front to back so that it catches the overhang of the next tread up. For a landing newel, the pocket positions the newel from front to back in the same manner. On the lower portion of the cut, however, the newel runs full width. — *J.D.*

## Landing Newel

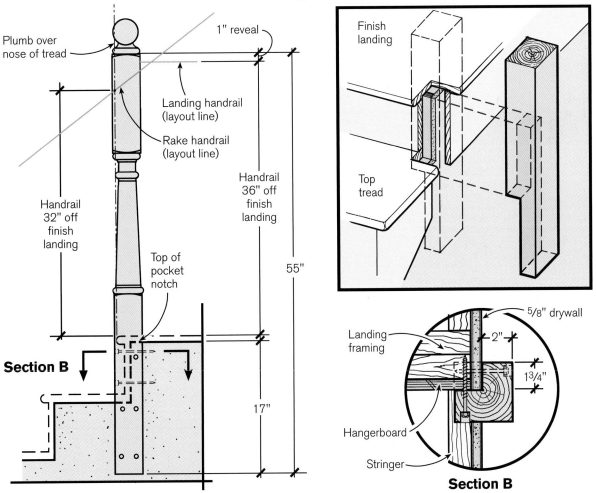

**Figure 29.** The author completes the newel pocket notches with a sharp chisel.

**Figure 30.** To notch the wall skirt around the landing framing, the author tacks the wall skirt along the nosings of the rough treads and marks a level line one standard rise above the landing floor.

## Mitering the Skirtboard

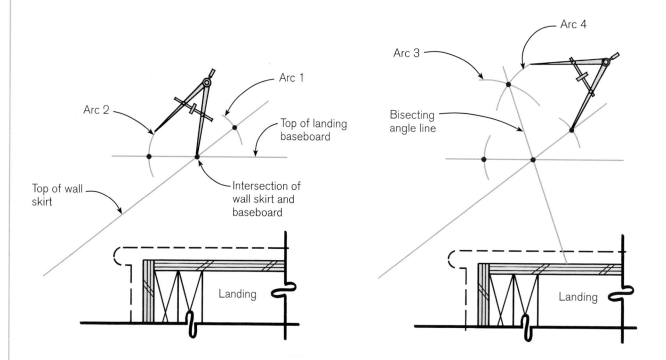

**Figure 31.** To bisect an angle where the wall skirt and baseboard meet, the author marks lines showing the tops of the wall skirt and landing baseboard and extends them several inches beyond where they intersect. After setting a compass to 4 inches, he strikes Arc 1 and Arc 2, then resets the compass to 8 inches before swinging intersecting Arc 3 and Arc 4. He bisects the angle by marking a line that connects the two points of intersection and runs to the floor. Finally, he picks up the angle using a bevel gauge and transfers it to a speed square.

with a dropped finial. To lay out the pocket notch, I follow the same rules as for the bottom newel, except that I allow 37 inches above the finish floor.

Before making these notch cuts, check the carriage and walls for plumb. You may have to rough-cut the pocket notches, then scribe the newels plumb to the plaster before making the final cuts.

*Cutting pocket notches.* To cut the notches, use a circular saw set to the proper depth. Before cutting, clamp the newel to a bench, because accuracy is essential on the cuts where the newel meets a tread or drywall. Finish the notch cuts little by little with a good, sharp chisel. I use cheap, all-steel chisels, so I can hit them hard (**Figure 29**). The steel in them is not bad, but you'll need to take the time to keep them sharp.

After the pocket notch is complete, drill for the screws. I use a 1/2-inch counterbore and come back later to fill with 1/2-inch bungs that match the grain of the wood. I line up the grain of the bungs, and pare them off smooth. If I'm making the bungs in my shop, I'll use a piece of scrap wood from the newel to cut them. That's especially important with mahogany, because the color varies quite a bit, and you can match the grain better if you use a bung cut from the same piece.

I use a level to plumb the newels, then I fasten them into the framing with 31/2- or 4-inch lag screws. I don't glue the newel to the framing because the lag screws are strong enough. However, I always glue all the other abutting trim, such as the risers and skirts, onto the newel so the joints stay tight over time.

## Skirtboards

Traditionally, a straight run of stairs gets a skirtboard on both sides. The wall skirt runs on the same plane as the flooring baseboard and gets finished out with the same base cap. On the open side, the face skirt acts as an apron running below the treads, and also gets finished out with base — except here the cap is run upside down.

*Wall skirt.* I've seen old-timers scribe and notch the wall skirt around each tread. I've tried it once or twice, and it's come out okay. But it's tricky, and if it doesn't come out right the first time, you can end up chasing an elusive good fit forever when you try to tune it up. I don't think it's worth it. Instead, I always leave a gap between my rough stair and the wall by installing a 2x4 between the bottom edge of my first rough stringer and the wall studs. This leaves room for the drywall to be slipped down first, followed by a 1x10 wall skirt.

To mark the cuts for the wall skirt, I temporarily tack the uncut board along the corners of the rough treads (**Figure 30**). I then set a compass to the distance of one rise and scribe level cuts at the main

floor and the landing floor. This scribe technique allows the cut wall skirt to slide down flush to the floor so that its bottom edge will be hidden behind the finish treads and risers. I use a level to mark a plumb cut line at the top where the skirt hits the landing. This plumb cut line intersects the landing level cut line and together they mark a notch that fits around the landing where it's attached to the wall (the landing is not spaced away from the wall the way the stringers are).

If you're tying into baseboard that is thinner than 3/4 inch, I recommend you plumb-cut the wall skirt at the top and bottom to simply catch the baseboard. But, if you're using two-piece or 3/4-inch baseboard, you'll want your baseboard to continue down the stairs as your wall skirt. Decide on the height of the baseboard first, then set the skirtboard so the top edges will meet in a smooth transition. Instead of making a plumb joint, which exposes end grain on the skirtboard, I prefer to make a miter cut. If you know the theoretical angle, you can simply halve it. If not, you can use a simple compass technique to manually bisect the angle (**Figure 31**).

*Face skirt.* The face skirt has level cuts at all tread overhangs and vertical miter cuts that will tie into the risers (**Figure 32**, next page). When installing the face skirt, I nail only along the bottom edge, so the top is "flapping in the wind." That way, later on, I can move the top of the board to align it with the miters on the risers. Don't forget to glue the ends of the face skirt to the newel posts.

To cut the face skirt to length, first make a plumb cut where the skirt meets the bottom newel. I usually cut this to the theoretical plumb cut for the stair — 36.9 degrees in this case. Then, I hold it in place and mark the top plumb cut where it meets the landing newel. At this point, I can't assume that my newel posts are perfectly parallel, so I cut the skirt slightly long, then scribe it to fit with a sharp block plane.

After fitting the face skirt to length, I tack it over the ends of the rough stair, holding it a little high to allow for the top corners of the finish risers, which are going to be 3/4 inch proud of the rough riser. I then use a level to mark the cuts for each rise and run. Because the framing may be slightly out of square, I center the bubble for each line I mark. Then I pull the board off, and using the same level, I transfer the lines back where the cut needs to be made.

These lines are on the inside of the skirtboard. The plumb cuts, which will miter into the risers, will be cut on a 45-degree bevel, and the horizontal cuts will be square. I start by cutting the miters. This is a right-hand stair (when you look up the stair, the handrail is on the right-hand side), so I can cut the miters with a circular saw, which usually has the blade set to the right. On a left-hand stair, I would need to use a saw with the blade set on the left side, like most worm

**Figure 32.** To scribe the face skirt, the author uses a level to mark true plumb and level cuts for each sub-riser and sub-tread.

drives. Cutting from the back side of the face skirt, where the marks are, you can overcut the miters a little in the corners, because the kerf won't show through on the face. This makes it possible to remove the triangles entirely when making the level cuts.

## Risers and Treads

At this point, the newel posts are up and the skirtboards are cut and installed. The bottom step has a radius-end tread, which installs on a premanufactured wraparound riser box that returns to the bottom newel post. On the second and top steps, the risers and treads must be scribed to the newel posts. The landing requires a special tread with a rabbeted underside so that its top is at the same level as the 3/4-inch strip flooring, but from the front it will appear to be as thick as a manufactured tread (1 1/16-inch).

*Installing risers.* Eventually, the risers will sit on and cover the treads. With the type of frame that I build, the treads are well supported and won't move up and down — so this gap along the riser edge is going to stay tight. But the treads are usually around a foot wide and they're going to move as the humidity varies. I run the tread under the riser edge so that any movement does not show up as a gap.

Risers can be ripped to a width equal to the net rise minus the tread thickness. For measuring and marking risers and other pieces that meet the wall skirt on one end and the newel post on the other end, I use my handmade stair gauge (**Figure 33**). Alternatively, you can use a scribe. Cut the risers with a 45-degree bevel to match the face skirt. Install them by spacing off the sub-tread with tread scraps, gluing the miter joints, and nailing off from the bottom working upwards.

After the risers are in place, there is one quick task to take care of — notching the face skirt where the

treads slide into place under the risers (**Figure 34**).

*Treads.* Manufactured treads are reversible because they are sanded on both sides. After scribing each tread to fit (**Figure 35**), I put construction adhesive on the underside of each of the treads and slide them underneath the already installed risers. If the fit is tight, try using a 5-lb. nonmarring rubber hammer to persuade them into place. I use my white rubber Porta-Nailer mallet (available from www.porta-nails.com). Be sure to double-check the overhang.

The risers will pin the treads to the frame on the back side, but the treads still have to be nailed off along the front to ensure a good glue bond. To finish out the treads, I glue and brad scotia molding under the tread nosing and nosing return.

## Handrail and Balusters

I cut the handrail the same way I cut the face skirt. First I cut the bottom to the theoretical angle, then I prop the rail into place and mark the other end. I cut it a little long on the first try so I can trim it until I have a good fit. While checking the fit, I'm careful not to push the newels out of plumb. I temporarily fasten the handrail with 3 1/2-inch countersunk screws through the newel posts. Later, I fill the holes on the newel posts with bungs taken from scraps of the same wood. However, before permanently installing the handrail, you need to lay out the balusters.

*Baluster spacing.* Most codes require a maximum 4-inch space between balusters (**Figure 36**, page 374).

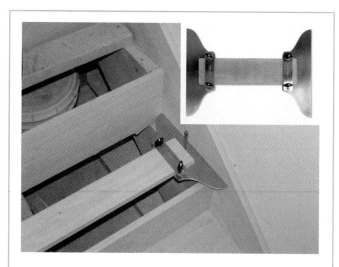

**Figure 33.** A stair gauge helps to mark cuts for both risers and treads. You can make a stair gauge out of two pieces of plywood, cut off at a bevel, screwed to a stick cut to the right length. You just push them into place and screw them together with the stick. Or you can make up a permanent adjustable gauge by routing an adjustment slot and attaching the bevel pieces with adjustable wing nuts. You can also buy a gauge like the one shown here, called the Tread Template, made by Collins Tool Co. (www.collinstool.com).

**Figure 34.** The author spaces the finish risers off the sub-treads before gluing the miter joint and nailing the riser off (left). He then notches the face skirt to make way for the treads later on (right). The depth of the notches equals the tread width minus the net run minus the overhang. For example, if the treads are 11½ inches, and the net run is 10 inches and there's a 1⅛ overhang, the face skirt needs to be notched ⅜ inch.

Remember that if you're using balusters that have been turned on a lathe, the maximum spacing rule applies to the thinnest portion along the profile. If you have a turned baluster with a 1¼-inch base on a 10-inch tread, you actually end up needing three balusters per tread. With 1¾-inch balusters on 9½-inch treads, you might only need two per tread.

The corner of the first baluster goes right over the corner of the riser and the face skirt. With 1¼-inch balusters and a 1⅛-inch overhang, the centerline is 1¾ inches in from the edge. After measuring in from both the side and the front, mark the centerpoint of the first baluster on each tread. To measure the other two baluster centerpoints on a tread, calculate the spacing based on the net run — so that the spacing is equal between all balusters in the run. With a 10-inch run and three balusters per tread, you can divide 10 by 3 using the 12th scale on your framing square.

Once you have centerpoints marked on the treads, you can transfer them up to the handrail with a level or plumb bob. At this point, the balusters need to be cut to length and holes drilled in the underside of the handrail, taking care not to blast through the top. I find drilling baluster holes while the rail is temporarily fastened in place works well.

With balusters, I like to see the detail of the turnings follow the pitch of the rail down the stairs. I do this by varying the height of the bottom baluster blocks. In addition, I think that manufactured stock balusters often have ridiculously long bottom squares. I like the longest bottom square on a baluster to be just one rise in height.

On a staircase with a net rise of 7½ inches, the three balusters on each tread will become successively shorter by one-third of the rise, or 2½ inches.

That makes the bottom squares 7½, 5, and 2½ inches, back to front. After the bottom squares are cut, pin-top balusters should be cut so that they extend at least ¾ inch into the rail. Square-top balusters should be individually fit and cut so that they butt into the underside of the rail.

For attaching balusters to the treads, all of the stair manufacturers provide a type of dowel screw (a screw

*continued on page 374*

**Figure 35.** To install treads, the author first cuts them approximately to length — to within scribing range. He then puts them each in place temporarily, making sure the overhang along the front is even. After setting a scribe to the distance between the nosing return and the face skirt, he marks that dimension against the wall skirt. On steps with newel posts, he also has to scribe around the newel post.

# Squeak-Free Stairs With Pocket-Hole Screws

**by Mark O'Neil**

Here's a method I use to keep nails — and squeaks — out of staircases I build on site (**A**). On a new-construction job, like the one shown here, it's a good idea to give the drywallers a heads up; they can cut the pieces that go on the bottom of the stringers and set them aside for installation after the stairs are finished.

I start by preparing the skirtboards, first fitting them in place (**B**). When transferring the locations of the treads and risers, I don't automatically copy the stringer's actual shape. Because the tips of a dimension-lumber rough stringer will naturally shrink, I make the marks on the skirt reflect the stringer's original shape, being careful to make the intersections of the treads and risers exactly 90 degrees. I also take care not to mark too low, so the parts don't bind and bow when I assemble them.

Next I use a Forstner bit and drill guide (available from Rockler, www.rockler.com) to drill a flat-bottomed hole where the tread noses will land (**C**), then rout the dadoes for treads and risers (**D**). I make the holes and dadoes ¼ to 5⁄16 inch deep, and about 1⁄16 inch wider than the tread and riser stock so that everything fits together easily.

Using my basic router, I have to take two passes with a ½-inch straight bit to get the desired depth, and two more passes to get the right width. On an enclosed stair, one of the skirtboards has to be "gutted" — that is, the material behind the dadoes has to be removed all the way

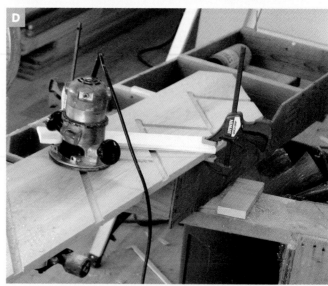

to the bottom edge. This allows that skirtboard to slide along the wall and into the finish treads and risers that have already been loosely installed into the dadoes on the other skirtboard.

With one of the skirtboards nailed to the wall (preferably the longer one) and the other clamped into position, I take measurements for the treads and risers. I cut them ⅛ inch short, then dry-assemble the whole stair (**E**).

Next I use a Kreg jig (www.kregtool.com) to drill pocket holes in the rough stringers — usually two holes at every tread and riser location (**F, G**). Having already done a dry fit, I'm ready to use glue; PL urethane has a long working time and fills gaps of up to ⅜ inch wide.

Armed with a bunch of shims and 1¼-inch screws, I

work from the top down, gluing and screwing the staircase together. Anywhere I have a gap greater than ¼ inch, I'll run in a 1½-inch screw. The shims wedge the parts tight against the front edge of the dadoes, and the urethane glue expands to fill the voids (**H**). I also use 1⅝-inch trim-head screws to secure the backs of the treads to the bottoms of the risers. Once everything is put together, I pack PL into any remaining voids.

By the way, it's a good idea to drill pocket-screw holes in the back of the bottom riser. This allows you to pocket-screw it to the wood floor before it gets covered with the tread.

*Mark O'Neil runs Xylem Construction in Wellfleet, Mass.*

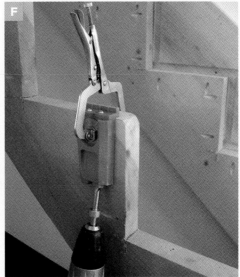

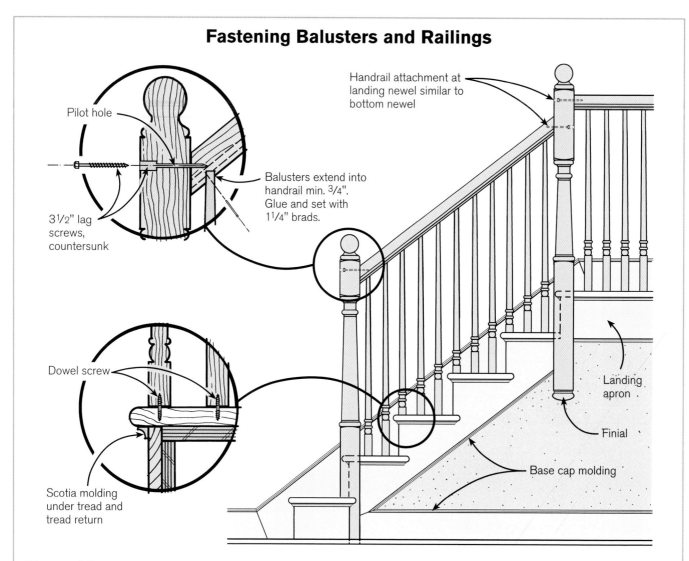

**Fastening Balusters and Railings**

Pilot hole

Handrail attachment at landing newel similar to bottom newel

Balusters extend into handrail min. 3/4". Glue and set with 11/4" brads.

3¹/2" lag screws, countersunk

Dowel screw

Landing apron

Finial

Base cap molding

Scotia molding under tread and tread return

**Figure 36.** After the baluster bottoms are tightened into place using dowel screws, the author installs the handrail over the pin-tops and runs lag screws through the newels to fasten the balustrade system together.

that has a lag-type thread on both ends). When screwed into the bottom of a tread, 1/4-by-2¹/4-inch dowel screws really hold a baluster down. To use dowel screws, you have to predrill holes in both the treads and balusters. Some manufacturers predrill the balusters.

To install the balusters, remove the handrail and use the dowel screws to attach the bottoms, making sure the squares line up. Using dowel screws with square-top balusters is harder because they need to tighten to one exact orientation. But with some fid-

dling, it's still the best possible option.

*Setting the handrail.* For pin-top balusters, place glue on the baluster tops and handrail ends. Set the handrail onto the balusters and permanently fasten it into position. Use 1¹/4-inch brads to hold the balusters in position. For square-top balusters, fasten the handrail into position and then plumb, glue, and nail each baluster to the underside of the rail, taking care to center the baluster on the rail.

*Jed Dixon operates North Road Woodshop in Foster, R.I.*

# Chapter 20: Wood & Laminate Flooring

■ **Installing Hardwood Strip Flooring**

■ **Prefinished Hardwood Flooring**

■ **Installing Laminate Floors**

■ **Floating Floor Options**

# Installing Hardwood Strip Flooring

by Howard Brickman

**Dry out the job site, prep the subfloor, and don't skimp on nails.**

Even after 30 years in the wood flooring industry, I still get immense satisfaction when my tools are packed up in the van and I can admire the natural beauty of a newly completed job. For that wood floor to perform flawlessly throughout its projected 50- to 80-year life span, however, there are many crucial steps I have to carefully perform.

## Moisture Control Is Critical

Accounting for moisture is the single most important factor when laying a hardwood floor. Understanding how moisture affects wood is not a mystical art, it's common sense. Simply put, wood reaches a state of equilibrium with the relative humidity (RH) of the surrounding materials and environment. When the RH of the surrounding air is low, wood loses water molecules and shrinks. When RH is high, wood gains water molecules and swells.

Wood scientists and lumber manufacturers long ago figured out the relationship between the amount of water in wood and the surrounding RH levels (**Figure 1**).

We call the amount of water contained in a wood sample its *moisture content* (MC), which is calculated for each type of wood as a percentage of its weight

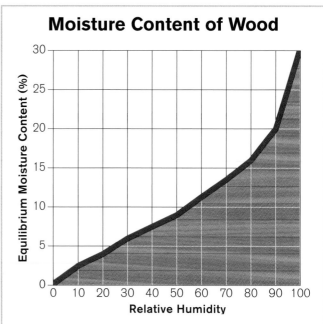

Figure 1. As relative humidity (RH) in the air rises, so does wood's moisture content (MC). Wood swells in size until it reaches its fiber saturation point, at an MC level of 28%.

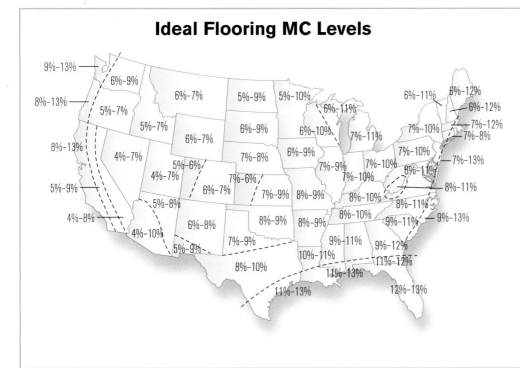

## Ideal Flooring MC Levels

**Figure 2.** Seasonal ranges in RH vary across the U.S. Optimally, both the subfloor and the strip flooring should be at mid-range MC levels shown on this map during installation. This means drying out new construction sites before delivering materials and acclimating materials only if you are in extremely dry or moist areas of the country.

when oven dry (OD). A sample is deemed oven dry when it has been baked in a 200°F oven for 24 to 48 hours and all of the water molecules have been removed.

A wood sample shrinks to its minimum dimensions at 0% RH and 0% MC. Maximum swelling occurs at 100% RH and 28% MC, at which point wood reaches its fiber saturation point (FSP). The FSP is the total amount of water molecules that can be absorbed within the microstructure of wood.

## At the Mill

Because of the shrinking and swelling that accompanies changes in RH, it makes no sense to manufacture any wood flooring product to its final dimensions and shape until it has been dried. The first step in lumber processing is to remove the excess moisture from the green wood. After the lumber is rough-cut, it's dried to an MC falling in the range of RH levels to which the wood will be exposed as a finished product.

During the 1930s, a nationwide survey of interior RH and MC by the USDA found regional variations based on local climatic conditions (**Figure 2**). Today, most manufacturers kiln-dry wood building materials to an MC of 7.5% at a corresponding RH of 40% — roughly the national average.

## Job-Site Moisture

Excessive moisture at the job site is the leading cause of problems with wood floors. All of the expense and effort to properly kiln-dry and precisely manufacture wood strip flooring are for naught if the flooring is later exposed to excessive moisture and swells before,

during, or after it is installed.

Much of the wood-flooring industry literature is misleading because it emphasizes acclimating wood flooring to job sites. In reality, the reverse is true: a job site needs to be dried out before any wood flooring arrives. There is nearly always excessive moisture on new construction sites and major remodeling job sites.

Wood flooring should never be delivered to the job until all excessive moisture has been eliminated. The quickest and most effective method for removing job-site moisture is to run the heating system and increase fresh air ventilation.

Wood flooring should be installed only after the interior MC level of a structure has been reduced to within the range that will prevail during the life of that structure after it is occupied. This prevents the excessive moisture present during any major renovation or new construction project from being absorbed into a kiln-dried wood floor. If the wood subfloor over which the wood floor is to be installed contains excessive moisture, then the wood flooring will absorb the moisture and swell.

One of the biggest lies I've been told in my 30 years as a flooring contractor is "This job is as dry as a bone — you can start laying the floor next Monday."

Even if there is no intent to deceive, you need to confirm that a job site is dry by measuring the moisture content of the subfloor. If you're acting as the flooring sub, don't rely on the contractor to control site moisture. In the end, it's the installer who needs to take responsibility for checking MC levels.

Water vapor is colorless and odorless, so it can only

**Figure 3.** Using a moisture meter is the only accurate way to check for excessive moisture in subfloors and finish flooring strips. A pocket-size meter is an essential tool for good wood flooring installations.

be reliably measured with moisture meters (**Figure 3**). Electrical resistance meters are the simplest type to use and provide the only practical nondestructive way to determine moisture content in wood-frame construction. Two pins are driven into a wood surface parallel to the grain and the meter gives an MC reading. Small pocket versions are available from several manufacturers for about $200.

## Wood Subfloors

Standard 3/4-inch-thick solid strip flooring must be nailed into a wood subfloor. This includes plywood, OSB, or plank subflooring — as long as certain conditions are met. My preference is 3/4-inch plywood; OSB can swell if it gets wet. Old plank subfloors are usually okay as long as there's not a moisture problem in the building. (As an aside, I do not recommend the use of fire-retardant-treated plywood as subflooring. The water used in the process is not always properly removed before delivery, and the salts used in the treatment process may cause fasteners to corrode and work loose over time.)

Beyond acceptable dryness, a few other qualities are important for a nailing substrate to function properly. First, the subfloor needs to be thick enough to allow the use of standard-length nails. There must be enough substrate area for plenty of nails throughout the floor, which is why two-by sleepers by themselves do not make an adequate nail base. Last, to prevent movement during seasonal changes in RH, a subfloor needs adequate strength and stiffness.

The key to prepping conventional subfloors is taking the time to get rid of any potential squeaks and uneven areas before the wood flooring goes down. In new construction, properly glue and nail tongue-and-groove plywood to floor joists to provide a uniform, squeak-free surface. On an existing subfloor, check for and nail off any loose spots and repair any unevenness at joints.

## Wood Floors Over Concrete

Concrete under a wood floor must be dry. If it's not dry, use heat and ventilation to dry it. Also, concrete should be level to 1/4 inch over 10 feet and should be clean and free of surface contamination before a flooring installation begins. Concrete in contact with the ground should be placed over at least 6 inches of crushed stone or gravel with a 6-mil polyethylene vapor barrier under the concrete.

A vapor barrier is vital because concrete is not waterproof but rather somewhat porous. Looked at under a microscope, concrete has tiny spaces throughout. If you doubt this, pour a cup of water on any unsealed concrete surface and watch the concrete absorb the water. The tiny voids in concrete allow water and especially water vapor to move through the concrete in a manner similar to capillary action.

Before delivering flooring to a wood-over-concrete job, check moisture levels. If there is excessive moisture present, it will continue to evaporate up through the surface of the concrete. There are basically three ways to test for moisture in concrete: electronic moisture meters, calcium chloride crystals, and the rubber mat/polyethylene test, which I use because it's easy and dependable. I simply place several solid, smooth-backed rubber or vinyl mats on the surface of the concrete. A variation of this test is to tape 2-by-2-foot squares of clear polyethylene to the surface of the concrete with duct tape. After 24 hours, any dampness or even slight darkness beneath the mat or polyethylene indicates excessive moisture. Many times you can observe the presence of excessive moisture in a slab by looking under boxes, ply-

**Figure 4.** The author screeds dry mason's sand to level a low spot on a slab before installing a plywood nailing substrate. The trick with this technique is to avoid stepping in the sand after you've screeded it level and covered it with a poly vapor barrier.

## Plywood Fastened to Slab

Wall Line

3/4"

1/2"

6-mil poly

#15 felt

3/4" plywood

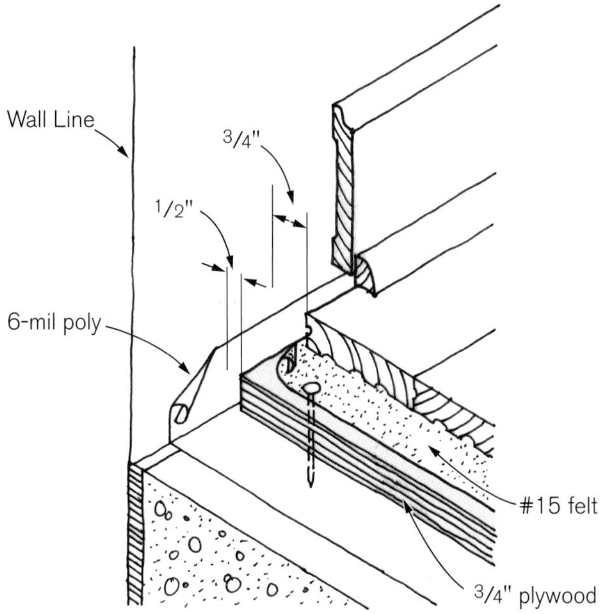

**Figure 5.** Where moisture is not a problem, the author installs hardwood flooring over 3/4-inch plywood nailed directly to the slab over a vapor barrier. The plywood sheets should be spaced 1/4 inch apart with a minimum 1/2-inch space around the room perimeter. The installer must use shorter flooring nails or tilt the nailing machine to keep flooring nails from hitting the concrete.

wood, or other items that may have been stacked on the surface overnight.

It is vital that you document the results of this test somewhere in your field notes or job file. Many times the customer wants work completed as quickly as possible and will try to push you to "Just do it!" If you fail to point out potential problems to the customer and make him or her understand the risks, you may assume the liability.

When my company encounters this problem, I write a letter explaining the situation and include an unconditional release of liability with signature blocks for the customers. I also request a meeting where I present the facts calmly and professionally. I then present the letter for their signatures and explain that I am unwilling to assume the increased risk of proceeding with the delivery of materials until the excessive moisture conditions are eliminated. If a customer won't accept the risk, I believe it's more cost effective to find some other work rather than to do a job twice but get paid only once.

## Plywood Substrate Over Concrete

I don't install wood flooring over 2x4 sleepers, and I don't recommend it under any circumstance. Instead, I provide a nailing substrate using fastened

or floating plywood systems laid over a poly vapor barrier right on top of the concrete. The reason often stated to justify sleeper systems is to provide space for the floor to breathe. If we agree that breathing is unnecessary because no excess moisture is present and that the use of sleepers without a plywood subfloor doesn't provide an adequate nailing substrate, then the extra cost and hassle of installing sleepers under plywood is unjustified.

*Leveling the slab.* Check to see that the slab is flat and does not vary more than a gradual 1/4 inch over 10 feet when checked with a straightedge. Fill any low spots with a leveling product — I usually just use clean dry sanitary mason's sand (**Figure 4**). Just be careful not to walk in the sand before you cover it with rigid foam insulation or plywood.

*Plywood fastened to slab.* After placing a poly vapor barrier over the slab, lay down sheets of 3/4-inch-thick plywood, leaving 1/4-inch spaces between panels and at least a 1/2-inch space around the room perimeter. Then fasten the plywood directly to the concrete with power-driven concrete nails (**Figure 5**). The poly vapor barrier is still 99% intact, with small punctures every square foot or so. Under normal conditions these punctures should not dramatically decrease moisture resistance.

Next, proceed with the normal installation by using #15 asphalt-saturated building paper or felt between the plywood and the finish flooring. It will be necessary either to use shorter 1 3/4-inch flooring fasteners or to slightly tilt the nailing machine so that nails don't strike the concrete and damage the tool (**Figure 6**).

*Floating plywood on slab.* Whenever I'm worried about future moisture intrusion through the slab, I

**Figure 6.** When installing flooring over a single sheet of plywood on a slab, a shim beneath the nailer shoe will angle the nail to prevent it from striking the concrete.

**Figure 7.** To insulate a floor installed over concrete, the author installs compression-rated rigid foam insulation under the floating plywood nailing substrate.

use the floating plywood method. First, place 6-mil poly over the concrete. To protect against anticipated moisture problems, take the extra steps of taping the overlaps with duct tape and extending the poly up the walls several inches. You may want to put down a layer of compression-rated rigid foam insulation (no gluing necessary) to limit heat loss through the floor (**Figure 7**). Next, place a layer of 1/2-inch plywood oriented with the long direction of the room. Space the panels 1/4 to 1/2 inch apart and leave at least 1/2 inch along the perimeter. Do not fasten this layer to the concrete.

Then lay a second layer of 1/2-inch plywood over the first, orienting these panels 45 degrees to the first layer with the same spacing at the edges and perimeter (**Figure 8**). The 45-degree orientation of the second layer keeps the joints of the two layers from lining up and helps to form a rigid monolithic system when the installation of the flooring is complete. Staple the two layers together with a pneumatic stapler, making sure that the staples don't

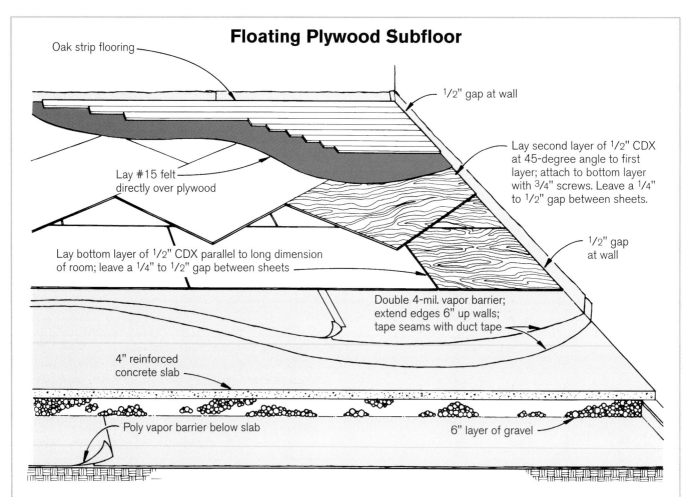

## Floating Plywood Subfloor

Oak strip flooring

1/2" gap at wall

Lay #15 felt directly over plywood

Lay second layer of 1/2" CDX at 45-degree angle to first layer; attach to bottom layer with 3/4" screws. Leave a 1/4" to 1/2" gap between sheets.

Lay bottom layer of 1/2" CDX parallel to long dimension of room; leave a 1/4" to 1/2" gap between sheets

1/2" gap at wall

Double 4-mil. vapor barrier; extend edges 6" up walls; tape seams with duct tape

4" reinforced concrete slab

Poly vapor barrier below slab

6" layer of gravel

**Figure 8.** To construct a floating plywood subfloor for strip flooring, the author places a double poly vapor barrier directly on the concrete. Then, he places two layers of 1/2-inch CDX plywood, one layer parallel to the length of the floor, the second at a 45-degree angle to the first. He leaves a 1/4- to 1/2-inch space between sheets, and screws or staples the two layers of plywood together, making sure not to puncture the poly. Finally, he rolls out #15 felt and installs the strip flooring with a standard floor nailer.

## Installer's Checklist

**Prep work.** Make sure the moisture content (MC) of the subfloor is within a normal range (no more than 2% beyond the maximum MC for the region). Be sure to eliminate all excessive moisture before you even deliver the flooring to the site.

Check the wood subfloor for looseness and proper nailing. Remove squeaks now! Repair any damaged areas in the subfloor. Point out any major uneven spots to the customer and find out if they want you to repair them.

Lay down #15 asphalt-saturated felt underlayment. This is the cheapest insurance policy you can buy.

Mark floor joist locations for the first and last courses of flooring.

**Figure B.** *The author makes splines to use whenever he has to run the flooring groove side to groove side.*

**Figure A.** *Snapping a chalk line to start the layout in a new room ensures that the flooring runs parallel to the walls.*

**Installation.** Pick out straight pieces of flooring to start and finish the floor. Nothing is quite as frustrating as trying to rip a warped and twisted piece of flooring to fit against the wall.

Use a string, chalk line, or straightedge to start the floor. Start straight to stay straight (**Figure A**). This, in conjunction with the straight boards, makes nailing easy.

Stagger the end joints at least 6 to 8 inches as you lay out the floor.

Nail every 6 to 8 inches for 2¼-inch strip flooring and even closer as width increases (see **Figure 9**, next page).

Use splines whenever you have to reverse direction — in other words, run the flooring groove to groove (**Figure B**). Be sure to nail down the groove edge so that it doesn't rise up from the pressure applied during installation. — *H.B.*

---

go completely through the bottom layer. You may substitute screws for staples, but be careful not to puncture the polyethylene vapor barrier. Then proceed with normal installation, using #15 asphalt-saturated felt between the plywood and finish flooring.

## Flooring Installation Basics

The checklist (above) gives the proper steps and sequence for installing a tongue-and-groove wood-strip floor. Four issues always seem to generate the most interest and discussion: acclimation of the flooring, use of #15 asphalt-saturated felt paper, frequency of nailing, and whether to leave an expansion space.

**To acclimate or not?** Ideally, the proper moisture content for the installation of any wood floor is midway between the seasonal high humidity, which occurs during the summer, and the seasonal low humidity, which occurs near the end of the first winter heating season after construction is completed. In

my 30 years of consulting in the wood flooring industry, I have often seen damage done to wood flooring from "acclimating" the flooring to the job before installation. Because the quality of kiln-drying within the wood flooring industry is high, acclimation is only appropriate in extreme climates where interior relative humidity levels are substantially above or below the 7.5% MC/40% RH manufacturing specifications. This includes the arid regions of the western U.S. and the humid southeastern U.S. Acclimating wood flooring in other regions actually risks exposing it to the high levels of relative humidity and moisture present during summer or on a new construction site. This will cause the wood flooring to swell before and during installation. Then, during the first heating season, it will shrink and permanent spaces will be left between the flooring strips. Instead, dry out the building before bringing the flooring on site.

**Felt paper.** I've often heard doubters ask, "Why

## Recommended Nailing for Strip Flooring

| Flooring Width (inches) | Nailing Interval (inches) |
|---|---|
| 1 1/2 | 10 to 11 |
| 2 1/4 | 6 to 8 |
| 3 | 5 to 6 |
| 3 1/4 | 5 |
| 4 | 4 |
| 5 | 3 to 4 |
| 6 | 3 |
| 7 | 2 to 3 |
| 8 | 2 |

**Figure 9.** You need to drive lots of nails into wood flooring to hold it firmly in place during regular seasonal climate swings. The wider the flooring, the more nails that need to be driven along the nailing edge of each board.

should I use #15 felt, and what does it really do?" It performs four functions:

**1. Felt slows the flow of water vapor.** It gradually absorbs moisture in the subflooring, allowing it to pass through the flooring slowly, instead of flooding the underside of the flooring and causing it to swell and possibly cup.

**2. Felt increases the friction between the flooring and the subfloor**, which in turn helps to resist lateral movement in the event that swelling occurs.

**3. Felt adheres to the subfloor** and wood flooring

and will help to eliminate any vertical looseness or movement that might occur.

**4. Finally, felt will help safeguard a manufacturer's warranty** in the event that you encounter a problem like cupping or large spaces between the boards. The majority of the wood flooring manufacturers consider the use of #15 felt to be mandatory and will deem your installation to be negligent if you don't use it.

The cost for materials and labor to include #15 asphalt-saturated felt underlayment is approximately 5¢ per square foot. That's cheap insurance even if its only function is to avoid warranty issues in the event of a problem.

*Nailing.* I go nuts when I hear a person say that you should not use too many nails because then the flooring can't move. There is no such thing as too many nails unless they start splitting the flooring strips into little pieces. Nails are what hold the flooring in place and keep it from moving.

I prefer to think in terms of nails per square foot to determine the proper fastening for flooring of different widths. If the optimal nailing interval for 2 1/4-inch-wide strip flooring is 6 to 8 inches, this is equal to 9 or more nails per square foot. The schedule in **Figure 9** gives the average nailing interval necessary for 9 nails per square foot for other flooring widths.

*Expansion gap.* Since wood shrinks and swells very little in length (with the grain direction), there is no need to allow any space at the ends of the flooring. In fact, I generally don't worry about leaving expansion spaces anywhere — sides or ends — when installing a traditional nail-down T&G floor (**Figure 10**). This is because, as mentioned above, I use enough nails to firmly hold the individual pieces of flooring in place.

As long as the moisture cycle stays within the nor-

**Figure 10.** Because he uses plenty of nails to keep the strip flooring from moving, the author doesn't leave perimeter expansion spaces on typical residential installations. Countersunk face nails hold the perimeter strips snug; the last strip is scribed tight to the wall. To prevent splitting these last courses, the author uses a nail spinner (left) from Vermont American, which chucks into a drill, to drive the finish nails (www.vermontamerican.com).

mal range for the region where the floor is installed, movement isn't usually a problem when the flooring shrinks and swells. Wood is somewhat elastic and can be slightly compressed without becoming permanently deformed. The exception is when there's an unexpected source of excessive moisture, such as a plumbing leak or an abnormally long period of extremely high humidity. In that case, the swelling of the floor can exert such pressure that the wood actually compresses permanently. Then, when the moisture subsides and the flooring shrinks, large gaps will result and the floor will creak and pop when it is walked on. In the case of excessive moisture, leaving a perimeter expansion gap will do nothing to prevent damage.

Expansion is typically less of a problem than shrinkage. In the Boston area, for example, most nail-down solid tongue-and-groove flooring is fit tight against pre-installed baseboards and other moldings. Later, during the first heating season, the flooring shrinks, leaving gaps between the perimeter flooring and the baseboards. To remedy at least part of this problem, it's wise to install baseboards over the already installed wood floor.

Remember, this discussion applies only to nail-down floors over attached subfloors. When installing floating or glue-down wood floors, however, you must be certain to leave adequate expansion spaces. Those are entirely different installations than those discussed here.

*Howard Brickman is a flooring contractor and consultant based in Norwell, Mass.*

# Prefinished Hardwood Flooring

by Don Bollinger

Wood floors are usually a simple matter. You nail 3/4-inch-thick planks or hardwood strips to a sound, dry, level subfloor, then hire a reputable sub to sand and finish them to perfection. When circumstances permit, this is the best option. That's because a solid wood floor is more than a covering. It adds strength to the floor system, and it can be repeatedly refinished.

But solid floors have limitations. For instance, what do you do if you've got a below-grade or concrete subfloor that might subject the hardwood to high humidity? Or a floor height that doesn't permit underlayment? Or a project that's too small to interest a sanding sub? Or a job where you don't want the mess or scheduling delays caused by sanding?

There are a growing number of prefinished wood flooring systems that solve these problems. Prefinished floors can be installed close to the project's completion date with minimal fuss and mess. They're available in a number of wood species, and with nearly any type of stain or finish. Many prefinished floors perform as well as conventional wood floors under more demanding conditions, yet don't require wood subflooring, sanding, finishing, or special skills to install.

Prefinished flooring can be classified by whether it's solid or laminated, and by whether it's nailed, glued, screwed, or "floated" in place. If the floor has to endure years of hard service and repeated refinishings, solid wood is probably your best choice. Solid prefinished flooring comes in thicknesses ranging from 1/4

**Factory-coated products install quickly and can provide a tough, guaranteed finish.**

C. BATES

to 3/4 inch. To permit even a single refinishing, the boards should have a minimum 1/8-inch-thick sanding surface (the amount of stock between the top of the tongue and the surface of the board); 3/4-inch boards should have a 1/4- to 5/16-inch sanding surface. Solid

**Figure 11.** The 1/8-inch-thick top veneer of this Robbins laminated floor is guaranteed for three sandings.

wood floors should be nailed, screwed, or glued to a structurally sound and dry wood subfloor.

## Laminated Floors

If refinishing isn't an issue or if there's a concrete subfloor, consider using a laminated product, often referred to as "engineered wood" flooring. Laminated wood floors are available in strip, plank, and parquet styles (**Figure 11**). They already dominate the market in many parts of the world. Laminated products are less demanding on our natural resources than solid wood and, given time, will no doubt become more plentiful and less expensive. For now, however, their cost varies from slightly less to a great deal more than solid wood. But just as there are times when a solid wood floor is best, there are other times where a laminated product is more appropriate. Laminated products are more stable and less prone to dimensional expansion and contraction, so they're my first choice for below-grade floors. In my opinion, a laminated product is also the best option for glue-down floors. (More on glue-down floors later.)

Here are some things to consider when comparing laminated flooring products:

• *The number of plies.* More plies generally means a stronger and more stable floor (three plies is typical).

• *The species of the face veneer.* Dense woods like jatoba or merbau will take a lot more punishment than softwoods like pine. A teak-faced product will be more dimensionally stable than an oak-faced one (see "Wood Flooring Species," page 387).

• *The cut of the face veneer.* Rotary-cut veneers (like those on a sheet of plywood) dent easily because they expose much of a board's early growth — its soft underbelly — to the ravages of floor traffic. Sliced veneers are much more durable. Rotary cuts are more common in American-made products, while sliced veneers are more common in European products.

• *The species of the core veneers.* The core and face laminates should be made from the same species, or at least from species that expand and contract at the same rate. Manufacturers use any of hundreds of species for the core veneers. If the face and core expand and contract at different rates, they could eventually delaminate. The use of different species is more common with imported than with American-made flooring.

• *The installation method — nailing, gluing, or floating.* How good a floor feels to the homeowner depends on how it's installed. Floating floors seldom feel as solid as nail-down or glue-down floors. I usually have customers walk on both types to see if they like them.

• *The type of finish.* A top-quality finish will last a long time but may also be quite expensive (see page 388 for more on finishes).

You should also be aware of special techniques used by the manufacturer. Bruce and Carlisle (www.wideplankflooring.com), for example, both make wide-plank prefinished flooring, while Hartco makes a five-ply laminated flooring that's exceptionally stable. (Bruce, Hartco, and Robbins are now divisions of Armstrong; www.armstrong.com.) Hartco also has a product called Pattern Plus that consists of strips of acrylic-impregnated red oak veneer glued over thin, noticeably spaced strips. The product fits the contours of uneven substrates remarkably well. Robbins Traditional Strip oak flooring features a 1/6-inch-thick sanding surface — guaranteed for three complete refinishings. Junckers has developed a process for condensing the cells of even fairly dense woods like beech. Its flooring can withstand extraordinary punishment without denting, yet is remarkably stable.

C. BATES

**Figure 12.** One advantage of a floating floor is that it can be installed over a continuous moisture barrier that doesn't get punctured by fasteners. A foam or felt pad must also be used as a gasket.

**Figure 13.** Instead of being fastened to the subfloor, most floating floors are installed by gluing adjacent boards to one another. The floor acts as a monolithic panel that's free to expand and contract.

## Nail-Down and Glue-Down Floors

Nailable products may be solid or laminated and come in a range of thicknesses. They include 1/4-inch parquet and 3/8- to 3/4-inch strip flooring. Though 3/4-inch-thick solid prefinished floors can be nailed in place just like standard strip flooring, there are some complications. If you're not careful, you can scratch the finish with the base of the metal nailer. One way to guard against this is to create a cushion by wrapping the bottom of the nailer with duct tape. Thinner panels — 3/8 and 1/4 inch — can also be nailed, but a wedge adapter must be attached to the flooring nailer. All nailable products must be installed over a wood subfloor.

Glue-down products can be installed over nearly any flat, dry subfloor, including concrete. Only laminated strip or plank products (with a few notable exceptions) can be successfully glued without nailing. Solid parquet is glued all the time.

A laminated strip or plank floor glues down faster and easier than a nailed floor. (Solid wood flooring can't be counted on to install snugly or to lay flat in a bed of mastic, much less to stay that way over time.) Glue-down solid boards must also be less than 2 feet long — anything longer would be too hard to straighten out without nailing.

If you're installing a glue-down floor, you can get an excellent moisture barrier by using a mastic to glue two layers of 4- or 6-mil poly to the substrate. Lay the poly layers in opposite directions and overlap the seams at least 6 inches. Then glue a layer of plywood to the poly. No fasteners should be allowed to penetrate the moisture barrier.

## Floating Floors

In a floating floor, the tongue-and-groove boards are fastened to each other rather than to the subfloor. Floating floors are fitted together without nails and are installed over a foam or felt pad and a continuous vapor barrier (**Figure 12**). Because the pad acts as a gasket, a floating floor can be installed over smooth tile or low-pile carpet. Although not altogether recommended by manufacturers, floating floors can in some cases perform well even over exposed aggregate (that is, concrete with a rough surface), an option that requires a 1/8-inch-thick layer of foam. If the job calls for it, you can even lay the flooring over a soundproof underlayment like homasote. Floating floors are perfect for use over radiant heat, in areas with above-average shifts in moisture levels, or over concrete.

Most floating floor products are installed by gluing the tongue to the groove (**Figure 13**). However, a number of no-glue "click-lock" products have been introduced that use special interlocking edges to hold the planks together. Most are laminated wood. One exception is Junckers (www.junckershardwood.com), which makes a solid-wood floating floor system that's held together with slightly bent metal clips that slide into slots cut in the underside of each plank (**Figure 14**). The clips exert enough tension to hold the boards together, yet permit seasonal expansion and contraction.

Though the edges of a floating floor are covered by

**Figure 14.** The only solid hardwood floating floor is made by Junckers. The boards are held in place with special metal clips instead of glue.

**Figure 15.** To prevent cracks from opening up between floorboards, the edges of a floating floor must have room to move freely with changes in temperature and moisture. A standard baseboard will cover the gap along the walls (far left). At thresholds, some installers notch the ends into a tongue-and-groove header board that's fastened to the floor (left), but even this can restrain movement enough to cause problems.

a standard baseboard (**Figure 15**), door openings must be finished with a threshold (called a header board) that's attached to the subfloor and has a lip that permits the flooring to slide freely beneath it. To eliminate this threshold, some contractors glue down the ends of the flooring. But gluing down a floating floor voids the warranty. Because the ends are restrained while the rest of the floor is free to move with changes in temperature and humidity, gaps tend to radiate out from the glued end to the center of the

floor. Many installers restrain the ends by notching them into a tongue-and-groove header board that's set perpendicular to the flooring and that's screwed or glued to the subfloor. The intent is to let the ends of the boards move as freely as the centers. But while this is better than gluing the ends, I've found that the tightness of the joint will inhibit movement enough that some gaps will still appear in the floor.

*Comparing floating-floor products.* Before choosing a floating floor, ask your supplier for samples of

## Micro-Bevel vs. Square Edges

**by Dave Holbrook**

Contrary to popular belief, not every factory-finished flooring strip has a pronounced beveled edge to conceal milling irregularities. In fact, manufacturers now compete to have the smallest eased edge, or "microbevel." The technology for producing prefinished wood flooring has advanced to the extent that many engineered wood lines are available with a true, square edge (**Figure A**). The mating edges and surfaces of some lines of engineered plank are so uniform that the manufacturer promises no "overwood," or difference in surface plane from plank to plank. Ironically, micro- and more exaggerated bevels thus become design options, described in certain product brochures as providing a "handcrafted look."

**Bevels and refinishing.** If you have to sand rather than recoat a floor's finish, strongly beveled plank styles may spell trouble. The sanding process eliminates the overwood, but there's no fast or simple method for removing the finish from the bevels. Superficial sanding

**Figure A.** *The micro-bevels in today's prefinished strip floors are barely perceptible (left). Engineered floors are also available with a true, square edge (right).*

results in a floor surface interrupted by dark bevel stripes that vary in width according to the degree of surface wood removed. There's little chance of matching these stripes in with the new stain and finish. Unless the old finish is beyond rescue, your best bet is to recoat, rather than sand, the floor (see section on "No-Sand Refinishing," in sidebar on page 389).

*Dave Holbrook is a builder on Cape Cod, Mass.*

the styles you're considering. Lay them out on a flat surface. Boards should be flat and straight, with little or no curvature along their length. Minor irregularities should disappear once the tongues are fitted into the grooves. If it's hard to keep the pieces flat, you'd do well to ask why or to make another selection. Longer pieces almost always have more bows than shorter ones, so if you see a lot of bowing in the shorter pieces, strike that product from your list of choices.

Next, slip the pieces together side by side on a smooth surface. If they go together easily yet snugly, and display minimal fissures along the sides and ends, you've got a winner. Unfortunately, samples are almost always better than the real thing, and radical changes in humidity can cause even the most superbly milled product to look and perform like waste.

Finally, look for any thickness variations between the strips, as these will leave ridges where the pieces come together — a condition called overwood. An uneven substrate can also cause overwood. Overwood is easily sanded out on a site-finished floor, but with a prefinished floor you're stuck with it. How much overwood is acceptable depends on the homeowner; I've found that the most dissatisfied home-

**Figure 16.** Many manufacturers reduce height discrepancies between adjacent floorboards by easing or V-grooving the edges.

owners are the ones who start with unreasonable expectations. You can lessen the chance that clients will be unhappy by telling them just how much overwood to expect. Many manufacturers lessen the effects of overwood by easing or V-grooving the edges, and sometimes the ends, of their floorboards (**Figure 16**). If your customer does not like the deep grooves, you can choose a "micro-bevel" product now offered by many manufacturers (see "Micro-Bevels vs. Square Edges," facing page).

## Wood Flooring Species

| Species | Color of Heartwood | Hardness (relative to Red Oak) | Dimensional Stability (relative to Red Oak) | Durability |
|---|---|---|---|---|
| Ash | Light tan | +2% | +26% | Excellent shock resistance, remains smooth under friction |
| Birch | Reddish brown | −2% | +8% | Stiff and very strong, excellent shock resistance |
| Doug Fir | Tan to light brown | −49% | +28% | Easily dented, somewhat brittle, splinters easily |
| Hickory | Tan or reddish | +41% | −11% | Strong, very shock resistant |
| Pecan | Reddish brown with dark brown stripes | +40% | +15% | Strong, very shock resistant |
| Hard Maple | Pale to creamy white | +12% | +4% | Dense, excellent shock resistance, resists wear |
| Mesquite | Light brown to dark reddish brown | +82% | +65% | Dense, very strong |
| Red Oak | Reddish brown | − | − | Dense, resists wear, high shock resistance, less durable than white oak |
| White Oak | Light brown | +5% | +1% | More durable than red oak, resistant to insects and fungi |
| American Black Walnut | Dark brown to purplish black | −22% | +26% | Moderately dense, very strong, good shock resistance, not as dent resistant as oak |
| Brazilian Cherry | Red to orange-brown | +82% | +19% | Dense and very strong |
| Jarrah | Pinkish to dark red | +48% | −7% | Dense and very strong, highly resistant to wear |
| Santos Mahogany | Dark reddish brown | +71% | +36% | Extremely durable |
| Padauk | Reddish or purple-brown or black | +34% | +51% | Average to high durability |

## Understanding Finishes

After narrowing your choices by flooring type, you should compare the finishes that manufacturers use. Today's factory-applied coatings rival, and in some cases surpass, practically anything a professional floor finisher can apply on site. Literally hundreds of floor finishes are available, from oil-based finishes to acid-curing Swedish finishes (see "High-Performance Factory Finishes," below). But urethanes are rapidly emerging as the standard for factory-applied finishes on wood flooring.

*UV-urethanes.* Most people have heard of oil-modified and aliphatic urethanes, but the lesser-known "UV-urethanes" are by far the most durable. These factory-applied coatings are made from 100% solids (though they go on wet), and are cured with ultraviolet light right after application. (Oil-modified urethanes can take months to fully cure.) A fully cured finish holds up better to abuse, a quality that's crucial during the final phase of construction, when

## High-Performance Factory Finishes

**by Dave Holbrook**

Site-applied finishes are no match for the latest generation of reinforced urethane coatings, available only as a factory-applied finish. Most manufacturers now offer some version of a urethane finish enhanced with aluminum oxide, making the wear surface far more durable than one with a standard site-applied coating.

### Aluminum Oxide

The aluminum-oxide crystals are suspended in multiple layers of UV-cured polyurethane, resulting in a surface that's claimed in more than one brochure to be "ten times more abrasion resistant than traditional urethane finishes." Some reinforced finishes are slightly rough to the touch, due to the hard crystal content. Mannington's "Scratch-Resist" finish employs two sizes of aluminum-oxide particulate, one far smaller than the other to act as a filler between the larger particles. This makes the surface more consistent, in terms of both hardness and smoothness of finish. Because aluminum-oxide crystals are clear, such finishes are just as clear as an ordinary urethane coating.

Conventional wisdom holds that a glossy urethane finish should be applied only on low-use areas, and that high-traffic floors require a satin finish. Aluminum-oxide-enhanced urethane is said to make those distinctions more or less irrelevant — you can choose your degree of shine without concern.

*Ceramic, diamond, and titanium* also turn up in various manufacturers' urethane finish formulations, alone or in combination with aluminum oxide. All are invisible in suspension and serve the same purpose. I see little evidence that one formula has a clear advantage over another. Manufacturers offer 10- to 25-year warranties on their enhanced finishes, assuming normal use and maintenance.

### Other Finishes

Many types of prefinished flooring can be ordered with a traditional finish coating. Among the coatings available are wax, urethane, water-borne acrylics, and penetrating oils. You can expect these finishes to perform identically to site-applied equivalents. The main advantages of prefinishing are uniform appearance and faster completed installation.

Acrylic-wood is a unique finish option, available in 3/8-inch-thick engineered strip and plank flooring. The nominal 1/8-inch-thick wear layer of an acrylic-wood floor is solid, natural, colorized acrylic-impregnated wood with a clear, satinlike finish. In the impregnation process, liquid acrylic is forced into the porous cell structure of the wood wear layer, then permanently hardened by heat or gamma irradiation. The flooring is designed to be installed by the direct glue-down method on concrete or plywood underlayment. Its primary application tends to be commercial, but it is also appropriate for residential use.

Because the color and acrylic finish run all the way through the wear layer, the surface is said to be anywhere from three to five times harder than ordinary hardwood and highly resistant to impact. Deep scratches can be spot-repaired by buffing or localized sanding. If you want a high-gloss surface, you can even buy acrylic-wood flooring with an aluminum-oxide urethane finish.

### Care and Feeding

To protect any wood floor from accidental scratches, homeowners should use felt pads under furniture legs and sweep or vacuum frequently to remove abrasive sand and dirt. Periodic waxing maintains and restores the original shine (but don't wax unless you've installed a wax-finish product in the first place).

Breathable, mesh-type rug underlays help prevent moisture entrapment and damage. To safely move a piano or other heavy furniture item, use protective, 1/4-inch hard-

seemingly every trade on a project runs roughshod over its freshly finished surfaces.

Some manufacturers advertise the fact that they apply two or three coats of UV-urethane. However, long-term durability hinges not on the number of coats but on total film build. I wouldn't buy a flooring product with a film build of less than 1.5 to 2 mils. Film build should be noted on the product's sales literature.

As good as UV-urethanes are, they have their draw-backs. Their performance is greatly affected by the underlying wood. Porous, early-growth wood grain soaks up more of the finish than does the more dense, late-growth wood. Since the ultraviolet light can't penetrate the wood grain, the urethane never fully cures. This can lead to a cracked surface and will give off toxic fumes. An uncured UV-urethane will give off a sickening solventlike odor that can be very unpleasant in an enclosed area. (Fully cured UV-urethanes have no odor.)

**Figure A.** *Because prefinished floors can be difficult to sand, manufacturers now offer sandless recoating systems, like Basic Coating's TyKote Dustless Recoating System, a three-step process that allows you to restore the finish using only water-based agents.*

board runner strips under the casters.

Avoid wetting or wet mopping any wood floor — instead, use proprietary or manufacturer-recommended cleaners — and try to dissuade your clients from choosing wood flooring for the bathroom.

Most manufacturers offer routine maintenance products for their prefinished wood flooring. There are proprietary cleaners for sticky food spills and rubber heel marks; touch-up kits are also available for light scratches, burns, and other kinds of minor damage. As a professional courtesy, leave a maintenance kit behind with every prefinished floor you install.

## Refinishing

The principal complaint from homeowners about any hardwood floor is the vulnerability of the finish to scratches. Shallow scratches can be spot-treated with various touch-up products. If not deeply scratched, flooring with an acrylic or urethane finish can be rotary screened and recoated with good results.

Deep scratches, however, leave the wood prone to water damage and staining. Once the floor has reached an overall degree of dullness from wear, the only option is to refinish. A badly worn or abused area, such as in an entry or hallway, probably requires resanding and refinishing of the entire floor. This is not a small job and defeats one of the main reasons for installing factory-finished flooring — avoiding the dust, disruption, odor, and scheduling of a site-finished floor.

## No-Sand Refinishing

Eventually, every finish shows signs of wear. The best way to restore a floor's finish is to periodically recoat before the wear pattern advances through to bare wood. Some flooring installers worry that a reinforced urethane finish might be difficult to abrade in preparation for recoating. Yet manufacturers affirm that conventional machine-screening with the equivalent of a 3M abrasive pad will effectively prepare a tired aluminum-oxide finish for an application of conventional polyurethane. Of course, this recoat, lacking the superior scratch resistance of the original finish, will provide only ordinary service.

Basic Coatings (www.basiccoatings.com) provides TyKote Dustless Recoating System, a three-step finishing process, specially formulated to eliminate sanding or screening of the old finish before recoating (**Figure A**). TyKote is a water-based agent that creates a chemical bond between the old finish and a proprietary water-based top coat. The system is compatible with all existing urethane finishes, including those containing aluminum oxide. BonaKemi (www.bonakemi.com) makes a similar recoat adhesion system, Bona Prep, for all types of polyurethane-finished hardwood floors. BonaKemi's proprietary top coat options include both water- and oil-based products. Neither company's system is compatible with floors that have a factory- or site-applied wax coating.

*Dave Holbrook is a builder on Cape Cod, Mass.*

Some manufacturers compensate by using grain fillers that prevent the urethane from soaking too deeply into the wood. This permits greater film build with the same amount of urethane or less. It also gives you a better-looking, better-performing product at less cost to both the purchaser and the environment.

UV-urethanes are also quite expensive, so not every manufacturer offers them. (It can cost several million dollars to set up a UV-urethane manufacturing line.) However, most of the big manufacturers offer at least one UV-urethane-finished product in their "top of the line" category.

***Other urethane products.*** If you can't afford a UV-urethane, consider using some other type of urethane coating, such as an oil-modified or waterborne urethane. This will more than likely provide an easy-to-clean, slip-resistant surface that holds up well in heavy wear areas like bathrooms, kitchens, and entries, where occasional but inescapable water can quickly ruin wax or oil finishes.

Beware the urethane with wax topping. Manufacturers that produce a lot of flooring may run their finish lines at speeds that retard proper drying and curing of many urethane finishes. To keep the uncured boards from sticking together in the package, they apply a thin coat of wax to the surface. In my opinion this defeats much of the purpose of applying a urethane, as such boards have all the maintenance problems of a waxed floor. Though the package should say that the flooring has a wax topping, it may not — you have to ask.

*Don Bollinger, of Seattle, Wash., has been a flooring installer for more than three decades.*

# Installing Laminate Floors

by Dave Kostansek

There are two basic types of laminate flooring: square or rectangular tiles, which are usually made to simulate stone or ceramic tile; and plank flooring, which resembles wood. In both cases, the laminate surface is bonded to a substrate of medium-density fiberboard. The individual planks or tiles have tongue-and-groove edges that are glued together and held with special strap clamps, resulting in a smooth, stable, gap-free floor.

The biggest difference between laminate flooring and traditional flooring materials is that laminate flooring is fastened to the subflooring only by gravity and allowed to "float" on a thin layer of foam underlayment. Quarter-inch expansion gaps at the edges of the floor allow it to expand and contract with seasonal changes in temperature and humidity.

I'm a flooring installer and woodworker in the Cleveland area, where laminate flooring has been steadily gaining in popularity for the past 10 to 12 years. Although I still work with vinyl, ceramic tile, and some hardwood strip flooring, laminate now accounts for about half of my business. Most of that increase has come at the expense of sheet vinyl. I find that homeowners who have had bad experiences with dents and gouges in cheap builder-grade vinyl seem to like the idea of hard-surfaced laminate flooring.

I use all three leading brands of laminate — Pergo, Wilsonart, and Formica — as well as numerous other brands. Each company has its own styles, and my client's choice of color and pattern usually determines

**Well-planned transitions are key to a good-looking installation.**

what brand I use on a given job. But my personal favorite is Pergo, because its gluing system permits easier cleanup and the manufacturer provides better transition pieces than any other company.

Generally speaking, I've found that the installation instructions supplied by manufacturers are pretty good — they're enough to get you going, at least. But

**Figure 17.** Laminate flooring can be applied over a variety of substrates, including existing flooring materials, as long as the surface is flat enough. Surface irregularities that exceed 3/16 inch in a 6-foot span (left) must be filled or cut down. Acrylic- or latex-fortified cement-based floor patching material used to fill low spots should be tapered to a feather edge (right).

they leave out a lot of the tricks and fine points that make the difference between a so-so installation and a professional job.

## Preparing the Subfloor

One of the great things about a floating laminate installation is that it can be put right on top of many existing materials, including wood, vinyl, and concrete. It can even be applied over some types of carpeting, such as short, dense commercial carpet. In most cases, though, the carpeting will have to come up anyway so the subfloor can be adequately prepared. Soft, thick carpeting always has to be removed. Laminate can go over wood flooring that has been installed over joists, but existing hardwood that's glued to concrete has to be torn up, because

the required vapor barrier under the laminate could create a moisture lock and cause the wood to rot or develop mold.

***Building up.*** Laminate isn't a structural material, so it can't bridge gaps or low spots. Each manufacturer specifies the maximum permitted height difference between high and low spots — typically 3/16 inch over a 6-foot span. To check the floor for level, I use the same 6-foot aluminum straightedge I use when installing ceramic tile (**Figure 17**). Once I've identified the low spots, I fill them with acrylic- or latex-fortified cement-based floor patching material, which adheres well to concrete and existing vinyl, as well as to plywood and OSB. Smaller low spots are easily built up with overlapping layers of #15 felt (**Figure 18**).

I also carry a lot of homemade shims of different

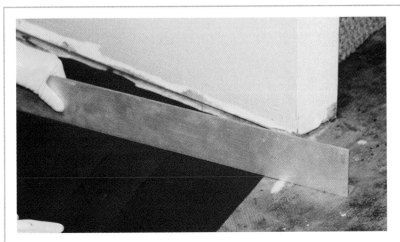

**Figure 18.** Minor low spots can be corrected with several layers of #15 felt (left). Cutting each successive piece smaller than the one before builds up the greatest thickness in the center and tapers the edges. If necessary, the felt can be taped in place until the weight of the laminate floor holds it in place permanently. The author also uses cedar shims to ease transitions at doors and stairways (right).

**Figure 19.** All laminate flooring manufacturers require a poly vapor barrier if the laminate will be applied over a concrete subfloor. Adjoining sheets of poly should be taped in position and must overlap by at least 8 inches (left). The vapor barrier is followed by a foam underlayment that provides cushioning and compensates for any remaining irregularities in the subfloor. Pergo offers the choice of a standard-grade underlayment (top layer in right photo) or a denser premium-grade material (bottom layer in right photo).

thicknesses and widths, which often come into play around doors and entryways.

*Lowering high spots.* High areas on joisted floors usually take the form of humps or ridges running the width of the floor. Coarse sandpaper in a floor edger with a dust collection system works very well for high spots on wood or plywood. On a vinyl floor, I outline the high spot with a grease pencil and score the material at close intervals with a sharp utility knife, then cut it down with a 4-inch razor-blade scraper. It's usually not practical to cut down high spots in concrete. Instead, I build up the rest of the floor with self-leveling concrete.

## Vapor Barriers and Underlayment

When laminate flooring is installed directly over concrete or vinyl-covered concrete, all laminate flooring manufacturers require a poly vapor barrier between the subfloor and the foam underlayment. (Some manufacturers offer a "two-in-one" underlayment that also serves as a vapor barrier.) Each manufacturer provides its own proprietary brand of 6-mil poly. There's probably little difference between them, and it can be tempting to use leftover poly from one job under a different brand of laminate; but to prevent possible warranty problems, I avoid mixing materials from different manufacturers. Adjacent sheets of poly should overlap by at least 8 inches.

Most manufacturers offer a choice of standard-grade foam underlayment or a denser premium grade (**Figure 19**). Prices vary from one manufacturer to the next, but the standard material typically sells for less than 50 cents a foot, while the better grade goes for two or three times that.

I recommend the better-quality underlayment,

because it provides better sound deadening and a more solid feel underfoot. This can be an important issue with customers, who often expect woodlike laminate to have the same distinctive "thud" underfoot as real wood. Educating them about what to expect can prevent disappointment later.

**Figure 20.** The first three rows of flooring are cut and dry-fitted to ensure an accurate and attractive layout. Note that the foam underlayment, unlike the vapor barrier, fits closely together but does not overlap.

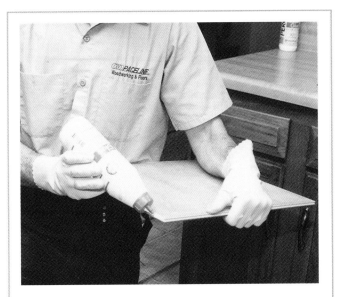

**Figure 21.** The grooved half of each joint between tiles or planks is carefully filled with a proprietary glue. Failure to use enough glue is the most common cause of laminate floor problems. Squeeze-out should be cleaned up according to the manufacturer's directions — in the case of the Pergo floor shown here, by wiping the joints immediately with a clean rag squeezed in a bucket of warm water.

## Layout, Gluing, and Clamping

The usual floor layout rules apply to laminates: center the tiles or planks on doors or in hallways, stagger joints between planks by at least 8 inches, and avoid slivers and U-shaped cutouts. I use a Gizmo III laser — which has a 90-degree function — to make sure that my initial layout is straight and square to the room. I cut and dry-fit the first three courses before I start gluing to make sure that everything lines up the way I want it (**Figure 20**).

*Glue joints and direction changes.* It's important to use enough glue. A continuous bead should be applied to the grooved side of each plank or tile (**Figure 21**); and when the joint has been tapped together and clamped, a thin line of squeeze-out should appear along the entire joint. Some brands have slightly different gluing procedures; for example, the directions may call for applying a bead of glue to the top of the groove and the bottom of the tongue. Depending on the manufacturer, the squeeze-out is either scraped off after it has partially set or immediately cleaned up with a damp rag.

The gluing and assembly process starts at one corner of the room, where a section several tiles or planks long and wide, with the grooves facing the walls, is glued, clamped, and allowed to set up for an hour (**Figure 22**). This provides a solid base to build onto one piece at a time, loosening and retightening the clamps as pieces are added.

Especially when I'm working with tile-type flooring, I check the alignment often, because any irregularities that creep in at the start will get worse as you move along. To maintain proper pressure on the joints, I keep the clamp straps neatly aligned with the seams between tiles. As in laying hardwood flooring, a slip tongue can be used to change direc-

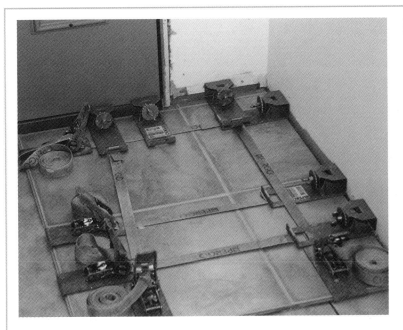 

**Figure 22.** Proprietary strap clamps secure the first rows of flooring (left). Clamps can be adjusted to alter the spacing between the edge of the flooring and the adjacent wall to compensate for any irregularities in the framing. A carefully aligned initial strip of flooring several tiles wide is glued, clamped, and allowed to set up for an hour. Clamps are then loosened and retightened as needed to place additional tiles (right).

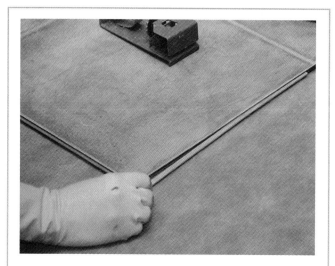

**Figure 23.** Tiles are typically installed from left to right, beginning with a grooved side against the wall. Slip tongues are used to change direction where needed to avoid an inefficient "backfill" installation.

**Figure 24.** Quarter-round trim strips are fastened to cabinet bases to conceal the required ¼-inch expansion gap between flooring and base. The kickspace can be finished with vinyl cove base.

tion when needed to keep an efficient work pattern (**Figure 23**).

## Cabinet Trim

There are several ways to conceal the quarter-inch expansion gap where the flooring meets kitchen or bathroom cabinets. The most popular approach is to enclose the cabinet base with base shoe or quarter-round molding, which is coped or mitered at the corners (**Figure 24**). Depending on what the customer

wants, I'll use a real wood molding that's stained or painted to match the cabinet, or a laminate-faced molding that matches the floor, available from the flooring manufacturer.

To avoid impairing the flooring's ability to expand and contract, the molding should be nailed only to the cabinet base, not the floor. I use Senco's air-free brad nailer for this job (www.senco.com), because it saves me from having to lug around a compressor and hoses to run a few feet of trim.

**Figure 25.** To eliminate the need for quarter-round at the base of the toe kick, the author scribes the combined thickness of the flooring and underlayment on the outside corners (left), which are then slightly undercut (center) and cleaned out with a chisel. Leaving a small amount of extra material in the corner of the adjoining L-shaped tile lets the flooring dive under the corner for a clean look with no visible gap (right). The expansion gap in the kickspace is covered with vinyl cove base, which is cut off flush with the side of the cabinet. The gap at the side is concealed by quarter-round that terminates just short of the corner with a back cut.

**Figure 26.** Here, the author trims the transition between flooring and a sliding door threshold with end molding (left). The vertical leg of the trim piece is embedded in a bead of silicone caulk in the gap between flooring and threshold; undercutting the side casings makes it possible to slip the molding beneath them, eliminating the need for complicated scribe cuts. End molding can also be used to trim the base of a carpeted riser (center). If the gap between flooring and riser is sized correctly, the pressure from the carpeted riser will hold the trim piece firmly in place but still allow the floor to move (right).

Another method, which I often use in bathrooms, does away with the quarter-round in the toe kick while still leaving a clean, gap-free corner (**Figure 25**). This requires undercutting the cabinet base at the outside corners and takes a little more time, but it's made much easier with a good undercutting saw. I use the Sinclair Ultrasaw (Sinclair Equipment, www.sineqco.com), which also comes in handy for dealing with door side casings and other tricky areas.

## Baseboards and Room Perimeter

It's especially important to leave an adequate perimeter expansion space in new construction. Framing lumber, drywall, and fresh concrete emit a lot of water vapor, which can cause a floor to buckle if it doesn't have room to expand.

But it's also important to prevent water from making its way into the expansion space and damaging

**Figure 27.** Transitions between laminate flooring and carpeting require a two-piece carpet reducer (left). After the U-shaped metal base is fastened to the concrete subfloor with expansion anchors and screws (center), the transition piece itself snaps into place. In a neat-looking installation, the lip of the trim piece should be pressed snugly against the carpet (right). If the height difference is too great — which is often the case where thin, dense carpeting is used — it may require "ramping up" the edge of the carpet to the proper height with cedar-shingle shims between carpet pad and subfloor.

the floor. In wet areas like bathrooms, the expansion gap and the area under the toilet flanges must be filled with 100% silicone caulk. The same goes for potentially wet areas in kitchens, such as along cabinets below a sink or dishwasher. I install moldings immediately after I fill those areas with sealant, because once the silicone sets up, it often has high spots that can keep the molding from sitting flat.

*Baseboard options.* The simplest way to deal with baseboards is to bring the laminate up to the existing base and cover the gap with quarter-round or base shoe. This is an easy and inexpensive approach, and it's the one that most of my customers seem to prefer. But this method does have a drawback. With narrow baseboard, the built-up height of the floor and the added height of the shoe molding can make the base seem awkwardly small and "buried." If the base is only 2 1/4 inches high to begin with, it can end up looking very skinny by the time you're done. I explain all this to my customers so they won't be surprised by the finished appearance.

A more labor-intensive option is to reuse the original baseboard by removing it before the flooring goes down and reinstalling it afterward. If it's too much trouble to save the old base, it can be replaced with matching new material. Either way, the base-

board itself covers the expansion gap, so there's no need to add a base shoe. A drawback to this method is that the reset or replaced baseboard will sit about 3/8 inch higher on the wall than it did originally, so it won't match the height of the base in areas where the floors haven't been covered with laminate. I often use plinth blocks or some other additional trim to conceal the height difference where the two levels meet.

## Other Transitions

Pergo makes a very versatile piece of trim called end molding, which is an L-shaped piece that is useful for trimming around door thresholds, hearths, and even carpeted stair risers (**Figure 26**, previous page). Other manufacturers also offer end molding, but I find that most of them are too bulky for my taste and need to be cut to produce the profile I like.

Transitions between laminate flooring and carpeted areas are trimmed with a two-piece carpet reducer (**Figure 27**, previous page). A similar hard-surface reducer is used for transitions between laminate and vinyl, wood, or tile.

*Dave Kostansek is a woodworking and flooring contractor in North Royalton, Ohio.*

# Floating Floor Options

by the *JLC* Staff

Traditional hardwood strip flooring has long been a staple of residential construction, but sanding and sealing the floor on site is messy and inconvenient. While prefinished strip flooring eliminates the need for on-site finishing, contractors looking for less labor-intensive alternatives are increasingly turning to "floating" floor systems. Designed to be laid over a vapor barrier and a thin foam pad, the planks or tiles of a floating floor are edge-glued to each other without the need for fasteners.

*Two types.* Most floating floors are either wood veneer or plastic laminate (**Figure 28**). Like plywood, wood veneer flooring is built up from several core layers, topped with a prefinished hardwood face veneer. Plastic laminate flooring has a composite core milled with tongue-and-groove edges, and topped with a layer of high-density plastic laminate similar to but thinner than that used on countertops. The decorative laminate most often simulates wood grain but is also available to imitate tile or stone.

Installation of plastic laminate and most wood veneer

flooring typically requires edge-gluing using special clamps and spacers (see "Installing Laminate Floors," page 390). While these accessories are usually available through the manufacturer, Crain Floor Covering Tools (www.craintools.com) makes a complete set of tools specially designed for floating floor installation.

*Glueless floors.* Installation of the only solid-sawn floating floor system, made by Junckers (www.junckershardwood.com), requires no glue — the planks are held together with metal clips (**Figure 29**, page 398). In addition, two laminate flooring lines (made by BHK and Norske Skog) use interlocking "click-lock" planks designed to be installed without glue. A number of similar click-lock flooring products using engineered wood have recently been introduced, due to the appeal of no-glue floors in the do-it-yourself market. Glueless floors are also popular in Europe, where people sometimes take their finish floors with them when they move, but no-glue flooring also saves time in permanent installations by eliminating the need for clamping. Repairs are much

**Edge-glued and glueless flooring performs well over slabs and radiant heating.**

easier, too, since the floor can be disassembled to the point of damage, then reassembled.

*Look and feel.* Properly installed, a floating floor is practically indistinguishable from a conventional wood floor. However, some clients may be dissatisfied with the way the foam underlayment compresses slightly under the weight of foot traffic, and may claim that a floating floor sounds hollow or doesn't feel solid. As a precaution, make sure your client has an opportunity to walk on a sample floating floor.

It's also important for clients to see more than a small material sample. With both wood and laminate flooring, manufacturers may visually divide wider planks into as many as three "strips" (**Figure 30**, next page). People accustomed to traditional strip flooring may not like the appearance of two- and three-strip plank designs, which create more conspicuous joints where planks butt.

## Pros and Cons

Besides offering a wide variety of surface patterns, floating floor systems have distinct advantages over conventional strip flooring.

**Figure 28.** Plastic laminate flooring has a composite core capped with a high-density plastic laminate that simulates wood grain, stone, or tile (far left); wood veneer flooring is built up in layers, like plywood, and capped with a solid wood veneer (left).

**Figure 29.** The Junckers solid-sawn flooring system is fastened with metal clips (far left). Norske Skog's Alloc flooring (left), uses an interlocking edge to hold planks together.

*Stability.* Both wood veneer and plastic laminate flooring are more stable than solid-sawn strip flooring, so they expand and contract less with seasonal changes. More important, any movement is more uniform, board to board, which keeps cracks from developing in the edge-glued joints. Most wood veneer or plastic laminate flooring is also rated for use over radiant heating, although manufacturers recommend the same precautions be taken as for solid-sawn flooring.

Neither material, however, is impervious to moisture and should always be installed over a vapor barrier. In addition, most wood veneer manufacturers do not warrant their products in fulls bath or other locations where puddled surface water may seep through joints in the floor and cause swelling or delamination. A few even prohibit damp mopping or require use of a proprietary cleaner. The reverse is true of plastic laminate flooring, most of which is approved for use in kitchens and baths. In full baths, however, some laminate manufacturers require sealing of the flooring edges at the room perimeter and at penetrations, often with a proprietary sealant.

*Cost.* Where prep work can be reduced, floating floors are without question the least expensive option. On a concrete slab, for example, laying strip flooring requires additional materials and labor to

**Figure 30.** Single-strip patterns, such as the antique heart pine shown at left, most closely approximate the look of real wood planks. Some people may object to two- and three-strip patterns, however, because the butt joints are more conspicuous (right).

prepare a subfloor, whereas a floating floor needs just a vapor barrier and a foam pad. The same holds true for floors laid over radiant heating systems embedded in lightweight concrete. A floating floor can also save demolition and disposal costs, as when planks are laid directly over short-fiber carpeting.

In general, material costs for plastic laminate flooring are competitive with traditional hardwood strip flooring. While engineered wood flooring is slightly more expensive than a comparable solid-wood product, the cost begins to even out with the more exotic wood species. A species that would be prohibitively expensive if purchased as solid-sawn strip flooring is much more affordable as wood veneer flooring because the face layer is only about $1/8$ inch thick.

Unlike solid-sawn floors, which can be sanded and refinished four times or more, longevity of floating floors is more difficult to measure. While most wood veneer floors will outlive their owners, the relatively thin face veneer can only be refinished once, possibly twice. Plastic laminate, on the other hand, can't be refinished at all; it can, however, be completely replaced for about twice what it would cost to sand and finish a wood floor.

prep work, 240–241, 244–251, 286–288
production methods, 286–292
rough trim crew, 240–241
running a business, 240–243, 257, 286
spec sheet, 240–241
stair and rail crew, 241–242
windows, 254, 256–257, 262
*See also* Baseboard; Casings; Crown; Doors; Flexible
moldings; Polymer moldings; Shelving; Wainscoting;
Windows
**Ipe,** hardwood decking, 230
**IRC,** top plate rules, 41
**Irregular hip roof,** layout, 69–75
**Irregular valley roof,** layout, 76–81

## J

**Jack rafters**
calculating length, 64, 67–69
gang-cutting, 92–94
layout, 83, 89, 101–102
**Jacks**
to lift beam, 162–163, 165
to lift dormer roof, 174–175
**Jamb extensions.** *See* Extension jambs
**Jambs.** *See* Door jambs; Extension jambs
**J-bolts.** *See* Anchor bolts
**Jigs**
for hanging fiber-cement, 203
for hinges, 258, 260, 265–267
for pocket screws, 315–317, 373
**Joint compound,** for polymer moldings, 305
**Joist hangers**
for I-joists, 25
installing with palm nailer, 7
**Junckers,** floating hardwood flooring, 384–385, 396

## K

**Kitchen cabinets**
clamp for face frames, 317, 323, 325
design review, 322–323
installation, 322–325
layout, 320–322
leg levelers, 325
mechanical lift for, 324
plumbing/electrical locations, 321–322
shimming level, 319–320
**Kitchens**
design review, 322–323
rough-in, 36–37
rough-in inspection, 248
*See also* Kitchen cabinets
**Kleer,** PVC trim, 184, 186
**Knee wall,** added to shed dormer, 174
**Kreg jig,** for pocket screws, 315–317, 373
**Kwik Bolts,** wedge anchors, 22

## L

**Labor Saver,** fiber-cement siding jig, 203
**Lag screws,** RSS, 234
**Laminate flooring**
installation, 393–396
subfloor prep, 391–392
underlayment for, 392
vs. floating wood floor, 396–399
**Landing tread,** installation, 352, 356, 358, 361–363
**Lap siding,** framing layout for, 38

**Laser,** for frame-and-panel layout, 331–332
**Lasers**
for framing layout, 6, 8
for girder post layout, 20
for sill layout, 16–19
to align jamb extensions, 284
to lay out laminate flooring, 393
to plumb walls, 43–44
to set sills, 14
**Laundry room,** rough-in, 36
**Layout**
arches for porch, 226
barrel-vault ceiling, 129–135
barrel-vault dormer, 114–115
bathroom framing, 33–36
cathedral hip roof, 112
check slab/deck, 10
circle, 193
conical roof, 58
curved portico, 187–189, 183
ellipse for ceiling, 129, 132–133
eyebrow dormer, 117–119
fiber-cement siding, 202
first-floor deck, 16–20, 30–38
floor joists, 20–21
hip tray ceiling, 122–126
kitchen framing, 33
mudsill, 13–14, 16–19
precut framing, 142–143
rake wall, 49–50
roof, by calculator, 64–69
roof, by scale drawing, 69–75
walls, 30–38
windows and doors, 32–33, 35, 38
**Layout sticks,** 5–6, 31
**L-bead,** drywall trim around doors/windows, 258
**Leaf blower,** for cleaning off deck, 7
**Ledger**
for curved porch, 190
for deck, 235
**Leg levelers,** for kitchen cabinets, 325
**Level,** Stabila, 43
**Lighting**
outdoor, 233
rough-in, 36–37
undercabinet, 324
**Lining.** *See* Straightening
**Loads,** checking in layout, 37
**Lockout crew,** 243
**Locks,** installed by lockout crew, 243
**Lumber**
breakdown framing package, 8–9
ordering for framing, 2–3
plastic cover for, 8
precutting framing, 4–5, 9
**LVL**
for flitch beam, 160–162
for hip/valley rafter, 76–77
for trimmer rafters, 114–115

## M

**Makita**
saws for fiber-cement, 201, 205, 206
screw gun for deck building, 236
**Mantels,** by production crew, 242
**Marvin,** curved windows, 60, 136–137